Frommer's®
Prague
& the Best of the Czech Republic

My Prague

by Hana Mastrini

WHILE GROWING UP IN A SMALL CZECH TOWN, I ALWAYS LOOKED TO MY country's capital with respect. Czechs have long dubbed Prague the "mother of all cities." It's here, the heart of Bohemia, where events have conspired to change kingdoms, regimes, and lives, again and again. From the grandeur of the Holy Roman Empire, which Charles IV ruled from this city, to the rise and fall of the Hapsburgs, Nazis, and Communists—Prague has seen it all, and historical landmarks are still found throughout its aged core.

In November 1989, I marched with other students, feeling that change was upon us. That peaceful event, the Velvet Revolution, led to the end of 4 decades of harsh Communist rule. Today, Prague is about the symbiosis of old and new. While historic objects have regained their original glory, modern architecture is also making its mark. More newcomers have added to the cultural mix, making this a truly cosmopolitan capital. I'm proud that Prague is the hometown of both my sons, and I'm sure they will see even more change in Mother Prague.

Legend has it that, during construction of the **CHARLES BRIDGE (left),** in the 14th century, eggs (an expensive commodity at the time) were mixed with mortar to strengthen the structure. Indeed the bridge has withstood several floods and wars. During the daytime, musicians perform and artists display their work. Cross the Vltava River early in the morning or during sunset, when crowds are sparse, and admire the 30 statues that stand sentry on each side of the bridge.

Prague's historic heart, **OLD TOWN SQUARE (above),** has witnessed numerous events over the centuries. Its ornate astronomical clock (orloj) on the city hall amuses crowds at the top of every hour with its show of marching apostles. It was on the famous cobblestones here that I brought my infant sons to take their first steps. During the holiday season, the city puts up a magnificent Christmas tree, with a market offering hot wine (svařák), grilled chestnuts, and small gifts.

In the past nearly 2 decades, I have always been happy to see buildings recover from Communist negligence. Hotel Imperial recently reopened on Na Poříčí and its grand Art Deco *kavárna,* **IMPERIAL CAFÉ (left),** now welcomes visitors again. Restoration has preserved its lovely pillars and colorful mosaic ceiling. It is popular for morning coffee and afternoon tea. You get a free *kobliha* (doughnut) with your coffee.

Leafy **PETŘÍN HILL (above)** has always served Praguers as a getaway from the loud city center. The park, close to Prague Castle, provides an expansive view of the city's spires and red rooftops. Traditionally, on May Day the pathways are filled with couples kissing under trees and paying a visit to the statue of Czech poet Karel Mácha. His tragic love poem *"Máj"* (May) has become the key work of Czech romanticism.

The Czechs have over 500 years of brewing tradition as the creators of golden lager. Czech pivo is good, and it's cheap. To experience a slice of Czech culture, find a local pub such as **U ZLATÉHO TYGRA (THE GOLDEN TIGER, above)** full of *"štamgasts"* (regulars). Each round is preceded by the toast *"Na zdraví!"* ("To your health!") and a clunk of the mug on the table.

After an American bomb destroyed a house on the waterfront of New Town at the end of WWII, the void remained for decades. In 1996, architects Frank Gehry and Vlado Milunic incorporated a progressively designed modern piece of architecture to a row of neoclassical apartment houses. Called the **DANCING HOUSE (right)** for its depiction of an abstract dancing couple (it is also called "Fred and Ginger," after the famous duo), it is best observed from across the river. Ex-President Václav Havel used to live next door in a building owned by his father.

My hometown. Holy Roman Emperor Charles IV, in the 14th century, knew where to build his holiday cottage. He found local hot springs while on a hunting expedition. Today, **KARLOVY VARY** (right) is one of the most popular spa towns in Europe. Pictured is Grandhotel Pupp, the most renowned hotel in town.

At the edge of Prague, **DIVOKÁ ŠÁRKA (WILD SARKA, below)** offers valleys and hills, woodsy paths, and open fields for great escapes from the city. Outdoor swimming in summer and cross-country skiing in winter are popular activities here for all age groups. You can walk, bike, hike, climb, or camp here throughout the year.

When touring the city, do not forget to look up. Look closely. Prague proudly displays its architectural jewels, and the most interesting features are often well above street level. This detail, part of a massive stained-glass window designed by Alfons Mucha, hangs above the high altar at **ST. VITUS CATHEDRAL.** *© Glenn Harper/Alamy*

Frommer's®

Prague & the Best of the Czech Republic

8th Edition

by Mark Baker & Hana Mastrini

WILEY

Wiley Publishing, Inc.

Published by:

WILEY PUBLISHING, INC.

111 River St.
Hoboken, NJ 07030-5774

ISBN 978-0-470-53772-5

Editor: Jamie Ehrlich
Production Editor: Michael Brumitt
Cartographer: Guy Ruggiero
Photo Editor: Richard Fox
Production by Wiley Indianapolis Composition Services

Front cover photo: Art Nouveau stained glass window at the Municipal House Theater in Prague's Old Town ©Martin Child / Robert Harding Photo Library
Back cover photo: Cobblestone streets with St. Nicholas Church in background, Old Town Square ©Ellen Rooney / Robert Harding Photo Library

For information on our other products and services or to obtain technical support, please contact our Customer Care Department within the U.S. at 877/762-2974, outside the U.S. at 317/572-3993 or fax 317/572-4002.

Wiley also publishes its books in a variety of electronic formats. Some content that appears in print may not be available in electronic formats.

Manufactured in the United States of America

5   4   3   2   1

CONTENTS

8 STROLLING AROUND PRAGUE 150

9 PRAGUE SHOPPING 172

10 PRAGUE AFTER DARK 184

11 DAY TRIPS FROM PRAGUE 202

12 THE BEST OF BOHEMIA 222

13 THE BEST OF MORAVIA 264

14 FAST FACTS: PRAGUE & THE CZECH REPUBLIC 283

15 USEFUL TERMS & PHRASES 289

INDEX 296

LIST OF MAPS

ABOUT THE AUTHORS

Mark Baker is a long-time American expat who lives in Prague. He's one of the original editors of *The Prague Post* and was for years a correspondent and editor for Radio Free Europe/Radio Liberty, based in Prague. He's now a freelance writer and reporter. He's the author of *Frommer's Prague Day by Day,* and coauthor of *Frommer's Eastern Europe* and *Frommer's Poland.*

Hana Mastrini is a native of the western Czech spa town of Karlovy Vary who became a veteran of the "Velvet Revolution" as a student in Prague in 1989.

ACKNOWLEDGMENTS

I'd like to thank my parents, Ed and Sandy Kurdziel, and my brother Scott who keep me motoring around Bohemia with them on their visits to Prague, and my friend Hana Klamkova for her insider's knowledge of Brno. I'd also like to thank my editor Jamie Ehrlich for giving me the assignment in the first place.

—Mark Baker

HOW TO CONTACT US

In researching this book, we discovered many wonderful places—hotels, restaurants, shops, and more. We're sure you'll find others. Please tell us about them, so we can share the information with your fellow travelers in upcoming editions. If you were disappointed with a recommendation, we'd love to know that, too. Please write to:

Frommer's Prague & the Best of the Czech Republic, 8th Edition
Wiley Publishing, Inc. • 111 River St. • Hoboken, NJ 07030-5774

AN ADDITIONAL NOTE

Please be advised that travel information is subject to change at any time—and this is especially true of prices. We therefore suggest that you write or call ahead for confirmation when making your travel plans. The authors, editors, and publisher cannot be held responsible for the experiences of readers while traveling. Your safety is important to us, however, so we encourage you to stay alert and be aware of your surroundings. Keep a close eye on cameras, purses, and wallets, all favorite targets of thieves and pickpockets.

FROMMER'S STAR RATINGS, ICONS & ABBREVIATIONS

Every hotel, restaurant, and attraction listing in this guide has been ranked for quality, value, service, amenities, and special features using a **star-rating system.** In country, state, and regional guides, we also rate towns and regions to help you narrow down your choices and budget your time accordingly. Hotels and restaurants are rated on a scale of zero (recommended) to three stars (exceptional). Attractions, shopping, nightlife, towns, and regions are rated according to the following scale: zero stars (recommended), one star (highly recommended), two stars (very highly recommended), and three stars (must-see).

In addition to the star-rating system, we also use **seven feature icons** that point you to the great deals, in-the-know advice, and unique experiences that separate travelers from tourists. Throughout the book, look for:

(**Finds**)	Special finds—those places only insiders know about
(**Fun Facts**)	Fun facts—details that make travelers more informed and their trips more fun
(**Kids**)	Best bets for kids, and advice for the whole family
(**Moments**)	Special moments—those experiences that memories are made of
(**Overrated**)	Places or experiences not worth your time or money
(**Tips**)	Insider tips—great ways to save time and money
(**Value**)	Great values—where to get the best deals

The following **abbreviations** are used for credit cards:

AE	American Express	**DISC**	Discover	**V**	Visa
DC	Diners Club	**MC**	MasterCard		

TRAVEL RESOURCES AT FROMMERS.COM

Frommer's travel resources don't end with this guide. Frommer's website, **www.frommers.com**, has travel information on more than 4,000 destinations. We update features regularly, giving you access to the most current trip-planning information and the best airfare, lodging, and car-rental bargains. You can also listen to podcasts, connect with other Frommers.com members through our active-reader forums, share your travel photos, read blogs from guidebook editors and fellow travelers, and much more.

The Best of Prague & the Czech Republic

"Bests" by their very nature are highly personalized affairs. One person's best might be a classical concert in a baroque church, while another person might relish a night of jazz in a club that's been around since the 1950s. Fortunately, Prague has a wide of selection of bests that are sure to cater to a range of interests, whether they be in music, art, architecture, nature, or just a glass of very good beer. Here are some of our suggestions below:

1 THE MOST UNFORGETTABLE TRAVEL EXPERIENCES

- **Stroll Across Charles Bridge at Dawn or Dusk:** The silhouettes of the statues lining the 600-year-old crown jewel of Czech heritage hover like ghosts in the still of the sunrise skyline. Early in the morning you can stroll across the bridge without encountering the crowds that appear by midday. With the changing light of dusk, the statues, the bridge, and the city panorama take on a whole different character. See "Walking Tour 1: Charles Bridge & Malá Strana (Lesser Town)" in chapter 8.

- **Make Your Own Procession Down the Royal Route:** The downhill jaunt from Prague Castle, through Malá Strana (Lesser Town), and across Charles Bridge to Old Town Square, is a day in itself. (If you want more exercise, start in the Old Town and walk up to the castle.) The trip recalls the route taken by the carriages of the Bohemian kings; today it's lined with quirky galleries, shops, and cafes. See chapter 8.

- **Take a Slow Boat Down the Vltava:** You can see many of the most striking architectural landmarks from the low-angle and low-stress vantage point of a rowboat you pilot yourself. Make the trip in the evening and rent a rowboat with a little lantern. See "Sightseeing Options" in chapter 7.

- **Get Lost in Prague's Old Town:** It happens to everyone, even people who have lived here for years. You think you're taking a shortcut down a back alley, and soon you're on a street you've never seen before and have no idea where you are. Old Town's winding lanes were carved out long before cities had rectilinear street grids, and that's a big part of the city's charm. See chapter 7, "The Art of Getting Lost," p. 120.

- **Catch a Performance of Smetana's Moldau Symphony:** Or any other piece of classical music, for that matter. Prague's Gothic spires and baroque cupolas provide the perfect backdrop for a classical concert, opera, or ballet, and the city's symphony halls and churches are just as beautiful as the music itself. See chapter 10, "Prague After Dark."

- **Have a Cold One in the City That "Invented" Beer:** We're not talking about Prague here, but the western Bohemian city of Plzeň (Pilsen) that's the birthplace of clear, golden modern lager. It's why we call beer "pilsner" or simply "pils." They're still making beer there and you can tour the brewery. If you can't make it to Plzeň, stop in at just about any pub in the country for some of the best beer you'll ever drink. See chapter 12, "The Best of Bohemia."

- **Step into History at Karlštejn Castle:** A 30-minute train ride southwest of Prague puts you in the most visited

Czech landmark in the environs, built by Charles IV (Karel IV in Czech—the namesake of Charles Bridge) in the 14th century to protect the Holy Roman Empire's crown jewels. This Romanesque hilltop bastion fits the image of the castles of medieval lore, though the exterior is more impressive than inside. See chapter 11.

2 THE BEST SPLURGE HOTELS

- **Four Seasons Hotel Prague** (Veleslavínova 2a, Prague 1; ℭ 221-427-000): Arguably the number-one luxury hotel in Old Town, with many rooms having a river view of Prague Castle and Charles Bridge. The house restaurant, Allegro, has won a Michelin star 2 years running, a first in all of central Europe. See chapter 5, p. 74, and chapter 6, p. 95.
- **Hotel Savoy** (Keplerova 6, Prague 1; ℭ 224-302-430): This opulent but tasteful small hotel suggests London more than Prague. Enjoy afternoon tea in the library, where you can read by a crackling fire. See p. 68.
- **Hotel Paříž** (U Obecního domu 1, Prague 1; ℭ 222-195-195): This restored Art Nouveau hotel recalls 1920s Prague, one of the wealthiest cities on earth at that time. It's across from another remodeled gem, the Municipal House (Obecní dům). See p. 76.
- **Hotel Aria** (Tržiště 9, Prague 1; ℭ 225-334-111): This reconverted baroque townhouse plays on Prague's musical heritage, with each one of its beautifully appointed rooms named after a composer or performer. Some rooms look

out over the Vrtbovská garden. Don't leave without having dinner or a drink on the rooftop terrace. See p. 72.
- **Hotel Josef** (Rybná 20, Prague 1; ℭ 221-700-111): For fans of clean lines, white walls, and minimalist chic, the Josef was Prague's first real boutique hotel and still arguably the best. See p. 75.
- **Hotel Mandarin Oriental** (Nebovidská 1, Prague 1; ℭ 233-088-888): This local branch of the international luxury chain occupies a sublime location in a converted monastery in a quiet corner of Malá Strana. This is no cookie-cutter chain; each room is funky and wonderful in its own unique way. See p. 72.
- **U zlaté studně** (U zlaté studně 4, Prague 1; ℭ 257-011-213): This reconstructed 17th-century townhouse sits just below Prague Castle, and many of the rooms afford stunning views out over Malá Strana and Old Town. Rumors were swirling in April 2009 during U.S. President Barack Obama's visit to Prague that he and Mrs. Obama were going to dine on the restaurant's terrace. He ended up staying (and eating) at the Hilton, but this would have been a more presidential choice. See p. 68.

3 THE BEST MODERATELY PRICED HOTELS

- **Hotel Cloister Inn** (Konviktská 14, Prague 1; ℭ 224-211-020): This freshly restored hotel in a former convent offers

a comfortable room at a fair price in Old Town near Jan Hus's 15th-century Bethlehem Chapel. See p. 77.

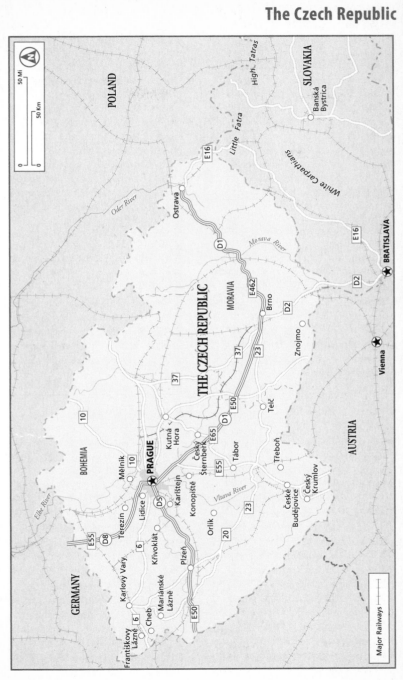

- **Pension Větrník** (U Větrníku 40, Prague 6; ✆ **220-612-404**): This family-run romantic hideaway is reachable in about 25 minutes by tram from the city center. Its atmosphere and price are unbeatable. See p. 82.

- **Czech Inn** (Francouzská 76, Prague 10; ✆ **267-267-600**): This place calls itself a hostel, but "budget boutique" would be more accurate. Great breakfasts, an upscale modern interior, a bank of convenient computers in the lobby for surfing, and friendly receptionists make this a great choice if value is a prime consideration. See p. 75.

- **Castle Steps** (Nerudova 7, Prague 1; ✆ **257-216-337**): These beautifully restored rooms in a series of town palaces along Nerudova in Malá Strana are quirky in the best sense of the word. You won't get this location—or drop-dead gorgeous chambers—for less money, but you may have to share a bathroom. See p. 73.

- **K+K Hotel Central** (Hybernská 10, Prague 1; ✆ **225-022-000**): Okay, it's absurd to put a four-star luxury hotel in the moderate category, but this stunningly restored Art Nouveau palace frequently discounts rates over its website, so it's always worth a click to see what's available. See p. 79.

- **Hotel Absolutum** (Jablonského 476, Prague 7; ✆ **222-541-406**): This is a sleek, modern hotel, with designer-style rooms at very reasonable prices. The location, across the street from the Holešovice train and metro station, won't win any beauty contests, but it's super convenient for getting to the center or for checking out Holešovice, one of Prague's up-and-coming neighborhoods. See p. 81.

- Staying in **Vinohrady,** a residential area above Wenceslas Square, will put you a bit off the Royal Route, but you can find no better price and selection in central Prague, especially if you arrive without reservations. One example is the **Orion** (Americká 9, Prague 2; ✆ **222-521-706**). This neighborhood teems with cafes and has easy metro access to the older quarters. See "Vinohrady" in chapter 5.

4 THE MOST UNFORGETTABLE DINING EXPERIENCES

- **Kampa Park** (Na Kampě 8b, Prague 1; ✆ **296-826-112**): On a warm evening in summer, Kampa Park's idyllic riverside setting will be etched in your memory for a long time to come. The food and service are pretty spectacular too, but give the place a pass if you can't book on the terrace since there's better value to be had elsewhere. See p. 89.

- **Pálffy Palác** (Valdštejnská 14, Prague 1; ✆ **257-530-522**): This renovated baroque townhouse restaurant is a Prague institution. The hardest part may be deciding where to sit: the luxurious main room feels like a dinner with Louis XIV, but the outdoor terrace floats just below Prague Castle and has striking views. See p. 93.

- **La Degustation** (Haštalská 18, Prague 1; ✆ **222-311-234**): How could you ever forget a full seven-course meal that seems to unfold without end over a long evening, interspersed with unexpected appetizers and bottles and bottles of wine? It's a meal you'll talk about for years to come. See p. 96.

- **Kavárna Obecní dům** (náměstí Republiky 5, Prague 1; ✆ **222-002-763**): This reinvigorated Art Nouveau cafe at the **Municipal House** has re-created the grandeur of Jazz Age afternoons. See p. 104.

- **Bellevue** (Smetanovo nábřeží 18, Prague 1; ✆ **222-221-443**): This is the best spot for an important lunch or dinner. It has artful international fare and impeccable business-friendly service, with a cozy atmosphere and super views near Charles Bridge. See p. 95.

- **Angel** (V kolkovně 7, Prague 1 ✆ **773-222-422**): Star chef Sofia Smith will have you coming back again and again for her alchemistic concoctions of Asian spices and central European staples such as lamb shank, pork belly, and duck. Angel's 2008 opening was the culinary event of the year and it's only gotten better since. See p. 96.

- **Bakeshop** (Kozí 1, Prague 1 ✆ **222-316-823**): Yes, it's pricey for a bakery, particularly one in central Europe, but who can resist those loaves of sourdough bread, muffins straight from the oven, cookies, and brownies, not to mention the range of lunch items like sandwiches, salads, and big bowls of chili? Eat at the counter along the window or take it with you. See p. 100.

5 THE BEST MUSEUMS

- **Šternberk Palace** (Hradčanské nám. 15, Prague 1; ✆ **233-090-570**): The country's best collection of European art, ranging from Byzantine-era icons straight through to Rembrandt, El Greco, Goya, and Van Dyck. See p. 122.

- **Alfons Mucha Museum** (Panská 7, Prague 1; ✆ **221-451-333**): Posters, decorative panels, objets d'art, and excerpts from sketchbooks, as well as oil paintings from this well-known Art Nouveau master, are displayed at the baroque Kaunický Palace near Václavské náměstí. See p. 125.

- **St. George's Convent** (Jiřské nám. 33, Prague 1; ✆ **257-531-644**): I never thought I'd have a weakness for 19th-century landscape paintings, but these are spectacular. While the Czech Republic lacks rugged mountains (not to mention a seashore), it's blessed with some of the most beautiful rolling countryside in Europe, and the painters displayed here knew how to capture that. See p. 122.

- **Veletržní Palác** (Veletržní at Dukelských hrdinů 47, Prague 7; ✆ **224-301-111**): Prague's museum of art of the 20th and 21st centuries is an underrated gem, filled with masterworks by Klimt, Munch, Schiele, and Picasso. But the real treats here are works by the Modernist Czech painters from the 1920s and '30s. See p. 122.

- **Jewish Museum** (U Starého hřbitova; enter from Široká 3, Prague 1; ✆ **221-711-511**): This "museum" is not just one building but a series of preserved synagogues and the Old Jewish Cemetery, which together bear witness to 7 centuries of Jewish life in this tiny part of Prague. The admission fee is regrettably high, but the memory of all those jagged tombstones jutting upward in that crowded plot will last a lifetime. See p. 119.

- **Museum of the Ghetto** (Terezín; ✆ **416-782-225**): This is a sobering space that tells the shocking tale of how the Nazis deceived the world into thinking their "Final Solution" was actually building vacation homes for Jews. How did the Nazis get away with it, and how did the world allow them to? See p. 218.

- **Bone Church (Kostnice)**, (Sedlec, near Kutná Hora; ✆ **728-125-488**): Three words: creepy, creepy, creepy. Thousands of human bones from the Middle Ages were used in the 19th century to construct this "gothic" interior of a rather ordinary looking (from the outside) church not far from Kutná Hora. You'll finally understand the term "bone chilling." See p. 212.

1

6 THE BEST THINGS TO DO FOR FREE (OR ALMOST)

- **Having a Cup and a Debate at the Kavárna Slavia:** (Národní at Smetanovo nábřeží, Prague 1; © 224-218-493). The reincarnation of Prague's favorite Communist-era dissident cafe retains its former Art Deco glory. The cloak-and-dagger interactions of secret police eavesdropping on political conversations may be gone, but there's still an energy that flows with the talk and java at the Slavia—and it comes with a great view. See p. 104.

- **Crossing the Charles Bridge at Night:** At night, the bridge takes on a completely different persona. The crowds thin out (a little) and musicians, street performers, and flower people come here to sit under the statues and sing or just hang out. Why not join them? See chapter 10 for more nightlife options.

- **Enjoying New Year's Eve in Český Krumlov:** At midnight in Bohemia's Český Krumlov, the Na Plášti Bridge at the castle overlooking the town turns into a mini–United Nations, as revelers from all over gather to watch and light fireworks, see who can uncork the champagne the fastest, and just plain celebrate. See "Český Krumlov" in chapter 12, p. 250.

- **Exploring Antiques Shops:** If you like old stuff, you'll enjoy finding something "out of this world" in many of Prague's antiques shops *(starožitnosti)* or bookstores selling more-or-less-old publications *(antikvariáts).* See chapter 9, "Prague Shopping" (p. 173) for shopping suggestions.

- **Have a Beer at Letná:** In summer, you'll find the city's best beer garden on the far eastern edge of Letná Park, across the river from Old Town. While the beer's not free (too bad!), it's not all that expensive either, and you're free to sit at one of the picnic tables or along the park benches. The views down to Old Town are simply superb. See "Other Top Sights" in chapter 7.

- **Treat Yourself to a *Svařák*:** *Svařák*, short for *svařené víno*, is the Czech version of mulled wine, a traditional Christmastime treat that's best drunk outside in the freezing cold from a plastic or Styrofoam cup. Vendors on Old Town Square start selling the stuff in early November and svařák season lasts through the new year or longer. Okay, it's not free, but a good-size cup of the stuff will only set you back about 40Kč.

- **Drop in at St. Vitus Cathedral:** Most of the Castle complex requires an expensive combined-entry ticket to visit, but not the biggest site of all, St. Vitus Cathedral. Be sure to take in the amazing stained glass windows and the St. Wenceslas Chapel. See p. 109.

- **Feed the Swans:** Okay, the bread won't exactly be free, but it's worth a couple of crowns to buy some rolls and head down to the river (for the best swan sightings, try the banks on the Malá Strana side just south of the Malostranská metro station along the street U Lužického semináře). The Vltava is home to hundreds of white swans (if not more), but be careful with the bread, since the birds might bite.

7 THE BEST ACTIVITIES FOR FAMILIES

- **Ride a Big Boat down the Vltava:** For those not willing to test their navigational skills or rowing strength in their own boat, large tour boats offer similar floating views, many with meals. Be sure to check the direction of your voyage to be certain it travels past the castles and palaces. See "Sightseeing Options" in chapter 7.

- **Picnic at Vyšehrad:** Of all the parks where you can picnic, the citadel above the Vltava standing guard over the south end of the Old Town is the calmest and most interesting spot close to the center. Its more remote location means less tourist traffic, and the gardens, city panoramas, and national cemetery provide pleasant walks and poignant history. See "Other Top Sights" in chapter 7.

- **Spend a Day at the Zoo:** Prague's zoo has improved immensely in recent years, after the 2002 flood severely damaged the grounds and even killed several animals. There's been lots of new investment and the setting by the river is great. Check out some of the biggest collections of giraffes and great apes in Central Europe. See "Other Top Sights" in chapter 7.

- **Gaze at the Stars:** For budding astronomers, Prague has two treats in store. A real live observatory on Petřín Hill is open on clear nights in summer or winter for checking out the moon, Jupiter,

Saturn, and even some other galaxies. The planetarium in Stromovka park is an indoor stellar spectacle. See "Other Top Sights" in chapter 7.

- **Hop Aboard the *Oldtimer:*** That's Prague's endearing name for Tram 91, a vintage streetcar from a bygone era that still plies the rails on Saturdays and Sundays during the summer. Hope aboard at any stop, buy a ticket from the conductor, and ride for as long as you want. See "Sightseeing Options" in chapter 7.

- **Visit the Technical Museum:** Older kids will enjoy a visit to Prague's National Technical Museum, a kind of miniature Smithsonian Institution, crammed with planes, trains, and automobiles. It's been closed now for several years while undergoing refurbishment, but was set for a grand reopening in 2010. See "Other Museums & Galleries" in chapter 7.

- **Get Lost in a Mirror Maze:** There are lots of offbeat attractions on Petřín Hill in addition to the mock "Eiffel Tower." The mirror maze is an old-fashioned house of mirrors—more disorienting for adults that it is for kids! But fun for all. See "Sightseeing Options" in chapter 7.

8 THE MOST ROMANTIC EXPERIENCES

- **Český Krumlov:** If you have time for only one excursion from Prague, make it Český Krumlov. This living gallery of Renaissance-era buildings housing many galleries, shops, and restaurants is 167km (104 miles) south of Prague. Above it towers the second-largest castle complex in the country, with the Vltava River running underneath. No wonder UNESCO named this town a World Heritage Site. See " Český Krumlov" in chapter 12.

- **Holding Hands on the Charles Bridge:** This is a no-brainer, but the real trick is to choose the right moment. In summer, shoot for an evening stroll just as the sun is setting behind Prague Castle. In winter, pray for snow, and then go out at night as the flakes swirl around and muffle the sounds of the city.

- **Take a Ride on the Metro:** There must be something in the air down there or about those long intervals between stations (especially along the C line), but

Czechs (particularly young couples) love to hold hands, kiss, and generally push the PDA envelope on the metro. As they say, "when in Rome . . ."

- **Dine on the River:** Several of the Prague's best restaurants are perched right next to the Vltava or command stunning views out over it (see chapter 6, "Where to Dine in Prague," for some suggestions). Or do the ultimate romantic thing and actually dine *on* the river. Buy a bottle of "Bohemia Sekt" (domestic sparkling wine), a picnic lunch from Bakeshop (p. 100), and rent a paddle boat from one of the rental outlets on the island across from the National Theater.

- **Visit Your Local Pub:** I know that it's bad form to kiss in a pub. Not only does the beer play tricks with your judgment, you risk the rest of the bar jangling their keys (a polite enjoinder to "get a room"). On the other hand, if you're lucky, the setting and the beer will conspire to create a moment that seems so right, the only logical response will be an amorous one. See chapter 10, "Prague After Dark," for a list of good Czech pubs.

- **Spend an Afternoon at Stromovka Park:** This is Prague's most secluded park and no one will look askance as you spread out your blanket, uncork a bottle of wine, and start whispering sweet nothings into your partner's ear. In fact, look around, everyone else seems to be doing the same thing. See "Other Top Sights" in chapter 7.

9 THE BEST CZECH BEER

- **Pilsner Urquell:** I can hear the catcalls already. Yes, this is the biggest brewer in the country (it's a little like choosing "Budweiser" as the best American beer), but Pilsner Urquell really might be the Czechs' best. It still wins lots of national beer prizes and the signature bitter taste and smooth follow-through of its main 12-degree lager sets the standard for beers around the world.

- **Budvar:** Possibly my personal favorite, since I like beers to have a slightly sweet (but not too much so) taste. By the way (and no slight to the good folks in St. Louis, Missouri), this is the original "Budweiser" and hails from České Budějovice (known as "Budweis" in German).

- **Staropramen:** Prague's home brewery would never have made this list in the old days—the quality was too inconsistent. But "Staro" is now owned by the giant InBev group (which also owns Bass Ale and Stella Artois, among other big names) and surprisingly it's gotten better, not worse.

- **Kozel:** This bitter brew has long been a favorite of Prague's rowdy expat drinkers, who admire the brand's signature label depicting a goat just as much as the taste. Now Kozel is owned by the Pilsner Urquell group and has lost a little of its cachet. The standard Kozel golden lager seems to be getting harder and harder to find, but the very good Kozel dark is available at nearly all Pilsner Urquell pubs.

- **Krušovice:** This is another decidedly bitter brew that seems to divide beer drinkers down the middle between those who love it and those who can only tolerate it. Count me among the former. It's brewed in the middle of hop country and seems to taste all the fresher for it.

- Naturally, this list could go on and on and doesn't even begin to crack the smaller regional breweries, of which there are nearly 100 around the country. To find a good selection of hard-to-find bottles from smaller brewers, check out **Galerie Piva** in Malá Strana. See "Wine & Beer" in chapter 9.

Prague & the Czech Republic in Depth

It's been 20 years since the 1989 Velvet Revolution that overthrew the Communist government in power, and for Prague and the Czech Republic it's been quite a ride. Practically overnight, the city went from an obscure capital of a small Warsaw Pact country to one of Europe's top urban destinations, alongside luminaries like Paris, London, Rome, and Amsterdam.

In retrospect, the first years after the revolution were a little rocky. While nothing could detract from the medieval setting of the Old Town, the beauty of the Charles Bridge, and the Disneyesque castle on the hill, Prague was not quite ready for prime time. The city suffered from a chronic shortage of hotel rooms, restaurant food was mediocre, and everything from the quality of the service to the state of the trains was, well, second-rate.

The good news is that Prague has *finally* arrived. The years 2008 and 2009 saw the opening of no less than three five-star hotels to add to an already impressive list of deluxe properties. Looking over the lodging choices in Malá Strana alone, many in restored Renaissance and baroque palaces, it's hard to find a more stylish bunch anywhere in Europe.

Prague's restaurants have now won two Michelin stars as well as several Michelin *bibs gourmand,* and while one of those restaurants has since gone belly up (the local branch of Gordon Ramsay's Maze chain collapsed in 2009 with the rest of his empire), the die has been cast. It's hard to imagine local foodies ever going back to the days of canned vegetables and factory-made dumplings.

Prague was always a first-rate cultural destination, as the enduring popularity of the Prague Spring music festival attests. But now, there's even more to see and do. Each month seems to bring another music festival; add to that international jazz and dance fests, four or five film fests, two writers' fests, and the expanding repertoire of icons like the National Theater and State Opera, and you'll be hard-pressed to decide how best to spend your evenings.

All this progress has come at a price—literally. Prague is no longer that bargain-basement tourist outlet of yesteryear, where a meal on the town would set you back a couple of dollars and a glass of beer 25¢. But that's okay. Those days were the product of a historic anomaly from a time when half of Europe was placed in a deep freeze. They were never going to last, and the country and its citizens are better off for it. Today's city is cleaner, livelier, more fun, and simply better than it was. Prague is worth the splurge.

1 PRAGUE & THE CZECH REPUBLIC TODAY

The Czech Republic, at the close of 2009, found itself in an uncharacteristically difficult position. For most of the 20 years since the fall of Communism, the country had it relatively easy. Helped by a massive influx of tourist dollars, billions more in foreign investment, and a post-revolutionary president, Václav Havel, admired around the world, the Czech Republic was arguably the most successful of the former

Eastern bloc states. The country was among the first former Soviet satellites to be brought into the NATO military alliance (1999) and entered the European Union in the first wave of Eastern expansion in 2004. The economy had been on a 20-year bender with no signs of letting up. Then came the 2008–2009 global economic downturn to crash the party (see "Economy" below). Though Czechs appear to have escaped the worst of the downturn, they nonetheless felt the global chill in trade and investment; 2009 was the economy's worst year since the Velvet Revolution.

To make matters worse, the Czech Republic's two main political parties are again at each other's throats as this book goes to press (see "Domestic Politics," below). Political infighting brought the government down in the middle of 2009 (inconveniently coming as the country held the E.U.'s rotating presidency), and as of late 2009 the parties were still squabbling over fresh elections to choose a new government. Fortunately for short-term visitors, none of this is likely to matter much. The Czechs have seen their share of unstable governments and the country continues to soldier on.

Not even the weak economy could prevent Prague from embarking on its most ambitious series of capital investments since the building of the metro in the 1970s and '80s. Everywhere you look these days, you see cranes, backhoes, and scaffolding. The Charles Bridge is being ripped up and reassembled in stages in a multiyear renovation project that officials say is needed to keep the bridge from falling apart. It's still crossable but the scaffolding mars the experience somewhat. Work was expected to be completed sometime in 2010.

The main train station, Hlavní nádraží, is in the midst of a 5-year rebuilding phase until 2013 that's hoped to clean it up and make it a more attractive gateway to the nation's capital. The building booms in the outlying neighborhoods of Holešovice, Karlín, and Smíchov continue apace. These riverside districts, paradoxically, got a new lease on life in the devastating flood that struck the city in 2002. The cleanup that followed focused public and private attention on areas that had previously been little more than slums.

The biggest project of all, and one of the costliest construction feats now underway in the entire E.U., is the Blanka Tunnel in Letná, north of the Old Town across the Vltava river. The tunnel stretches several miles underground and one day will form part of an ambitious ring-road system to route vehicles away from the center.

DOMESTIC POLITICS

While the average visitor isn't likely to notice, the Czech Republic is blessed (if that's the right word!) with perhaps Europe's most dysfunctional government (and with Poland, Slovakia, and Hungary in the mix, that says a lot). The two main parties, the center-right Civic Democratic Party (ODS) and the center-left Social Democratic Party (ČSSD), are locked in constant battle, though neither party commands a sufficient majority to form a stable government. The result has been a succession of weak coalitions involving one or the other main party and linking smaller parties with often-contradictory aims.

These dysfunctions were on display for the whole world to see in 2009 when the Czech Republic held the rotating presidency of the European Union. Just as the Czech government was engaged in fighting the global economic crisis and flare-ups in the Middle East and everything else, the opposition party (in this case, the Social Democrats) called a no-confidence vote and the government collapsed. The E.U. was essentially without a presidency for 3 months running. As 2009 was drawing to a close, the country was still without an elected government.

Add to this volatile mix President Václav Klaus, the man who succeeded Václav Havel as president in 2003. Apart from having the same first name, Klaus bears absolutely no resemblance to his predecessor. He's carved out a niche as a right-wing iconoclast (some would even say "kook"), firmly anti-E.U. in his politics and a strong opponent of climate-change legislation or anything else that in his eyes smacks of "Bolshevism." Though he's far to the right of most of his countrymen, he continues to enjoy broad support.

ECONOMY

The global economic downturn of 2008–2009 hit the high-flying Czech economy disproportionately hard. Before the crisis, the economy was growing on the order of 5% to 6% a year. This level of growth was considered necessary if the country hoped to catch up with western Europe in a generation. While annual figures for 2009 were not available as this book was being researched, the economy for the year was expected to *contract* by around 4%. While you're not likely to notice while strolling through Prague, the Czech economy is actually highly industrialized. Exports include automobiles and big-ticket capital goods like trams, trains, and buses. Orders for all of these dried up as the downturn swept across Europe and the rest of the world.

Still, the Czech Republic appeared to be weathering the storm better than its peers in central Europe. There was no run on the Czech crown, for example, comparable to Polish zloty or Hungarian forint. Indeed, the crown held its own with respect to the euro and strengthened against the U.S. dollar. Prague, with its reliance on tourism, was partially buffered from the economic malaise, but the capital too suffered from a drop in the number of visitors. Many restaurants and shops dependent on the tourist trade suffered through what was generally viewed as the worst year in a decade, and several properties went belly up. Hotels responded by discounting room rates to a fraction of 2008 levels, and depending on the night, in 2009 it was possible to snag a four-star room in the center of town for under $100.

It's not clear if these discounts will continue to be available. Much will depend on the speed and timing of the economic recovery. Already in the fall of 2009, there were signs the tourist trade was coming back. If the world economy continues to deteriorate, expect continued low rates for hotels. One note of caution: because of the economic crisis, some of the properties listed in this book may no longer be in business by the time you are reading this. At press time it was impossible to predict with any accuracy who might and might not survive.

2 LOOKING BACK AT PRAGUE & THE CZECH REPUBLIC

IN THE BEGINNING

The word "Bohemia," now used to describe the westernmost province of the country, comes from an ancient Celtic tribe, the *Boii,* who once lived on the territory of the modern-day Czech Republic. The Boii settled here some 300 years before Christ in the land around the Vltava River. The Latin term *Bohemia* (land of the Boii) became etched in history.

Those early years were marked by strife between local Celtic tribes and Germanic tribes, like the Marcomanni, who managed to expel the Boii around 100 B.C., only to be chucked out in turn by the Huns by A.D. 450. The Huns were then expelled by a Turkic tribe, the Avars, a century later.

Shortly after this began the great Slavic migration of peoples westward from parts of Asia across the Carpathian Mountains into Europe. The westernmost of these Slavic tribes tried to set up a kingdom in Bohemia. The farming Slavs often fell prey to the nomadic Avars, but in 624 a Franconian merchant named Samo united the Slavs and began expelling the Avars from central Europe.

THE GREAT MORAVIAN EMPIRE

Throughout the 9th century, the Slavs around the Morava River consolidated their power. Mojmír I declared his Great Moravian Empire—a kingdom that eventually encompassed Bohemia, Slovakia, and parts of modern-day Poland and Hungary—as a Christian organization still outside the boundaries of the Holy Roman Empire.

In 863, the Greek brothers Cyril and Methodius arrived in Moravia to preach the Eastern Christian rite to a people who didn't understand them. They created a new language mixing Slavic with a separate script, Cyrillic. When Methodius died in 885, the Moravian rulers reestablished the Latin liturgy, though followers of Cyril and Methodius continued to preach their faith in missions to the east. Ultimately the Slavonic rite took hold in Kiev and Russia, where the Cyrillic alphabet is still used, while western Slavs kept the Latin script and followed Rome.

The Great Moravian Empire lasted about a century—until the Magyar invasion of 896—and not until the 20th century would the Czechs and Slovaks unite again under a single government. After the invasion, the Slavs living east of the Morava River swore allegiance to the Magyars, while the Czechs, who lived west of the river, fell under the authority of the Holy Roman Empire.

BOHEMIA LOOKS TO THE WEST

Bořivoj, the first king of the now-separate Bohemia and Moravia, built Prague's first royal palace at the end of the 9th century on the site of the present Prague Castle on Hradčany Hill. In 973, a bishopric was established in Prague, answering to the archbishopric of Mainz. Thus, before the end of the first millennium, the German influence in Bohemia was firmly established.

The kings who followed Bořivoj in the Přemyslid dynasty ruled over Bohemia for more than 300 years, during which time Prague became a major commercial area along central Europe's trade routes. In the 12th century, two fortified castles were built at Vyšehrad and Hradčany, and a wooden plank bridge stood near where the stone Charles Bridge spans the Vltava today. Václavské náměstí (Wenceslas Sq.) was a horse market, and the city's 3,500 residents rarely lived to the age of 45. In 1234, Staré Město (Old Town), the first of Prague's historic five towns, was founded.

Encouraged by Bohemia's rulers, who guaranteed German civic rights to western settlers, Germans founded entire towns around Prague, including Malá Strana (Lesser Town) in 1257. The Přemyslid dynasty of the Czechs ended with the 1306 death of teenage Václav III, who had no heirs. After much debate, the throne was offered to John of Luxembourg, husband of Václav III's younger sister, a foreigner who knew little of Bohemia. It was John's firstborn son who left the most lasting marks on Prague.

PRAGUE'S FIRST GOLDEN AGE

Charles IV (Karel IV) took the throne when his father died fighting in France in 1346. Educated among French royalty and fluent in four languages (but not initially Czech), Charles almost single-handedly ushered in Prague's first golden age (the second occurred in the late 16th c.). Even before his reign, Charles wanted to make Prague a glorious city. In 1344, he won an archbishopric for Prague independent of Mainz. When he became king of

Bohemia, Charles also became, by election, Holy Roman Emperor.

During the next 30 years, Charles transformed Prague into the bustling capital of the Holy Roman Empire and one of Europe's most important cities, with some of the most glorious architecture of the day. He commissioned St. Vitus Cathedral's construction at Prague Castle as well as the bridge that would eventually bear his name. He was most proud of founding Prague University in 1348, the first higher-education institution in central Europe, now known as Charles University. In 1378, Charles died of natural causes at age 62.

PROTESTANT REFORMATION & THE HUSSITE WARS

While Charles IV was the most heralded of the Bohemian kings, the short reign of his son Václav IV was marked by social upheaval, a devastating plague, and the advent of turbulent religious dissent.

Reformist priest Jan Hus drew large crowds to Bethlehem Chapel, where he preached against what he considered the corrupt tendencies of Prague's bishopric. Hus became widely popular among Czech nationals who rallied behind his crusade against the German-dominated establishment. Excommunicated in 1412 and charged with heresy 2 years later, Hus was burned at the stake on July 6, 1415, in Konstanz (Constance), Germany, an event that sparked widespread riots and ultimately civil war. Czechs still commemorate the day as a national holiday.

The hostilities began simply enough. Rioting Hussites (followers of Jan Hus) threw several Roman Catholic councilors to their deaths from the windows of Prague's New Town Hall (Novoměstská radnice) in 1419, a deed known as the "First Defenestration." It didn't take long for the pope to declare a crusade against the Czech heretics. The conflict widened

and by 1420 several major battles were being fought between the peasant Hussites and the Catholic crusaders, who were supported by the nobility. A schism split the Hussites when a more moderate faction, known as the Utraquists, signed a 1433 peace agreement with Rome at the Council of Basel. Still, the more radical Taborites continued to fight, until they were decisively defeated at the Battle of Lipany a year later.

RUDOLF II & THE SECOND GOLDEN AGE

Following this period of hostility, the nobility of Bohemia concentrated its power, forming fiefdoms called the Estates. In 1526, the nobles elected Archduke Ferdinand king of Bohemia, marking the beginning of Roman Catholic rule by the Vienna-based Habsburg family, which continued until the end of World War I.

Habsburg Emperor Rudolf II ascended to the throne in 1576 but uncharacteristically for a Habsburg chose to live in Prague rather than Vienna. This led to what became Prague's second golden age. Rudolf invited the great astronomers Johannes Kepler and Tycho Brahe to Prague and endowed the city's museums with some of Europe's finest art. The Rudolfinum, which was recently restored and houses the Czech Philharmonic, pays tribute to Rudolf's opulence.

Rudolf was relatively tolerant to the city's Jews, even hiring for a time the head of the Jewish community, Mordechai Maisel, to manage his financial affairs. Many of the splendors of Prague Jewish quarter, Josefov, were built during this time.

Rudolf brought many benefits to Prague but ultimately failed to resolve the ever-present split between Catholics and Protestants, setting the stage for the coming Thirty Years' War in Europe, a conflagration that eventually torched the entire continent and had no peer in terms of

Famous Czechs

- **Princess Libuše** (pre–9th c.) Fabled mother of Bohemia. Legend holds that the clairvoyant Libuše, the daughter of Bohemian philosopher Krok, stood on Vyšehrad Hill and foretold that on this land a great city would stand. She and Prince Přemysl Oráč declared the first Bohemian state, launching the Přemyslid dynasty, which lasted from the 10th to the 12th century.

- **St. Wenceslas (Svatý Václav;** ca. 907–35) Patron saint of Bohemia. Prince Wenceslas was executed at the site of the present-day city of Stará Boleslav—on the orders of his younger brother, Boleslav, who took over the Bohemian throne. A popular cult arose proclaiming the affable and learned Prince Wenceslas as the perpetual spiritual ruler of all Czechs. A statue of him at the top of the square erected in 1912.

- **Charles IV (Karel IV;** 1316–78) Bohemian king, Holy Roman Emperor, and chief patron of Prague. Born to John of Luxembourg and Eliška, the sister of the last Přemyslid king, Charles ascended the throne in 1346, and during his reign he made Prague the seat of the Holy Roman Empire and one of Europe's most advanced cities. He also inspired several key sites through the country, including Prague's university (Univerzita Karlova), stone bridge (Karlův most), largest New Town park (Karlovo nám.), and the spa town of Karlovy Vary.

- **Master Jan Hus** (1369 or 1370–1415) Religious reformer, university lecturer, and Czech nationalist symbol. Hus questioned the authority of the pope and called for the formation of a Bohemian National Church. From his stronghold at Bethlehem Chapel in Old Town, he declared that the powerful clergy should cede their property and influence to the people. In 1414, he was summoned to explain his views before the Ecclesiastic Council at Konstanz in Germany but was arrested on arrival. He was burned at the stake as a heretic on July 6, 1415, a day considered the precursor to the Hussite Wars and now a Czech national holiday. His church lives on today in the faith called the Czech Brethren.

- **Bedrich Smetana** (1824–84) Nationalist composer. After studying piano and musical theory in Prague, Smetana became one of Bohemia's most revered composers, famous for his fierce nationalism. His *Vltava* movement in the symphony *Má Vlast (My Country)* is performed on the opening night of the Prague Spring Music Festival. His opera *The Bartered Bride* takes a jaunty look at Czech farm life.

- **Antonín Dvořák** (1841–1904) Neo-Romantic composer and head of Prague Conservatory. Dvořák is best known for his symphony *From the New World,* which was inspired by a tour of the United States. His opera about a girl trapped in a water world, *Rusalka,* remains an international favorite; it became a popular film in Europe, starring Slovak actress Magda Vášáryová.

- **Franz Kafka** (1883–1924) Writer. Kafka was a German-Jewish Praguer who for much of his adult life worked in relative obscurity as a sad Prague insurance clerk. In works such as *The Metamorphosis, The Castle,* and *Amerika,* Kafka described surreal and suffocating worlds of confusion. Now many use the adjective *Kafkaesque* to mean "living in absurdity."

- **Tomáš G. Masaryk** (1850–1937)   Philosopher, professor, and Czechoslovakia's first president. Educated in Vienna and Leipzig, Masaryk spent decades advocating Czech statehood. In 1915, he made a landmark speech in Geneva calling for the end of the Habsburg monarchy. He received the backing of President Woodrow Wilson at the end of World War I for a sovereign republic of Czechs and Slovaks, which was founded in October 1918. He served nearly 17 years as president.

- **Alexander Dubček** (1921–92)   Government leader. Though he's not a Czech, Dubček is a key figure in the history of Prague and the country. A Slovak Communist, he became the first secretary of the Communist Party in January 1968, presiding over the "Prague Spring" reforms. After he was ousted in the August 1968 Soviet-led invasion, Dubček faded from view, only later to stand with Havel to declare the end of hard-line Communist rule in 1989. He returned to become speaker of Parliament after the Velvet Revolution but was killed in a car accident in 1992.

- **Václav Havel** (b. 1936)   Author, dissident, ex-president. Absurdist playwright in the 1960s, Havel became a leading figure in the prodemocracy movement Charter 77 and the first president after leading the Velvet Revolution. See the box "Václav Havel & the 1970s," p. 18.

Among other famous Czech expats are Oscar-winning film director **Miloš Forman** *(Amadeus, One Flew Over the Cuckoo's Nest)* and **Milan Kundera,** the author of *The Unbearable Lightness of Being* and other widely admired works about 20th-century Czech life. Kundera is now a French citizen and bitterly refuses to make a public return to his homeland, after having left during the dark days of Communist "normalization."

The Czech Republic is the homeland of many supermodels. Former Wonderbra icon **Eva Herzigová** hails from the blue-collar northern Bohemian industrial berg of Litvínov—whose smokestacks are about as far removed as you can get from the catwalks. Model, actress, and writer **Paulina Pořízková** is from the town of Prostějov; recently crowned the "Sexiest Woman Alive," **Karolína Kurková** is from Děčín, near the German border; and tsunami survivor and activist **Petra Němcová** is from Karviná, in Moravia.

Mention should also be made of **Ivana Trump,** born in Gottwaldov (now known again as Zlín), east of Prague in Moravia. The woman who first defined to the term "Velvet Divorce" was a skier on the Czechoslovak National Team and a model before marrying billionaire husband "The Donald" in 1977 (divorcing in 1991). Her first novel, *For Love Alone,* took place partly in Bohemia.

destruction until the world wars of the 20th century.

Prague has the dubious distinction as being the place where the war started. Conflicts between the Catholic Habsburgs and Bohemia's ever-present Protestant nobility came to a head on May 23, 1618, when two Catholic governors were thrown out of the windows of Prague Castle, in the Second Defenestration. The war eventually lasted until 1648, with the defeat of the Swedish army on the Charles Bridge (you can still see war damage on the side of the Old Town Bridge Tower). The war came to an end with the Peace of Westphalia.

THE BATTLE OF WHITE MOUNTAIN & THE AUSTRIAN OCCUPATION

The Thirty Years' War was a tragic setback for the Czechs and the Czech nation. One of the early decisive battles, presaging the Habsburg Catholics' sweeping victory in the Czech lands, was fought in 1620 on a hill in western Prague known as "Bílá Hora" (White Mountain).

The Czechs were ruled by their Protestant king, Frederick V of Palatinate. But Frederick was a lackluster commander-in-chief and the Habsburgs won decisively in a battle that lasted just 2 hours. The immediate repercussions were severe. The Austrians arrested some 47 Bohemian noblemen and publicly executed 27. Today, you'll find 27 crosses on the ground of Old Town Square to commemorate the executions. Following the battle, Frederick was run out of town to be forever known mockingly as the "Winter King," since he lasted just one winter on the throne. The Habsburgs went on to rule over the Czech lands for the next 300 years.

Vienna's triumph was Prague's loss, and the empire's focus shifted back to Vienna. Fresh waves of immigrants turned Prague and other towns into Germanic cities. By the end of the 18th century, Prague was dominated by Germans and the Czech language was on the verge of dying out.

INTO THE 20TH CENTURY & THE FOUNDING OF CZECHOSLOVAKIA

In the 19th century, the Industrial Revolution drew Czechs from the countryside into Prague, where a Czech national revival began.

As the economy grew, Prague's Czech population increased in number and power, eventually overtaking the Germans by around midcentury. In 1868, the Czech people threw open the doors to the gilded symbol of their revival, the neo-Renaissance National Theater (Národní divadlo), with the bold proclamation NÁROD SOBĚ ("The Nation for Itself") inscribed over the proscenium. Then, in 1890, at the top of Wenceslas Square, the massive National Museum Building (Národní muzeum) opened, packed with exhibits celebrating the rich history and culture of the Czech people.

As Czech political parties continued to call for more autonomy from Vienna, Archduke Ferdinand and his wife, Sophie, were assassinated in Sarajevo, setting off World War I. Meanwhile, a 65-year-old philosophy professor named Tomáš G. Masaryk seized the opportunity to tour Europe and America, speaking in favor of creating a combined democratic Czech and Slovak state.

As the German and Austrian armies wore down in 1918, the concept of "Czechoslovakia" gained international support. U.S. President Woodrow Wilson backed Masaryk on October 18, 1918, in Washington, D.C., as the professor proclaimed the independence of the Czechoslovak Republic in the Washington Declaration. On October 28, 1918, the sovereign Republic of Czechoslovakia was founded in Prague. Masaryk returned home in December after being elected (in absentia) Czechoslovakia's first president.

THE FIRST REPUBLIC: 1918–38

The 1920s ushered in an exceptional but brief period of freedom and prosperity in Prague. Czechoslovakia, its industrial strength intact after the war, was one of the 10 strongest economies in the world. Prague's capitalists lived the Jazz Age on a par with New York's industrial barons. Palatial Art Nouveau villas graced the fashionable Bubeneč and Hanspaulka districts, where smart parties were held nonstop.

The Great Depression gradually spread to Prague, however, drawing sharper lines between the classes and nationalities. As ethnic Germans in Czech border regions found a champion in the new German Chancellor Adolf Hitler in 1933, their calls to unify under the Third Reich grew louder.

In 1938, Britain's Neville Chamberlain and France's Edouard Daladier, seeking to avoid conflict with the increasingly belligerent Germans, met Hitler and Italy's Benito Mussolini in Munich. With the signing of the "Munich Accord" they agreed to cede the Bohemian border areas (which Germans called the "Sudetenland") to Hitler on September 30 and marked one of the darkest days in Czech history. Chamberlain returned to London to tell a cheering crowd that he'd achieved "peace in our time." But within a year, Hitler had absorbed the rest of the Czech lands and installed a puppet government in Slovakia. Soon Europe was again at war.

WORLD WAR II

During the next 6 years, more than 130,000 Czechs were killed, including more than 80,000 Jews. Though Hitler ordered devastation for other cities, he sought to preserve Prague and its Jewish ghetto as part of his planned museum of the extinct race.

The Nazi concentration camp at Terezín, about 48km (30 miles) northwest of Prague, became a way station for many Czech Jews bound for death camps at Auschwitz and points east. Thousands died of starvation and disease at Terezín even though the Nazis managed to dress it up as a "show" camp for Red Cross investigators.

Meanwhile, the Czechoslovak government in exile, led by Masaryk's successor, Edvard Beneš, tried to organize resistance from friendly territory in London. One initiative came in May 1942, when Czechoslovak paratroopers were flown in to assassinate Hitler's lead man in Prague, Reich Protector Reinhard Heydrich. The paratroopers managed to set a charge to blow up Heydrich's motorcade as it passed along a road north of Prague. Heydrich survived the initial blast, but died in the hospital days later. Hitler retaliated by ordering the total liquidation of a nearby Czech village, Lidice, where 192 men were shot dead and more than 300 women and children were sent to concentration camps. Every building in the town was bulldozed to the ground. The paratroopers, Jozef Gabčík and Jan Kubiš, and some of their civilian helpers, were hunted down by Nazi police and trapped in the Cyril and Methodius church on Resslova Street in Nové Město near the Vltava. They reportedly shot themselves to avoid being captured. The debate still rages on whether the assassination brought anything but more terror to occupied Bohemia.

THE ADVENT OF COMMUNISM

The final act of World War II in Europe played out where the Nazis started it, in Bohemia. As U.S. troops liberated the western part of the country, Gen. George Patton was told to hold his troops at Plzeň and wait for the Soviet army to sweep through Prague because of the Allied Powers' agreement made at Yalta months before. Soviet soldiers and Czech civilians liberated Prague in a bloody street battle on the last days of the war. Throughout Prague you can see small wall memorials on the spots where Czechs fell battling the Germans.

Václav Havel & the 1970s

In 1976, during the worst of "normalization," the Communists arrested a popular underground rock band called the Plastic People of the Universe on charges of disturbing the peace. This motivated some of Prague's most prominent artists, writers, and intellectuals, led by playwright Václav Havel, to establish Charter 77, a human-rights advocacy group formed to pressure the government—then Europe's most repressive—into observing the human rights principles of the 1975 Helsinki Accords. In the years that followed, Havel, the group's perceived leader, was constantly monitored by the secret police, the StB. He was put under house arrest and jailed several times for "threatening public order."

On his return from exile in England, Edvard Beneš ordered the expulsion of 2.5 million Germans from Czechoslovakia and the confiscation of all their property. Many thousands of Germans were killed in reprisal attacks. The "Beneš Decrees" are still an occasional bone of contention between the Czech and German governments. Meanwhile, the Czechoslovak government, exhausted and bewildered by fascism, nationalized 60% of the country's industries, and many looked to Soviet-style Communism as a new model. Elections were held in 1946, and Communist leader Klement Gottwald became prime minister after his party won about one-third of the vote.

Through a series of cabinet maneuvers, Communists seized full control of the government in a bloodless coup in February 1948, and Beneš was ousted. Little dissent was tolerated, and a series of show trials began, purging hundreds of perceived threats to Stalinist Communist authority. Another wave of political refugees fled the country. The sterile, centrally planned Communist architecture began seeping into classical Prague.

1968 & THE PRAGUE SPRING

In January 1968, Alexander Dubček, a career Slovak Communist, became first secretary of the Czechoslovak Communist Party. Long before Mikhail Gorbachev,

Dubček tinkered with Communist reforms that he called "socialism with a human face." His program of political, economic, and social reform (while seeking to maintain one-party rule) blossomed into a brief intellectual and artistic renaissance known as the "Prague Spring."

Increasingly nervous about what seemed to them a loss of party control, Communist hard-liners in Prague and other eastern European capitals conspired with the Soviet Union to remove Dubček and his government from power. On August 21, 1968, Prague awoke to the rumble of tanks and 200,000 invading Warsaw Pact soldiers claiming "fraternal assistance." Believing that they'd be welcomed as liberators, these soldiers from the Soviet Union, Poland, East Germany, Bulgaria, and Hungary were bewildered when angry Czechs confronted them with rocks and flaming torches. The Communist grip tightened, however, and Prague fell deeper into the Soviet sphere of influence. Another wave of refugees fled. The following January, a university student named Jan Palach, in a lonely protest to Soviet occupation, doused himself with gasoline and set himself afire in Wenceslas Square. He died days later, becoming a martyr for the dissident movement. But the Soviet soldiers stayed for more than 2 decades during the gray period the Communists called "normalization."

THE VELVET REVOLUTION & BEYOND

Just after the Berlin Wall fell, and with major change imminent in the rest of central and eastern Europe, thousands of students set out on a chilly candlelit march on November 17, 1989. As part of their nonviolent campaign, they held signs calling for a dialogue with the government. Against police warnings, they paraded from the southern citadel at Vyšehrad and turned up National Boulevard (Národní třída), where they soon met columns of helmeted riot police. Holding their fingers in peace signs and chanting, "Our hands are free," the bravest 500 sat down at the feet of the police. After an excruciating standoff, the police moved in, squeezing the students against buildings and beating them with clubs.

Although nobody was killed and the official Communist-run media presented the story as the quiet, justified end to the whims of student radicals, clandestine videotapes and accounts of the incident blanketed the country. By the next day, Praguers began organizing their outrage. Havel and his artistic allies seized the moment and called a meeting of intellectuals at the Laterna Magika on Národní, where they planned more nonviolent protests. Students and theaters went on strike, and hundreds of thousands of Praguers began pouring into Wenceslas Square, chanting for the end of Communist rule. Within days, factory workers and citizens in towns throughout the country joined in a general strike. On Wenceslas Square, the protesters jingled their keys, a signal to the Politburo that it was time to go. By the end of the year, the Communist government fell and on New Year's Eve, Havel, joined by Dubček, gave his first speech as president of a free Czechoslovakia. Because hardly any blood was spilled, the coup was dubbed "the Velvet Revolution."

The 1990s brought both democracy and free-market capitalism to the country, with the early phases marked by wild corruption sprees, when the whole of eastern Europe was known as "the Wild East." Czechoslovakia as a country was unable to resist the pressures of freedom as Slovaks stepped up their demands for an independent state. Czechoslovakia split peacefully into the independent Czech and Slovak republics on January 1, 1993.

Prosperity eventually returned to the country by the end of the end of the 1990s and the Czechs realized a long-held foreign policy goal in 2004 of joining the European Union. One major setback came in 2002, with the tragic flooding of the Vltava that inundated large parts of Malá Strana and other riverside districts, but luckily spared much of the Old Town. The damage ran into the billions of euros, but the city managed to turn the tragedy into a boon, using the reconstruction effort to rebuild large sections of the city, like Smíchov, Holešovice, and Karlín, that had been neglected for decades. Much transformation work still needs to be done and corruption remains a chronic problem, but the general consensus is that the Czechs have somehow clawed their way back into the Western family of nations and this time may be there to stay.

3 THE CZECH REPUBLIC IN POPULAR CULTURE

Czech contributions to Western culture are not widely recognized outside the country's borders. That's a shame since despite being a relatively small country, the output in film, literature, and music has been nothing short of remarkable.

FILM

Czech filmmaking has a long tradition, but the heyday came in the mid-1960s when a group of young directors made quirky films that managed to capture both the pathos of life under Communism and the Czechs' innate pluck and humor under adverse circumstances. These "New Wave" films as they were called took the world by storm, garnering two Oscars for best foreign film and several other nominations.

Jiří Menzel and Miloš Forman were the leading directors at the time. An easy-to-find example of this period's work (with English subtitles) is Menzel's Oscar-winning *Closely Watched Trains,* a snapshot of the odd routine at a rural Czech train station.

Forman made his splash with a quirky look at a night in the life of a town trying to have fun despite itself. *The Fireman's Ball* shows Forman's true mastery as he captures the essence of being stone-bored in a gray world, yet he still makes it thoughtful and funny. Of course, this was made before Forman emigrated to the big budgets of Hollywood and first shocked Americans with *Hair.* He then directed the Oscar-winning *One Flew Over the Cuckoo's Nest* and *Amadeus.* For *Amadeus,* Forman sought authenticity, so he received special permission from the Communists to return to Prague; while filming, he brought back to life the original Estates' Theater (Stavovské divadlo), where Mozart first performed.

Czech-based directors after the New Wave mostly disappeared from view, but one stunningly brave film was made in 1970, as the repressive post-invasion period known as "normalization" began its long, cold freeze of talent. In *The Ear (Ucho),* director Karel Kachyňa presents the anguished story of a man trapped in an apartment wired for sound, subject to the Communist leaders' obsession and paranoia with Moscow. That *The Ear* was made in the political environment of the time was astounding. That it was quickly banned wasn't. Fortunately, local TV has dusted off copies from the archives, and it has begun playing to art-house audiences again.

The film about Prague probably most familiar to American audiences is *The Unbearable Lightness of Being,* based on the book by émigré author Milan Kundera. Set in the days surrounding the 1968 Soviet invasion, the story draws on the psychology of three Czechs who can't escape their personal obsessions while the political world outside collapses around them. Many Czechs find the film disturbing, some because it hits home, others because they say it portrays a Western stereotype.

Nowadays, modern Czech directors are trying to get back some of that old mojo, but with only hit-and-miss successes. The father-and-son team of Zdeněk and Jan Svěrák did manage to win the Best Foreign Film Oscar in 1996 for *Kolja,* the bittersweet tale of an abandoned Russian boy grudgingly adopted by an aging Czech bachelor on the cusp of the 1989 revolution. Other important younger directors include Jan Hřebejk, who tends to make tough, unsympathetic films about modern life, like his 2004 *Horem Pádem* (Up and Down), and Petr Zelenka, who's made a series of offbeat, cult films that while all very different nevertheless manage to capture some of the absurdity of the 1960s' New Wave, such as 2002's *Rok dábla* (Year of the Devil), and *Knoflíkáři* (Buttoners). Many of these are available on DVD.

Prague has also become a popular location for shooting major motion pictures. Producer/actor Tom Cruise and director Brian De Palma chose it for the stunning night shots around Charles Bridge in the early scenes of *Mission: Impossible.* During shooting, a verbal brawl broke out with Czech officials, who jacked up the rent for use of the riverside palace that acts as the American Embassy in the film (the palace is actually claimed by the von Liechtenstein family). *Immortal Beloved,* a story of Beethoven, made use of Prague's timeless streets (shooting around the graffiti).

Five Czech Films to Rent on DVD

A list of great Czechoslovak and Czech films could run well into the several dozen, but these five convey a good flavor of Czech life over the decades, complete with ample doses of Czech sardonic wit seen as necessary to making sense of it all. All five are available with English subtitles through services such as Amazon (www.amazon.com) or Netflix (www.netflix.com).

1. *Loves of a Blonde* (1966). Miloš Forman's New Wave masterwork artfully combines the tender sadness of unrequited love and the frustrations felt by a group of single women stuck in dead-end jobs in a Czech factory town.
2. *Amadeus* (1984). Forman's absorbing Oscar-winning Mozart drama was partly filmed in Prague, an homage to the city that appreciated Amadeus's genius long before Vienna and the rest of the world caught on.
3. *Closely Watched Trains* (1965). Jiří Menzel charmed the world with this Oscar-winning tragicomedy about Miloš, a young man with "issues" who only discovers his manhood in a futile act of resistance against the Nazis in World War II.
4. *The Unbearable Lightness of Being* (1988). Imperfect yet highly watchable adaptation of the Milan Kundera novel of the same name manages to capture something of Czech humor under adverse circumstances in the days before the Warsaw Pact invasion of 1968.
5. *Czech Dream* (Český sen; 2004). Offbeat documentary is a brilliant send-up of consumer capitalism and shows what can happen when a new shopping center offers impossibly low prices. The problem is, it's just a "dream."

More recently, the fields and forests around the Barrandov film studios south of the city center were transformed into idyllic Narnia for 2008's *Prince Caspian: The Return to Narnia*, based on the C. S. Lewis classic.

BOOKS
Fiction

Any discussion of Czech literature with visiting foreigners usually begins and ends with Milan Kundera. Reviled among some Czechs who didn't emigrate, Kundera creates a visceral, personal sense of the world he chose to leave in the 1970s for the freedom of Paris. In *The Unbearable Lightness of Being,* the anguish over escaping the Soviet-occupied Prague he loves tears the libidinous protagonist Dr. Tomáš in the same way the love for his wife and the lust for his lover does. More Czech post-normalization angst can be found in *The Book of Laughter*

and Forgetting and *Laughable Loves.* Kundera's biting satire of Stalinist-style purges in the 1950s, *The Joke,* however, is regarded by Czech critics as his best work.

Arnošt Lustig, a survivor of the Nazi-era Terezín concentration camp and author of many works, including *Street of Lost Brothers,* shared the 1991 Publishers Weekly Award for best literary work with John Updike and Norman Mailer. In 1995, he became the editor of the Czech edition of *Playboy.*

The best work of renowned Ivan Klíma, also a survivor of Terezín, is translated as *Judge on Trial,* a study of justice and the death penalty.

Jaroslav Hašek wrote the Czech harbinger to *Forrest Gump* in *The Good Soldier Švejk,* a post–World War I satire about a simpleton soldier who wreaks havoc in the Austro-Hungarian army during the war.

2

Five Czech Books for the Plane or Backpack

Though publishers have dropped the ball in recent years when it comes to publishing English translations of Czech literature, fortunately there's a good body of work available in English, including most of the classics from the Communist period. Here is a highly subjective list of five "musts."

1. *The Joke,* Milan Kundera. Kundera's first novel was written in the brief period of relative freedom in the mid-1960s and tells the story of Ludvík, an enthusiastic young Communist whose sarcastic sense of humor puts him at odds with the party faithful and changes his life forever. Funny and moving in equal measure.

2. *I Served the King of England,* Bohumil Hrabal. Far more than Kundera, Czechs identify with Hrabal and his themes of quirkiness, absurdity, and human folly. This is his most accessible book in English and describes the hilarious rise and fall of an ambitious waiter during the Nazi occupation and the years immediately after.

3. *Life With a Star,* Jiří Weil. Weil wrote two classics on the fate of Jews in Nazi-occupied Prague during World War II. This book tells the story of a young Jewish banker who goes undercover to save his life. The other. *Mendelssohn is On the Roof,* is equally gripping.

4. *The Good Soldier Švejk,* Jaroslav Hašek. Humorous tale of a Czech army recruit who'll do anything to avoid military service in Austrian army during World War I, including acting the half-wit. Or maybe he really is that stupid? Czechs laugh too but tend to resent the portrayal; after reading it at least you'll understand all those restaurants named "Švejk" around the country.

5. *The Castle,* Franz Kafka. Kafka is more widely appreciated than read, but give this book or his short-story collections a try to understand the complexities of modern life as viewed by a prescient German-speaking Jewish insurance salesman in the years during and after World War I. The ending is unsatisfying but chilling.

Bohumil Hrabal, noted for writing about the Czech "everyman" and maybe the country's all-time favorite author, died in 1997 when he fell (so they said officially) out of a fifth-story window while trying to feed pigeons. His death was eerily similar to the fate of a character in one of his stories. He had two internationally acclaimed hits: *Closely Watched Trains* (also translated as *Closely Observed Trains,* on which the Menzel film was based), and *I Served the King of England.* When then-President Bill Clinton visited Prague in 1994, he asked to have a beer with Hrabal in the author's favorite Old Town haunt, the pub U Zlatého tygra (At the Golden Tiger).

No reading list would be complete without reference to Franz Kafka, Prague's most famous novelist, who wrote his originals in his native German. *The Collected Novels of Franz Kafka,* which includes *The Castle* and *The Trial,* binds his most claustrophobic works into a single volume.

Nonfiction

If it's contemporary philosophy you want, there is, of course, the philosopher ex-president. Václav Havel's heralded dissident essay, "The Power of the Powerless," explained how the lethargic masses were allowing their complacency with communism to sap their souls. His "Letters to Olga," written to his wife while in prison in the 1980s, takes you into his cell and his view of a moral world. Available are two solid English-translated compilations of his dissident writings: *Living in Truth* and *Open Letters*. *Disturbing the Peace* is an autobiographical meditation on childhood, the events of 1968, and Havel's involvement with Charter 77. His first recollections about entering politics are in "Summer Meditations," a long essay written during a vacation. Havel's most recent work *To the Castle and Back* (2008) recounts his ups and downs in high office as president of Czechoslovakia and later the Czech Republic from 1989 to 2003.

For an epic intellectual tour of the long, colorful, and often tragic history of the city, try the 1997 release of *Prague in Black and Gold* by native son and Yale literature professor Peter Demetz. His follow-up book, *Prague in Danger* (2008), is an absorbing history of Prague life during the Nazi occupation interwoven with poignant tales of Demetz's own family.

MUSIC

Czechs have bequeathed the world at least three household names in classical music: **Antonín Dvořák, Bedřich Smetana,** and **Leoš Janáček,** as well as heaps of pop tunes that are mostly unknown beyond the country's borders but still fun to listen to.

Dvořák is best known to visitors for his Symphony No. 9 *(From the New World)*, which was written during his stay in the United States in the 19th century and was so beloved it was taken to the moon by astronaut Neil Armstrong during his Apollo mission in 1969.

Smetana wrote probably the best-known piece of Czech classical music, the Moldau Symphony *(Vltava)*, whose ominous low notes (like thunder rolls) will be instantly recognizable to any classical music lover. Smetana's composition was

---

Five Czech Songs for the iPod or MP3 Player

Google and YouTube have made it easier than ever before to find and sample Czech music ahead of your visit. Simple searches like "best Czech songs" or "Czech music hits" bring up hundreds of tunes that you can listen to, watch performed, or note for downloading on sites such as iTunes. If anything, the variety is overwhelming and you'll have to look around to find your niche. Some places to start:

1. *Proměny (Changes)*, Čechomor. Dreamy ballad by the country's leading folk, or "world music," band whose phrasing and harmonies sound as if they could have drifted straight out of the Middle Ages.
2. *Lady Carneval*, Karel Gott. One of the best-known songs from the 1960s by a Czech crooner who's been likened to Tom Jones, Frank Sinatra, and Engelbert Humperdinck all rolled into one. He's still at it well into his seventh decade.
3. *Porcelánový prasata (Piggy Bank)*, Kabát. Don't blast this through your ear buds if you want to keep year hearing. This is loud, aggressive rock that touches both an anarchic and nationalistic chord and remains wildly (inexplicably) popular.
4. *Srdce (Heart)*, Kryštof. One of a number of likable teen-rock tunes from arguably the best pop band to emerge in the past decade.
5. *Oh Baby, Baby*, Marta Kubišová. Nostalgic '60s tune brings back those optimistic days before the 1968 Warsaw Pact invasion. Kubišová's music was banned by the Communists in the '70s and '80s and she was only permitted to perform publicly after 1989.

part of six symphonic poems entitled *Má Vlast* (My Homeland) that sums up perfectly in bars and measures Czechs' yearning for their own national identity in the 19th century.

Janáček, an early 20th century composer from Moravia, will be less familiar to most, but better known perhaps to hardcore opera lovers for compositions such *Káťa Kabanová* and *The Cunning Little Vixen*. His works mix traditional Moravian folk melodies with modern impulses to create music that initially sounds discordant but soon grow on you.

Czech popular music came into its own in the 1960s with singers like Karel Gott (who recently celebrated his 70th birthday and is still going strong), Marta Kubišová, and Helena Vondráčková. Czech pop at the time was heavily influenced by Western bands like the Beatles, but nevertheless retains something of the naïve hope and optimism of those days before the 1968 Warsaw Pact invasion when it seemed Czechoslovakia might actually break free of communism.

Modern Czech popular music mimics international trends in rock, pop, electronic, and hip-hop. Some of the more popular bands include Čechomor (beautifully rendered folk ballads), Kabát (hardcore rock), and Support Lesbiens (tongue-in-cheek pop sung in English, and, yes, the misspelling is intentional).

4 ART & ARCHITECTURE IN THE CZECH REPUBLIC

ARCHITECTURE

Prague wears its history on its sleeve. Spared large-scale destruction during World War II, the city's medieval core remains largely intact. For history buffs, a walk down nearly any street in the Old Town is a real-life power-point presentation on 8 centuries of history. A little knowledge of architecture goes a long way toward helping to decode it.

Romanesque

Romanesque architecture dates from the turn of the first millennium and is the style of the oldest buildings still standing in Prague. Romanesque exteriors are often circular (a rotunda), and the interiors are starker and simpler than Gothic. Prague's finest Romanesque building is **St. George's Basilica** at the Prague Castle complex (see chapter 8, p. 114). Look past the building's misleading 17th-century facade to find a starkly beautiful stone interior with a lovely vaulted ceiling.

Gothic

Ask any Praguer what his or her favorite architectural style is and chances are they will say Gothic. It's no wonder. Gothic's signature soaring towers, spires, and buttresses are deeply connected to Prague's rise in the 14th century as one of Europe's great cities and its brief but impressive period as capital of the Holy Roman Empire under Charles IV.

In Prague's heyday the best architects of the time came here to build Charles's vision for a capital worthy of the empire. These included Peter Parler, who oversaw the building of **St. Vitus Cathedral** (p. 109), and Benedikt Ried, whose soaring ceiling in the **Vladislav Hall** (p. 112) at Prague Castle is consider a highpoint of late Gothic. Ried was also involved in building Kutná Hora's great **St. Barbara's Cathedral.**

Great Gothic buildings read like a greatest hits collection of the city's architecture. In addition to St. Vitus and the

Old Royal Palace, there's the **Týn Church,** the **Old Town Hall and Astronomical Clock,** and even the foundations of **Charles Bridge** itself (but not the statues—they came later). See chapter 7 for more on these structures.

Renaissance

Bohemia also participated in the great European renaissance of the 16th century, with its emphasis on classical and mythical figures, and above all harmony and symmetry in architectural design. Renaissance came to Prague via the Habsburgs and the nobility and their love of Italian style.

Renaissance buildings are easy to spot, just look for the trademark *sgraffito*—geometric or figurative designs etched into a building's stucco exterior. The **Schwarzenberg Palace** on Hradčanské náměstí, across from the entrance to Prague Castle, is the city's best example of Renaissance architecture.

Baroque

Baroque architecture is inevitably linked to the twin triumphs of the Austrian Habsburg Empire and the Roman Catholic Church following the 1620 Battle of White Mountain and efforts to reindoctrinate the Czechs with over-the-top displays of power and wealth. You can forget the architectural adage "less is more"; with baroque more is definitely more. Signature elements include big cupolas, marble columns, ornately painted frescoes, and all manner of marble and gold.

The most important baroque buildings in Prague are doubtless the **St. Nicholas Cathedral** in Malá Strana (p. 117) and the bright pink **Goltz-Kinský Palace** on Old Town Square, as well as many of the palaces in Malá Strana. The baroque period was an intensively active one; many church interiors in Prague (regardless of the exterior style) will have lavish baroque interiors.

19th-Century Neoclassical & Other "Neos"

The 19th century saw the reemergence of the Czech nation, and 19th-century buildings are invariably tied up with Czech nationalism. Unfortunately, the century was a relatively boring period for architectural invention. Prague architects took their cues from Vienna, which was in the thrall of "historicism"—basically copying historic styles such as Gothic, Classic, and Renaissance and appending the prefix "neo" to the front.

Landmark buildings from this time include the neo-Renaissance **National Theater, National Museum,** and **Rudolfinum** (p. 188). This is also when Prague received all of those Gothic spires that inspired its nickname of "City of a Thousand Spires." During the latter part of the 19th century, "neo-Gothic" was all the rage.

Art Nouveau & "Cubist"

The turn of the 19th century elicited a strong reaction from Prague architects, tired of the sterility of the previous decades. Art Nouveau, with its wavy lines, florid designs and conscious ornamentation, was everything neoclassical was not. Prague Art Nouveau emerged as a synthesis of the prevailing Parisian style mixed in elements of the more subdued Viennese Secession style. Today, buildings of both types can be found in the city center.

The best example of the Parisian variant is the **Obecní Dům** (Municipal House), just off of Náměstí Republiky (p. 128). For Secession, check out the **turn-of-the-19th-century apartment buildings** in Josefov, along Pařížská and around the former Jewish quarter. You can't help but notice the inlaid jewel- and tile-work embedded into the facades like a finely crafted jewelry box.

Cubism came a few years later and like Art Nouveau was a reaction to the sterility of the 19th century. Cubism was a purely Czech invention that never caught on outside the country's borders; nevertheless the Cubist effects are striking. Check out the facade on the **House of the Black Mother of God,** just off of Celetná in the Old Town (p. 163).

Functionalist & Communist

These styles bear a superficial resemblance, but in fact have nothing to do with each other. Functionalism was a style that arose in the 1920s, greatly influenced by Germany's Bauhaus, that sought to strip away all unnecessary ornamentation from a building, leaving in its place clean, horizontal lines and spare but pleasing boxy shapes.

Arguably, the best Functionalist building in Prague is the 1928 **Veletržní palác** in Holešovice, originally built as an exhibition space for trade fairs and now housing the National Gallery's Museum of 20th and 21st Century Art.

Communist style, by contrast, came after World War II with the ascendancy of the communist regime. These buildings are boxy too, but the boxes reflect more a lack of imagination and money more than any conscious style choice. One of the more celebrated (and controversial) Communist buildings is the 1975 **Kotva** department store, built in Brutalist style, just off of Náměstí Republiky in the Old Town.

The brief exception to the uniformity of Communist architecture came with 1950s' Socialist-Realist style, where architects tried consciously to imitate Stalin's tastes. One of the very few examples of Socialist Realist architecture in Prague is the former **Hotel International** in Dejvice (now home to the **Crowne Plaza Hotel**).

ART IN THE CZECH REPUBLIC

The Czech contribution to painting and the visual arts has not been as profound as in other areas, like literature, film, and architecture. Czech painters, in general, didn't break out in a big way until the 19th

century and the coming of the Czech National Revival movement, with painters like Mikuláš Aleš and Antonín and Josef Mánes. The best of these mainly realist and landscape paintings can be found in the Museum of Czech 19th-Century Art at St. George's Convent in the Prague Castle complex (see chapter 7, p. 108). The Art Nouveau style of the early 20th century saw the emergence of the country's first (and possibly only) household name in painting, Alfons Mucha. Mucha's work can be viewed in the stained-glass windows at St. Vitus Cathedral, as well as at the Obecní Dům and at the Alfons Mucha Museum in Nové Město (New Town; see chapter 7).

The first decades of the 20th century, the early Modern period, saw an explosion of Czech talent working in styles like Cubism, Constructivism, and Surrealism. Check out painters such as Bohumil Kubišta, Josef Šíma, and the female Surrealist Toyen at the National Gallery's Museum of 20th and 21st Century art in Holešovice (p. 122).

World War II and the Communist takeover put an end to much of this output and for several years, Czech painters were constrained to working in the "Socialist-Realist" style (essentially mimicking Soviet art and extolling the virtues of workers, peasants and the Communist Party).

Against this relatively modest backdrop, it may come as a surprise that one of the biggest names in contemporary art these days is a Czech, David Černý, whose irreverent, tongue-in-cheek murals, statues, and installations have been exhibited around the world. Černý first came to fame in the early 1990s, when he painted a Russian tank—an official monument to commemorate the country's liberation after World War II by the Soviet Union— the very unmilitary color pink. Since then, he's gone on to do several more public installations around Prague that mostly mock the powers that be or are meant to question modern assumptions. The best of these include an installation of giant babies crawling up the Žižkov TV tower (possibly meant to suggest our dependence on the media for sustenance); a hanging statue of St. Wenceslas astride an upside-down horse (perhaps mocking Czechs' uncritical worship of their own history) inside the Lucerna shopping arcade (p. 133); and a statue of two men urinating together into a basin shaped like the Czech Republic (possibly a comment on the self-deprecating nature of Czechs or perhaps their propensity to urinate outside whenever or wherever the urge strikes) just near the entrance to the Hergetova Cihelna restaurant (p. 93).

Černý's most notorious and best-known installation is doubtless "Entropa," mounted in Brussels in 2009 to coincide with the Czech Republic's holding of the rotating European Union presidency. In an obvious breach of E.U. decorum, the installation viciously lampooned each of the E.U.'s 27 member states, depicting Germany, for example, covered in highways zigzagging vaguely in the shape of a swastika, or Romania as a Dracula theme park. Depending on your point of view, it was either deeply insulting or a brilliant send-up of European stereotypes. Neither the Czech government nor the bureaucrats in Brussels were amused and Bulgaria, portrayed by Černý as a squat toilet, even demanded that the installation be taken down. It was removed at the end of the Czech presidency in mid-2009 and has yet to find a permanent home.

5 EATING & DRINKING IN THE CZECH REPUBLIC

Czech food is filling and hearty, and when it's done well is reminiscent of a good home-cooked meal. Not surprisingly, given the country's long period as part of the Austro-Hungarian Empire, Czech cuisine borrows heavily from its neighbors. The schnitzels, strudels, and goulashes you'll see on menus here have all been gently appropriated but often given a local twist. Czech goulash, for example, is milder than its Hungarian cousin and comes in a number of variations depending on whether the main ingredient is beef or pork. Schnitzels are typically built around fried chicken or pork instead of veal, normally the heart of a Viennese schnitzel.

If there's a uniquely Czech contribution in all of this, it's likely to be the bread or potato dumplings, *knedliky,* that accompany many main dishes. These are essentially big balls of dough prepared in boiling water that come sliced and (hopefully) steaming hot to your plate. They are great for soaking up the extra gravy or sauce from the goulash.

TRADITIONAL MEALS
Starters
Traditional Czech meals invariable start out with a soup, often beef or chicken broth or maybe something heartier like *kulajda,* a potato-mushroom cream soup, seasoned with dill and a shot of vinegar to make it slightly sour. The herb soups are often the most piquant part of the meal, but the meat-based broths, whether chicken or beef, are frequently served without filtering the heavy renderings.

Appetizers are often passed over to get to the main course, but traditional starters are likely to include salads, ham rolls, and sometimes imported dishes like beef carpaccio or smoked salmon.

Main Courses
No self-respecting Czech restaurant could open its doors without serving at least

some version of the three national foods: *vepřo, knedlo,* and *zelo* (pork, dumplings, and cabbage). The **pork** *(vepřové maso)* is usually a shoulder or brisket that is baked and lightly seasoned or breaded and fried like a schnitzel *(řízek)*. Unlike German sauerkraut, the **cabbage** *(zelí)* is boiled with a light sugar sauce. The **dumplings** are light and spongy if made from flour and bread *(houskové knedlíky)*, or dense and pasty if made from flour and potatoes *(bramborové knedlíky)*. This "VKZ" combo cries out for an original **Budweiser (Budvar), Kozel,** or **Pilsner Urquell** beer to wash it down.

Other standard main courses include *svíčková na smetaně,* slices of beef that are baked and served in a vegetable-based cream sauce served over tender, spongy, sliced dumplings; roast beef *(roštěná);* baked chicken *(grilované kuře);* and smoked ham and other spicy cured meats *(uzeniny).*

A local favorite is *cmunda,* found at the pub U medvídků (p. 196): a steaming potato pancake topped with sweet boiled red cabbage and spicy Moravian smoked pork. Also popular is **wild game,** such as venison, goose, rabbit, and duck, and the more exotic, like the wild boar goulash

served at U modré kachničky (one of the better Czech-centric restaurants; p. 93). Czech sauces can be heavy and characterless but occasionally they are prepared with daring doses of spice.

There's also usually a good selection of indigenous freshwater fish, such as trout, perch, and carp, the Christmas favorite. People worry about the safety of waterways, but most fish served in Prague come from controlled fish farms. Since the country has no coastline, you'll find most **seafood** at the more expensive restaurants, but a growing selection of salmon, sea bass, shark, and shellfish is shipped in on ice.

BEER

Beer, called *pivo,* is the Czech national beverage. It's a perfectly acceptable accompaniment to either lunch or dinner (and occasionally even breakfast). You'll find it not only at the lowliest pubs but also the finest restaurants. Indeed, wherever Czechs congregate, you can be sure there will be pub or a beer stand somewhere nearby. And it's not just a guy thing either; it's very popular with women too.

Beer goes back a long way. It's been served in pubs for centuries, often made

---

Ordering a Beer in a Czech Pub

Ordering a beer Czech-style is simple and takes just a few words to master. After sitting down at a pub or restaurant, when the barman or waiter comes to take your order, simply say *pivo prosím* (beer please) and indicate with your fingers how many you want. A thumb is one, a thumb and index finger is two, and so on in order. The next question, invariably, will be "large or small?" *Velké* (vel-keh) means "large" and refers to a half liter (about 16 oz.); *malé* (mall-eh) means "small," or a third of a liter (about 10 oz.). It will be taken for granted that you want the golden Pilsner-style lager; so if you'd like a dark beer, make a point of saying *"tmavé"* (tuh-*mah*-veh). The last question might be what octane you want. If you'd like the lighter, less-alcoholic 10-degree beer, say *"desítku"* (des-*seet*-koo). Standard 12-degree brew is *dvanáctku* (duh-vah-naht-skoo). After you've finished, if you'd like another, say *ještě jedno* (yesh-tye yed-no) for "one more." If you'd like to pay up and move on, say *zaplatím prosím* (zah-plaht-*eem* pro-*seem*), which translates awkwardly as "I will pay now, please."

by monks who lived off the proceeds. The earliest incarnations bore only a faint resemblance to what we consider beer nowadays. Modern-day Pilsner-style pale lager was first brewed in the western Bohemian city of Plzeň (or *Pilsen,* hence the name) in 1842, and the beer industry hasn't looked back since. That brewery, Pilsner Urquell, by the way, is still going strong. See p. 240 for a tour of the Pilsner Urquell brewery.

Typical Czech beer is not exactly the same as you're used to back home. Czech beer tends to be heavier and hoppier than standard American or English lagers, and even a bit zippier than German beers. There are also not as many varieties here. While Czechs do dabble occasionally in dark beer *(tmavé pivo),* stouts, and porters, the main diet invariably consists of the pale Pilsner-style beers known locally as "light" beer *(světlé pivo).* That said, you won't find American-style "light," or low-calorie, beer. Instead, beer is sold according to degree (a technical term that refers to the amount of malt extract used in brewing). The two most common strengths are 10-degree (often confusingly written as 10%—though it doesn't mean 10% alcohol content) and 12-degree. Ten-degree beers typically contain less alcohol (about 3.5% by volume as opposed to 4% for a standard 12-degree beer).

WINE

Wine, called *víno,* is not quite as storied as beer in the Czech Republic. Nearly all of the drinkable wines come from a small grape-growing area in southern Moravia, just across the border from the Austrian *Weinviertel.* For years, the big wineries were mostly state-owned and suffered from overproduction. Now, smaller vintners are setting up shop and quality is on the rise. Many Prague restaurants stock the better Czech varieties, and so don't be afraid to dabble. Czech wines have the virtue of being much cheaper than imported wines, and the quality is getting closer every year.

Czech wines come in both white and red, with most of the better bottles in white. Popular whites include *Tramín* (better known abroad by its German name, "Gewürztraminer"), Sauvignon, and *Rulandské bíle,* which seems to sound better as "Pinot Blanc"). The best reds include *Frankovka* (sometimes known abroad as "Blaufränkisch") and *Rulandské červené* ("Pinot Noir").

In Prague, at least, wines take a distinct back seat to beer. That situation is reversed in Moravia, where wine and beer seem at least equally appreciated. On hot days in the summer, though, Praguers do enjoy sitting back with a *bílý střik,* a glass of white wine cut with soda water. In winter, a cup of mulled wine, called *svařené víno* (or *svařák* for short), is great for cupping your hands around during a chilly stroll of Prague's Christmas market. In season, you'll find it at vendors everywhere. Also, in the fall, look out for *burčák,* young wine that's still in the process of fermenting. It looks and tastes like juice but packs a powerful wallop.

3

Planning Your Trip to Prague & the Czech Republic

Visiting Prague and the Czech Republic has never been easier. Short-term visitors from the U.S., Canada, Australia, and the European Union, including the U.K., don't require visas or need to take any particular health or safety precautions. Indeed, the Czech Republic is a member of the "Schengen Zone," the European Union's common customs and border area. That means if you're arriving from another E.U. member state by road or by rail, you won't even have to show a passport at the border.

As far as packing goes, your suitcase or backpack will look pretty much the same as for any U.S. or Continental European destination with four distinct seasons. If you forget anything, rest assured that just like at home, there's likely to be a shopping mall or convenience store down the street where you can find a suitable substitute. Even in midsummer, though, you'll want to pack some warm clothes, like a sweater or jacket for evening. And always prepare for rain at any day, any time.

More challenging than packing might be deciding how to divide your time between Prague and the rest of the country. What you are able to do depends largely on the length of your stay, but first-time visitors will want to focus most of their attention on Prague, the country's undisputed tourist jewel. Plan on at least 2 full days in the capital, and ideally longer if possible. If you don't have much time but would still like to see some of the rest of the country, it's easy to use Prague as a base for day trips. If you're a repeat visitor, no doubt you'll want to get out and see more of the rest of the Czech Republic. Even here, though, Prague makes a convenient base. It's centrally located and usually no more than a few hours by car or train from wherever you might want to go.

Whatever the plan is, don't forget to bring comfortable walking shoes and be ready to use them. Although there's great public transportation everywhere, you're probably going to do a lot more walking than you think. For additional help in planning your trip and for more on-the-ground resources in Prague and the Czech Republic, turn to chapter 14, "Fast Facts."

1 WHEN TO GO

THE BEST TIMES TO GO

Spring and fall are considered high season in Prague. Of the two, spring is the more beautiful. The magnolia trees begin to flower in early April and if you're blessed with a few sunny days, you're going to think you died and went to heaven. Fall (Sept–Oct) can be pleasant as well, with long, warm days and usually reliably sunny weather. Avoid travel over the Christmas, New Year's, and Easter holidays, when the city fills to brimming with tour groups from Germany and Italy. Midsummer (July–Aug) is considered shoulder (in-between) season. On the plus side, hotels usually discount prices 20% or more. On the minus, summers can be surprisingly iffy weather-wise. Some years bring weeks of hot sunshine; others, day after day of cold rain. You might also consider coming during the off-season: January and February and from November to mid-December. Yes, it's cold and often rainy or snowy, but the crowds thin out and you finally feel like you have this beautiful city to yourself.

THE WEATHER

Spring and fall generally bring the best weather for touring, with warm days and cool nights. Summers can be hit or miss, with some years bringing lots of rain and others weeklong stretches of hot sunshine. Winters can be cold and unusually long, sometimes lasting into April or even May.

Rain is a possibility any time of year, so be sure to pack an umbrella.

Prague's Average Temperatures & Rainfall

Month	High (F/C)	Low (F/C)	Rain (in./cm.)
January	34/1.1	24/–4.4	0.8/2
February	36/2.2	25/–3.8	0.7/1.8
March	46/7.8	32/0	1/2.5
April	54/12.2	36/2.2	1.4/3.6
May	64/17.8	45/7.2	2.3/5.8
June	69/20.5	51/10.5	2.7/6.9
July	72/22.2	54/12.2	2.6/6.6
August	73/22.8	53/11.6	2.5/6.4
September	65/18.3	48/8.8	1.6/4.1
October	54/12.2	39/3.8	1.2/3
November	41/5	32/0	1.1/2.8
December	36/2.2	28/–2.2	0.9/2.3

CALENDAR OF EVENTS

Prague has an active cultural calendar year-round. For an exhaustive list of events, check out our website at http://events.frommers.com

SPRING The **Prague Spring Music Festival** (www.festival.cz) held in late spring (late May, early June) is a world-famous, 3-week series of symphony, opera, and chamber performances. **Prague Khamoro** (www.khamoro.cz), usually held at the end of May, is a celebration of Roma (gypsy) culture. **Febiofest** (www.febiofest.cz), in March, is one of the largest noncompetitive film and video festivals in central Europe. Many of the films are shown in English or with English subtitles. The **One World** film festival (www.jedensvet.cz), also in March, brings together the best human rights and documentary films of the past year. Many of the screenings are in English. Late spring (late May to early June) brings the annual **Prague Fringe Fest** (www.praguefringe.com), a week of offbeat music, happenings, and theater at scattered venues around town.

SUMMER The summer kicks off with the **Prague Writers' Festival** (www.pwf.cz) in June. A handful of contemporary writers from around Europe and the United States, including usually a couple of big names, hold readings, book-signings, lectures, and happenings. **Tanec Praha** (Dance Prague; www.tanecpraha.cz) is an international dance festival in June that focuses on contemporary dance and movement theater. **United Islands** (www.unitedislands.cz) festival, usually a long weekend in June, is a carnival of jazz, rock, folk, and house music spread out over several islands in the Vltava River.

FALL The **Prague Autumn Music Festival,** in late September and early October, is similar to the spring festival but the focus is more on orchestral music, bringing some of Europe's best ensembles to play at Prague's Rudolfinum. The weeklong **Prague International Jazz Festival** (www.jazzfestivalpraha.cz), usually in November, attracts some big names in jazz. Performances are usually held in the Lucerna Music Hall and the city's oldest jazz venue, Reduta.

WINTER The **Christmas** season begins on St. Nicholas Eve (Dec. 5), when children traditionally dress as **St. Nicholas,** the devil, or an angel. The annual **Prague Christmas Market** in Old Town Square gets going about then. Stalls hawk all manner of food, mulled wine, ornaments, and cheap gifts in a festive atmosphere that toes a fine line between traditional and tacky. New Year's Eve is literally a blowout, and the entire town comes out to light firecrackers on Old Town Square, Wenceslas Square, and Charles Bridge. Watch your head, as every year hundreds of people are injured by errant bottle rockets.

For an exhaustive list of events beyond those listed here, check http://events.frommers.com, where you'll find a searchable, up-to-the-minute roster of what's happening in cities all over the world.

2 ENTRY REQUIREMENTS

PASSPORTS

All visitors to the Czech Republic are required to have a passport valid for 6 months from the date of entry. This applies as well to visitors from the European Union. The Czech Republic is a member of the European Union's Schengen common border area, meaning that if you arrive in the country by road or rail from another Schengen-member country (including Austria, Germany, Poland, Slovakia) you will not normally have to show a passport or pass through customs control.

VISAS

Visitors from the U.S., Canada, the European Union, including the U.K., and Australia do not need a visa to enter the Czech Republic. Visitors are permitted to stay in the country for 90 days of a 6-month period; E.U. visitors can stay 180 days. Visitors from other countries may need to obtain a visa before entering. A list of countries requiring entry visas as well as steps necessary to acquire a visa can be found on the website of the Czech Ministry of Foreign Affairs: www.mzv.cz.

CUSTOMS
What You Can Bring into the Czech Republic

Customs checks are relatively rare and most likely on arrival at Prague Airport you will be waved through without ever having to open your suitcase. Visitors are allowed to freely import the following: 200 cigarettes or 50 cigars or 250 grams of tobacco; 1 liter of spirits over 22% volume or 2 liters of fortified wine or sparkling wine, or 2 liters of still wine; 50 grams of perfume; 250ml of eau de toilette; as well as other goods to a value of about $225 (175€). Restricted items include meat, meat products, milk and dairy products, certain plants, and wildlife as well as illegal narcotics (including marijuana), weapons, explosives, and pornographic materials. Travelers entering or leaving the country with more than 10,000€ in cash are required by law to make a currency declaration.

What You Can Take Home from the Czech Republic

For information on what you're allowed to bring home, contact one of the following agencies:

U.S. Citizens: U.S. Customs & Border Protection (CBP), 1300 Pennsylvania Ave., NW, Washington, DC 20229 (© 877/287-8667; www.cbp.gov).

Canadian Citizens: Canada Border Services Agency (© 800/461-9999 in Canada, or 204/983-3500; www.cbsa-asfc.gc.ca).

U.K. Citizens: HM Customs & Excise at © 0845/010-9000, or 020/8929-0152 from outside the U.K.), or consult their website at www.hmce.gov.uk.

Australian Citizens: Australian Customs Service at © 1300/363-263, or log on to www.customs.gov.au.

New Zealand Citizens: New Zealand Customs, The Customhouse, 17–21 Whitmore St., Box 2218, Wellington (© 04/473-6099 or 0800/428-786; www.customs.govt.nz).

Medical Requirements

There are no special inoculations or preparations required to enter the Czech Republic. Tick-borne encephalitis can be a problem and if you're planning to camp or hike extensively in wilderness areas, you should get vaccinated.

---

3 GETTING THERE & GETTING AROUND

GETTING TO PRAGUE
By Plane

Prague Airport (code PRG; © 220-113-314; www.prg.aero) is the main international air gateway to the Czech Republic. The airport lies in the suburb of Ruzyně about 18km (12 miles) northwest of the center. The airport has two passenger terminals: North 1 and North 2 (in Czech: *Severin 1* and *Severin 2*). North 1 handles destinations outside the European Union, including overseas flights to and from the U.S. as well as flights from the U.K. (which is outside the E.U.'s Schengen common border zone). North 2 handles what are considered to be internal flights within the European Union, including flights to and from France, Germany, Italy, and Switzerland.

Prague is well served by the major European and international carriers, including several budget airlines. The Czech national carrier, **CSA** (www.czechairlines.com) operates regular direct service to New York's JFK airport, as well as Toronto. **Delta Airlines** (www.delta.com) offers regular direct service between Prague and both New York JFK and Atlanta.

To find a list of major airlines that travel to Prague, see "Airline, Hotel & Car-Rental Websites" on p. 287.

Getting into Town from the Airport

Taxis are the quickest but most expensive option. Two cab companies are licensed to operate at the airport. The more reliable of the two is **AAA Radiotaxi** (© 222-333-222; www.aaa-taxi.cz), look for the yellow cabs lined up outside both main terminals, North 1 and North 2. Fares with AAA average about 600Kč to the center. The trip normally takes about 25 minutes, but the drive can run as long as an hour during rush hour.

If you're staying in the immediate center of town, a cheaper alternative is to share a minibus operated by **CEDAZ** (© 221-111-111; www.cedaz.cz). Minibuses run regularly between the airport and the center for a flat fee of 480Kč for groups of one to four persons. CEDAZ also takes individual passengers from the airport to V celnici street in central Prague (near Náměstí Republiky) for 120Kč per person.

The most affordable option is public transportation. City bus no. 119 stops at both terminals and runs regularly from the airport to the Dejvická metro station (on Line A), from where the center is just three metro stops away. Bus no. 100 runs south from the airport to the area of Zličín and connects to metro Line B. Travel on both requires a 26Kč ticket purchased from yellow ticketing machines at the bus stop (note that the machines only accept change), or 30Kč if bought from the driver (exact change appreciated). Buy two tickets if you're carrying large luggage. A special **Airport Express** (designated "AE" on buses) runs to and from Prague's main train station and costs 50Kč per person each way. This is convenient if you are connecting directly to an international train.

By Car

Prague is easily accessible by major highway from around Europe. The main four-lane highways leading into and out of the city include the D1 motorway running south and east to Brno (2 hr.), Bratislava (3 hr.), and with connections to Kraków (8 hr.) and Budapest (6 hr.); the D5 motorway running southwest to Plzeň (Pilsen; 1 hr.) and Nuremberg (3 hr.), with connections to Italy and points in southern and western Europe; and the D8 running north to Dresden (2 hr.) and eventually Berlin (5 hr.). Vienna is about 5 hours by car, with most of the way along crowded two-lane highway.

Rentals

Rental cars are widely available and many of the big international agencies have offices either in town or at Prague Airport. To find a list of major rental car agencies in Prague, please see "Airline, Hotel & Car-Rental Websites," p. 287. To rent a car you must be at least 18 years old (though many rental agencies require drivers to be at least 23 or even 25) and hold a valid driver's license from your home country (U.S. states' licenses are acceptable).

Rental prices can be high, with daily rates starting at around 750Kč a day/unlimited mileage for an economy car, rising to about 1,500Kč per day for a full-sized car. Tips for getting a lower rate include renting in advance over the Internet or through Internet aggregators like Expedia.com, or opting for local agencies rather than the big internationals. It's also cheaper to rent from in-town agencies rather than the airport, since airport rentals must pay an airport surcharge.

Rental prices normally include unlimited mileage, VAT, and obligatory liability insurance, though the vehicle itself may not be insured against damage (be sure to ask). Some credit card companies insure cardholders against collision damage at no extra charge when they rent a car using the company's card. The car's insurance green card is required if you intend to drive the car outside the Czech Republic.

By Train

Prague lies on major European rail lines, with good connections to Dresden (2 hr.) and Berlin (5 hr.) to the north, and Brno (2–3 hr.), Vienna (4–5 hr.), Bratislava (3 hr.), and Budapest (7 hr.) to the south and east. New high-speed rail service, the Pendolino, has been introduced on the Prague-Vienna run, shortening the travel time on some trains to as little as 4 hours. More high-speed rail links are on the drawing board.

Prague has two international train stations, so makes sure to ask which station your train is using when you buy your ticket. Most international trains arrive at the main station, **Hlavní nádraží** (Wilsonova 80, Prague 1; ✆ **224-614-071;** www.cd.cz; metro stop: Hlavní] nádraží, Line C). Trains to and from Berlin, Vienna, and Budapest, however, often stop at the northern suburban station, **Nádraží Holešovice** (Vrbenského ul., Prague 7; ✆ **224-615-865;** www.cd.cz; metro stop: Nádraží] Holešovice, Line C).

Train information is available at ℂ 840-112-113 or on the web at http://jizdnirady.idnes.cz.

Of the two main stations, Hlavní nádraží is the larger and more popular, but it's also seedier. Built in 1909, this once beautiful four-story Art Nouveau structure was one of the city's beloved architectural gems before it was connected to a darkly modern dispatch hall in the mid-1970s. It has been neglected for years, but at this writing a massive reconstruction of the building complex and its surroundings is underway. From the train platform, you'll walk down a flight of stairs and through a tunnel before arriving in the ground-level main hall, which contains ticket windows,

a useful **Prague Information Service** office that sells city maps and dispenses information, and restrooms. Also useful is the **ČD center** (ℂ 840-112-113; www.cd.cz) run by the Czech Railways. It provides domestic and international train information as well as currency exchange and accommodations services. It is open daily 7 to 11am, 11:30am to 2pm, and 2:30 to 5:45pm. Visa and MasterCard are accepted. The station's basement has luggage lockers, but they aren't secure and should be avoided.

After you leave the modern terminal hall, a 5- to 10-minute walk to the left puts you at the top of Wenceslas Square and 15 minutes by foot from Old Town

Riding the Rails in the Czech Capital

While Prague has a fine metro and an extensive bus network, it's the tram—
tramvaj in Czech—that sets the transportation tone for the city. Any visitor will
be familiar with the sight of these (mostly) red and cream whales on rails, glid-
ing smoothly over the cobblestones and pushing their girth through impossibly narrow streets that were originally built to accommodate horses but are
now packed with cars, trucks, buses, and an endless stream of streetcars.

Tram no. 22 is a visitor's favorite. For the price of a 90-minute ticket—
26Kč —you can ride all the way from Prague Castle, down through the Lesser
Quarter, across the Vltava (with stunning views of Charles Bridge to the left)
and into the very center of town. Stay on the line and you're transported in
minutes through the gentrifying suburb of Vinohrady, and out to the Communist-era, high-rise housing projects of Hostívař and beyond. You may even have
some time left on your ticket to return to the center free of charge.

Prague's trams remain a repository of civility that long ago vanished from
other aspects of city life. Visitors—forced mostly to interact with waiters and
shop clerks—can sometimes get the impression that Czechs are gruff or rude.
But step onto a tram and it's like going back 50 years in time. For example, it's
still considered the height of ill manners on a crowded tram for a man to fail to
offer his seat to women of a certain age. This societal nicety curiously doesn't
apply as strictly to the city's newer and less-mannered metro.

The calculation of when and whether to offer a seat is not always easy in
practice. It's clear if a woman is elderly, enfeebled, or with child in arms, but
what if she's simply older and otherwise able-bodied? If you offer your seat too
quickly, you risk reminding her of her age; too slowly and you might elicit the
wrath of the rest of the car.

Younger women, too, are expected to yield their seats to older men, but an
added dose of sensitivity is required. Male egos are notoriously fragile. A former work colleague of mine—a man of about 60 and in pretty good shape—
once told me how depressed he became after an attractive young woman, on
seeing him standing, immediately leapt out of her seat and offered it to him.
He'd originally interpreted her smile and eye contact as flirtatious interest—not
unknown on Prague's trams.

Men are also expected to learn the delicate art of assisting young mothers
with baby carriages. Though some of the newer trams stand fairly low to the
ground, the older models are a good three steps up and in (or down and out).

Square. Metro line C connects the station easily to the other two subway lines and the rest of the city. Metro trains depart from the lower level, and tickets are avail-able from the newsstand near the metro entrance. Gouging taxi drivers line up outside the station and are plentiful throughout the day and night but are not recommended.

Prague has two smaller train stations. **Masaryk Station,** Hybernská ul., Prague 1 (© **221-111-122**), is primarily for travel-ers arriving on trains originating from other Bohemian cities. Situated about 10

Once a woman has locked eyes on you as the carriage-holder, there's no polite way of refusing. To properly off-load a pram, wait for the tram to come to a complete stop, precede the carriage down the steps, take firm hold of the front axle, and deliver the baby gently to the ground.

Prague's trams are generally quiet and there's not much banter among the riders. This changes after 11pm, when the city's day fleet retires to the garages, and special night trams are brought into service to ferry revelers from pubs in the center to the housing projects on the outskirts. The mood at 3 or 4am can get raucous, and night trams are often little more than pubs on wheels. There are no laws against carrying open containers of alcohol (at least none rigorously enforced). Unlike in New York, for example, there's no need to swill from a paper bag.

Prague's extensive tram network sprang up in the early years of the 20th century, more or less concurrent with the country's independence from the Austro-Hungarian Empire. The original electronic genius behind the system was a Czech, František Křížík, though it must be admitted the tram culture shares much in common with the empire's former capital, Vienna. Anyone who's spent much time there will feel easily at home here.

In a city that's now in the throes of remarkable change, the trams add a welcome sense of permanence. Looking at old tram maps from the 1920s and '30s, it's reassuring to see how little the basic layout has changed. The no. 12 tram still wends its way northward from the suburb of Smíchov in the southwest across town to the neighborhood of Holešovice and beyond—just as it did 70 years ago. The no. 17 tram still hugs the eastern bank of the Vltava for much of its run, as it always has. It's no stretch to say that a Czech Rip Van Winkle returning to the city from the 1930s would, in turns, be horrified and amazed to hear about the Nazi occupation, the Communist period, the Velvet Revolution, and now the European Union, but would have no trouble at all making his way home that night on the tram.

The future for Prague's trams looks secure. After a long period of neglect, the city appears committed to improving the tram infrastructure, including adding a new generation of super-sleek cars designed by none other than the Porsche group. These oversized, red and gray cars recall a kind of comic-book bullet train (even though trams top out at just 30 mph).

—Mark Baker

minutes by foot from the main train station, Masaryk is near Staré Město, just a stone's throw from náměstí Republiky metro station. **Smíchov Station,** Nádražní ul. at Rozkošného, Prague 5 (© **224-617-686**), is the terminus for commuter trains from western and southern Bohemia, though it's a convenient station for getting to popular day trip destinations like Karlštejn and Plzeň. The station has a 24-hour baggage check and is serviced by metro line B.

By Bus

The **Central Bus Station–Florenc,** Křižíkova 4–6, Prague 8 (℃ **900-144-444;** www.florenc.cz for timetable info), is a few blocks north of the main train station. Most local and long-distance buses arrive here. The adjacent Florenc metro station is on both lines B (yellow) and C (red). Florenc station is relatively small and doesn't have many visitor services. There are even smaller bus depots at **Želivského** (metro line A), **Smíchovské nádraží** (metro line B), and **Nádraží Holešovice** (metro line C).

GETTING AROUND

On Foot

Prepare to do plenty of walking. Most of the center of the city is closed to vehicles, including taxis, meaning you'll have to walk pretty much everywhere. Distances are relatively close, but always wear comfortable shoes since many of the streets are *paved* (if that's the right word) with cobblestones.

By Public Transportation

Prague's highly efficient public transportation network of metros (subways), trams, and buses (www.dpp.cz) is one of the few sound Communist-era legacies. In central Prague, metro stations abound. Trams and buses offer a cheap sightseeing experience but also require a strong stomach for jostling with fellow passengers in close quarters.

TICKETS & PASSES For single-use **tickets,** there are two choices. The first is a discount ticket, which costs 18Kč, or 9Kč for 6- to 15-year-olds (children 6 and under ride free), and this allows travel to up to five stations on the metro (not including the station of validation) or 20 minutes on a tram or bus. A full-price ticket costs 26Kč and allows for unlimited travel on metros, trams, and buses for up to 75 minutes (90 min. on Sat–Sun, public holidays, and after 8pm on workdays). The cheaper ticket is usually sufficient for short hops within the center, but note that

you can't use it to transfer from metros to trams or between trams.

A **1-day pass** good for unlimited travel is 100Kč, a **3-day pass** 330Kč, and a **5-day pass** is 500Kč. The 3- and 5-day passes include travel with one child from 6 to 15 years of age and only make sense if you are traveling with a child.

You can buy tickets from yellow coin-operated machines in metro stations or at most newsstands marked TABÁK or TRAFIKA. The machines have English instructions but are a little clunky to operate. First push the button for the ticket you want (either 18Kč or 26Kč) and then insert the money in the slot. Validate your ticket in little the stamping machine before you descend the escalator in the metro or as you enter the tram or bus. Hold on to your validated ticket throughout your ride—you'll need to show it if a ticket collector (be sure to check for his or her badge) asks you. If you're caught without a valid ticket, you'll be asked, and not so kindly, to pay a fine on the spot while all the locals look on, shaking their heads in disgust. The fine is 700Kč if paid on the spot and 950Kč if paid later.

BY METRO Metro trains operate daily from 5am to midnight and run every 2 to 10 minutes depending on the time of day. The three lines are identified by both letter and color: A (green), B (yellow), and C (red). The most convenient central stations are Muzeum, on both the A and C lines at the top of Václavské náměstí (Wenceslas Square); Můstek, on both the A and B lines at the foot of Václavské náměstí; Staroměstská on the A line, for Old Town Square and the Charles Bridge; and Malostranská, on the A line, serving Malá Strana and the Castle District. Refer to the metro map on the inside back cover for details.

BY TRAM & BUS The city's 24 tram lines run practically everywhere, and there's always another tram with the same number traveling back. You never have to

---

If you're taking tram no. 22 to Prague Castle from Národní or anywhere farther from the castle, I recommend getting a 26Kč ticket. It is valid for 75 minutes of tram ride on weekdays (up to 90 min. after 8pm and on weekends). Use the 18Kč ticket only for a short travel distance (one or two tram stops) since it is only good for 20 minutes and you may get caught beyond this limit.

---

hail trams; they make every stop. The most popular tram, no. 22 (aka the "tourist tram" or the "pickpocket express"), runs past top sights like the National Theater and Prague Castle. Regular bus and tram service stops at midnight, after which selected routes run reduced night schedules, usually only once per hour. Schedules are posted at stops. If you miss a night connection, expect a long wait for the next.

Buses tend to be used only outside the older districts of Prague and have three-digit numbers. Both the buses and tram-lines begin their morning runs around 4:30am.

BY FUNICULAR The funicular (cog railway) makes the scenic run up and down Petřín Hill every 10 minutes (15 min. in winter season) daily from 9am to 11:30pm with an intermediate stop at the Nebozízek restaurant halfway up the hill, which overlooks the city. It requires the 26Kč ticket or any of the same transport passes as other modes of public transport and departs from a small house in the park near the Újezd tram stop (trams no. 12, 20, 22) in Malá Strana.

By Taxi

While the situation has gotten marginally better in recent years, you still run the risk of getting ripped off by a taxi driver if you hail a taxi off the street in a heavily touristy area like Václavské náměstí or take one of the cabs parked at the main train station or at major hotels. A better idea is to call a taxi by phone or have your hotel or restau-

rant call one for you. Reputable companies with English-speaking dispatchers include: **AAA Radiotaxi** (✆ **14014** or 222-333-222; www.aaa-taxi.cz); **ProfiTaxi** (✆ **844-700-800;** www.profitaxi.cz); or **SEDOP** (✆ **841-666-333;** www.sedop. cz). AAA operates a few dedicated taxi stands around town, including ones conveniently located on Václavské náměstí and Malostranské náměstí, where you will find honest drivers.

The meter in an honest cab starts at 40Kč, 30Kč if you've ordered by phone, and it increases by 28Kč per kilometer. Fares around the center typically run from 100Kč to 200Kč, depending on the journey. A taxi from the center to the airport will cost around 600Kč.

Some tips for avoiding being ripped off: never get into an unmarked cab; ask the driver on entering what the approximate fare will be to your destination (he may not know exactly, but should be able to give some idea); make sure the driver has switched on the meter; and tell the driver you will need a receipt at the end of the ride. If you do get ripped off, it's better to pay the fare and learn a lesson than argue and end up with a bloody nose.

By Car

Driving in Prague isn't worth the money or effort. The roads are crowded and the high number of one-way streets can be incredibly frustrating. What's more, parking in the center is often restricted and available only to residents with pre-paid parking stickers. The only time you *might* want a car is if you only have a few days and plan to explore other parts of the Czech Republic.

RENTAL COMPANIES Try **Europcar,** Elišky Krásnohorské 9, Prague 1 (℃ **224-811-290;** www.europcar.cz). There's also **Hertz,** Karlovo nám. 15, Prague 2 (℃ **225-345-031;** www.hertz.cz). **Budget** is at Prague Airport (℃ **220-560-443;** www.budget.cz) and in the Hotel Inter-Continental, náměstí Curieových 5, Prague 1 (℃ **222-319-595**).

Local car-rental companies sometimes offer lower rates than the big international firms. Compare **CS Czechocar,** Kongresové centrum (Congress Center at Vyšehrad metro stop on the C line), Prague 4 (℃ **261-222-079** or 261-222-143; www.czechocar.cz), or at Prague Airport, Prague 6 (℃ **220-113-454**); or try **SeccoCar,** Přístavní 39, Prague 7 (℃ **220-800-647;** www.seccocar.cz).

Car rates can be negotiable. Try to obtain the best possible deal with the rental company by asking about discounts. Special deals are often offered for keeping the car for an extended period, for unlimited mileage (or at least getting some miles thrown in free), or for a bigger car at a lower price. You can usually get some sort of discount for a company or an association affiliation. Check before you leave home and take a member ID card with you.

ROADWAYS & EMERGENCIES Major roadways radiate from Prague like spokes on a wheel, so touring the country is easy if you make the capital your base. The Prague-Brno (D1) motorway *(dálnice)* is the most traveled, but the new Prague–Nürnberg (D5) motorway has opened a 2-hour express route into western Germany. In addition, the D-8 motorway is now complete all the way to Dresden to the north. You are advised to check the most recent map before you travel. Alternatively, see www.ceskedalnice.cz, where you will find updates on the newly built

motorways. If you are going to use any of these, you have to purchase a special stamp-sticker *(dálniční známky),* which goes on your windshield. Most filling stations and post offices sell them. The sticker costs 220Kč for 1 week, 330Kč for 1 month, or 1,000Kč for the calendar year. Rental cars should come with a valid stamp already.

Czech roads are often narrow and in need of repair. Add to this drivers who live out their Formula One race fantasies on these potholed beauties, and taking the train sounds a lot more appealing. The few superhighways that do exist are in good shape, so whenever possible, stick to them, especially at night. If you have car trouble, major highways have **SOS emergency phones** to call for assistance, located about every 1km (half mile). There's also the ÚAMK, a 24-hour auto club like AAA that can provide service for a fee. You can summon its bright yellow pickup trucks on the main highways by using the emergency phones. If you're not near an SOS phone or are on a road without them, you can contact ÚAMK at ℃ **1230** (www.uamk.cz), or **ABA,** another emergency assistance company, at ℃ **1240** (www.aba.cz).

In theory, foreign drivers are required to have an international driver's license, though this is often overlooked in practice and short-term visitors are fine with a valid national driver's licenses. Cars must also carry **proof of insurance** (a green card issued with rental cars), **registration** (in Czech *technický průkaz*), as well as a **first aid kit** in the trunk. Czech police are infamous for stopping cars with foreign plates, and the "fines" they exact are often negotiable. If you're stopped, expect to pay at least 1,000Kč for speeding or other common infractions like not having your headlights on during the day. Those caught by the police should ask for some type of receipt *(účet* in Czech, pronounced *oo*-chet); this can help cut down on overpayment.

GASOLINE Not only are car rentals expensive, gasoline *(benzín)* in the Czech Republic costs much more than you're accustomed to paying—around 30Kč per liter, or 120Kč per gallon. Filling stations can be found on all major highways. Most are open 24 hours, and many have mini-markets with food and drink as well. If you're leaving the country, fill up near the border, as the price of gas in Austria and Germany can be higher still.

PARKING Finding a parking spot in Prague can be more challenging than driving in this maze of a city. Fines for illegal parking can be stiff, but worse are "Denver Boots," which immobilize cars until a fine is paid. If you find your car booted, call the number on the ticket, tell them where you are, wait for the clamp removers, and pay them 1,500Kč or more depending on the violation. Much of the center of Prague has restricted parking available only to residents (these are marked out by blue lines painted on the curb and street). Here and there you'll find a few zones where paid street parking is permitted. In these areas, you will have to feed coins into a central parking meter, which will then issue a slip that you place on the dashboard so that it is visible through the windshield.

SPECIAL DRIVING RULES Drivers are required to use headlights night and day year-round. Seat belts are required, and you *cannot* legally make a right turn when a traffic light is red. Automobiles must stop when a pedestrian steps into a cross-walk (however, they often don't, as you'll find when you're walking around). Children under 1.5m (about 5 ft.) tall are not permitted to ride in the front seat. On major highways, the speed limit is 130kmph (81 mph). The yellow diamond road sign denotes the right of way at an unregulated intersection. When approaching an intersection, always check to see who has the right of way, since the "main" road can change several times within blocks on the same street. Drinking and driving is strictly prohibited and the allowable blood-alcohol content is zero. You'll get a very steep fine if you're caught.

By Bike

Prague has a growing number of specially marked bike lanes, including a long and popular run that follows the Vltava River south of the center from the National Theater and another that starts around the Prague Zoo and follows the Vltava northward toward Germany. The city's ubiquitous cobblestones make mountain bikes (with fat tires) the natural choice. Two companies in central Prague specialize in rentals (and also give organized bike tours): Praha Bike, Dlouhá 24, Prague 1 (© **732-388-880;** www.prahabike.cz) and City Bike, Králodvorská 5, Prague 1 (© **776-180-284;** www.citybike-prague.com).

---

4 MONEY & COSTS

The Czech Republic is not as cheap a destination as it was a few years ago but remains generally less expensive than western Europe. Prices for everyday travel expenses like food and drink (especially beer), hotels, and museum admissions are substantially less than they would be in Paris or London. The exceptions are rental

The Value of the Czech Crown *(koruna)* vs. Other Popular Currencies

Kč	US$	Can$	UK£	Euro (€)	Aus$
100Kč	$5.55	C$6.15	£3.50	€3.90	A$6.60

What Things Cost in Prague	Kč	US$
Cup of good espresso	40Kč	$2.20
Hot dog on the street	20Kč	$1.10
Taxi from the airport	600Kč	$33
Metro ticket (full price)	26Kč	$1.40
Movie ticket	160Kč	$8.90
Gallon of gasoline (4 liters)	120Kč	$6.60
Three-course meal without alcohol	450Kč	$25
Moderate hotel room	2,000Kč	$110

cars (and gasoline), hotels, and imported clothing and other luxury goods, for which prices are as high as anywhere else.

At press time, one U.S. dollar was worth about 18Kč, one euro about 25Kč and one British pound about 30Kč.

Frommer's lists exact prices in the local currency. The currency conversions quoted above were correct at press time. However, rates fluctuate, so before departing consult a currency exchange website such as **www. oanda.com/convert/classic** to check up-to-the-minute rates.

The Czech currency is the crown (*koruna* in Czech). It is usually noted as "Kč" in shops and "CZK" in banks. One crown, in theory, is divided into 100 haler, though halers no longer circulate. Coins come in denominations of 1, 2, 5, 10, 20, and 50 crowns. Bills come in denominations of 50, 100, 200, 500, 1,000, and 5,000 crowns. The euro is not in circulation in the Czech Republic, though euros are sometimes accepted at large hotels and larger shops. Many hotels list their rates in euros for the convenience of foreign guests, though of course you always have the option of paying in crowns. Long gone are the days when Czech merchants would accept U.S. dollars as payment for goods.

Changing money is not a problem in the Czech Republic. If you're arriving at Prague Airport, skip the currency-exchange booths in the arrivals hall and instead use the ATMs that are lined up just as you enter the main airport hall

from customs clearance. Banks and ATM machines generally offer the best rates and lowest commissions. Local ATMs work with a four-digit PIN; before leaving home make sure that you have a four-digit PIN and let your bank or credit card company know that you will be abroad so they don't protectively block your account once they see a few foreign transactions come through.

Resist the temptation to use one of the private currency-exchange offices that line Václavské náměstí and other areas with heavy tourist concentrations. These outfits seldom pay the rates they advertise on the outside and the commissions (and hidden commissions) can be prohibitive, especially on relatively small amounts of money. If you must use one of these private currency exchanges, before surrendering your bills, show them to the teller through the window and then ask him or her to write down the amount in Czech crowns that you will receive. Once you've handed over the money, it's too late.

Komerční banka has three convenient Prague 1 locations with ATMs that accept Visa, MasterCard, and American Express: Na Příkopě 33, Spálená 51, and Václavské nám. 42 (© **800-111-055,** central switchboard for all branches; www.kb.cz). The exchange offices are open Monday to Friday from 8am to 5pm, but the ATMs are accessible 24 hours.

Credit and debit cards are increasingly common and many shops, restaurants and hotels accept them. Stores may impose a minimum purchase amount for using a card. Traveler's checks, on the other hand, have become much less common in recent years and much harder to use. As a rule, only large banks will cash traveler's checks; hotels and restaurants are not likely to accept them.

5 HEALTH

STAYING HEALTHY

The Czech Republic presents no unusual health concerns and proof of vaccinations and inoculations is not required to enter the country. As with any destination, you could experience a minor bout of food poisoning (usually a short-lived case of an upset stomach or diarrhea). If you're planning to spend time in the bright sunshine, you should apply sunscreen. Mosquitoes and ticks are a problem in wooded areas, particularly near water, in the warmer months.

Pharmacies are abundant and sell both over-the-counter (OTC) medications like aspirin as well as prescription drugs. OTC medicines are not available in grocery stores, convenience stores, or gas stations but must be purchased at a licensed pharmacy. Stock up on prescription drugs before leaving home, as a Czech pharmacist may not recognize your doctor's prescription. In any event, use generic names instead of trade names when describing drugs (such as acetaminophen instead of Tylenol), as trade names change from market to market and may not be the same in the Czech Republic.

Common Ailments

DIETARY RED FLAGS Czech food tends to be hearty and heavy and not advisable for anyone on a low-fat or low-cholesterol diet. Vegetarian restaurants are few and far between, but Prague has a couple of decent vegetarian options. Nearly any restaurant will offer omelets, salads, and items like fried cheese *(smažený sýr)*, which may not necessarily be healthy but at least are nominally vegetarian.

Bugs, Bites & Other Wildlife Concerns

Tick-bite encephalitis is a rare but serious disease caused by a bite from an infected tick. If you plan on camping or hiking in wilderness areas, you're best advised to get vaccinated. Spiders are common, but bites are infrequent. Snakes are practically unheard of.

What to Do If You Get Sick Away from Home

Medical treatment in the Czech Republic is good and cost-effective. In an emergency, immediately call ✆ 112 (general emergency). Most operators are trained to understand at least a little bit of English. Slowly explain the problem and your location, and an ambulance will come as quickly as possible to take you to the nearest hospital. Be sure to take along with you your passport as well as some means of payment (cash or credit card).

Note that U.S., Canadian, and Australian citizens may be required to prepay for any services required, even if they are carrying valid medical insurance. In this case, be sure to save all of the paperwork for later reimbursement. European Union citizens, including those from the U.K., are covered for emergency hospital treatment provided they have a valid European Health Insurance Card (EHIC).

In any emergency situation, an ambulance would usually take you to the nearest available hospital. If you have a choice of which hospital to go to, ask for Nemocnice Na Homolce (Hospital Na Homolce) at Roentgenova 2, in the Prague district of Smíchov (✆ 257-271-111; www.homolka.cz). They maintain a high standard of medical care and are accustomed to dealing with foreigners.

If you are seeking nonurgent medical attention, practitioners in many fields can be found at the Canadian Medical Care center at Veleslavínská 1, Prague 6, Dejvice (✆ **235-360-133;** www.cmcpraha.cz).

We list additional **emergency numbers** in chapter 14, "Fast Facts," p. 283.

6 SAFETY

In Prague's center you'll feel generally safer than in most big cities, but always take common-sense precautions. Be aware of your immediate surroundings. Don't walk alone at night around Wenceslas Square—one of the main areas for prostitution and where a lot of unexplainable loitering takes place. All visitors should be watchful of pickpockets in heavily touristed areas, especially on Charles Bridge, in Old Town Square, and in front of the main train station. Be especially wary on crowded buses, trams, and trains. Don't keep your wallet in a back pocket and don't flash a lot of cash or jewelry. Riding the metro or trams at night feels just as safe as during the day. Petty crime, especially car break-ins and bike theft, are serious problems and are underreported in official statistics. Don't leave valuable items in parked cars overnight or leave bikes, even if they're securely locked, unattended for more than a few minutes.

Drug laws tend to be more lenient than in other countries. Marijuana has been decriminalized; possession of a few marijuana cigarettes is a low-level misdemeanor and the police are usually tolerant about outdoor smoking (those most bars and clubs will not allow you to smoke pot indoors). Possession of larger amounts of cannabis or any amount of harder drugs can land you in big trouble. If you're caught, you are best off phoning your embassy to figure out your legal options.

Prostitution is technically legal, though it's only loosely regulated and potentially high-risk. Václavské náměstí (Wenceslas Square), at night, is filled with touts pushing various "cabarets" and "nightclubs," code words for strip clubs and occasionally bordellos. If you choose to patronize one, don't take in lots of big bills with you and leave your credit cards back at the hotel. Most of the women working at these places are not likely to be Czechs, but Russians, Romanians, Ukrainians, and others, some brought here via organized crime networks. Public health checks are infrequent, if ever, so exercise extreme caution.

There are very few serious discrimination issues and most travelers won't have any problems. The only exception may be Roma (gypsies) or travelers with darker skin and dark hair who could conceivably be misidentified as Roma. Anti-Roma discrimination in the Czech Republic runs deep, and while such travelers are unlikely to meet with any overt violence, they might experience unfriendly treatment at the hand of shop-owners.

Czechs are remarkably tolerant when it comes to gays, and while same-sex handholding is rare, homosexuals are not likely to experience any overt discrimination.

Women traveling alone are not likely to experience any serious problems or unwanted attention. Women are generally safe walking alone at night, though of course bad things can happen anywhere and if there's any doubt, proper precautions should be taken.

In addition to the destination-specific resources listed below, please visit Frommers.com for additional specialized travel resources.

GAY & LESBIAN TRAVELERS

Prague and the Czech Republic are relatively tolerant, and gay and lesbian travelers are not likely to encounter any problems. The Prague neighborhood of Vinohrady is particularly gay-friendly, and several gay clubs and bars have opened up in recent years. For a list of popular gay clubs, please see "Gay & Lesbian Clubs" on p. 199.

In addition, there are a couple of hotels and guesthouses around town that cater to a largely or exclusively gay clientele. For more lodging options, see chapter 5.

The legal situation for gays and lesbians is relatively good. Same-sex partnerships are protected under Czech law and contain many of the legal protections of marriage, though same-sex couples are not permitted to adopt children. Overt discrimination on the basis of sexual preference is against the law.

The Czech GayGuide (www.czechgayguide.org) and GayGuide Prague (www.prague.gayguide.net) are both excellent resources for happenings, bars, restaurants, and clubs. Both are in English and written with visitors in mind. The latter site includes information on the gay scene in Warsaw, Kraków, and Sofia as well as Prague.

TRAVELERS WITH DISABILITIES

Prague remains a difficult city to negotiate for travelers with disabilities. Few sidewalks have curb cuts, the cobblestones are difficult to walk and wheel over, and many older buildings do not have elevators (or if they do, the elevator is not wide enough to accommodate a wheelchair). New hotels and buildings built in the past 5 years must now conform to more disabled-friendly standards, but they remain in the minority. We've identified hotels that offer special services for guests with disabilities in "Where to Stay in Prague," on p. 65.

The main umbrella organization for the rights of those with disabilities is the **Prague Association of Wheelchair Users** (Pražská organizace vozíčkářů) at Benediktská 6, Prague 1 (✆ **224-827-210;** www.pov.cz). Unfortunately, the website is in Czech only, but has several useful maps showing wheelchair-friendly parts of the city.

The Prague public transit company (DPP) continues to expand facilities for passengers with disabilities. Several, but not all, metro stations have accessible elevators. A handful of new trams and buses have street-level entry doors to allow for wheelchair entry. For further information, contact the DPP website with information on barrier-free travel in English (www.dpp.cz).

FAMILY TRAVEL

Prague is not a particularly child-friendly destination. Certainly, kids will get a kick out of riding around on the trams and metros and younger children may show an interest in the fairy-tale castles and ancient history, but this isn't Disneyland, and after a few hours of hitting the cobblestones a little boredom is likely to set in.

Fortunately, Prague is not just dusty museums and history lessons on Gothic architecture. Some ideas for kids include the Prague Zoo (p. 141), the National Technical Museum (stuffed with old trains and cars; p. 126), an afternoon swimming at the Podolí public pool and even just feeding the swans on the banks of the

Vltava. For a longer list of "Best Activities for Families," see p. 6.

To locate accommodations, restaurants, and attractions that are particularly kid-friendly, refer to the "Kids" icon throughout this guide. For a list of more family-friendly travel resources, visit www.frommers.com/planning.

SENIOR TRAVEL

Seniors are normally entitled to reductions at museums, galleries, and castles. Usually the reduction is half the standard admission price for people aged 60 or over, though some attractions only discount above age 65.

Seniors (over 60) pay half price on Prague metros, trams, and buses. To get the senior discount, simply produce your passport at the ticket window and say "senior." Often you can get the discount simply for asking for it without having to show any documentation.

STUDENT TRAVEL

Czech clubs, restaurants, hotels, and museums frequently offer discounts for students and young people. Check out the International Student Travel Confederation (ISTC; www.istc.org) website for comprehensive travel services information and details on how to get an International Student Identity Card (ISIC), which qualifies students for substantial savings on rail passes, plane tickets, entrance fees, and more. It also provides students with basic health and life insurance and a 24-hour helpline. The card is valid for a maximum of 18 months. You can apply for the card online or in person at STA Travel (© **800/781-4040** in North America; 132 782 in Australia; or 0871 2 300 040 in the U.K.; www.statravel.com), the biggest student travel agency in the world; check out the website to locate STA Travel offices worldwide.

If you're no longer a student but are still under 26, you can get an International Youth Travel Card (IYTC) from the same people that entitles you to some discounts. Travel CUTS (© **800/592-2887;** www.travelcuts.com) offers similar services for both Canadians and U.S. residents. Irish students may prefer to turn to USIT (© **01/602-1906;** www.usit.ie), an Ireland-based specialist in student, youth, and independent travel.

---

8 SUSTAINABLE TOURISM

Prague and the Czech Republic have been slow to encourage and adopt sustainable tourism practices. Part of the blame, like everything else, goes to Communism. For 40 years from 1948 to 1989, industries, roads, and vast public housing tracts were built up with scant concern for their effect on the environment. By the time of the Velvet Revolution in 1989, the city and country were on a downward ecological spiral. Large areas in the north of the country had been destroyed by strip mining and acid rain produced by rampant coal burning. In Prague, the air was unbreathable during winter inversions, when slow-moving high-pressure systems would trap dirty air in the lower atmosphere. On those days children would be bused out of the city to camps in the countryside. The city was still pumping raw sewage into the Vltava River.

The good news is that the city authorities have taken big steps toward cleaning up the air and the river. Much of the city is now heated by natural gas, not coal, leaving the air much cleaner in the winter months—though a huge increase in car ownership has mitigated some of these gains. Sewage is now treated before it's released into the river. The water is still too polluted to swim in, but every year brings an improvement in water quality.

More Resources

In addition to the above, the following websites provide valuable wide-ranging information on sustainable travel. For a list of even more sustainable resources, as well as tips and explanations on how to travel greener, visit www.frommers.com/planning.

- **Responsible Travel** (www.responsibletravel.com) is a great source of sustainable travel ideas; the site is run by a spokesperson for ethical tourism in the travel industry. **Sustainable Travel International** (www.sustainabletravelinternational. org) promotes ethical tourism practices, and manages an extensive directory of sustainable properties and tour operators around the world.
- In the U.K., **Tourism Concern** (www.tourismconcern.org.uk) works to reduce social and environmental problems connected to tourism. The **Association of Independent Tour Operators** (**AITO;** www.aito.co.uk) is a group of specialist operators leading the field in making vacations sustainable.
- In Canada, **www.greenlivingonline.com** offers extensive content on how to travel sustainably, including a travel and transport section and profiles of the best green shops and services in Toronto, Vancouver, and Calgary.
- In Australia, the national body that sets guidelines and standards for eco-tourism is **Ecotourism Australia** (www.ecotourism.org.au). **The Green Directory** (www. thegreendirectory.com.au), **Green Pages** (www.thegreenpages.com.au), and **Eco Directory** (www.ecodirectory.com.au) offer sustainable travel tips and directories of green businesses.
- **Carbonfund** (www.carbonfund.org), **TerraPass** (www.terrapass.org), and **Carbon Neutral** (www.carbonneutral.org) provide info on "carbon offsetting," or offsetting the greenhouse gas emitted during flights.
- **Greenhotels** (www.greenhotels.com) recommends green-rated member hotels around the world that fulfill the company's stringent environmental requirements. **Environmentally Friendly Hotels** (www.environmentallyfriendlyhotels.com) offers more green accommodation ratings. The **Hotel Association of Canada** (www.hacgreenhotels.com) has a Green Key Eco-Rating Program, which audits the environmental performance of Canadian hotels, motels, and resorts.
- **Sustain Lane** (www.sustainlane.com) lists sustainable eating and drinking choices around the U.S.; also visit **www.eatwellguide.org** for tips on eating sustainably in the U.S. and Canada.
- For information on animal-friendly issues throughout the world, visit **Tread Lightly** (www.treadlightly.org). For information about the ethics of swimming with dolphins, visit the **Whale and Dolphin Conservation Society** (www.wdcs.org).
- **Volunteer International** (www.volunteerinternational.org) has a list of questions to help you determine the intentions and the nature of a volunteer program. For general info on volunteer travel, visit www.volunteerabroad.org and www.idealist.org.

Much remains to be done. Auto exhaust, for one, remains a significant source of air pollution. In the outlying areas, property developers have transformed large swaths of land into residential and office complexes, destroying green areas and adding more roads and cars to the mix. On a more subtle note, the massive increase in tourism in the past 20 years has contributed to a form of cultural environmental damage, where once thriving urban areas in the center have been transformed into largely tourist-only zones. High-rent souvenir shops, selling cheap glass and T-shirts, have forced out legitimate shops and services, and high rents have pushed ordinary Czechs into other parts of town.

There are signs that the national and municipal authorities are aware of the problems, but are still at odds at how best to solve the problems while keeping the city's economy, particularly its very important tourism industry, on track. The 2009 global economic recession didn't help matters.

While there is not much you can do as a short-term visitor, it's at least good to be aware of the impact your trip is having on the local economy. In general, when shopping, try to avoid the dozens of shops in the center, especially along Karlova street, that traffic in cheap, mass-produced items like factory-made puppets, Russian nesting dolls, and fake KGB hats that are not made locally and have little connection to the Czech Republic. Seek out instead the smaller stores, away from the action, that offer genuine, high-quality Czech made goods, like handmade puppets and jewelry from Czech garnets. In our shopping section, we've identified some of these places. A small but growing number of hotels have adopted sustainable practices, such as curbing unnecessary water use and recycling, but there's still much room for improvement on this front. For further information on steps the Czech government is taking toward protecting the environment, turn to the website of the **Czech Ministry of the Environment** (www.mzp.cz).

The not-for-profit **Friends of Czech Greenways** (www.pragueviennagreenways.org) is a foundation dedicated to promoting ecofriendly tourism by building up an infrastructure of hiking, biking, and water routes around the country, including several projects in Prague.

9 SPECIAL TRIPS & GENERAL-INTEREST TOURS

ESCORTED GENERAL-INTEREST TOURS

Several international travel agencies offer travel packages that focus exclusively on Prague and the Czech Republic or offer Czech destinations as part of a "Central European" or "Eastern European" tour. A few of the best are described below.

U.S.-based **Kensington Tours** (300 Delaware Ave, Suite 1704, Wilmington, DE 19801; © **888/903-2001;** fax 866/613-7599; www.kensingtontours.com) offers a luxury "Five Days in Prague" tour that includes day trips to Karlovy Vary and Kutná Hora, and a 10-day discovery tour that includes Budapest and Vienna.

U.S. operator **Tauck's** (© 800-788-7885; www.tauck.com) 2-week eastern European tour that includes Prague, Warsaw, Budapest, and Vienna. Another tour, called "A Week in Imperial Europe," focuses on the capital cities of central Europe.

The Czech domestic operator **Čedok** (Na Příkopě 18; © **221-447-242;** www.cedok.com) offers several highly rated Czech packages, including to the best-known castles in Bohemia and to the country's UNESCO-listed cities.

ADVENTURE & WELLNESS TRIPS

The Bohemian and Moravian countryside is covered with bike paths and organized bike trips have become very popular. These usually include airport pickups, hotels along the way, bike and helmet rentals, and a van to carry your belongings as you cycle. One of the most popular rides is the 400km run from Prague to Vienna along mostly dedicated bike paths and country roads. The Czech-based **Greenways Travel Club** (© **519-511-572;** www.gtc.cz) maintains a list of organized bike trips, including the Prague-Vienna trail and several specialty bike tours that mix cycling with exploring the beer region of southern Bohemia or the wine region of southern Moravia.

FOOD & WINE TRIPS

Trips that combine sightseeing with wine-tasting or eating and/or cooking are only starting to get going in the Czech Republic. Čedok, Greenways Travel Club (see above), and other operators run tours to the wine areas of southern Moravia.

The U.S.-based operator **Ipswich Tours** (8 Herrick Dr, Ipswich, MA 01938; © **877/356-5163;** fax 978/356-0382; www.ipswichtours.com) runs a 15-day "Gourmet" tour of the Czech Republic, Poland, and Hungary that combines traditional sightseeing with a special emphasis on local foods.

For more information on Package Tours and for tips on booking your trip, see www.frommers.com/planning.

10 STAYING CONNECTED

TELEPHONES

The country code for the Czech Republic is 420. To dial the Czech Republic from abroad, dial the international access code (011 in the United States) plus 420 and then the unique nine-digit local number (there are no area or city codes in the Czech Republic). Once you are here, to dial any number anywhere in the Czech Republic, simply dial the nine-digit number.

To make a direct international call from the Czech Republic, dial 00 plus the country code of the country you are calling and then the area code and number. The country code for the U.S. and Canada is 1; Great Britain, 44; Ireland, 353; Australia, 61; and New Zealand, 64. To dial a number in New York from Prague, for example, you would dial 001-212-xxx-xxxx.

For directory inquiries regarding phone numbers within the Czech Republic, dial © **1180.** For information about services and rates abroad, call © **1181.**

Working public phones are few and far between thanks to the rapid growth of mobile phones. A few public telephones around town still accept coins, but they are being slowly phased out. Most public phones require a prepaid magnetic stripe calling card that you can buy from tobacco and magazine kiosks. The cards are available for 200Kč to 500Kč worth of credit. Simply insert the card, listen for the dial tone, and dial. You can use pay phones with prepaid cards to dial abroad.

Long-distance phone charges are higher in the Czech Republic than they are in the United States, and hotels usually add their own surcharge, sometimes as hefty as 100% to 200%, of which you may be unaware until you're presented with the bill. Ask before placing a call from a hotel.

Even if you're not calling person-to-person, collect calls are charged with the hotel fees, making them pricey, too. Charging a long-distance call to your phone credit card from a public telephone is often the most economical way to phone home.

A fast, convenient way to call the United States from Europe is via services like AT&T USA Direct. This bypasses the foreign operator and automatically links you to an operator with your long-distance carrier in your home country. The access number in the Czech Republic for AT&T USA Direct is © **00-800-222-55288.** For MCI CALL USA, dial

© **00-800-001-112.** Canadians can connect with Canada Direct at *©* **00-800-001-115.** From a pay phone in the Czech Republic, your local phone card will be debited only for a local call.

Other ways to beat high-cost long-distance calls from your hotel include calling from the main post office (see "Mail" in chapter 14) or over the Internet at many Internet cafes (see "Internet & E-mail" below).

Telephone books are printed in two editions: A separate set of White Pages contains alphabetical lists of household phone owners, while the Yellow Pages list businesses according to trade, with an alphabetical listing in more White Pages upfront. The Yellow Pages include an English-language index.

CELLPHONES

Czech cellphones operate on a GSM band of 900/1800MHz. This is the same standard in use throughout Europe but different from the one used in the U.S. American cellphones will work here provided they are triband phones (not all phones are triband) and that you've contacted your service provider to allow for international roaming. Keep calls to a minimum, however, since roaming charges can be steep.

U.K. cellphones should work without any problem provided that you've contacted your service provider to activate international roaming (the same precautions about steep roaming charges apply to U.K. cellphones).

One way of avoiding international roaming charges is to purchase a pay-as-you-go SIM card for your cellphone and a prepaid calling card. This provides you with a local number and allows you to make calls and send text messages at local rates. All of the major local telephone operators: Telefónica 02 (www.cz.02.com); T-mobile (www1.t-mobile.cz); and Vodafone (www.vodafone.cz), offer pay-as-you-go SIM cards and telephone number services.

For iPhone travelers, at press time, Telefónica 02 was the only Czech operator offering 3G network services, though the other major providers had plans to launch 3G networks of their own. Wi-Fi networks are plentiful and easy to find for surfing the net with the iPhone, though keep in mind that downloading data over a 3G network outside of your payment plan can be prohibitively expensive. To be safe, switch off data roaming the moment you arrive.

VOICE-OVER INTERNET PROTOCOL (VOIP)

If you have Web access while traveling, consider a broadband-based telephone service (in technical terms, Voice over Internet protocol, or VoIP) such as **Skype** (www.skype.com) or **Vonage** (www.vonage.com), which allow you to make free international calls from your laptop or in a cybercafe. Neither service requires the people you're calling to also have that service (though there are fees if they do not). Check the websites for details

INTERNET & E-MAIL
With Your Own Computer

Nearly every hotel from a three-star property on up will offer some kind of in-room Internet access, though many hotels will charge for the service. Most often these days this will be a wireless connection, though occasionally it will be a LAN (dataport) connection. If the hotel offers LAN connections, they will usually also loan out Ethernet cables for guests to use during their stay. Check with the reception desk.

If having a good in-room Internet connection is important to you, make this clear when you register for your room. Wi-Fi signal strength drops off considerably the further your room is from the router. Though the hotel may generally offer Wi-Fi, some rooms may not be close enough to make this practical.

Even if your hotel doesn't offer in-room Internet, there are usually lots of options for logging on with your own laptop. A surprising number of cafes, restaurants, and bars now offer free Wi-Fi to customers with a purchase. You may have to finagle a bit with the password, but you'll normally be able to get it to work.

To locate Wi-Fi hotspots in the Czech Republic (and around the world), go to www.jiwire.com; its Hotspot Finder holds the world's largest directory of public wireless hotspots.

Without Your Own Computer

Many hotels will have a public computer or a business center for guests to use. If your hotel doesn't and you just want to check e-mail, it's sometimes worth asking at the reception desk whether you can use the hotel's computer for a couple of minutes. The answer is likely to be yes if it's a small place and the reception desk is not busy at the time.

Prague has several centrally located Internet cafes and your hotel receptionist will certainly know the location of the nearest one. Surfing, however, can be relatively expensive. Rates average around 1Kč to 2Kč a minute.

The **Globe Bookstore and Coffeeshop** at Pštrossova 6, Prague 1, Nové Město (© **224 934 203;** www.globebookstore. cz) is one of the better deals in town; it's both a free Wi-Fi hotspot and offers surfing on its own computers for 1Kč per minute. **Bohemia Bagel** at Masná 2, Prague 1, Staré Město (© **224-812-560;** www.bohemiabagel.cz) charges 2Kč per minute for surfing, and also offers low-cost phone calls. **Spika** at Dlážděná 4, Prague 1, Nové Město (© **224-211-521;** http://netcafe.spika.cz) is open Monday to Friday 8am to midnight, and Saturday and Sunday 10am to 11pm. They charge 20Kč for 15 minutes and offer cheap, Internet-based international phone calls.

11 TIPS ON ACCOMMODATIONS

The past 5 years have seen a boom in hotel construction in Prague. The room shortage that plagued the city in the 1990s has been overcome and if anything the city now has a surplus of rooms. That's good news for travelers, since it means the overly high prices for lodging might start to fall. That already started to happen somewhat in the summer of 2009, when the global recession cut demand for rooms and hotels were suddenly offering deeply discounted prices over their Internet websites.

Most of the boom in hotels has come in the high-end segment, and Prague now has some of central Europe's most beautiful hotels. Many of the best are in reconstructed town palaces that combine fabled historic settings and architecture with modern comfort and services. The years

2008 and 2009 alone saw the opening of several new five-star properties, including a Buddha Bar, a Kempinski, and a new Sheraton (see chapter 5 for more details). The openings, however, couldn't have come at a worse time given the global economy, and as this book was being researched all three were offering big reductions on the rack rate just to generate traffic. That may continue to hold in 2010, but the lesson remains that it's always a good idea to check in for deals at the hotel website and it never hurts to bargain for a lower rate.

The number and range of medium-priced and cheaper options has not kept pace with the growth of more expensive properties, and Prague continues to have a shortage of low-cost accommodation.

Fortunately, the past few years have seen the arrival on the market of a new breed of luxury hostel, offering boutique hotel ambience at prices that are not much higher than a youth hostel. Another way to beat the high cost of lodging is to book an apartment. These make sense if you're staying 3 days or longer. While you sacrifice something in terms of hotel services, you often get significantly lower rates per night as well as an efficiency kitchen to prepare some of your own meals.

With a very efficient metro and tram system, it is relatively easy to stay in one part of Prague and quickly visit another quarter, but if you want to awaken with the Golden City glowing in your window, a room with a view in Old Town or Malá Strana is worth the splurge. For tips on surfing for hotel deals online, visit www.frommers.com/planning.

Suggested Itineraries

Prague's most intriguing aspects are its architecture and atmosphere, best enjoyed while slowly wandering through the city's heart. So, with that in mind, your itinerary should be a loose one. If you have the time and energy, go to Charles Bridge at sunrise and then at sunset to view the grand architecture of Prague Castle and the Old Town skyline. You'll see two completely different cities.

1 NEIGHBORHOODS IN BRIEF

Prague was originally developed as four adjacent self-governing boroughs, plus a walled Jewish ghetto. Central Prague's neighborhoods have maintained their individual identities along with their medieval street plans.

HRADČANY (CASTLE DISTRICT) The Castle District dominates the hilltop above Malá Strana. Here you'll find not only the fortress that remains the presidential palace and national seat of power, but also the seat of religious authority in the country, St. Vitus Cathedral, as well as the Loreto Church, Strahov Monastery, and the European masters branch of the national art gallery. You can take a scenic walk down the hill via Nerudova or through the lush Petřín Hill gardens.

MALÁ STRANA (LESSER TOWN) Prague's storybook Lesser Town was founded in 1257 by Germanic merchants who set up shop at the base of the castle. Nestled between the bastion and the river Vltava, Malá Strana is laced with narrow, winding lanes boasting palaces, and red-roofed town houses (see "Walking Tour 1: Charles Bridge & Malá Strana [Lesser Town]," in chapter 8). The parliament and government and several embassies reside in palaces here. Kampa Park, on the riverbank just south of Charles Bridge, forms the southeastern edge of Lesser Town. Nerudova is the steep, shop-lined alley leading from the town square to the castle. Alternate castle routes for the strong of heart are the New Castle Stairs (Nové zámecké schody), 1 block north of Nerudova, and the Old Castle Stairs (Staré zámecké schody), just northwest from the Malostranská metro station. Tram no. 22 will take you up the hill if you don't want to make the heart-pounding hike.

> ## Impressions
>
> Prague is a priceless asset, which surely deserves to be spared from the worst excesses of modern development, which have so ravaged the other cities of Europe. The challenge must be to find ways of ensuring . . . that it becomes once again the thriving prosperous heart of Europe, not merely a crumbling museum exhibit.
>
> —Prince Charles to Prague's leaders, May 1991

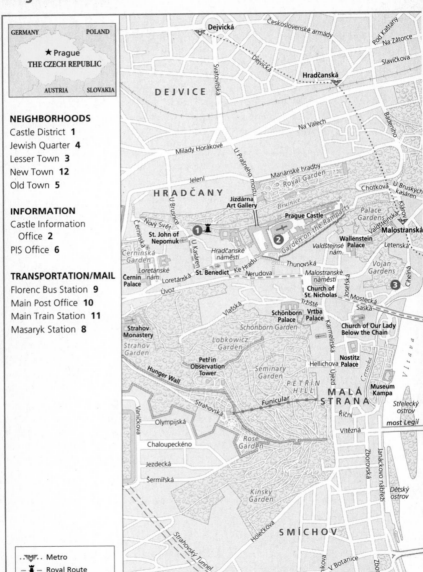

GERMANY   POLAND

★ Prague
THE CZECH REPUBLIC

AUSTRIA   SLOVAKIA

NEIGHBORHOODS
Castle District **1**
Jewish Quarter **4**
Lesser Town **3**
New Town **12**
Old Town **5**

INFORMATION
Castle Information
Office **2**
PIS Office **6**

TRANSPORTATION/MAIL
Florenc Bus Station **9**
Main Post Office **10**
Main Train Station **11**
Masaryk Station **8**

..🚇.. Metro
– 🛡 – Royal Route
===== Pedestrian passage
xxxxxx Steps

0   1/5 mi
0   0.2 km

N

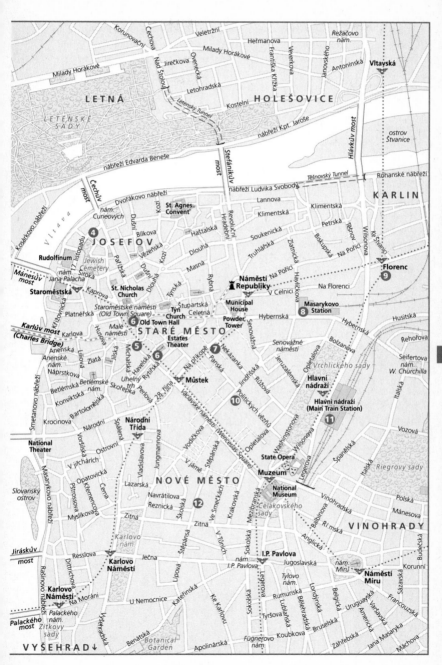

Finding an Address

Don't worry about getting lost—everyone does temporarily, even lifelong Praguers. If you're pressed for time and can't enjoy an aimless wander, you'll find that street signs are emblazoned on red Art Nouveau frames, usually bolted to buildings. House numbers generally increase as you get farther from the Vltava or the square from which the street begins.

Note that Prague street names always precede the numbers, like Václavské nám. 25. Ulice (abbreviated ul. or often omitted) means "street," třída (abbreviated tr.) means "avenue," náměstí (abbreviated nám.) is "square" or "plaza," most is "bridge," and nábřeží is "quay."

Prague is divided into 10 postal districts whose numbers are routinely included in addresses. The districts forming the main tourist areas are listed below with their corresponding neighborhoods.

Prague 1   Hradčany, Malá Strana, Staré Město, Josefov, northern Nové Město.
Prague 2   Southern Nové Město, Vyšehrad, western Vinohrady.
Prague 3   Eastern Vinohrady, Žižkov.
Prague 6   Western Bubeneč, Dejvice, Vokovice, Střešovice, Břevnov, Veleslavín, Liboc, Ruzyně, Řepy, Nebušice, Lysolaje, Sedlec, Suchdol.
Prague 7   Holešovice, Letná

STARÉ MĚSTO (OLD TOWN)   Staré Město was chartered in 1234, as Prague became a stop on important trade routes. Its meandering streets, radiating from Staroměstské náměstí (Old Town Sq.), are still big visitor draws. Old Town is compact, bordered by the Vltava on the north and west and Revoluční and Národní streets on the east and south. You can wander safely without having to worry about straying into danger. Once here, stick to the cobblestone streets and don't cross any bridges, any streets containing tram tracks, or any rivers, and you'll know that you're still in Old Town. You'll stumble across beautiful Gothic, Renaissance, and baroque architecture and find some wonderful restaurants, shops, bars, cafes, and pubs. For a detailed walking tour, see "Walking Tour 3: Staré Město (Old Town)," in chapter 8.

JOSEFOV   Prague's Jewish ghetto, entirely within Staré Město, was surrounded by a wall before almost being completely destroyed to make way for more modern 19th-century apartment buildings. The Old-New Synagogue is in the geographical center of Josefov, and the surrounding streets are wonderful for strolling. Prague is one of Europe's great historic Jewish cities, and exploring this remarkable area will make it clear why. For details, see "Walking Tour 4: Josefov (Jewish Quarter)," in chapter 8.

NOVÉ MĚSTO (NEW TOWN)   Draped like a crescent around Staré Město, Nové Město is where you'll find Václavské náměstí (Wenceslas Square), the National Theater, and the central business district. When it was founded by Charles IV in 1348, Nové Město was Europe's largest wholly planned municipal development. The street layout has remained largely unchanged, but many of Nové Město's structures were razed in the late 19th century and replaced with the offices and apartment buildings you see today. New Town lacks the classical allure of Old Town and Malá Strana, but if you venture beyond Wenceslas Square into Vinohrady you'll find restaurants, interesting shops, and a part of Prague that feels more like a normal city instead of a tourist attraction.

In order to digest enough of Prague's wonders, do what visiting kings and potentates do on a 1-day visit: Walk the Royal Route (or at least part of it). From the top of the castle hill in Hradčany, tour Prague Castle in the morning. After lunch, begin your slow descent through the odd hill-bound architecture of Lesser Town (Malá Strana).

Then stroll across Charles Bridge, on the way to the winding alleys of Old Town (Staré Město). You can happily get lost finding Old Town Square (Staroměstské nám.), stopping at private galleries and cafes along the way. From Old Town Square, take Celetná street to Ovocný trh, and you'll reach Mozart's Prague venue, the Estates' Theater. Dinner and your evening entertainment are all probably within a 10-minute walk from anywhere in this area. Start: tram no. 22 or take a taxi ride up the castle hill.

❶ Prague Castle ★★★

Since the 9th century, the castle has been the seat of the central state and church. It witnessed the first central unifying power, the Přemyslids, and the reigns of the Luxembourg and the Jagiellos, as well as the Habsburg dynasty. The castle is now the official seat of the Czech president. See p. 108.

❷ St. Vitus Cathedral ★★★

King John of Luxembourg and his even more famous son Charles IV laid the foundation stone in 1344 in the place of the original Romanesque rotunda. The first Gothic building period was led by Matyas of Arras, and then Peter Parléř and his sons continued through 1399. The construction of this impressive architectural piece was not completed until 1929. See p. 109.

❸ The Royal Palace ★★★

The oldest part of the palace dates from 1135. Famous Czech kings Přemysl Otakar II, Charles IV, Wenceslas IV, and Vladislav Jagiello then initiated additional reconstructions. The central part, the late Gothic Vladislav Hall, with its ribbed-star-vaulting ceiling, was the largest secular hall in medieval Prague. Still today, every 5 years, the presidential elections take place here. See p. 112.

❹ St. George's Basilica ★★

This is the oldest preserved church building of the castle. The originally Romanesque structure gained its baroque facade in the 17th century. Now, as a part of the National Gallery, this venue houses a permanent exhibition of 19th-century Czech art. See p. 114.

❺ Golden Lane ★

This bizarre conglomeration of mini townhouses within the castle complex was once briefly home to writer Franz Kafka (no. 22). See p. 114.

❻ Lobkowicz Palace ★★

This splendid palace, owned by the noble Lobkowicz family, houses the "Princely Collections," the family's valuable holdings of European art, original music scores, rare books, and other fascinating objects.

> **❼ LOBKOWICZ PALACE CAFÉ & RESTAURANT**
> Even if you don't decide to tour the palace, be sure to take your midday meal or a coffee here, easily the best restaurant in the entire castle complex.

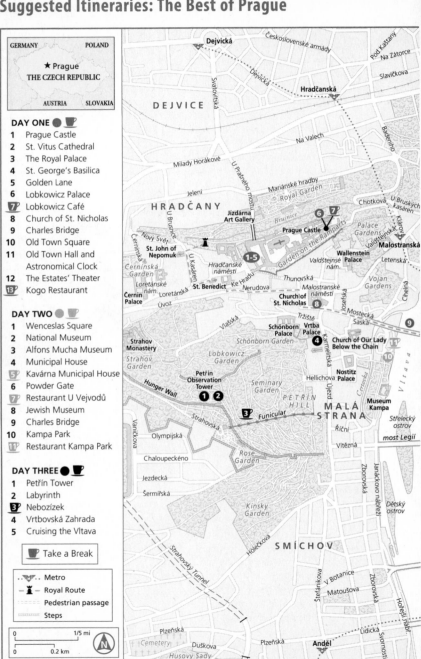

GERMANY   POLAND

★ Prague
THE CZECH REPUBLIC

AUSTRIA   SLOVAKIA

DAY ONE ● ☕
1   Prague Castle
2   St. Vitus Cathedral
3   The Royal Palace
4   St. George's Basilica
5   Golden Lane
6   Lobkowicz Palace
7   Lobkowicz Café
8   Church of St. Nicholas
9   Charles Bridge
10 Old Town Square
11 Old Town Hall and
    Astronomical Clock
12 The Estates' Theater
13 Kogo Restaurant

DAY TWO ● ☕
1   Wenceslas Square
2   National Museum
3   Alfons Mucha Museum
4   Municipal House
5   Kavárna Municipal House
6   Powder Gate
7   Restaurant U Vejvodů
8   Jewish Museum
9   Charles Bridge
10 Kampa Park
11 Restaurant Kampa Park

DAY THREE ● ☕
1   Petřín Tower
2   Labyrinth
3   Nebozízek
4   Vrtbovská Zahrada
5   Cruising the Vltava

☕ Take a Break

···▼··· Metro
— ✠ — Royal Route
······· Pedestrian passage
▨▨▨▨ Steps

0   1/5 mi
0   0.2 km

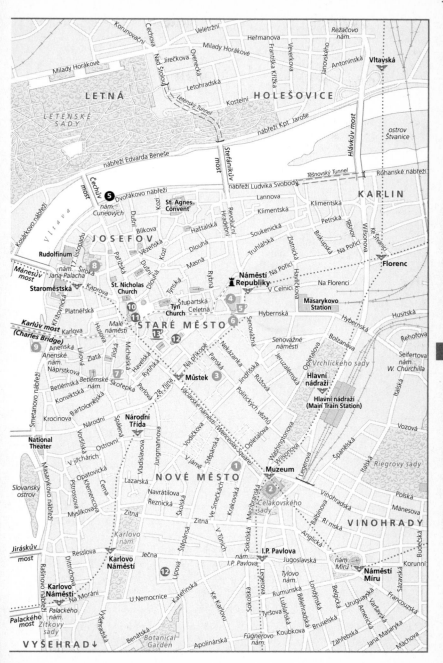

Start making your way back through the castle's courtyards to Hradčanské náměstí, from which you'll be able to see Prague in its panoramic beauty (if it's not foggy that day). Then as you walk down Nerudova, the road leading to the Lesser Town, you'll find small shops and galleries tucked into every narrow nook.

❽ Church of St. Nicholas ★★

The dome of the Church of St. Nicholas, with its gilded baroque interior, dominates the view from Lesser Town Square (Malostranské nám.). Organ concerts are held here throughout the year. Note that the interior is not heated in winter. See p. 117.

❾ Charles Bridge ★★★

Early on, this pedestrian path became one of the centers of town life. Now it's a promenade best known for its open-air gallery of sculptures, and, of course, the magic views of Prague Castle and Lesser Town. See p. 115.

❿ Old Town Square ★★★

The very center of the Old Town life, this square is constantly crowded in high season, but definitely one of the "must-dos." See p. 132.

⓫ Old Town Hall & Astronomical Clock ★★★

In Old Town Square, you can watch a performance of the astronomical clock at the top of each hour. If you aren't tired by now, climb to the top of the Old Town Hall tower for a panoramic view (or take the elevator). See p. 118.

⓬ Estates' Theater ★

If you still have the time and you like opera, try to catch a performance here in the theater that first staged Mozart's Don Giovanni in October 1787. Mozart himself was on hand that night to conduct the world premiere of his masterpiece. Don Giovanni is still occasionally performed here (usually during the summer for tourists), but there's almost always something interesting on hand. Buy tickets at the National Theater box office (p. 191) or at Ticketpro outlets (p. 185).

⓭ KOGO ★

Whether you make it here before the theater or for a late-night, after-opera dinner, you'll not be disappointed by the well-prepared and well-presented Italian food. Havelská 27. ℂ **224-214-543.** See p. 98.

---

3 THE BEST OF PRAGUE IN 2 DAYS

On your second day, explore the varied sights of New Town, Old Town, the Jewish Quarter, and Lesser Town—what you didn't have time for the day before. Just wander and browse. Throughout Old Town you'll find numerous shops and galleries offering the finest Bohemian crystal, porcelain, and modern artwork, as well as top fashion boutiques, cafes, and restaurants. While the shops aren't that much different from those in other European cities, the setting is.

From Old Town, it's just a short walk across Charles Bridge to the Lesser Town, Malá Strana. This was once the neighborhood for diplomats, merchants, and those who served the castle, with narrow houses squeezed between palaces and embassies. Finish the day by getting a riverside view of the city and Charles Bridge from Kampa Park. Start: metro A, Muzeum.

❶ Wenceslas Square ★★

As a trade center of Prague this has been the liveliest and busiest part of the city since the

18th century, witnessing several loud political demonstrations over the years. Here you'll find excellent opportunities for shopping, dining, and day or (more lascivious) evening entertainment. See "Historic Squares" in chapter 7.

If you're traveling with children, I recommend a visit to the National Museum at the top of the square. If you are an art lover, the Mucha Museum on Panská street, parallel to this square, might be more compelling.

❷ National Museum
This iconic hulk of a building is another example of Czech architecture of the second half of the 19th century. Its hall of fame is devoted to the memory of outstanding Czech personalities throughout history. Expansive collections of minerals and various zoological and paleontological displays are part of the permanent exhibition here. See p. 125.

❸ Alfons Mucha Museum ★
This is a pleasant oasis in a busy neighborhood. You can slow down here and relax by stepping into a world of this famous turn-of-the-20th-century artist and his archetypical Art Nouveau designs. See p. 125.

❹ Municipal House ★★
Prague's Art Nouveau jewel! At the end of Na Příkopě street, in the middle of the shopping district, this beautiful corner building, built on the site of the former Royal Court, was reconstructed in the 1990s. It houses the Prague Symphony Orchestra and offers numerous concerts in its Smetana Hall throughout the year. See p. 128.

---

❺ KAVÁRNA OBECNÍ DŮM (AT THE MUNICIPAL HOUSE) ★★
This is a good time to have coffee or even a little snack. Stop here and take in the unique interior and atmosphere of the Art Nouveau era. Náměstí Republiky 5. 𝒞 **222-002-763**. See chapter 7, "Exploring Prague," p. 124.

---

❻ Powder Gate ★
You can't miss the Old Town Powder Tower, just next to the Municipal House. This is where the Royal Route ends (or starts). If you have enough energy, you can climb up the 186 stairs to have a look at Old Town's rooftops. *Note:* It is closed in winter. See p. 130.

Continue walking through the pedestrian zone of Na Příkopě and 28. října. Turn right onto Perlová street and you'll get to a little square, Uhelný trh. Skořepka street will lead you from there to Jilská. If you get lost around these Old Town winding streets, I'm sure you'll stumble upon a pub or restaurant. I recommend:

---

❼ U VEJVODŮ ★
One of the original restaurants of the Pilsner brewery, this spot serves an authentic goulash for 139Kč, and even though you probably won't meet many locals here anymore, you'll still have a good Czech pub experience. Jilská 4. 𝒞 **224-219-999**. See p. 107.

Make your way through Jilská, Malé náměstí, and U Radnice, to Maiselova street.

❽ Jewish Museum ★★★
In the Jewish quarter of Josefov, you can visit the Jewish Museum with its wide array of religious artifacts, as well as the Old Jewish Cemetery and its clusters of headstones stacked grave upon grave. The Pinkas Synagogue displays heart-wrenching sketches by the children held at the Terezín concentration camp during World War II. See p. 119.

❾ Charles Bridge ★★★
Try to pace your walk toward Charles Bridge so you stroll across at dusk and witness the unforgettable view of Prague panorama at twilight. See p. 115.

⑩ Kampa ★★

Kampa is the Lesser Town embankment of the Vltava, with a series of quaint shops and restaurants. You can reach it by taking the stairs down from Charles Bridge (on the left side, before you exit the bridge itself).

---

⑪ KAMPA PARK ★★

There are several choice spots around here for an evening meal. If money is no object, splurge for a riverside table at elegant Na Kampě 8b; ☎ **296-826-112.** A slightly cheaper option, though the view is just as good, is at nearby Hergetova Cihelna ★★, at Cihelná 2b; ☎ **296-826-103.** See p. 89 and 93.

---

4 THE BEST OF PRAGUE IN 3 DAYS

On your third day, after visiting the most important Prague sights, go for a day's excursion to Karlštejn Castle. See p. 205 for details.

Alternatively, if you're staying in Prague, on a warm, sunny day, pack yourself a picnic and stroll over to Petřín Hill, the leafy park where kids will enjoy the tower view and mirrored labyrinth. Before you leave Lesser Town, visit its well-hidden secret, the Vrtbovská garden. Try to work in a cruise on the Vltava or pilot your own rowboat ride in the late afternoon or evening. Start: tram no. 12, 20, or 22 to Újezd.

Begin by walking up the Petřín Hill, or take the funicular from Újezd halfway up to Nebozízek, or all the way up. See p. 139.

❶ Petřín Tower ★

In the morning you'll probably be rested enough to climb the 299 steps up to the top platform of this reduced copy of the Eiffel Tower built in 1891. When the weather cooperates, the bird's-eye view of Prague is worth the hike. There is an elevator, but only seniors over 70 and people with disabilities may use it. See p. 131.

❷ Labyrinth

This funhouse was originally built as a pavilion for the Prague Exhibition in 1891 and later transferred to Petřín. It was fitted with mirrors and made into a maze. See p. 140.

After you find your way out, start looking for a picnic spot. You can have a walk around on the top of the hill or begin your slow descent to the town. There are plenty of benches along the way down.

If you are not ready for a picnic or a walk, use the funicular and go to the midway stop:

❸ NEBOZÍZEK ★

This restaurant has a great hillside location, and you probably will forget what you're eating (a pity because the food is actually pretty good) since your attention will be drawn to the view. Petřínské sady 411. ☎ **257-315-329.** See p. 94.

Take tram no. 12, 20, or 22 or walk 10 minutes from Újezd to the Karmelitská stop.

❹ Vrtbovská Zahrada ★

The entrance to this baroque terraced garden is not well marked, and you won't quite imagine what kind of "backyard" is hidden behind the door at no. 25 on Karmelitská. *Note:* It is closed in winter. See p. 139.

❺ Cruising the Vltava

Cruising upstream and enjoying the sights of Prague as dusk descends is a memorable experience. You'll see it all from a low angle surrounded by reflections on the water, providing a new perspective on the city. Choose the 3-hour cruise,

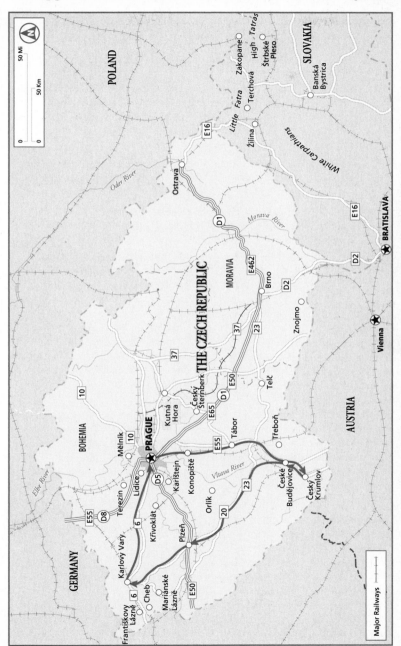

which departs from a port under Čechův Bridge at 7pm. Buffet dinner, aperitif, and live music are included in the price. See p. 144.

5 THE BEST OF THE CZECH REPUBLIC IN 1 WEEK

The Czech lands offer many historic and cultural monuments. Castles and châteaux dominating the picturesque natural landscape represent the most important part of Czech attractions. For those travelers with more time to discover Bohemia and even Moravia, see chapters 11, 12, and 13 to learn about visits to other Czech towns. Below I give you one example out of many possible itineraries.

Days ❶–❷: Arrive in Prague

Spend the first 2 days as recommended above in "The Best of Prague in 2 Days." Then rent a car from one of the rental agencies recommended on p. 40. Keep in mind that the speed limit is 90kmph (56 mph) on two-lane highways and 50kmph (31 mph) in villages, and that you must keep your headlights switched on while driving. Before setting out, review the other Czech rules for driving on p. 41.

Day ❸: Český Krumlov ★★★

Leave for this romantic destination in southern Bohemia early in the morning to give yourself plenty of time to walk around once you get there. Take Hwy. D1 and then E55. The trip takes about 3 hours. Once there, visit the castle first, then just wander, and finally relax in a local restaurant. Spend the night in one of the recommended hotels or pensions. But book early, as Krumlov is the most popular Czech destination after Prague. See details in chapter 12.

Day ❹: České Budějovice, Castle Hluboká nad Vltavou ★

On this day start heading for Plzeň via České Budějovice, the home of Budvar beer. Upon arrival at České Budějovice, have a quick stroll and look around one of central Europe's largest squares, where you can also have lunch. In the early afternoon, take Hwy. E49 and then Hwy. 105 north for 30 minutes (this includes parking time) to the tiny town Hluboká nad Vltavou, where you'll see a castle fashioned after the Windsor Castle in England towering above the green meadows. For more information, see p. 245 in chapter 12.

Next, take Hwy. E49 to Plzeň. You'll get there in about 2 hours. Spend the night there. See p. 241.

Day ❺: Plzeň ★

Explore Plzeň's center in the morning, when it is the least crowded. If you're interested in the beer-making process, visit the Pilsner Breweries in the early afternoon. Just outside the factory is a restaurant that serves traditional Czech food. See chapter 12 for more details.

After your break, hit the road again. Hwy. E49 will take you to the most popular Czech spa town, Karlovy Vary, in about 1 hour. Spend the night there.

Day ❻: Karlovy Vary ★★

This town was built for relaxation, which makes it the perfect place to end your Bohemian week.

Start slowly with a stroll around the city's historic center. Then, get your "cup" and taste the mineral waters that make this destination so famous. Find out more about Karlovy Vary in chapter 12.

Day ❼: Karlovy Vary to Prague

It's time to return to Prague. Take Hwy. E48. You should reach the capital in 2 hours. Be warned that this two-lane highway is one of the busiest and most accident-prone in the country.

Where to Stay in Prague

Not so long ago, Prague used to have a shortage of hotel rooms, and if you arrived in town without reservations there was a good chance you would be without a place to stay. That's no longer the case (though it always pays to reserve in advance if you find a good place at a good price). Hotel construction became a boom industry during the past decade, and if anything, the city now has too many beds, not too few. That's great news for travelers. It means that prices might someday start to come down from their lofty peaks. Inexplicably, hotel prices in Prague the past decade or so have been higher on average than in Paris or Amsterdam, for facilities that were usually inferior.

The combination of new hotels plus the worldwide economic recession in 2009 succeeded in driving down prices somewhat, meaning that, depending on the night, it was possible to snag a good place in the center for under $100 for the first time in many years. It's not clear what the future will bring, but it always pays to shop around. Bargains are out there.

The highest demand and highest prices are for properties in Malá Strana and Staré Město, widely considered the two most desirable places to stay. They offer the closest proximity to the main sites and the possibility of a castle or river view out your window. Of the two, Malá Strana is the quieter and more upscale. Nové Město, the city's commercial heart, is also a popular lodging choice. A hotel here will probably offer the same walk-to proximity to the major sites, but may lack some of the innate charm of Malá Strana or Staré Město. The leafy inner suburb of Vinohrady has increasingly evolved into an alternative lodging locale. This is an upscale and highly desirable area, but requires a metro or tram ride to get to the center. For other outlying districts, look at the map carefully before booking your room. Try to get as close to a metro or tramline as possible, or you'll spend too much time trying to figure out your transit routes and not enough time enjoying the sights.

Tips **What's for Breakfast?**

In most hotels and B&Bs the room rate includes breakfast—usually heavy bread or rolls *(rohlíky)*, jam, butter, cheese spreads, and sometimes liver pâté, plus yogurt, cereal, juice, milk, and coffee or tea. Occasionally, slices of Prague ham or smoked pork *(debrecínka)*, hard-boiled eggs, local cheeses, and fresh fruit will join the buffet. The better places will also offer bacon and eggs cooked to order. Don't expect, however, to get drinkable coffee. It's invariably of the black-sludge variety. Better to eat your breakfast and grab a coffee somewhere after you leave the hotel.

Websites with Online Reservations

In addition to the room-finding agencies listed above, the following travel agencies also provide online room-booking services. It's always a good idea to check prices on several different websites. In addition, be sure to check out individual hotel websites, since hotels frequently post seasonal or last-minute discounts that may not be available elsewhere:

- **www.euroagentur.cz**
- **www.praguehotels.cz**
- **www.hotelline.cz**

HOTELS Prague offers everything from five stars on down to modest mom and pops perched on the side of the road. Most hotels in the center fall in the three- to four-star range, where rooms are normally clean and secure with attached bathrooms and modern conveniences like TVs, telephones, and occasionally (but not usually) air-conditioning. Most, but not all, hotels will offer some form of in-room Internet (whether Wi-Fi or LAN connection). This may or may not be free (always ask before booking).

Nearly all hotels are now smoke-free or at a minimum offer smoke-free rooms (be sure to make your request known upfront). Most hotels won't have on-site parking but are likely to have a pay garage or lot nearby. Figure on shelling out an additional 500Kč a day, on average, for parking.

Wheelchair access remains a problem and most older or smaller hotels are not likely to be accessible for persons with disabilities. The best bets are chains and larger hotels built or remodeled in the past couple of years. Contact the hotel directly for up-to-date information on accessibility. See chapter 3, "Planning Your Trip to Prague & the Czech Republic," for more information on traveling with disabilities, p. 30.

Most of the big international hotel chains, including Hilton, Marriott, Sheraton, and several others now have properties in Prague. A complete list is included in chapter 14, "Fast Facts."

PENSIONS These are typically guesthouses, often family-owned, which offer fewer services than hotels but tend to be cheaper. In practice, there is little difference between a pension and a two- or three-star hotel.

SHORT-TERM APARTMENT RENTALS An increasingly popular option is to pass up high-priced hotel rooms and opt instead for private apartments. Several agencies now offer short-term rentals for what are surprisingly nice places in high-demand areas like Malá Strana, Staré Město, and Nové Město. These often can accommodate up to four people (usually more) and have modest kitchens. Services, however, are limited to things like pickup and drop-off at the airport. You will usually have to arrange a time in advance to pick up the keys, since there's no reception.

Local real estate agency **Svoboda & Williams** at Benediktská 3, Prague 1 (© **257-328-281;** www.svoboda-williams. com) offers luxury short-term rentals starting at about 2,000Kč a night for properties in the center. **Apartments in Prague** at Petřínská 4, Prague 5 (© **251-512-502;** http://apartments-in-prague.org) has some beautiful properties in Malá Strana and elsewhere starting at 1,500Kč during the off-season up to 4,000Kč a night and higher for New Year's Eve. Check both companies' websites for apartment photos.

ROOM-FINDING AGENCIES Prague has several agencies that can assist in helping to find a room in a hotel or pension, or even book a short-term apartment rental or a private room in someone's house. These agencies normally offer a wide selection of properties and allow for online selection and payment. One of the market leaders is Prague-based **E-Travel.cz** (www.travel.cz or www.apartments.cz). Its office is near the National Theater at Divadelní 24 (© **224-990-990;** fax 224-990-999). **Mary's Travel & Tourism** at Italská 31, Prague 2 (© **222-254-007;** www.marys.cz) has an excellent range of hotels from two to five stars and a well-organized website. Simply choose how many stars you want and what district you want to stay in, then type in the data and you're set.

BEST HOTEL BETS

- **Best Panoramic Views:** The **Corinthia Hotel Prague** (© **261-191-111**) is a bit out of the center and the high-rise architecture won't appeal to everyone, but each north-facing room provides a gorgeous wide-angle view stretching to Prague Castle and beyond. See p. 81.
- **Best Malá Strana Views:** The terrace at the hotel **U Zlaté studně** (© **257-011-213**), the Golden Well, offer some of the best old-world views over Malá Strana's red rooftops. See p. 69.
- **Best Bohemian Country Setting:** The **Romantik Hotel U raka** (© **220-511-100**), in a secret ravine minutes from the castle in Hradčany, has cozy rustic rooms and a tastefully folksy atmosphere. See p. 69.
- **Best Hotel Closest to Prague Castle:** The **U Krále Karla** (© **257-531-211**), on the main castle-bound thoroughfare Nerudova, tries hard to provide a stay to match its Renaissance motif. It's a few steps above the main turn to the castle, avoiding much of the tourist commotion below. The **Castle Steps** (© **257-216-337**) puts you literally, well, on the castle's steps for a fraction of the price you'd pay elsewhere. See p. 73.
- **Best for Business Travelers:** Just off Náměstí Republiky near the imposing Czech National Bank, the **Prague Marriott Hotel** (© **222-888-888**) comfortably fits the bill for those who need to get in, cut a deal, and then get out to see the city (especially if the firm is paying the bill). The **Kempinski Hotel** (© **226-226-111**) in Nové Město is bolder, brasher, and has a better restaurant. See p. 79.
- **Best for Stressed-Out Business Travelers:** The **Buddha Bar** (© **221-776-300**), in Staré Město, is all about lifestyle and finding that right balance between work and spirit. So after you've amassed your fortune, spend it here to decompress. See p. 74.
- **Best Romantic Pension:** Although the **Pension Větrník** (© **220-612-404**) is well outside the city center, this family-run B&B is a very friendly and romantic place, easily accessible by tram or taxi. It's built into an antique windmill amid lush gardens, and you can't beat it for charm and price. See p. 82.
- **Best Throwback to Prague's First Republic:** The restored Art Nouveau **Hotel Paříž** (© **222-195-195**) recalls 1920s Prague, one of the wealthiest cities on earth at the time. The hotel's beauty oozes with period elegance. It's across from another remodeled gem, the Municipal House (Obecní dům). **The K+K Central** (© **225-022-000**) has an even more impressive Art Nouveau exterior and the rooms convey a Functionalist 1920 and 1930s feel. See p. 76.

- **Best for Families:** Consider a **private apartment** from an agency (see "Short-Term Apartment Rentals," above). Larger and cheaper than hotel rooms, these apartments come with kitchens so you can fix your own meals. (For more options, see "Family-Friendly Accommodations," later in the chapter.)

- **Best Health Clubs:** The **Hotel InterContinental Prague** (© 296-631-111) has a fully equipped gym with modern machines and free weights and is home to a variety of workout and aerobics classes. There's also a smallish pool on hand and a hot tub. The gym is primarily for hotel guests, but it's possible to buy day passes, as well as short- and long-term memberships. See p. 74.

- **Best Tom Cruise/Leonid Brezhnev Haunt:** The **Hotel Praha** (© 224-341-111) was once a heavily guarded bastion for visiting Communist bigwigs. The lingering chintz of the Praha has unexpectedly emerged as a refuge for luminaries who want to lie low, including the star of *Risky Business, Top Gun,* and *Mission: Impossible.* A wacky choice. See p. 82.

1 HRADČANY

VERY EXPENSIVE

Hotel Savoy ★   One of Prague's finest hotels, the Savoy occupies a quiet spot behind the Foreign Ministry and Černín Palace, and is just a few blocks from the castle. The guest rooms are richly decorated and boast every amenity as well as spacious marble bathrooms. The beds are huge, which contrasts with the customary central European style of two twin beds shoved together. The pleasant staff provides an attention to detail that's a cut above that at most hotels in Prague. The Hradčany restaurant is excellent.

Keplerova 6, Prague 1. © **224-302-430.** Fax 224-302-128. www.savoyhotel.cz. 61 units. From 4,500Kč double; from 8,000Kč suite. Rates include breakfast. AE, DC, MC, V. Tram: 22. **Amenities:** Restaurant; bar; concierge; "relaxation" center w/small set of exercise machines; room service; sauna; whirlpool. *In room:* A/C, TV, DVD, hair dryer, minibar.

U Zlaté studně ★★   The "Golden Well" is a reconstructed Renaissance townhouse that occupies a perch high above Malá Strana and just below Prague Castle. Many of the rooms afford stunning views out over the river and the Old Town in the distance. The guest rooms are traditional in style and outfitted with antiques and reproductions. The overall effect is of a high-quality guesthouse. Rumors were swirling in April 2009 during U.S. President Barack Obama's visit to Prague that he and First Lady Michelle Obama were going to dine on the restaurant's terrace. He ended up staying (and eating) at the Hilton, but this would have been a more presidential choice.

U zlaté studně 4, Prague 1. © **257-011-213.** www.goldenwell.cz. 19 units. From 4,500Kč double. Rates include breakfast. AE, DC, MC, V. Tram: 12, 20, or 22 to Malostranské nám. plus a steep hike. **Amenities:** Restaurant; bar; concierge; "relaxation" center w/small set of exercise machines. *In room:* TV, hair dryer, minibar.

EXPENSIVE

Hotel Neruda ★   Another great writer/philosopher who left his mark on Prague was Jan Neruda, but the street that bears his name—Nerudova—is hardly remembered as the scene of his 19th-century literary greatness. Instead, it is a cozy alley of stores and pubs leading up to the castle. Squeezed into the long row of curiosity shops is a strong

Value   Money-Saving Tips

The best way to save money on a hotel room is to book as far in advance as possible and make use of the local room-finding services (listed above) or big hotel aggregators, like Expedia.com. Their customer-finding clout gives them leverage to extract discounts from hotel owners, part of which they can pass on to you. In addition, always **check out the hotel's own website.** This is where hotels post their special offers as well as last-minute and seasonal discounts. Rates can be shockingly low as hotels, seemingly, will stoop to any level to fill beds. So much the better for you.

Czech hotel receptionists have little interest in haggling over room rates, but sometimes you can still get a deal by simply asking at the end: "Is this the best price you can offer me?" Hotels are under increasing pressure from the competition, and last-minute rate cuts have become the norm and not the exception. Your bargaining position is stronger if you're planning a longer stay.

contender for the best boutique hotel in Malá Strana—the Hotel Neruda. This refurbished 42-room villa has combined a high level of modern elegance with the original accents of its 14th-century shell. Most of the fixtures—from the fresh new bathrooms to the beds and dining tables—suggest a bold sense of Prague's promising future, but enveloped within its Renaissance past. With the recent summers setting new records for heat, you will appreciate the air-conditioning. Check the website for last-minute discounts.

Nerudova 44, Prague 1. © **257-535-557.** Fax 257-531-492. www.hotelneruda-praha.cz. 42 units. From 4,200Kč double. Rates include breakfast. AE, DC, MC, V. Tram: 12, 20, or 22 to Malostranské nám. **Amenities:** Cafe-restaurant; concierge. *In room:* A/C, TV, hair dryer, minibar.

Romantik Hotel U raka ★   Hidden among the stucco houses and cobblestone streets of a pristine medieval neighborhood below Prague Castle is this pleasant surprise. The Romantik Hotel U raka (At the Crayfish), in a ravine beneath the Foreign Ministry gardens, has been lovingly reconstructed as an old-world farmhouse. It is the quietest getaway in this tightly packed city. The rustic rooms have heavy wooden furniture, open-beamed ceilings, and stone walls. The much-sought-after suite has a fireplace and adjoins a private manicured garden, making it a favorite with honeymooners. Water trickles through the Japanese garden that surrounds the hotel.

The owners are relaxed but attentive and will help you navigate the phalanx of nearby streets. Prague Castle is a 10-minute walk away, and you can catch a tram into the city center by walking up ancient steps at the side of the hotel. Reservations well in advance are recommended.

Černínská 10, Prague 1. © **220-511-100.** Fax 233-358-041. www.romantikhotel-uraka.cz. 6 units (5 with shower only). From 3,800Kč double; from 7,000Kč suite. Rates include breakfast. AE, MC, V. Tram: 22. *In room:* A/C, TV, hair dryer, minibar.

U Krále Karla ★   This castle hill property does so much to drive home its Renaissance roots, King Charles's heirs should be getting royalties. Replete with period prints, open-beamed ceilings, and stained-glass windows, the atmosphere is almost Disneyesque in its

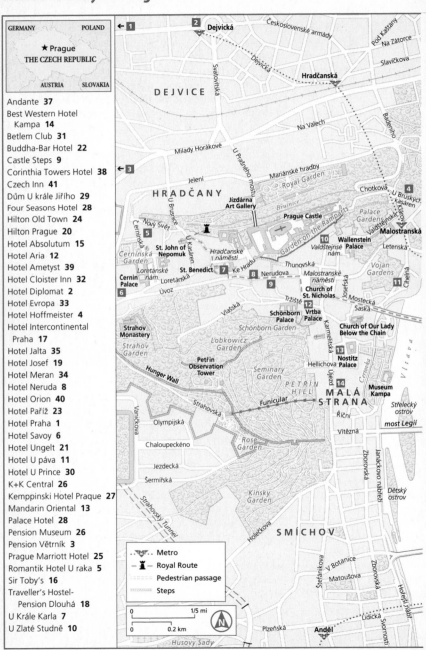

GERMANY   POLAND

★ Prague
THE CZECH REPUBLIC

AUSTRIA   SLOVAKIA

Andante **37**
Best Western Hotel
  Kampa **14**
Betlem Club **31**
Buddha-Bar Hotel **22**
Castle Steps **9**
Corinthia Towers Hotel **38**
Czech Inn **41**
Dům U krále Jiřího **29**
Four Seasons Hotel **28**
Hilton Old Town **24**
Hilton Prague **20**
Hotel Absolutum **15**
Hotel Aria **12**
Hotel Ametyst **39**
Hotel Cloister Inn **32**
Hotel Diplomat **2**
Hotel Evropa **33**
Hotel Hoffmeister **4**
Hotel Intercontinental
  Praha **17**
Hotel Jalta **35**
Hotel Josef **19**
Hotel Meran **34**
Hotel Neruda **8**
Hotel Orion **40**
Hotel Paříž **23**
Hotel Praha **1**
Hotel Savoy **6**
Hotel Ungelt **21**
Hotel U páva **11**
Hotel U Prince **30**
K+K Central **26**
Kemppinski Hotel Praque **27**
Mandarin Oriental **13**
Palace Hotel **28**
Pension Museum **26**
Pension Větrník **3**
Prague Marriott Hotel **25**
Romantik Hotel U raka **5**
Sir Toby's **16**
Traveller's Hostel-
  Pension Dlouhá **18**
U Krále Karla **7**
U Zlaté Studně **10**

Metro
Royal Route
Pedestrian passage
Steps

0   1/5 mi
0   0.2 km

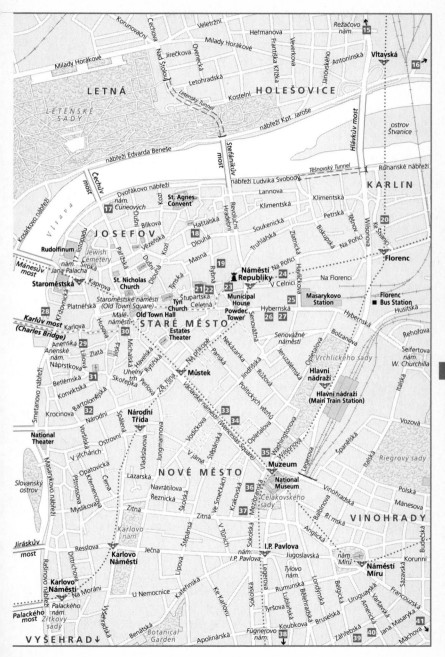

pretense, but somehow appropriate for this location at the foot of Prague Castle. The rooms offer plenty of space, heavy period furniture, and bed frames with firm mattresses as well as clean bathrooms with a tub/shower combination or shower only. This is a fun, comfortable choice with colorful angelic accents everywhere.

Nerudova-Úvoz 4, Prague 1. © **257-531-211.** www.romantichotels.cz. 19 units (13 with shower only). From 3,000Kč double; 4,500Kč suite. Rates include breakfast. AE, MC, V. Tram: 12, 20, or 22 to Malostranské nám. and then walk up the hill. **Amenities:** Restaurant; babysitting; Internet; room service; solarium. *In room:* TV, hair dryer, kitchenette, minibar.

2 MALÁ STRANA (LESSER TOWN)

VERY EXPENSIVE

Hotel Aria ★   This music-themed hotel occupies a luxuriously reconstructed town-house in the heart of Malá Strana, just around the corner from the St. Nicholas Cathedral. Each of its four floors is tastefully decorated to evoke a different genre of music, famous composer, or musician. The rooms and bathrooms vary in their size and layout, and all are kept to the same exceptionally high standard evident through-out the hotel. There is an impressive library of CDs, DVDs, and books about music off the lobby, and a full-time resident musicologist is available to help you choose a concert in the city. The Aria will delight newlyweds or any romantic soul with its luxurious but cozy atmosphere, and the extensive list of amenities, which includes a roof terrace garden with spectacular views of Malá Strana, a screening room, and music salon.

Tržiště 9, Prague 1. © **225-334-111.** Fax 225-334-666. www.aria.cz. 52 units. From 5,800Kč double; 9,500Kč suite. Rates include breakfast. AE, MC, V. Metro: Malostranská and then tram no. 12, 20, or 22 to Malostranské nám. **Amenities:** Restaurant; bar; exercise room; courtesy car from the airport; room service. *In room:* A/C, DVD/CD player, Internet, PC, hair dryer, minibar.

Mandarin Oriental Hotel ★★   The Mandarin offers superior accommodations and service in a converted, former Dominican in Malá Strana. Smart, sleek design underlines the relaxing Far East ambience throughout the building. Large rooms and suites are well equipped and some include impressive views. The hotel boasts a spa in what was a Renaissance chapel, so you can heal your body and soul at the same time, while the Essensia restaurant fuses Eastern and Western cuisines. This booking would be a great choice for a business traveler who can take his or her spouse along (and charge it to the expense account).

Nebovidská 1, Prague 1. © **233-088-888.** Fax 233-088-668. www.mandarinoriental.com/prague. 99 units. 4,400Kč double; from 9,000Kč suite. Rates include breakfast. AE, MC, V. Metro: Malostranská; then take tram no. 12, 20, or 22 to the Hellichova stop. **Amenities:** Restaurant; bar; tea lounge; spa-relaxation center; room service. *In room:* A/C, TV, CD/DVD player, Internet, minibar.

EXPENSIVE

Best Western–Hotel Kampa   On the edge of the park where troops once camped along the banks of the Vltava, the Kampa occupies what was a 17th-century armory. It has a choice location on a quiet, winding alley off the park, with easy access to Malá Strana and Charles Bridge. The plain rooms suggest a bit of Communist chintz without much attention to aesthetics, but they're comfortable enough if you don't expect first-class surroundings. The best rooms boast a park view—request one of these when booking or checking in. There's a restaurant, but you'd be better off visiting one of those nearby, like Kampa Park under Charles Bridge (p. 89). The hotel also rents its large hall for private parties and that might become a disturbing factor in your stay here. Ask beforehand about planned events at the hall.

Všehrdova 16, Prague 1. ℂ **257-404-444.** Fax 257-404-333. www.euroagentur.cz. 84 units (shower only). From 4,100Kč double. Rates include breakfast. AE, DC, MC, V. Metro: Malostranská; then take tram no. 12, 20, or 22 to the Hellichova stop. **Amenities:** Restaurant w/garden; bar; Internet; room service. *In room:* TV, hair dryer, minibar.

Hotel Hoffmeister Conceived by the son of Adolph Hoffmeister, an artist and former diplomat, the hotel's bold style is striking. Sketches by the father adorn the walls and depict acquaintances of the late artist with celebrities at the time such as Charlie Chaplin, Salvador Dalí, and George Bernard Shaw. The rooms are solid and well equipped. Each has a unique color scheme, with rich fabrics, matching draperies, and even bed canopies. For the ultimate relaxation, visit the wellness center, where massages and other body treatments are on the menu. The in-house restaurant, Ada, is highly recommended and even won a mention in the 2009 Michelin guide for its interior.

Pod Bruskou 9, Prague 1. ℂ **251-017-111.** Fax 251-017-120. www.hoffmeister.cz. 41 units (tub/shower combination in bathrooms). From 3,600Kč double; from 4,800Kč suite. Rates include breakfast. AE, MC, V. Metro: Malostranská. **Amenities:** Restaurant; cafe; bar; wellness center; concierge; room service. *In room:* A/C, TV, hair dryer, minibar.

Hotel U páva ★ The "Peacock" is a fine B&B in Malá Strana managed by the same group as the King Charles. On the narrow street across from the walled Vojanov Gardens, a stone's throw from Charles Bridge, this family-run hotel has the intimacy of a farmhouse and offers room service from its decent kitchen. Original wooden ceilings, antique chairs, and comfortable beds accent the reasonably spacious rooms. The best rooms on the top floor facing the front have a fantastic low-angle view of Prague Castle. The fully tiled bathrooms of adequate size have tub/shower combinations.

U Lužického semináře 32, Prague 1. ℂ **257-533-360.** Fax 257-530-919. www.romantichotels.cz. 27 units (tub/shower combination in bathrooms). From 4,000Kč double. Rates include breakfast. AE, MC, V. Metro: Malostranská. **Amenities:** Restaurant; cafe; bar; babysitting; room service; sauna. *In room:* TV, hair dryer, minibar.

MODERATE

Castle Steps ★ (Value) A nontraditional hotel in that it occupies not just one building but a series of rooms and apartments in several beautifully restored town palaces along Nerudova and in and around Malá Strana. It is quirky in a good way, though that also extends to the sometimes overly friendly staff, the vegan breakfasts, and the fact you may have to share a bathroom (be sure to say in advance if this is an issue). Still, and it's a big *still,* you won't get these kind of drop-dead gorgeous rooms (many done up in 19th-century period style), or the walk-out-the-door-and-gaze-up-to-the-castle location for less money, period.

Nerudova 7, Prague 1. ℂ **257-216-337.** www.castlesteps.com. 60 units. From 1,800Kč double; from 2,800Kč apt. Rates include breakfast. AE, DC, MC, V. Metro: Malostranská plus tram no. 12, 20, or 22 to Malostranské nám and a steep hike. **Amenities:** Concierge.

3 STARÉ MĚSTO (OLD TOWN) & JOSEFOV

VERY EXPENSIVE

Buddha Bar ★★   The ultraluxurious Buddha Bar was one of several five-star properties to open its doors in 2008 and 2009, just as the world economy was cratering and the number of people who could drop a grand per night on a room was dwindling fast. Still, if you've got the crowns you can hardly do better than this chic French-Asian-inspired inn in the middle of the Old Town. The rooms are furnished in a style that might be described as tastefully exotic, with warm reds and golds and bright tiles that recall the best of India or the Middle East. The in-house Buddha Bar restaurant features very good Asian-inspired cuisine, including a sushi bar, in a setting that manages to be both hip and high-end at the same time.

Jakubská 8, Prague 1. ℂ **221-776-300.** Fax 221-776-310. www.buddha-bar-hotel.cz. 39 units. From 11,000Kč double; from 22,000Kč suite. AE, DC, MC, V. Metro: Náměstí Republiky. **Amenities:** Restaurant; cafe, bar; concierge; health club; room service. *In room:* A/C, TV, CD, DVD player, hair dryer, minibar.

Four Seasons Hotel ★★★   Located in an imposing position on the banks of the Vltava River right next to Charles Bridge, the Four Seasons provides an elegant base for exploring Old Town and enjoying the symphonies at the nearby Rudolfinum, while taking in a wonderful panoramic view of Prague Castle across the river.

The property actually melds three historic buildings from the city's most important architectural periods—baroque, Renaissance, and Art Nouveau. The most impressive wing, the 17th-century baroque villa, houses the Presidential Suite with a cozy fireplace, a private dining room, and the privilege of peering into the castle's ornate staterooms across the way. The surrounding executive suites and guest rooms are smaller but still nicely appointed. The best have sweeping views and sunken marble tubs. The Art Nouveau wing is less expensive but the street-side views are less impressive. All rooms are fitted with fine solid wood furniture: some with antique pieces, others with more modern avant-garde accents. The house restaurant, the Allegro, is a two-time Michelin star winner.

Veleslavínova 2a, Prague 1. ℂ **221-427-000.** Fax 221-426-000. www.fourseasons.com. 161 units. From 9,600Kč double; from 20,000Kč suite. AE, DC, MC, V. Metro: Staroměstská. **Amenities:** Restaurant; bar; health club; concierge; room service. *In room:* A/C, TV, CD, DVD player, hair dryer, minibar.

EXPENSIVE

Hotel InterContinental Prague   The upper suites of this hotel have hosted luminaries including former U.S. Secretary of State Madeleine Albright, and legend has it global terrorist Carlos the Jackal. Secretary Albright came for the comfortably reconstructed rooms; the Jackal apparently came because during the Communist era the hotel was a safe house with decent room and board. The 1970s facade is unappealing, but the interior has been updated with modern rooms, a glittering fitness center, and an atrium restaurant. The standard guest rooms aren't very large but are comfortable, with decent but not exceptional upholstered furniture, computer ports, and marble bathrooms. A riverside window might give you a glimpse of the castle or at least the metronome at the top of Letná Park across the river, where a massive statue of Joseph Stalin once stood in the late 1950s and early '60s.

Prague's Best Hostels

Hostels aren't what they used to be, at least not in Prague. These days, backpackers with a little spare cash are demanding more style for their money, and hotel owners have responded with a new breed of "flashpacker" hostels, combining the stripped-down basics of a hostel (like dorm beds and shared bathrooms) with services and style you might associate more with a boutique hotel.

In Prague, two names to look out for include the **Czech Inn** ★★ at Francouzská 76, Prague 10 (℃ **267-267-600;** www.czech-inn.com) and **Sir Toby's** ★ at Dělnická 24, Prague 7 (℃ **246-032-610;** www.sirtobys.com). Both offer beds in shared dorm rooms for around 390Kč per person, and private doubles from around 1,500Kč—in other words, excellent value for what's available. Prices include a hearty breakfast, and there are thoughtful touches like big banks of computers for checking e-mail and modern efficiency kitchens. Though both are situated outside the center, they are close enough to public transportation that this is not an issue.

Travellers' Hostel-Pension Dlouhá ★ (Dlouhá 33, Prague 1; ℃ **224-826-662;** fax 224-826-665; www.travellers.cz) is one of the best hostels in the city center. This flagship in the local Travellers' group of hostels is open year-round, just a few blocks off Old Town Square and a few floors above one of the better music clubs in town, the Roxy. The hostel offers shared accommodation in dorm rooms or private singles and doubles, and attracts a mix of backpackers and veteran tourists taking advantage of the clean, affordable setting. Travellers' offers other hostels at dormitories throughout town during the high season. Check the website for more info. Rates including breakfast are 690Kč per person in a double room.

Pařížská 30, Prague 1. ℃ **296-631-111.** Fax 224-811-216. www.icprague.com. 364 units. From 4,161Kč double; from 7,605Kč suite. Rates include buffet breakfast. AE, DC, MC, V. Metro: Staroměstská. **Amenities:** 2 restaurants; cafe; concierge; fitness center; indoor pool; room service. *In room:* TV, hair dryer, minibar.

Hotel Josef ★★   The Josef is the hippest of Prague's hip hotels. British-based Czech architect Eva Jiřičná brings a new study on the interior use of glass to her native land with its own long history of the glazier's craft. Every piece of space breathes with life and light, breaking the stuffy mold of most high-end hotels. She uses modern glass walls, tables, and chairs bathed with the light of modern lighting fixtures to offset funky yellows and greens, and even rust-colored bedspreads are thrown in. There is a daring and dramatic effect in every room. Superior rooms are so bold as to offer transparent bath nooks, shower stalls, and washrooms with a full view of grooming activities for your partner to absorb in the main sleeping chamber. Room no. 801, a penthouse suite with a magnificent vista of the Prague skyline, is highly sought-after for those who want to absorb the Golden City in its full glory.

Rybná 20, Prague 1. ℃ **221-700-111.** Fax 221-700-999. www.hoteljosef.com. 109 units. From 4,300Kč double. AE, DC, MC, V. Metro: Náměstí Republiky. **Amenities:** Restaurant; babysitting; concierge; health club; room service. *In room:* A/C, TV, DVD, CD player, hair dryer, Internet, minibar.

(Kids) **Family-Friendly Accommodations**

Private apartments where you can fix your own meals are the most convenient option for families (p. 66), but if you would prefer more hotel-like services and settings, try:

Orion (p. 80) This affordable apartment-style hotel in Vinohrady has plenty of space for kids as well as kitchens for meals the way you want them.

Corinthia Hotel (p. 81) This is one of the few hotels anywhere to offer its own Western-style bowling alley complete with automatic scoring. Vyšehrad Park, with playgrounds and beautiful views for picnicking, is a short walk away.

Hotel Ungelt (p. 76) A convenient location in the heart of Old Town, and large apartment suites, make this hotel a good choice for a short or long family stay.

Pension Větrník (p. 82) This country inn has plenty of fresh air and forests for the kids to run around. Mom and Dad will like the price and made-to-order meals.

Hotel Paříž ★ At the edge of Náměstí Republiky and across from the Municipal House, the 100-year-old Paříž provides a rare chance to put yourself back in the gilded First Republic. Each light fixture, etching, and curve at this Art Nouveau landmark recalls the days when Prague was one of the world's richest cities. The sinuous banister leading past the reception area is an intricate piece of ironwork, and the lobby is tastefully furnished in the Art Nouveau style known here as the *secese* motif. The high-ceilinged guest rooms are done in a purplish theme; they aren't plush but are comfortable and adequately equipped, with more modern furnishings than the lobby would suggest. It's the ground floor that really maintains an authentic period elegance.

U Obecního domu 1, Prague 1. (*) **222-195-195.** Fax 222-195-907. www.hotel-pariz.cz. 86 units (most with tub/shower combination). 4,000Kč double; 8,000Kč suite. AE, DC, MC, V. Metro: Náměstí Republiky. **Amenities:** Restaurant; cafe; babysitting; concierge; room service. *In room:* A/C, TV, hair dryer, minibar.

Hotel Ungelt ★★ (Value) (Kids) In the afternoon shadow of the Týn Church, just off Old Town Square, you'll find a place not as opulent as the Paříž (see above), but a good value. The three-story Ungelt offers full apartments that are airy, spacious, and very comfortable for families. Each unit contains a bedroom, a living room, a full kitchen, and a bathroom. The bedrooms have standard-issue beds and not-too-attractive upholstered couches, but do boast luxurious accents like huge chandeliers and antique dressers. Some also have magnificent hand-painted ceilings. Because the Ungelt is in a tightly constructed neighborhood behind the church, there are no great exterior views. However, the back rooms overlook a quaint courtyard. The Gothic Suite is apparently a favorite of British writer Dick Francis.

Štupartská 7, Prague 1. (*) **222-745-900.** Fax 222-745-901. www.ungelt.cz. 6 units. From 2,700Kč 1-bed-room suite; from 3,600Kč 2-bedroom suite. Rates include breakfast. AE, MC, V. Metro: Staroměstská or line B to Náměstí Republiky. **Amenities:** Bar; Internet. *In room:* TV, hair dryer, minibar.

Hotel U Prince ★ (**Value**) Sometimes with a location this good a hotel will fall short of expectations, but the Hotel U Prince has reformed itself into a worthy choice for its price range. Directly across from the Astronomical Clock in Old Town Square, a complete reconstruction of the 12th-century building has given its once ragged rooms and salons a new lease on life. They are spacious and equipped with heavy period furniture, including beds with soft mattresses. The bathrooms offer tub/shower combinations. The double glazing has locked out most of the constant buzz from the square below. Rooms in the back are even more secluded. However, the showstopper of this property is the roof terrace bar and restaurant, which offers exceptional views for dining in Prague during the high season.

Staroměstské nám. 29, Prague 1. ℂ/fax **224-213-807.** www.hoteluprince.cz. 24 units. 3,000Kč double; from 4,800Kč suite. Rates include breakfast. AE, MC, V. Metro: Staroměstská. **Amenities:** 2 restaurants, including 1 rooftop restaurant open year-round; bar; summer garden; room service. *In room:* A/C, minibar.

MODERATE

Betlem Club (**Value**) Protestant firebrand Jan Hus launched his reformation drive at the reconstructed chapel across the street, but other than the vaulted medieval cellar where breakfast is served, little about the Betlem Club recalls those heady 15th-century days. Still, this small hotel has a great location on a cobblestone square. The rooms are unimaginatively decorated with bland modern pieces but are comfortable and fairly priced. The bathrooms are small but clean.

Betlémské nám. 9, Prague 1. ℂ **222-221-575.** Fax 222-220-580. www.betlemclub.cz. 22 units (tub/ shower combination). From 2,600Kč double; from 3,100Kč suite. Rates include breakfast. AE, MC, V. Metro: Národní třída. **Amenities:** Babysitting; Internet. *In room:* TV, hair dryer, minibar.

Dům U krále Jiřího The "King George" perches above a pub and a jazz club on a narrow side street. The rooms are pretty bare but have a bit more charm than they used to. The ceilings are high, and the dark wooden furniture is another improvement. Charles Bridge is a few dozen steps away and a swing to the left from the pension, but this narrow alley has become more like Bourbon Street than the Royal Route. Ask for a room in back if you want to deaden the clamor of the pubs below. Breakfast is served in the wine cellar, which lacks character despite a remodeling.

Liliová 10, Prague 1. ℂ **221-466-100.** Fax 221-466-166. www.hotelkinggeorge.com. 11 units. From 2,500Kč double or suite. Rates include breakfast. AE, MC, V. Metro: Staroměstská. *In room:* TV, fridge, minibar.

Hotel Cloister Inn ★★ (**Value**) Between Old Town Square and the National Theater, this property has been renovated into a good-value, midrange hotel. The original rooms of this unique spot were developed from holding cells used by the Communist secret police, the StB; the cells themselves were converted from a convent. It sounds ominous, but the Cloister Inn rooms are actually very inviting. A new proprietor has taken over management from the secret police and has refurbished and expanded the hotel with smart colors and comfortable Nordic furniture. The rooms offer enough space, beds with firm mattresses, and reasonably sized bathrooms with showers only. All is maintained to a high standard. It is just a short walk from both Charles Bridge and Old Town Square.

Konviktská 14, Prague 1. ℂ **224-211-020.** Fax 224-210-800. www.cloister-inn.cz. 73 units (showers only). From 2,100Kč double. Rates include breakfast. AE, DC, MC, V. Metro: Národní třída. **Amenities:** Concierge; Internet. *In room:* A/C, TV, hair dryer, minibar.

4 NOVÉ MĚSTO (NEW TOWN)

NEAR WENCESLAS SQUARE

Expensive

Hotel Jalta ★   Recently reconstructed, the Jalta has put on a fresh face and a new attitude. The lobby is pretty cold and unwelcoming, but the rooms have high ceilings and decent upholstered chairs. An infusion of Japanese money has improved the hotel furnishings, which were formerly depressing Communist-issue pieces. The Jalta is just below the statue of St. Wenceslas, where the masses gathered to ring out the Communist government in 1989. The rooms facing the square have balconies, allowing a broad view of the busy square and a chance to imagine the scene on those historic, revolutionary November nights.

Václavské nám. 45, Prague 1. © **222-822-111.** Fax 222-822-833. www.hoteljalta.com. 94 units. From 3,500Kč double; 5,000Kč suite. Rates include breakfast. AE, DC, MC, V. Metro: Muzeum. **Amenities:** 2 restaurants; concierge; fitness center; room service; casino. *In room:* A/C, TV, hair dryer, minibar.

Moderate

Andante ⓥ**Value**   This best-value choice near Wenceslas Square is tucked away on a dark side street, about 2 blocks off the top of the square. Despite the unappealing neighborhood, this is the most comfortable property at this price. With modern beds and good firm mattresses, as well as high-grade Scandinavian furniture and colorful decorations, the rooms are extremely comfortable. They offer plenty of space and white, well-kept bathrooms with tub/shower combinations, some with shower only.

Ve Smečkách 4, Prague 1. © **222-210-021.** Fax 222-210-591. www.andante.cz. 32 units (some with shower only, some with tub only). From 2,700Kč double; 3,600Kč suite. Rates include breakfast. AE, MC, V. Metro: Muzeum. **Amenities:** Restaurant; room service. *In room:* TV, hair dryer, minibar.

Hotel Meran   This used to be part of the Hotel Evropa next door (see below), but the Meran is a bit brighter and more inviting than its bigger Art Nouveau neighbor, which draws so much attention to its gilded facade. The Meran has had a facelift to make it a fair but not spectacular midrange choice on Wenceslas Square, a walkable distance to the main train station. The lobby interior has retained some original Art Nouveau accents, although the rooms have few. They are unimaginatively decorated and seem cramped. The tiny bathrooms have tub/shower combinations or shower only. Like the Hotel Jalta (see above), front windows overlook the place where hundreds of thousands demonstrated until the Communist government fell in a peaceful coup in 1989.

Václavské nám. 27, Prague 1. © **224-238-440.** Fax 224-230-411. www.hotelmeran.cz. 20 units with bathroom (tub or shower). From 2,400Kč double. Rates include breakfast. AE, DC, MC, V. Metro: Muzeum or Můstek. **Amenities:** Concierge; Internet. *In room:* TV.

Inexpensive

Hotel Evropa   Established in 1889 as the Hotel Archduke Stephan, the Evropa was recast in the early 1900s as a gleaming Art Nouveau hotel. However, this is yet another classic that has seen much better days. Though the statue-studded exterior, still one of the most striking landmarks on Wenceslas Square, has recently been polished, the rooms are aging; most don't have bathrooms and some are just plain shabby. The best choice is a room facing the square with a balcony. The hotel's famous cafe, a wood-encased former masterpiece that no longer glows, furthers the theme. Still, this is an affordable way to stay in one of Wenceslas Square's once grand addresses.

Václavské nám. 25, Prague 1. © **224-215-387.** www.evropahotel.cz. 90 units, 20 with bathroom (tub only). 1,600Kč double without bathroom; 2,500Kč double with bathroom. Rates include continental breakfast. AE, MC, V. Metro: Můstek or Muzeum. **Amenities:** Restaurant; cafe; concierge; luggage storage.

Pension Museum ★ (**Value** This is yet another example of a successful renovation of a 19th-century building in the very center of the city. Located just across the National Museum, the pension offers clean and comfortable rooms with modern furniture. Do not be put off by the busy road in front, however. There are actually only two rooms facing it, and their new double-glazed windows block the noise very well. The private cozy courtyard garden serves as an oasis for relaxation, which is otherwise hard to find around Václavské náměstí, the city's most lively shopping area.

Mezibranská 15, Prague 1. © **296-325-186.** Fax 296-325-188. www.pension-museum.cz. 12 units with bathroom (shower only). From 1,970Kč double; 2,440Kč suite. Rates include breakfast. AE, MC, V. Metro: Muzeum. **Amenities:** Atrium garden; concierge; Internet; luggage storage. *In room:* A/C, TV, fridge, hair dryer.

NEAR NÁMĚSTÍ REPUBLIKY/BANKING DISTRICT
Very Expensive
Kempinski ★ The Kempinski is another relatively recent entry into Prague's high-end accommodation market. It arrived just in time for the world economic downturn, but has enough going for it that it will surely outlast the bad times. The setting is a jaw-dropping refurbished 17th-century townhouse. The public areas are all polished stone and glass. The rooms feature a stylish contemporary interior with retro hints, and all the modern conveniences you'd expect at this price. The bathrooms are huge with the de rigueur see-through shower glass (it seems no one wants privacy anymore when they take a shower). The restaurant's Le Grill restaurant is easily one of the best in the city.

Hybernská 12, Prague 1. © **226-226-111.** Fax 226-226-123. www.kempinski-prague.com. 74 units. From 4,700Kč double; 8,125Kč suite. Rates include breakfast. AE, DC, MC, V. Metro: Náměstí Republiky. **Amenities:** 2 restaurants; cafe; concierge; conference hall; room service. *In room:* A/C, TV, hair dryer, Internet, minibar.

Expensive
Hilton Prague Old Town ★ Formerly known as the Renaissance Prague and now newly refurbished and run by Hilton, this is a top-level business hotel. Like the Marriott, it's around the corner from the central bank and caters to conference-goers. Each room is strategically lit, with warm woods and contemporary earth tones, but without any of the accents found at the Old Town's Art Nouveau hotels. The rooms include comfortable modern beds, flat-panel TVs, and clean, fully tiled bathrooms. The hotel enjoyed a brief vogue in 2008 and early 2009 as the site of Gordon Ramsay's fabled Maze restaurant—a Michelin-star winner that closed abruptly after Ramsay's global empire crashed and burned. The restaurant that replaced it, Zinc, is still pretty good, however.

V Celnici 7, Prague 1. © **221-822-100.** Fax 221-822-200. www1.hilton.com. 305 units. From 3,900Kč double; from 8,000Kč suite. Rates for suites and executive rooms include breakfast. AE, DC, MC, V. Metro: náměstí Republiky. **Amenities:** 2 restaurants; bar; ballroom; concierge; small exercise room; indoor pool; meeting rooms; sauna; room service; whirlpool. *In room:* A/C, TV, hair dryer, Internet, minibar.

K+K Hotel Central ★★ (**Value** It wasn't that long ago that Hybernská street, which runs beside the Masaryk train station, was a forgotten corner of the city and slightly derelict at night. Now it's one of the hottest properties for upscale hotels, including the

Kempinski (reviewed above), and this ornate Art Nouveau palace that may even be the better of the two. Fans of early-20th-century architecture will love the highly stylized exterior and public areas. The rooms are on the small side, but done up in a kind of low-slung Functionalist style that recalls the 1920s. The dining and breakfast areas are opulent in the extreme, a series of archways carved into the wall and festooned with 1920s period lighting. Check the website for discounts; the hotel frequently offers rooms that would put this in the moderate category. In other words: a steal.

Hybernská 10, Prague 1. ✆ **225-022-000.** Fax 225-022-999. www.kkhotels.com. 127 units. From 2,800Kč double; from 6,800Kč suite. Rates include breakfast. AE, DC, MC, V. Metro: Náměstí Republiky. **Amenities:** Restaurant; bar; cafe/lounge; babysitting; concierge; executive-level rooms; room service; sauna. *In room:* TV, hair dryer, minibar.

Prague Marriott Hotel ★ (Kids) A major addition to the thin ranks of full-service business hotels, the Marriott provides just what you would expect—a high standard. The large rooms have bright colors, tasteful (if homogenized) furniture, and comfortable beds, as well as phones, faxes, laptop connections, and other services. The bathrooms are spacious and immaculately maintained. In an effort to attract families, the Marriott offers Sunday family brunches in the in-house restaurant, where kids are welcome and PC games are available.

V Celnici 8, Prague 1. ✆ **222-888-888.** Fax 222-888-889. www.marriott.com. 328 units. 3,600Kč double; 5,400Kč executive-level double. Rates for executive rooms include breakfast. AE, DC, MC, V. Metro: Náměstí Republiky. **Amenities:** Restaurant; cafe; bar; concierge; well-equipped, largest fitness center in town; indoor pool; room service; saunas; spa rooms; whirlpools. *In room:* A/C, TV, hair dryer, minibar.

5 VINOHRADY

EXPENSIVE

Hotel Ametyst Though a little pricey for the location—a quiet backstreet about 5 blocks from náměstí Míru—the Hotel Ametyst is spotless and decorated in a warm contemporary style. The top-floor rooms are especially bright and cheery, with pitched ceilings and balconies overlooking the peaceful residential neighborhood. The rooms are smartly decorated in contemporary style, with big beds, flat-screen TVs, and wooden floors.

Jana Masaryka 11, Prague 2. ✆ **222-921-921.** Fax 222-921-999. www.hotelametyst.cz. 84 units (some with tub only, some with shower only). 5,625Kč double. Rates include breakfast. AE, DC, MC, V. Metro: Náměstí Míru. **Amenities:** 2 restaurants; bar; conference room; small fitness center; sauna. *In room:* TV, hair dryer, Internet, minibar.

INEXPENSIVE

Orion ★ (Kids) The best family value close to the city center, the Orion is an apartment hotel with each unit sporting a well-equipped kitchen. All accommodations have either one bedroom (sleeps two) or two bedrooms (sleeps up to six). The spacious guest rooms are comfortable but not very imaginative, bordered in pale blue with leather armchairs and dark wooden bed frames without much on the walls. The beds vary in the firmness of their mattresses. The bathrooms are small, basic white, and modern, as are the kitchens. In this friendly neighborhood, fruit and vegetable shops and corner grocery stores can be found around náměstí Míru, just up the street.

Americká 9, Prague 2. ☏ **222-521-706.** Fax 222-521-707. www.okhotels.cz/en/hotel-orion. 26 apts with bathroom (tub/shower combination). From 1,600Kč 1 bedroom; 2,400Kč 2 bedrooms. Breakfast 160Kč. AE, MC, V. Metro: Náměstí Míru. **Amenities:** Room service; sauna. *In room:* TV, fridge, kitchen.

6 ELSEWHERE IN PRAGUE

VERY EXPENSIVE

Corinthia Hotel Prague ★ **Kids**   Opened in the mid-1980s, this hotel was one of the last "achievements" of Communist central planners. Reserved occasionally for delegates attending Party Congress meetings at the Palace of Culture next door (now the Congress Center), the hotel juts up from a hill with a gorgeous panorama of the city. The medium-size rooms have undergone a recent renovation and are fitted out with solid furniture and firm mattresses on the beds. One of the more unusual amenities is a pub with a bowling alley in the basement, and the top-floor pool has a panoramic city view. Though the city center isn't within walking distance, the Vyšehrad metro station is just below the hotel entrance.

Kongresová 1, Prague 4. ☏ **261-191-111.** Fax 261-225-011. www.corinthia.com. 583 units. 4,000Kč double; from 6,000Kč suite. Rates include breakfast. AE, DC, MC, V. Metro: Vyšehrad. **Amenities:** 2 restaurants; cafe; babysitting; concierge; well-equipped fitness center w/pool, sauna, and exercise machines; game room; room service; bowling alley. *In room:* A/C, TV, minibar.

Hilton Prague   With its jarring 1980s galleria style, the Hilton looks like a huge ice cube outside and a greenhouse inside. The guest rooms are relatively cushy and functional, somewhat like those in an upscale U.S. motel. The building is packed with amenities that include a tennis club, pool, fitness center, and arguably the city's most elegant cocktail bar, the Cloud 9 Sky Bar and Lounge. The 700-plus rooms make this place a natural choice for the largest conferences and conventions; it's also the hotel of choice for visiting U.S. presidents, including Bill Clinton, George W. Bush, and in 2009, Barack Obama and his wife, Michelle. The location just outside the city center isn't ideal, but it's just a short walk to the Florenc metro station.

Pobřežní 1, Prague 8. ☏ **224-841-111.** Fax 224-842-378. www.hilton.com. 788 units (tub/shower combination). From 5,200Kč double; from 7,200Kč suite. AE, DC, MC, V. Metro: Florenc. **Amenities:** Cafe/restaurant; concierge; health club; indoor pool; putting greens; room service; sauna; tennis club. *In room:* A/C, TV, hair dryer, Internet, minibar.

MODERATE

Hotel Absolutum ★ **Value**   This is a sleek, modern hotel, with designer-style rooms at reasonable prices. The racks rates aren't particularly great, but the reception desk will usually offer decent discounts on slow nights (be sure to ask). The location, across the

---

Tips   **A Note on Floors**

Remember that Europe's floor-numbering system differs from that in North America. European buildings have a ground floor (corresponding to the first floor in the U.S.), then a first floor (the second floor in the U.S.), a second floor, and so on.

street from the Holešovice train and metro station, won't win any beauty contests, but it's super convenient for getting to the center or for checking out Holešovice, one of Prague's up-and-coming neighborhoods. The house restaurant is the best around, and a good place to get a bite if you're stuck waiting on a train at Holešovice nádraží.

Jablonského 476, Prague 7. ✆ **222-541-406.** Fax 222 541 407. www.absolutumhotel.cz. 34 units (some with tub/shower combination). 4,000Kč double. Rates include breakfast. MC. Metro: Nádraží Holešovice. **Amenities:** Cafe/restaurant; health club next door; limited room service. *In room:* A/C, TV, hair dryer, Internet, minibar.

INEXPENSIVE

Pension Větrník ★ (Value) (Kids)   A mostly scenic half-hour tram ride (or metro-tram combo) from the city center takes you to this romantic country hideaway. After getting off the tram, walk back behind a bunch of large concrete dorms to find a painstakingly restored 18th-century white windmill house. Once you buzz at the metal gate (be careful to avoid the buzzer for the door to the family residence), the owner will greet you. Lush gardens and a tennis court lead to a quaint guesthouse with a stone staircase and spacious rooms with big beds, open-beamed ceilings, and modern amenities. The bathrooms are roomy, with stand-up showers, and the windows are shuttered and boast flower boxes. If you opt for dinner at the pension, the owner will whip up a traditional Czech country meal (for around 200Kč) and serve it in a small medieval stone cellar with a crackling fire. There's a patio for drinks outside during pleasant weather. You can't get more romantic than this, especially for the price.

U Větrníku 40, Prague 6. ✆ **220-612-404.** Fax 220-513-390. www.pensionvetrnik.wz.cz. 6 units (4 shower only, 2 tub/shower combination). 2,200Kč double; 3,300Kč suite. Rates include breakfast. MC. Metro: Line A to Hradčanská station, then tram no. 1 or 18 to Větrník. **Amenities:** Tennis court. *In room:* TV, hair dryer.

---

7 NEAR THE AIRPORT

VERY EXPENSIVE

Hotel Praha ★   The Praha is a former luxury hotel for high-ranking Communist party members and is kind of a kitsch choice if you want to know how the other half once lived. Everything is oversized and the retro-futuristic cocktail bar has to be seen to be believed. The hotel is built into the hillside in a wealthy suburb on the city's western end, and all the rooms face east toward the center. The hotel has all the brass, chrome, and marble veneer that Brezhnev and Castro could ever have wanted, but before you dismiss it as a relic, you might be interested to know that Tom Cruise, Johnny Depp, and other celebrities have stayed here while filming in Prague. The draws are the fortresslike setting, private balconies, magnificent views of the city, and proximity to the airport. The rooms are spacious but on the plain side compared with the lavish public areas.

Sušická 20, Prague 6. ✆ **224-341-111.** Fax 224-311-218. www.htlpraha.cz. 124 units (tub/shower combination). From 7,200Kč double; from 9,800Kč suite. Rates include breakfast. AE, DC, MC, V. Metro: Dejvická. **Amenities:** 2 restaurants; babysitting; concierge; exercise room; indoor pool; 2 tennis courts; sauna; room service. *In room:* A/C, TV, hair dryer, Internet, minibar.

EXPENSIVE

Hotel Diplomat   The clean and functional Diplomat is a good choice if access to the airport is important. While it's not next to the airport, it does lie next to the main trunk road about 15 minutes away. It's also convenient for getting into town, situated just next to the Dejvická metro station, about 10 minutes by metro to the center. While it won't win any design awards, the Diplomat achieves what it sets out to do: provide an array of business services and spacious rooms with comfortable beds. The colorful decorations and furnishings give the rooms a warm atmosphere. The bathrooms are of adequate size, fitted with tub/shower combinations, and are well maintained.

Evropská 15, Prague 6. (℡ **296-559-111.** Fax 296-559-215. www.diplomathotel.cz. 398 units (tub/shower combination). 3,600Kč double; 5,200Kč suite. Rates include breakfast. AE, DC, MC, V. Metro: Dejvická. **Amenities:** 2 restaurants; cafe/bar; concierge; conference center; executive-level rooms; health club w/ sauna; whirlpool. *In room:* A/C, TV, hair dryer, Internet, minibar.

WHERE TO STAY IN PRAGUE

5

NEAR THE AIRPORT

Where to Dine in Prague

Prague still has a long way to go before people travel here just for the food, but the quality and variety of restaurants have improved tremendously in the past decade. Not that long ago, dining out meant choosing between a pizza covered in ketchup, listless pub grub, or a handful of overpriced "luxury" restaurants—the kind where stiff waiters wheel around tired appetizers on a little cart.

Today, thanks to a massive influx of tourist dollars as well as rising incomes of ordinary Czechs, Prague now supports many very good restaurants, with traditional Czech places supplemented by French, Italian, Japanese, Chinese, and Indian restaurants. The past couple of years have also even seen the country's first Michelin star awarded to **Allegro,** the house restaurant of the Four Seasons Hotel (p. 95).

But that doesn't mean every place is good. For every decent restaurant that has opened its doors in the past couple of years, it seems at least two inferior restaurants—tourist traps aimed squarely at fooling unwitting visitors—have popped up. More than ever, it pays to be careful. Avoid places in the heavily touristy areas of town around Old Town Square and Karlova street. These are pallid imitations of real Czech restaurants that are meant to empty your wallet, not satisfy your palate. Many of the best places are located outside of the center, so be prepared to hit the metro or grab a taxi if serious food is on the agenda.

The list below includes some of the city's best restaurants. To supplement our picks and see what Prague's expats are saying, check out two English-language restaurant blogs: the "Prague Spoon" (http://praguespoon.blogspot.com) by local critic Laura Baranik; and "Czech Please" (http://czechoutchannel.blogspot.com), by an American known as "Brewsta."

RESERVATIONS The economic recession in 2009 hit Prague's restaurants hard. In the boom days, reservations at the best places were often a requirement for getting a table. Harder economic times have eased demand substantially, though to avoid unpleasant surprises it's always best to phone ahead. Most restaurants should be able to handle a reservation request in English. Alternatively, ask your hotel reception desk to make the call.

SERVICE Service remains abysmal in Czech restaurants, a fact that needs to be stated bluntly upfront. Restaurant owners seem unwilling to commit the resources to proper training, and the result is often impossibly slow service, messed up orders, unfriendly staff, and long waits to pay your bill. The good news is that you're on vacation and time won't usually be a main concern. Just be sure to check your expectations at the door.

Some tips for getting better service are as follows: Be sure to greet the staff as you enter the restaurant. This lets everyone know you're here. Also, have a pretty good idea of what you might want (even before you enter the restaurant). That way you'll be ready to place your food order as soon as the first round of drinks arrives. Finally, resist the temptation to wave or call out loudly to the staff. There is no surer way to put yourself on the blacklist.

TIPPING & TAX   A tip of 10% of the bill is considered standard for good service in a tablecloth restaurant, but don't feel obliged to go the full amount if service was poor. Most Czechs tip considerably less and simply round up the bill to the next logical point. For example, on a 480Kč check, they might hand the waiter a 500Kč bill and tell him to keep the change. Tips are usually handed directly to the waiter or left discreetly in the little pouch or wallet that the bill is delivered in.

Some restaurants have begun the irritating practice of adding the tip—usually 10% but sometimes more for groups— directly to the bill. It's a good idea to look over the tab carefully to make sure you understand all of the charges.

DINING CUSTOMS   Traditional Czech custom is simply to find whatever seats are available without the assistance of a hostess or maitre d', but newer restaurants have started to employ staff to seat you. Barring this, just point at the table you want and nod at a nearby waiter to make sure it's available. Don't be afraid to sit in open seats at large tables where others are already seated, as is the case in many pubs and casual restaurants. However, it's customary to ask *"Je tu volno?"* ("Is this spot free?") before joining a large table. Likewise, don't be surprised if others ask to sit at your table. Just nod or say *"Ano, je"* ("Yes, it's free"), and make some new friends.

BEST DINING BETS

- **Best Splurge:** This is a tough call, but if you're into Michelin stars, give **Allegro** (℃ 221-427-000) in the Four Seasons Hotel a try. A big drop in price, but only a modest decline in quality, **Angel** (℃ 773-222-422) offers memorable Asian-inspired meals at prices that, while not cheap, are at least within reach. See p. 96.
- **Best Fancy Italian:** There's only one real game in town when it comes to the best Italy has to offer: **Aromi** (℃ 222-713-222) in Vinohrady. Come for dinner or for a remarkably good value lunch special on the terrace. See p. 102.
- **Best Czech Cuisine:** In an intricate flower-embellished setting, **U modré kachničky** (℃ 257-320-308) brings delicacy to Czech fare, including savvy spins on heavy sauces and wild game. See p. 93.
- **Best Pub Guláš (Goulash):** Old Town's boisterous **U Vejvodů** (℃ 224-219-999) dishes out a fine spicy goulash along with Pilsner Urquell. See p. 107.
- **Best All-You-Can-Eat Buffet:** I don't know how they make any money on this, but the antipasto buffet at **Pizza Nuova** (℃ 221-803-308), next to Kotva, is filled with mouthwatering grilled vegetables, meats, cheeses, and fish. Add all the fresh bread and salad you can eat for just 285Kč. See p. 98.
- **Best Bar Food:** It's loud and crude and filled with a boisterous mix of traveling Americans and Czechs bingeing after work, but **Jáma** (℃ 224-222-383) in Nové Město has, hands down, Prague's best bacon cheeseburger. See p. 101.
- **Best Sushi:** The appropriately named **Sushi Bar** (℃ 603-244-882) at the southern edge of Malá Strana consistently offers the freshest sushi in a town in the grips of a sushi craze. See p. 92.
- **Best Bagels:** Bohemia Bagel (℃ 257-218-192) at Lázeňská in Malá Strana and on Masná Street in Staré Město (℃ 224-812-560) has filled what was a curious vacuum. See p. 95.
- **Best Hot Dog:** *Párek v rohlíku* (hot dog in a roll) is a popular street food, and arguably the best in town are to be found at the little stand on **Náměstí Míru** square. When strolling around Vinohrady, take a break here. There are plenty of benches. See p. 99.

Tips on Tipping

Guidelines on tipping are in a state of flux. Under the old Communist regime, tipping was not encouraged, and tips tended to be on the low side—usually no more than a few crowns no matter what the size of the bill or the quality of service. Many Czechs, particularly older people, *still* tip like it's 1985.

That modest-tipping rule, sadly, doesn't extend to visitors. Although Prague waiters will rarely expect the 15 to 20% that's become common in the U.S., they do tend to get a bit peeved with tips of less than 10%, especially if they put in a hard night.

A good rule of thumb is as follows: For tabs under 100Kč, round up to the nearest 10Kč increment. If the bill comes to 75Kč, for example, hand the waiter your money and tell him or her the amount. On larger tabs of over 100Kč or so, a tip of 10% is considered standard for decent service (don't be afraid to go less for lousy service). Resist the temptation to go much higher, save for those times when the service is truly outstanding or the restaurant has gone to great lengths to honor a special request. You can hand the tip directly to the waiter or simply leave it on the table.

- **Best Kosher:** There are now a few kosher places around the Jewish Quarter but the **King Solomon Restaurant** (© **224-818-752**), across from the Pinkas Synagogue, gets it right. See p. 96.
- **Best for Kids/Best Pizza:** You can please the kids and satisfy your own cravings at **Pizzeria Rugantino** (© **222-318-172**), a friendly and energetic Old Town room run by an Italian family that loves kids. See p. 100.
- **Best for Vegetarians:** The venerable **Radost FX Café** (© **603-181-500**) still dishes out veggie burgers, burritos, and salads to the trendy postclub crowd until 5am. See p. 103.

1 RESTAURANTS BY CUISINE

American
Bakeshop ★★ (Staré Město, $, p. 100)
Jáma ★ (Nové Město, $, p. 101)

Bagels
Bohemia Bagel (Malá Strana or Staré Město, $, p. 95)

Cafes/Tearooms
Blatouch ★ (Vinohrady, $, p. 106)
Cafe Evropa (Nové Město, $, p. 105)

Café Imperial ★ (Nové Město, $$, p. 105)
Café Louvre (Nové Město, $, p. 105)
Dobrá čajovna ★ (Nové Město, $, p. 105)
The Globe Bookstore and Café ★★ (Nové Město, $, p. 105)
Grand Café (Staré Město, $, p. 104)
Grand Café Orient ★★ (Staré Město, $, p. 104)
Kavárna Medúza (Vinohrady, $, p. 106)

Key to Abbreviations: $$$$ = Very Expensive $$$ = Expensive $$ = Moderate $ = Inexpensive

Kavárna Obecní dům ★★ (Staré Město, $, p. 104)
Kavárna Slavia ★ (Staré Město, $, p. 104)
Velryba (Nové Město, $, p. 105)

Continental
Café de Paris ★ (Malá Strana, $$, p. 93)
Café Savoy ★★ (Malá Strana, $$, p. 93)
Kampa Park ★ (Malá Strana, $$$$, p. 89)
La Degustation ★★★ (Staré Město, $$$$, p. 96)
Nebozízek (Malá Strana, $$, p. 94)
Pálffy Palác ★★ (Malá Strana, $$$, p. 93)
U Medvídků ★★ (Staré Město, $, p. 106)
U Vejvodů ★ (Staré Město, $, p. 107)
U zlaté hrušky ★ (Hradčany, $$$$, p. 88)
Villa Richter ★ (Hradčany, $$$$, p. 88)

Czech
Café Louvre (Nové Město, $, p. 105)
Café Savoy ★★ (Malá Strana, $$, p. 93)
Hergetova Cihelna ★ (Malá Strana, $$$, p. 93)
Klub Architektů (Staré Město, $, p. 100)
La Degustation ★★★ (Staré Město, $$$$, p. 96)
Nebozízek (Malá Strana, $$, p. 94)
Pivovarský dům ★★ (Nové Město, $, p. 101)
U Medvídků ★★ (Staré Město, $, p. 106)
U modré kachničky ★ (Malá Strana or Staré Město, $$$, p. 93)
U Vejvodů ★ (Staré Město, $, p. 107)
U zlaté hrušky ★ (Hradčany, $$$$, p. 88)
Vikárka ★ (Hradčany, $$, p. 89)
Villa Richter ★ (Hradčany, $$$$, p. 88)

Vinárna U Maltézských rytířů (At Knights of Malta) ★ (Malá Strana, $$, p. 94)

Deli
Bakeshop ★★ (Staré Město, $, p. 100)
Lahůdky Zlatý Kříž (Nové Město, $, p. 99)

French
Café de Paris ★ (Malá Strana, $$, p. 93)
Chez Marcel (Staré Město, $, p. 100)
La Provence (Staré Město, $$$, p. 98)
Le Café Colonial ★ (Staré Město, $$, p. 99)
Les Moules ★ (Staré Město, $$, p. 99)
U Malířů (Malá Strana, $$$$, p. 92)

Greek
Taverna Olympos ★ (Vinohrady, $$, p. 102)

Indian
Masala ★★ (Vinohrady, $$, p. 102)

International
Allegro ★★ (Staré Město, $$$$, p. 95)
Angel ★★ (Staré Město, $$$, p. 96)
Bellevue ★★ (Staré Město, $$$$, p. 95)
Bonante (Vinohrady, $$$, p. 102)
Café Louvre (Nové Město, $, p. 105)
Cukrkávalimonáda ★★ (Malá Strana, $, p. 95)
Hergetova Cihelna ★ (Malá Strana, $$$, p. 93)
Jarmark (Staré Město, $, p. 100)
Klub Architektů (Staré Město, $, p. 100)
Mlýnec ★ (Staré Město, $$$, p. 98)
Vinárna V zátiší (Staré Město, $$$$, p. 96)
Zahrada v Opeře (Garden at the Opera) ★★ (Nové Město, $$, p. 101)

Internet Cafes

Bohemia Bagel (Staré Město, $, p. 106)

The Globe Bookstore and Cafe ★★ (Nové Město, $, p. 106)

Spika (Nové Město, $, p. 106)

Italian

Allegro ★★ (Staré Město, $$$$, p. 95)

Aromi ★★ (Vinohrady, $$$$, p. 102)

Grosseto ★ (Dejvice, $$, p. 103)

Kogo ★ (Staré Město, $$, p. 98)

Mirellie ★★ (Dejvice, $$, p. 103)

Pizza Nuova ★ (Staré Město, $$, p. 98)

Japanese

Sushi Bar ★★ (Malá Strana, $$$$, p. 92)

Kosher

King Solomon Restaurant ★ (Staré Město, $$$, p. 96)

Pizza

Grosseto ★ (Dejvice, $$, p. 103)

Pizza Nuova ★ (Staré Město, $$, p. 98)

Pizzeria Rugantino ★★ (Staré Město, $, p. 100)

Seafood

Rybí trh (Staré Město, $$$$, p. 96)

Sports Bar

Sport Bar Prague-Zlatá Hvězda (Nové Město, $, p. 101)

Vegetarian

Country Life (Staré Město, $, p. 99)

Radost FX Café (Vinohrady, $, p. 103)

2 HRADČANY

VERY EXPENSIVE

U zlaté hrušky ★ CZECH/CONTINENTAL   The best part of a meal here is finding your way to this beautifully hidden alleyway in the Castle quarter. The "Golden Pear" has been here for several years and will not disappoint if you're looking for old-world charm and atmosphere. The menu mixes international favorites like grilled chicken breast and filet mignon with dishes that have a more local cast such as roast leg of goose served with dumplings. But truth be told, the romantic setting—and not the food—is the main draw here.

Nový Svět 3, Prague 1. ✆ **220-941-244.** www.uzlatehrusky.cz. Reservations recommended. Main courses lunch 450Kč–650Kč, dinner 590Kč–790Kč. AE, DC, MC, V. Daily 11am–1am. Tram: 22 one stop past Prague Castle.

Villa Richter ★ CONTINENTAL/CZECH   A relatively recent entry into Prague's top echelon is this luxury restaurant in a hilltop vineyard just as you exit the Prague Castle complex on the eastern end. There are actually three restaurants here, including a relatively inexpensive option that serves burgers and has wine tastings for 45Kč a glass, but the big culinary draw is the "Piano Nobile," a gourmet restaurant offering the best of Czech and international cooking and a wine vault with some 2,000 bottles. There's a five-course tasting menu for 1,690Kč. In winter, dress up for the fancy dining room; in summer, it's more relaxed, with dining on the terrace overlooking Malá Strana to your right and the Old Town across the river.

Staré zámecké schody 6, Prague 1. ✆ **257-219-079.** www.villarichter.cz. Reservations recommended. Main courses 610Kč–690Kč, 1,690 Kč (five-course tasting menu). AE, DC, MC, V. Daily 11am–1am. Metro: Malostranská plus a walk up the stairs.

A Few Dining Warnings

Though the practice is declining, in the past some Czech restaurants have tried to raise a little extra revenue by placing seemingly free bowls of nuts or olives on the table or offering platters of appetizers or aperitifs that appeared to be on the house. Needless to say they were not and diners were often surprised to find they were paying the equivalent of $5 or more for a bowl of stale cashews.

These days it's more common for dining establishments to simply charge a cover, labeled *couvert* on the menu, of anywhere from 30Kč to 50Kč per person to cover things like the bread basket, spreads, and condiments. Regardless, it's good to be aware of the practice and if in doubt ask the waiter before touching any food on the table.

Many restaurants now accept credit cards, but waiters may not be adept at tricks like dividing a bill between two or three cards. It's best to keep it simple. Leave tips in cash on the table rather than charging them to the card; otherwise the server may never get them. Stories of credit card fraud by waiters are rare, but still it's always a good idea to keep a close watch on credit card statements.

MODERATE

Vikárka ★ **Kids** CZECH   Decent places to eat in Hradčany are rare. This wonderfully restored Romanesque and Gothic cellar restaurant within the castle walls not only offers good Czech and international dishes at decent prices, you get to eat amid more than 600 years of history. The staff gets into the mood with period costumes, but this is no tourist trap. For a real Czech treat, try the pork knee baked on dark beer served in the traditional style with slices of brown bread, horseradish, and mustard.

Vikářská 39, inside the Prague Castle complex, Prague 1. ✆ **233-311-962.** http://vikarka.cz. Main courses 180Kč–250Kč. AE, DC, MC, V. Daily 11am–9pm. Tram: 22 to Prague Castle.

3 MALÁ STRANA (LESSER TOWN)

VERY EXPENSIVE

Kampa Park ★ CONTINENTAL   This restaurant is worth the considerable splurge, but only if you can snag one of the highly coveted riverside tables. If you can't, move on and try for the terrace at Pálffy Palác or Hergetova Cihelna (both below). For years, Kampa Park was considered Prague's premier restaurant and lured its fair share of visiting celebs (check out the photos on the wall). These days, there's lots more competition, but the setting on the Vltava is still arguably the best in town. The menu, with items like seared monkfish and roast saddle of lamb, looks relatively tame, but the quality of the food is excellent.

Na Kampě 8b, Prague 1. ✆ **296-826-112.** www.kampagroup.com. Reservations recommended. Main courses 495Kč–895Kč. AE, DC, MC, V. Daily 11:30am–1am. Metro: Malostranská.

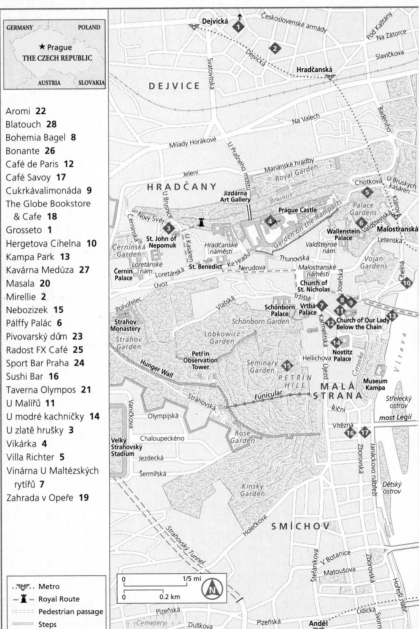

WHERE TO DINE IN PRAGUE

6

MALÁ STRANA (LESSER TOWN)

Aromi **22**
Blatouch **28**
Bohemia Bagel **8**
Bonante **26**
Café de Paris **12**
Café Savoy **17**
Cukrkávalimonáda **9**
The Globe Bookstore
   & Cafe **18**
Grosseto **1**
Hergetova Cihelna **10**
Kampa Park **13**
Kavárna Medúza **27**
Masala **20**
Mirellie **2**
Nebozizek **15**
Pálffy Palác **6**
Pivovarský dům **23**
Radost FX Café **25**
Sport Bar Praha **24**
Sushi Bar **16**
Taverna Olympos **21**
U Malířů **11**
U modré kachničky **14**
U zlaté hrušky **3**
Vikárka **4**
Villa Richter **5**
Vinárna U Maltézských
   rytířů **7**
Zahrada v Opeře **19**

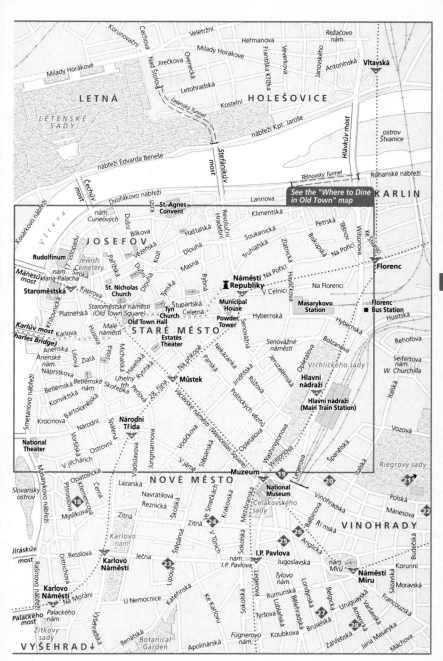

(Value) Money-Saving Tips

Restaurant prices in Prague have skyrocketed, and the unfavorable exchange rates for both the dollar and the pound have only added to the pain. These days, if you're not careful, it's quite easy to drop $50 a person on a meal that's only average. There are some tried and true techniques, however, for keeping the tab manageable.

By far the highest prices (and lowest quality) are to be found in the tourist joints around Old Town Square, so try to be as far away as possible from the throngs at mealtimes. Restaurants that use touts to haul in customers, have colorful plastic menus with photos, or are plastered with the words "Air Condition" on the front door are usually best avoided. You'll find the cheapest meals at traditional Czech pubs outside of the center. These offer a daily menu *(denní nabídka)* of a soup and main course for as little as 150Kč.

Other ways to save money include having your main meal at lunch and not dinner to take advantage of fixed-price luncheon specials around town. The same good food is available but for a fraction of the evening price. If you do happen to be out at a pricey tourist place in the evening, remember to politely refuse any offers of aperitifs or appetizers before seeing the menu. Keep in mind that Czech dinner portions are pretty big and there's often no need to order a separate appetizer. For the beverage, choose a local Czech wine. The quality is nearly as good and the price will be around half of what you'd pay for an imported bottle of wine. For very cheap meals, try the places covered in "Inexpensive Meals on the Run" (p. 99).

Sushi Bar ★★ JAPANESE   Sushi came late to the Czech Republic, but now it's here with a vengeance, and you can find sushi and maki on menus all across the city. If you care about truly good sushi, however, this is the only address in town. Conveniently, Sushi Bar is situated next to the city's best fish market, so sourcing is not an issue. Everything is fresh, and the "exclusive" jumbo maki are to die for. The dining area is tiny, so reservations are a must.

Zborovská 49. Prague 5. (℃) **603-244-882.** www.sushi.cz. Reservations recommended. Sushi menu 999Kč, exclusive maki 1,190Kč. AE, MC, V. Daily noon–11:30pm. Metro: Malostranská plus tram no. 12, 20, or 22 to Újezd.

U Malířů FRENCH   This is arguably the most romantic setting in one of the loveliest parts of Malá Strana. Surrounded by Romance-age murals and gorgeously appointed tables in three intimate dining rooms, you're faced with some tough choices, including a delicious baked duck breast and tuna served on roast noodles in a tomato mousse. Three-course set menus and a bottle of Czech wine, instead of French, can help keep the costs manageable, but if you want a truly old-world evening of elegant romance and French specialties, U Malířů may be worth it.

Maltézské nám. 11, Prague 1. (℃) **257-530-318.** www.umaliru.cz. Reservations recommended. Main courses 480Kč–690Kč, 3-course rotating summer menu 490Kč. AE, DC, MC, V. Daily 6–11pm. Metro: Malostranská.

EXPENSIVE

Hergetova Cihelna ★ INTERNATIONAL/CZECH   The main draw here is the riverside terrace with an unparalleled view of the Charles Bridge—plus the very good food (from the same people who run the more expensive Kampa Park). The building, dating from the 18th century, once served as a brick factory *(cihelna)* before it was renovated into this stylish modern restaurant around a decade ago. The first dining concept here was burgers and pizza, which the owners quickly ditched for more expensive items like rib-eye steaks with maple-glazed carrots (525Kč). Still, it's possible to eat cheaply if you stick to the Czech specialties and pasta dishes. Reserve several days in advance for the terrace.

Cihelná 2b, Prague 1. ✆ **296-826-103.** www.kampagroup.com. Reservations recommended. Main courses 215Kč–695Kč. AE, MC, V. Daily 11:30am–1am. Metro: Malostranská.

Pálffy Palác ★★ CONTINENTAL   This restaurant is a real treat, rain or shine. In bad weather, eat in the 17th-century baroque dining room, complete with candles, crystal chandeliers, and impossibly beautiful place settings—it's like having dinner with a wealthy count. In summer, sit on the terrace just below the lights of Prague Castle. Either way, you can't lose. The mostly high-end international dishes, built around standards like lamb and steak, are very good but miss the heights of truly haute cuisine.

Valdštejnská 14, Prague 1. ✆ **257-530-522.** www.palffy.cz. Reservations recommended. Main courses 490Kč–690Kč. AE, DC, MC, V. Daily 11am–11pm. Metro: Malostranská.

U modré kachničky ★ CZECH/WILD GAME   The "Blue Duckling," on a narrow Malá Strana street, comes close to refining standard Czech dishes into true Bohemian haute cuisine. This series of small dining rooms with vaulted ceilings and playfully frescoed walls is packed with antique furniture and pastel-flowered linen upholstery. The menu is loaded with an array of wild game and quirky spins on Czech village favorites. Starters include lightly spiced venison pâté and duck liver on toast. You can choose from six different duck main courses. Finally, the ubiquitous *palačinky* crepes are thin and tender and filled with fruit, nuts, and chocolate. There is an even more popular sister to the first "kachnička," at Michalská 16, Prague 1 (✆ **224-213-418**), with a similar menu and prices. Reservations are recommended (daily 11:30am–11:30pm; metro: Můstek).

Nebovidská 6, Prague 1. ✆ **257-320-308.** www.umodrekachnicky.cz. Reservations recommended for lunch, required for dinner. Main courses 290Kč–690Kč. AE, MC, V. Daily noon–4pm and 6:30pm–midnight. Metro: Malostranská.

MODERATE

Café de Paris FRENCH/CONTINENTAL ★   This delightful French bistro perched on pretty Maltézské náměstí is a perfect addition to a beautiful part of Prague. The menu is tiny with just a few items, though there are daily specials marked on the board outside. The specialty is grilled steak, entrecôte, served with salad, homemade fries, and a secret sauce known as "Café de Paris" sauce. The service is informal but attentive and the wine list is extensive and good value. An ideal spot for a long lunch or unfussy but good dinner.

Maltézské náměstí 4, Prague 1. ✆ **603-160-718.** www.cafedeparis.cz. Reservations recommended. Main courses 250Kč–350Kč. AE, MC, V. Daily noon–midnight. Metro: Malostranská plus tram no. 12, 20, or 22 to Malostranské náměstí.

Café Savoy CZECH/CONTINENTAL ★★   This lovingly restored 19th-century cafe recalls Prague's coffeehouse heyday under the Austro-Hungarian Empire. Inside, the

Family-Friendly Restaurants

Bohemia Bagel (p. 95)   The one on Masná street has a tiny garden with outside seating and a playroom for children, which makes family dining more pleasant and relaxed. Bagels and sandwiches are on the menu together with selections for small children.

Pizzeria Rugantino (p. 100)   A long list of crispy individual pizzas and salads, a seldom-seen nonsmoking section, and childproof tables make this noisy Old Town stop a staple for families.

Pizza Nuova (p. 98)   The pizzas are great, the menu offers all-you-can eat specials for hungry teens, and there's a small supervised play area in the corner for younger kids.

kitchen means business, serving a mix of international specialties and well-priced "Czech" entrees like Viennese-style goulash and Wiener schnitzel (made here from chicken breast or pork). It's run by the locally owned Ambiente chain, which also manages Pizza Nuova (p. 98). The cafe is open early for breakfast, with some rather creative menu items such as an "American-style" breakfast served with grilled chicken (which tastes better than it sounds).

Vítězná 5, Prague 5. ✆ **257-311-562.** www.ambi.cz. Reservations recommended. Main courses 150Kč–340Kč. AE, MC, V. Daily 11am–11pm. Metro: Malostranská plus tram no. 12, 20, or 22 to Újezd.

Nebozízek CZECH/CONTINENTAL   The rap on Nebozízek is that it relies too much on its unique location to draw crowds and not enough on the food. You can see their point. The restaurant's hillside setting looking east over Prague is one of the very best vantage points for a city panorama. Nevertheless, the chef is trying to make amends with a menu featuring well-done Continental standards and an exciting mix of Czech dishes like rabbit, shoulder of venison, and duck liver (served with spinach and balsamic vinegar). You get to this white Victorian house midway up Petřín Hill by taking the funicular to the interim stop. Call several days in advance to reserve a table with a view.

Petřínské sady 411, Prague 1. ✆ **257-315-329.** www.nebozizek.cz. Reservations recommended. Main courses 150Kč–560Kč. AE, MC, V. Daily 11am–11pm. Tram: 22 or 23 to Újezd, then take funicular up the hill.

Vinárna U Maltézských rytířů (At Knights of Malta) ★ CZECH   This restaurant on the ground floor and in the cellar of a charming house provides one of the friendliest and most reasonable home-cooked Czech meals in central Prague. The atmosphere makes you feel as if you've been invited into the family's home for a cozy candlelit dinner. The menu offers a fine and affordable chateaubriand for two and a breast of duck with saffron apples. Save room for the flaky strudel served with egg cognac.

Prokopská 10, Prague 1. ✆ **257-530-075.** www.umaltezskychrytiru.cz. Reservations recommended. Main courses 325Kč–600Kč. AE, MC, V. Daily 1–11pm. Metro: Malostranská plus tram no. 12, 20, or 22 to Malostranské náměstí.

Bohemia Bagel (Kids) BAGELS/SANDWICHES   The local Bohemia Bagel chain is a solid choice for breakfast or lunch, with several outlets scattered around town. Breakfast offerings include the standard bagel with cream cheese as well as more items like bacon and eggs. The lunch menu is filled with soups and fresh sandwiches, served on a bagel or French bread. Another branch is located just off Old Town Square at Masná 2 (Staré Město; ℭ **224-812-560;** Mon–Fri 7am–midnight, Sat–Sun 8am–midnight; metro: Staroměstská), which includes an Internet cafe with 15 terminals, a small garden with outside seating, and a playroom for children.

Lázeňská 19, Prague 1 (Malá Strana). ℭ **257-218-192.** www.bohemiabagel.cz. Bagels and sandwiches 60Kč–175Kč. No credit cards. Daily 7:30am–11pm. Metro: Malostranská plus tram no. 12, 20, or 22 to Malostranské náměstí.

Cukrkávalimonáda ★★ INTERNATIONAL   This cozy spot serves simple but excellent salads, sandwiches, and pasta dishes. The warm atmosphere is accentuated by exposed beams in the ceiling. It's perfect for a quick and easy lunch, and also ideal for coffee on the go or for killer hot chocolate on a cold day.

Lázeňská 7, Prague 1. ℭ **257-530-628.** Main dishes 140Kč–200Kč. No credit cards. Daily 9am–11pm. Metro: Malostranská plus tram no. 12, 20, or 22 to Malostranské náměstí.

4 STARÉ MĚSTO (OLD TOWN)

Staré Město has Prague's largest concentration of restaurants, but be sure to choose wisely. Be especially careful around Old Town Square, where a dozen different restaurants set out tables in warm weather to take advantage of the incredible views. The problem is these are mostly undistinguished kitchens and prices are high. If you're only here for the views and don't mind the food, then by all means sit back and enjoy. If you're looking for an excellent meal, however, have a beer on the square and choose one of the places below.

VERY EXPENSIVE

Allegro ★★ ITALIAN/INTERNATIONAL   The house restaurant of the Four Seasons hotel has been at the forefront of Prague dining since opening its doors a few years ago. It was the first recipient of a Michelin star in central Europe and has now grabbed the prize 2 years running. Chef Andrea Accordi's cooking mixes northern Italian influences with international trends and even a few local influences. Dinners can be prohibitively expensive for anyone not traveling on the company's dime, though the daily prix-fixe lunch specials, 750Kč for two courses and 950Kč for three courses, help bring the food within reach of mere mortals.

Veleslavínova 2a, Prague 1. ℭ **221-427-000.** www.fourseasons.com. Reservations recommended. Main courses 750Kc–1,250Kc. AE, DC, MC, V. Daily 11:30am–5pm and 5:30–10:30pm; Sun brunch 11:30am–3pm. Metro: Staroměstská.

Bellevue ★★ INTERNATIONAL   With its excellent views of Prague Castle, the Bellevue is a perennial top choice. The ambitious owners have put all their energy into the intelligent menu: beef, nouvelle sauces, well-dressed fish and duck, delicate pastas, and artistic desserts. For a tamer but extraordinary treat, try the roasted veal cheek with potato puree. Desserts feature a vanilla-bean crème brûlée. Reserve in advance to snag a coveted table with a castle view.

Smetanovo nábřeží 18, Prague 1. ℭ **222-221-443.** www.bellevuerestaurant.cz. Reservations recommended. Set meals (2-course) from 990Kč to (5-course) 1,390Kč, excluding wine. AE, DC, MC, V. Daily noon–3pm and 5:30–11pm; Sun brunch 11am–3pm. Metro: Staroměstská.

La Degustation ★★★ CONTINENTAL/CZECH Without a doubt, this is one of the city's best dining spots. It is housed in an Old Town corner building and has a minimalist interior. Two different prix-fixe, seven-course menus are served, as diners are invited to sample a wide array of food and wine. The *Bohême Bourgeois* menu finds inspiration in old Czech cookbooks and raises by miles the level of Czech cuisine usually served in restaurants here. The *Chef's Menu* adds more exotic items such as Kobe beef. Each dish is accompanied by an excellent selection of wines served by experienced sommeliers. Daily lunch specials can bring the price down to a more manageable 600Kc per meal.

Haštalská 18, Prague 1. ℭ **222-311-234.** www.ladegustation.cz. Reservations recommended. Fixed-price menu 2,250Kč–2,750Kč. AE, MC, V. Mon–Sat 6pm–midnight; Tues–Thurs noon–2:30pm. Metro: Staroměstská.

Rybí trh SEAFOOD The "Fish Market" has carved out a niche for itself as home to some of the freshest and most expensive seafood in the city, with items like an appetizer of scallops au gratin for 590Kc. But skipping the starters and choosing the delicious and relatively good value mains like crispy pike perch in creamed spinach sauce and mashed potatoes, also 590Kč, can help keep prices at least civilized. Service is attentive and the location, in the secluded Týn courtyard, is ideal.

Týnský Dvůr 5, Prague 1. ℭ **224-895-447.** www.rybitrh.cz. Reservations recommended. Main courses 590Kč–1,190Kč. AE, MC, V. Daily 11am–midnight. Metro: Staroměstská.

Vinárna V zátiší ★★ INTERNATIONAL This is a safe choice for an excellent meal, at a price, in a sophisticated yet still inviting environment. The menu and prices are similar to this restaurant's sister establishments, Mlýnec and Bellevue (also reviewed here), with items such as sea bass, lamb chops, and roasted farm chicken. Two- and three-course set menus help keep the tab relatively reasonable for the quality of the food.

Liliová 1, Prague 1. ℭ **222-221-155.** www.vzatisi.cz. Reservations recommended. Main courses 495Kč–795Kč, 3-course set menu 990Kč ($55), excluding wine. AE, DC, MC, V. Daily noon–3pm and 5:30–11pm. Metro: Národní třída.

EXPENSIVE

Angel ★★ INTERNATIONAL Head chef Sofia Smith has carved out a niche for herself, taking traditional Czech staples like duck and Moravian lamb and seasoning them with Asian-inflected ingredients including tamarind, ginger, and turmeric, that you'd be hard-pressed to find in a typical Czech kitchen. The result is a meal you'll remember for a long time. The atmosphere is casual and the service is first-rate. The business lunch specials offer great value.

V kolkovně 7, Prague 1. ℭ **773-222-422.** www.angelrestaurant.cz. Main dishes 375Kč–485Kč. AE, MC, V. Mon–Sat 11:30am–midnight. Tram: 17 or 18. Metro: Staroměstská.

King Solomon Restaurant ★ KOSHER Under the supervision of the Orthodox Council of Kashrut, the King Solomon has brought to Prague a truly kosher restaurant, across from the Pinkas Synagogue. The restaurant's dozen booths are camped under an industrial-looking atrium. During dining hours, which strictly adhere to the Sabbath, you can choose from a variety of fresh vegetable and meat dishes following kosher dietary

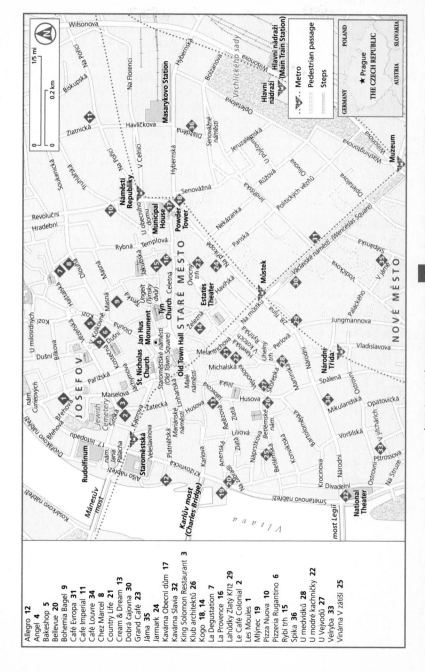

Allegro **12**
Angel **4**
Bakeshop **5**
Bellevue **20**
Bohemia Bagel **9**
Café Evropa **31**
Café Imperial **11**
Café Louvre **34**
Chez Marcel **8**
Country Life **21**
Cream & Dream **13**
Dobrá Čajovna **30**
Grand Café **23**
Jáma **35**
Jarmark **24**
Kavárna Obecní dům **17**
Kavárna Slavia **32**
King Solomon Restaurant **3**
Klub architektů **26**
Kogo **18, 14**
La Degustation **7**
La Provence **16**
Lahůdky Zlatý Kříž **29**
Le Café Colonial **2**
Les Moules **1**
Mlýnec **19**
Pizza Nuova **10**
Pizzeria Rugantino **6**
Rybí trh **15**
Spika **36**
U medvídků **28**
U modré kachničky **22**
U Vejvodů **27**
Velryba **33**
Vinárna V zátiší **25**

rules. The broad menu ranges from a vegetable béchamel to a stuffed roast quail. Selections of Israeli, American, and Moravian kosher wine include the restaurant's pride: a Frankovka red from the Baron Aaron Günsberger Moravian cellars.

Široká 8, Prague 1. (C) **224-818-752.** www.kosher.cz. Reservations recommended. Main courses 250Kč–1,600Kč. AE, MC, V. Sun–Thurs noon–11pm; Fri dinner and Sat lunch by arrangement only. Metro: Staroměstská.

La Provence FRENCH   A French country wine cellar meets urban kitsch in this loud subterranean haunt. Tables have been squeezed in, making a once-comfortable setting a little too intimate. Still, the din of the crowd allows you to discuss private matters without too much eavesdropping. A lunch choice of the local banking crowd, La Provence offers a wide array of French Provençal dishes, including a very good cassoulet with duck confit. Escargots, easily accessible on a tray in drawn butter, are garlicky and surprisingly good. Salads are large and fresh; they come with fresh French bread and garlic butter. Upstairs, the Parisian Brasserie offers traditional French classics.

Štupartská 9, Prague 1. (C) **296-826-155.** www.kampagroup.com. Reservations recommended. Main courses 395Kč–695Kč. AE, MC, V. Daily 11am–11pm. Metro: Náměstí Republiky.

Mlýnec ★ INTERNATIONAL   The "Mill" is owned by the V zátiší group, which is also responsible for Bellevue and V zátiší. Mlýnec is a more casual venture, with comfortable, clubby setting and a fantastic side-angle view of Charles Bridge. I recommend the New Zealand lamb chops with a spicy lemon sauce.

Novotného lávka 9, Prague 1. (C) **277-000-777.** www.mlynec.cz. Main dishes 395Kč–745Kč. AE, MC, V. Daily noon–3pm and 5:30–11pm. Tram: 17 or 18. Metro: Staroměstská.

MODERATE

Pizza Nuova ★ (Kids) ITALIAN/PIZZA   Ambiente Restaurants Group has brought the concept of "tasting restaurant" to Prague. Here you pay a set price and then eat what you can. You can choose from the exquisite antipasto salad bar with a wide selection of meats, cheeses and fish, or the Pasta & Pizza "dégustation"—basically unlimited servings of pizza and pasta brought to your table until you burst. The restaurant is on the first floor of the corner building next to the Kotva department store. For smaller kids there is a play corner with toys and activities, so you will have a better chance to fully enjoy the tasting.

Revoluční 1, Prague 1. (C) **221-803-308.** www.ambi.cz. "Eat what you can" cold buffet 285Kč; Main courses 265Kč. AE, MC, V. Daily 11:30am–11:30pm. Metro: Náměstí Republiky.

Kogo ★ ITALIAN   This modern, upscale trattoria for years has been a local favorite for brokers and bankers who work nearby. Tucked away on a side street just opposite the Havel Market, Kogo manages to combine the warmth and boisterousness of a family restaurant with a high culinary standard in its pastas, meaty entrees, and desserts. Try the fresh, zesty mussels in white wine and garlic *(cozze al vino bianco e aglio)* or the tangy grilled salmon. The wine list is extensive, and the tiramisu is light and sweet without being soggy.

Kogo has a second, even more popular, location in the atrium of the Slovanský Dům shopping center at Na Příkopě 22 ((C) **221-451-259**). The prices are higher here but the location makes it a logical choice for a pre- or postfilm repast after taking in a movie at the multiplex cinema.

Havelská 27, Prague 1. (C) **224-214-543.** www.kogo.cz. Reservations recommended. Main courses 210Kč–480Kč. AE, MC, V. Daily 9am–midnight. Metro: Můstek.

(Value) Inexpensive Meals on the Run

The Czech-style delicatessen **Lahůdky Zlatý Kříž,** Jungmannovo nám. 19 (entrance from Jungmannova 34), Prague 1 (© **221-191-801**), offers the typical Czech snack food *chlebíčky*—a slice of white bread with ham or salami and cheese or potato salad. You have to eat standing up, but prices are pure Czech. Or take it with you and go eat in the cozy garden behind the corner of this building (enter from the square). It's open Monday to Friday from 6:30am to 7pm and Saturday from 9am to 3pm. No credit cards are accepted.

Vegetarians will like **Country Life,** Melantrichova 15, Prague 1 (© **224-213-373**), a health-food store run by the Seventh-Day Adventists; it offers a strictly meatless menu to go. You'll find tofu, tomato, cucumber, and shredded cabbage salads; zesty wheat-bread pizzas topped with red pepper, garlic, and onions; and vegetable burgers on multigrain buns with garlic-yogurt dressing. Selections are 30Kč to 90Kč. It's open Monday to Thursday from 9am to 8:30pm, Friday 9am to 6pm, and Sunday 11am to 8:30pm. No credit cards are accepted.

At Old Town's **Cream & Dream,** Husova 12, Prague 1 (© **224-211-035**), you will definitely revive your mind and body after a tiring tour of the city, or just please your sweet tooth. The gelato here is world-class quality, and you will not get better ice cream in Prague, or perhaps even in Italy. This creamery, cafe, and chocolate shop is open daily 9am until midnight.

If you are visiting Prague's Vinohrady quarter, you can't avoid its main square, Náměstí Míru, with St. Ludmila's Church. On the right side of the church, when facing it, near the metro entrance, there is usually a stand with possibly the **best hot dog** in Prague. The dog is topped with ketchup or two kinds of tasty Czech mustard and served on a fresh white roll. It costs 20Kč and it is available Monday to Friday from 9:30am until the supply for that day runs out.

Le Café Colonial ★ FRENCH   This is a safe place for a break at any time of the day, but it is especially convenient after a stroll around the Jewish quarter (Josefov) and Staré Město. The menu features a nice range of salads and pastas as well as grilled fish and meat dishes. The restaurant is divided into two sections, with a more refined dining room to the left and an informal cafe to the right, though the food is the same on both sides.

Široká 6, Prague 1. © **224-818-322.** www.lecafecolonial.cz. Main courses 195Kč–415Kč. AE, MC, V. Daily 10am–midnight. Metro: Staroměstská.

Les Moules ★ FRENCH   Here's a little piece of Belgium tossed into the center of Prague, which includes a range of that country's very good beer (not that we need any more beer, but if you're looking for a little variety . . .). The mussels are the specialty (hence the name), but all of the French-inspired bistro food is very good. It's a great spot to plop down after long day spent walking through the Jewish Museum.

Pařížská 19, Prague 1. © **222-315-022.** www.lesmoules.cz. Reservations recommended. Main courses 300Kč–500Kč, AE, MC, V. 11:30am–midnight. Metro: Staroměstská.

Bakeshop ★★ AMERICAN/DELI   Prague's lucky enough to have an American-style bakery and sandwich shop that would be the envy of many an American town or city. Bakeshop is simply the best bakery for miles. Come here for soups, salads, ready-made sandwiches, yogurt cups, and, naturally, bread, cakes, brownies, and cookies. It's one-stop shopping for the perfect picnic lunch. You can eat in at the counter or get it to go.

Kozí 1, Prague 1. *©* **222-316-823.** www.bakeshop.cz. Sandwiches 90Kc–145Kč. AE, MC, V. Daily 7am–7pm. Metro: Staroměstská.

Chez Marcel FRENCH   This is a popular, informal French bistro—the kind of place where the house wine is served in carafes and the fresh French bread is always served with a bowl of mustard. Though the menu ventures into more exotic fare such as tuna sashimi, it's best to stick with the tried and true like pepper steak and fries or grilled chicken. The atmosphere is convivial and you'll want to linger after dinner.

Haštalské nám. 12, Prague 1. *©* **222-315-676.** www.chezmarcel.cz. Main courses 90Kč–300Kč. No credit cards. Mon–Fri 8am–1am; Sat–Sun 9am–1am. Metro: Staroměstská.

Jarmark (Kids) INTERNATIONAL   This is one cafeteria that serves a really tasty variety of meats, sides, salads, and, of course, beer. Oh, but this one is not, *repeat not,* all-you-can-eat for one price despite its convenient come-and-shove-it-in system. Upon entering Jarmark, everyone gets a ticket, which is validated at each pit stop you make among the various rows of steaming hot tables, veggie carts, and drink dispensers. The seating of the cafeteria and cafe is set on the first floor of the Myslbek shopping arcade.

Na Příkopě 19–21, Prague 1, Palác Myslbek. *©* **224-835-000.** Reservations not accepted. Main courses 70Kč–300Kč. AE, MC, V. Mon–Fri 8:30am–8:30pm; Sat–Sun 8:30am–4pm (cafe 4–8:30pm). Metro: Můstek.

Klub Architektů CZECH/INTERNATIONAL   Tucked into the alcoves of a 12th-century cellar across the courtyard from Jan Hus's Bethlehem Chapel, this eclectic club-house for the city's progressive architects' society is the best nonpub deal in Old Town. Among the exposed air ducts and industrial swag lights hovering above the tables in the stone dungeon, you can choose from baked chicken, pork steaks, pasta, stir-fried chicken, and even vegetarian burritos. It's not really spectacular, but the large portions and variety will satisfy a range of tastes. The wicker seating in the courtyard makes a summer night among the torches enjoyable, though the alfresco menu is limited.

Betlémské nám. 5a, Prague 1. *©* **224-401-214.** Reservations recommended. Main courses 110Kč–160Kč. AE, MC, V. Daily 11:30am–midnight. Metro: Národní třída.

Pizzeria Rugantino ★★ (Kids) PIZZA   Pizzeria Rugantino serves generous salads and the best selection of individual pizzas in Prague. Wood-fired stoves and handmade dough result in a crisp and delicate crust. The pizza "calabrese," with hot chili peppers and spicy pepperoni, is as close as you'll find to American-style pepperoni pizza in this part of Europe. A more spacious Rugantino II is located at Klimentská 40, Prague 1 (*©* **224-815-192;** metro: Florenc or Náměstí Republiky), with a children's corner and plasma TV. The constant buzz, nonsmoking area, heavy childproof wooden tables, and lots of baby chairs make this a family favorite.

Dušní 4, Prague 1. *©* **222-318-172.** Individual pizzas 120Kč–220Kč. AE, MC, V. Mon–Sat 11am–11pm; Sun noon–11pm. Metro: Staroměstská.

5 NOVÉ MĚSTO (NEW TOWN)

MODERATE

Zahrada v Opeře (Garden at the Opera) ★★ (Value) INTERNATIONAL   Czech designer Bořek Šípek, the man who remodeled former president Havel's offices in Prague Castle, has created a restaurant with a pleasant earthy interior mixing dark and light wood, rattan chairs, and intricate floral arrangements. In this calm oasis, you can relax and enjoy a truly excellent meal (and possibly the best price/quality ratio in town). Highly recommended among the light (but lively) salads and fish and vegetarian dishes is the filet of salmon boiled in champagne with an egg yolk tarragon sauce and served with ginger rice and sautéed vegetables.

Legerova 75, Prague 1 (beside National Museum). ✆ **224-239-685.** www.zahradavopere.cz. Main courses 150Kč–530Kč. AE, MC, V. Daily 11:30am–1am (kitchen open until midnight). Metro: Muzeum.

INEXPENSIVE

Jáma ★ AMERICAN   Jáma gets its share of abuse from longtime residents for being a kind of American-style college bar in Prague, but there's no denying it is a fun place to grab a beer, and the burgers and bar food items are some of the best around. Tuesdays are "burger day," when the gourmet cheddar-bacon burger shares menu space with exotics like a Cajun burger, a Cowboy Jack burger (made with Jack Daniel's), and a Black Pepper burger. Lunchtime brings a selection of classic Czech dishes at very good prices.

V Jámě 7, Prague 2. ✆ **224-222-383.** www.jamapub.cz. Reservations not necessary. Burgers and main courses 175Kč–250Kč. AE, MC, V. Daily 11am–1am. Metro: Můstek.

Pivovarský dům ★★ CZECH   Good Czech beer is not made only by the big brewers. This very popular microbrewery produces its own excellent lager as well as harder-to-find varieties like dark beer and wheat beer. The "Brewery House" also dabbles in borderline-blasphemous (but still pretty good) concoctions such as coffee-, cherry-, and banana-flavored beer. Sharing the spotlight with the beer is excellent traditional Czech food including pork, dumplings, rabbit, goulash, and schnitzel, served in an upscale pub-like setting. The dining areas are all nonsmoking. You'll need reservations to walk in the door—it's that popular.

Lípová 15 (corner of Ječná), Prague 2. ✆ **296-216-666.** www.gastroinfo.cz/pivodum. Reservations recommended. Main courses 135Kč–275Kč. AE, MC, V. Daily 11am–11:30pm. Metro: I. P. Pavlova plus tram no. 4, 6, 10, or 22 one stop to Štěpánská.

Sports, Spuds & Suds

The **Sport Bar Prague-Zlatá Hvězda** (✆ **296-222-292**), on Ve smečkách 12, Prague 2, is about 3 blocks from the top of Wenceslas Square. Here you'll find lots of big screens, decent bar food, and sports action—with local prices. A half liter of beer costs as little as 35Kč. It normally closes around midnight, but will stay open late for big games.

6 VINOHRADY

VERY EXPENSIVE

Aromi ★★ ITALIAN   Definitely worth the splurge and trip out to residential Vino-hrady for easily the best Italian cooking and possibly the best seafood in Prague. The swank interior manages to be both fancy and inviting at the same time, lending any meal the feeling of an occasion. The waitstaff is professional yet surprisingly unpretentious for a restaurant of this caliber. My favorite is the homemade ravioli stuffed with potatoes and sea bass, but everything is delicious. Sticking to the pastas can keep the bill manageable. The daily lunch special is a steal at around 200Kč per person.

Mánesova 78, Prague 2. ℂ **222-713-222.** www.aromi.cz. Reservations recommended. Pastas and main courses 345Kč–600Kč. AE, MC, V. Daily noon–11pm. Metro: Jiřího z Poděbrad or Muzeum plus tram no. 11.

EXPENSIVE

Bonante Restaurant ★ Value INTERNATIONAL   Bonante is great for shunning the cold of an autumn or winter evening near the roaring fire in the brick-cellar dining room. This place is a bridge between French cuisine and other Continental foods. You can start with a fish soup with salmon and mussels, or deep-fried jalapeños. There are several vegetarian and low-calorie chicken-based selections. When reserving, ask for a table within view of, but not too close to, the fireplace. If you do break into a sweat, it's not because of the check, as Bonante provides one of the best values in a full-service restaurant in Prague.

Anglická 15, Prague 2. ℂ **224-221-665.** www.bonante.cz. Reservations recommended. Main courses 120Kč–300Kč. AE, MC, V. Daily 11am–11pm. Metro: I. P. Pavlova or Náměstí Míru.

MODERATE

Masala ★★ INDIAN   This Indian mom-and-pop place is just what the doctor ordered if you have a taste for a well-made curry. Be sure to reserve, especially on a Friday or Saturday night, since there's only a handful of tables and they fill up quickly. The engaging staff will ask you how much spice you want—go for broke, since even "very spicy" would only qualify as "medium" in the U.S. or England, let alone back home in India. All of the classics are offered, including crispy nan bread and flavored yogurt drinks to start.

Mánesova 13, Prague 2 (behind the National Museum). ℂ **222-251-601.** www.masala.cz. Reservations recommended. Main courses 175Kč–395Kč. AE, MC, V. Mon–Fri 11:30am–10:30pm; Sat–Sun 12:30–10:30pm. Metro: Muzeum.

Taverna Olympos ★ GREEK   This convivial Greek restaurant in Žižkov, just on the Vinohrady line, always feels festive. In summer, sit out in the garden; in winter, bask in the enclosed winter garden. The highlights here are the appetizers like *tzatziki* and baked cheese in foil. The calamari is fresh; my favorite is the baked calamari stuffed with cheese and red pepper. House wine flows from carafes, and the staff is cheerful, if occasionally forgetful.

Kubelíkova 9, Prague 3. ℂ **222-722-239.** www.taverna-olympos.eu. Reservations recommended. Main courses 180Kč–290Kč. AE, DC, MC, V. Daily 11:30am–11pm. Metro: Jiřího z Poděbrad.

Radost FX VEGETARIAN   Radost has been coasting for years on a menu that was considered daring when it was introduced in 1993, but it's still one of the few—and best—vegetarian options in Prague. The veggie burger served on a grain bun is well seasoned and substantial, and the soups, like lentil and onion, are light and full of flavor. Sautéed vegetable dishes, tofu, and huge Greek salads round out the health-conscious menu. The hipster interior draws a stylish clientele, but the offhand waitstaff lends an impression they are a little too cool to work hard. The bill already includes an obligatory 10% tip, so no need to leave any extra money on the table.

Bělehradská 120, Prague 2. ✆ **603-181-500.** www.radostfx.cz. Main courses 80Kč–285Kč. AE, MC, V. Daily 11:30am–5am. Metro: I. P. Pavlova.

7 ELSEWHERE IN PRAGUE

MODERATE

Grosseto ★ ITALIAN/PIZZA   Grosseto is a very popular (reservations a must) pizzeria and Italian-style restaurant in the neighborhood around the Dejvická metro station. This is one of Prague's most desirable areas, yet inexplicably it's short on quality places to eat (hence the huge crowds here). The pizzas, cooked in an oven brought in from Italy, are some of the best in town. The pastas are usually very good. The main dining area is nonsmoking, with a smaller smoking section in the back. The only drawback, a minor one, is the often slow and error-prone service.

Jugoslávských partyzánů 8, Prague 6. ✆ **233-342-694.** Reservations recommended. Main courses 130Kč–250Kč. AE, DC, MC, V. Daily 11:30am–11pm. Metro: Dejvická.

Mirellie ★★ ITALIAN   If you like Kogo (p. 98), you'll love Mirellie. It has the same great Yugo-inspired pizzas, seafood, and grilled meats, but at little more than half the price. Try the spicy pappardelle with lamb ragout or the seafood risotto if you're starting to tire of pork and dumplings. The interior is sleekly modern but cozy enough to feel intimate. The only problem is the name—I simply cannot keep it in my head.

V.P. Čkalova 14, Prague 6. ✆ **222-959-999.** www.mirellie.cz. Reservations recommended. Main courses 180Kč–280Kč. AE, MC, V. Daily 11am–11pm. Metro: Hradčanská or Dejvická.

8 CAFE SOCIETY

In their heyday in the late 19th and early 20th centuries, Prague's elegant *kavárny* (cafes) rivaled Vienna's as places to be seen and perhaps have a carefree afternoon chat. The Bohemian intellectuals, much as their Viennese counterparts, laid claim to many of the local cafes, turning them into smoky parlors for pondering and debating the anxieties of the day.

Today, most of Prague's cafes have lost the indigenous charm of the Jazz Age or, strangely enough, the Communist era. During the Cold War, the venerable **Café Slavia,** across from the National Theater, became a de facto clubhouse in which dissidents passed the time, often within listening range of the not-so-secret police. It's here that Václav

Havel and the arts community often gathered to keep a flicker of the Civic Society alive. The Slavia is still thriving today, though the tables, more than likely, will be filled with tourists pouring through maps and guidebooks, rather than monocled dandies or angst-ridden intellectuals bent over the latest *feuilleton*.

That doesn't mean that cafes don't have a role to play. Old standbys like the **Café Louvre** are more popular than ever, and a great spot to relax or have a coffee and a light meal. Many of the gems have been newly spruced up, and a visit to gorgeous **Kavárna Obecní dům,** the **Grand Café Orient,** or the **Café Imperial** is worth it simply for the wow factor.

STARÉ MĚSTO (OLD TOWN)

Grand Café CAFE FARE   The biggest draw of this quaint cafe, the former Café Milena, is a great view of the Orloj, an astronomical clock with an hourly parade of saints on the side of Old Town Square's city hall. With a new management came wider selection of main courses as well as higher prices. Make sure you get a table at the window.

Staroměstské nám. 22, Prague 1 (1st floor). 𝄐 **221-632-522.** www.grandcafe.cz. Cappuccino 70Kč; sandwiches 110Kč–140Kč. AE, MC, V. Daily 7am–10pm. Metro: Staroměstská.

Grand Café Orient ★★ CAFE FARE   Round off your visit to the cubist House of the Black Madonna with a pit stop at this lovingly restored 1920s gem on the building's second floor. A 2005 restoration remained faithful to the cafe's original layout, and as you climb the stairs your eyes will glaze over in sepia tones at a picture perfect shot from a bygone era. Good coffee and cakes round out the charms.

Ovocný trh 19, Prague 1. 𝄐 **224-224-220.** www.grandcafeorient.cz. Cakes and coffees 50Kč–80Kč. AE, MC, V. Daily 10am–10pm. Metro: náměstí Republiky.

Kavárna Obecní dům ★★ CAFE FARE   An afternoon here feels like a trip back to the time when Art Nouveau was all the rage. The refurbishment of the entire Municipal House in the late 1990s was a treat for those who love this style of architecture, and the *kavárna* might be its most spectacular public room. Witness the lofty ceilings, marble wall accents and tables, altarlike mantle at the far end, and huge windows and period chandeliers. Coffee, tea, and other drinks come with pastries and light sandwiches.

In the Municipal House, Náměstí Republiky 5, Prague 1. 𝄐 **222-002-763.** www.vysehrad2000.cz. Cakes and coffees 55Kč–135Kč. AE, MC, V. Daily 7:30am–11pm. Metro: Náměstí Republiky.

Kavárna Slavia ★ CAFE FARE   You'll most certainly walk by this Prague landmark across from the National Theater, so why not stop in? The restored crisp Art Deco room recalls the Slavia's 100 years as a meeting place for the city's cultural and intellectual corps. The cafe still has a relatively affordable menu accompanying the gorgeous river-front panoramic views of Prague Castle.

Impressions

Today's (re-)opening of Café Slavia, one of the places that played such a fundamental role in my life, I understand as a step toward renovation of the natural structure of Czech spiritual life.

—Former president Václav Havel's proclamation at the Slavia's reopening, November 17, 1997

Národní at Smetanovo nábřeží, Prague 1. ✆ **224-218-493.** www.cafeslavia.cz. Coffees and pastries **105**
40Kč–60Kč; salad bar and light menu items 129Kč–180Kč. AE, MC, V. Daily 8am–midnight. Metro: Národní
třída.

NOVÉ MĚSTO (NEW TOWN)

Cafe Evropa CAFE FARE   This Art Nouveau gem was once the grande dame of cafes
on Wenceslas Square. Inexplicably, the owners have allowed the Evropa to fall into disrepair, but it's still worth a look at its etched-glass grandeur.

Václavské nám. 25, Prague 1. ✆ **224-228-215.** Coffee 70Kč; pastries 80Kč. AE, MC, V. Daily 10am–
11:30pm; Sat–Sun 9am–11:30pm. Metro: Můstek.

Café Imperial ★ CAFE FARE   One of Prague's many Art Deco gems that was left
neglected for years, it now has been reopened in its full beauty. You'll be immediately
stunned by high ceilings completely covered with original ceramic tiles and mosaics.
Enjoy morning coffee or afternoon tea and feel the regained First Republic atmosphere.
The food has greatly improved in the past couple of years and is easily worth a lunch or
dinner stop.

Na Poříčí 15, Prague 1. ✆ **246-011-600.** www.hotel-imperial.cz. Cappuccino 59Kč; English breakfast
198Kč; snacks, sandwiches 150Kč–245Kč. AE, MC, V. Daily 9am–11pm. Metro: Náměstí Republiky.

Café Louvre CZECH/INTERNATIONAL/CAFE FARE   A big, breezy upstairs hall,
Café Louvre is great for breakfast, coffee, an inexpensive pretheater meal, or an upscale
game of pool. A fabulous Art Nouveau interior, with huge original chandeliers, buzzes
with the noise of local coffee talk, the shopping crowd, business lunches, and students.
Starters include smoked salmon or Greek *tzatziki* (yogurt and cucumber). Main dishes
range from grilled steak of salmon to lamb filets with rosemary. In the snazzy billiards
parlor in back, you can enjoy drinks and light meals.

Národní 22, Prague 1. ✆ **224-930-949.** www.cafelouvre.cz. Reservations accepted. Main courses
79Kč–259Kč. AE, DC, MC, V. Daily 8am–11:30pm. Metro: Národní třída.

Dobrá Čajovna ★ CAFE FARE   On the walk toward the National Museum on the
right side of Wenceslas Square, there is an island of serenity in the courtyard at no. 14.
Inside the Dobrá Čajovna (Good Tearoom), a pungent bouquet of herb teas, throw pil-
lows, and sitar music welcomes visitors to this very understated Bohemian corner. The
extensive tea menu includes Japanese green tea for 60Kč a cup.

Václavské nám. 14, Prague 1. ✆ **224-231-480.** 40Kč–120Kč for a pot of tea. No credit cards. Mon–Fri
10am–9:30pm; Sat–Sun 2–9:30pm. Metro: Můstek.

The Globe Bookstore and Cafe ★ CAFE FARE   The Globe remains a popular
mainstay for English-speaking expats and a great place for coffee, light food, and books.
The front end of the store is a big bookstore on two levels, while the cavernous back
room serves coffee, cakes, great sandwiches, and light hot meals. The 89Kč lunch special
is excellent value.

Pštrossova 6, Prague 1. ✆ **224-934-203.** www.globebookstore.cz. Salads, sandwiches, pastas, and desserts 60Kč–195Kč. AE, MC, V. Daily 9:30am–1am. Metro: Národní třída.

Velryba CAFE FARE   If you're looking for place where people still occasionally meet
to discuss ideas, this smoky haunt on a back street off Národní třída might fit the bill.
Though the cafe's vogue has waned in the face of stiff competition, it still draws a mix of

intellectuals, journalists, and actors. The kitchen serves good light meals including pastas and salads.

Opatovická 24, Prague 1. ✆ **224-931-444**. www.kavarnavelryba.cz. Light meals 75Kč–135Kč. No credit cards. Daily 11am–midnight. Metro: Národní třída.

VINOHRADY

Blatouch ★ CAFE FARE   This is a comfortable, laid-back student cafe on one of Vinohrady's nicest residential streets. Come here for an excellent espresso or a glass of wine. The food offerings are meager, but most people come to relax, hang out, and chat. It also does double duty as a gallery and small Czech bookstore.

Americká 17, Prague 2. ✆ **222-328-643.** Cappuccino 40Kč; snacks and sandwiches 80Kč–180Kč. AE, MC, V. Daily 11am–midnight. Metro: náměstí Míru.

Kavárna Medúza CAFE FARE   With the feeling of an elderly lady's parlor, the Medúza, situated near several Vinohrady hotels and pensions, has a comfortable mix of visitors and students. The cappuccino comes in bowls, not cups, and the garlic bread hits the spot.

Belgická 17, Prague 2. ✆ **222-515-107.** Cappuccino 39Kč; pastries/light meals 50Kč–95Kč. No credit cards. Mon–Fri 10am–1am; Sat–Sun noon–1am. Metro: Náměstí Míru.

INTERNET CAFES

The **Globe Bookstore and Cafe** at Pstrossova 6, Prague 1, Nové Město (✆ **224-934-203;** www.globebookstore.cz) is one of the better deals in town; it's both a free Wi-Fi hotspot and offers surfing on its own computers for 1Kč per minute. **Bohemia Bagel** at Masná 2, Prague 1, Staré Město (✆ **224-812-560;** www.bohemiabagel.cz) charges 2Kč per minute for surfing, and also offers low-cost phone calls. **Spika** at Dlážděná 4, Prague 1, Nové Město (✆ **224-211-521;** http://netcafe.spika.cz) is open Monday to Friday 8am to midnight and Saturday and Sunday 10am to 11pm, and charges 20Kč for 15 minutes, and offers Internet-based cheap international phone calls.

9 THE PICK OF THE PUBS

Besides being the center of extracurricular activity, *hospody* are the best places for a fulfilling, inexpensive meal and a true Czech experience—not to mention the beer. Food selections are typically the same: *svíčková, guláš, roštěná na roštu*, or breaded fried hermelín cheese *(smažený sýr)*. Reservations aren't usually accepted, though, so you'll usually just have to show up and hope for an empty seat.

Below I've listed two top Old Town pub choices based on atmosphere, authenticity, and price. For more pub selections, see chapter 10, "Prague After Dark," p. 196.

U Medvídků ★★ CZECH/CONTINENTAL   The "House at the Little Bear" is one of the few big Czech pubs in the center where locals and tourists mix happily together, and the mood most evenings is festive. Several varieties of Budvar are on tap as well as the pub's own microbrews. The menu is bigger and better than is usually found in a pub, with several varieties of goulash, Czech standards like pork schnitzel, and more exotic offerings such as venison and boar. In high season, an "oompah" band sometimes plays in the beer wagon in the center of the pub.

Na Perštýně 7, Prague 1. ✆ **224-211-916.** www.umedvidku.cz. Main courses 90Kč–250Kč. AE, MC, V. Daily 11:30am–11pm. Metro: Národní třída.

U Vejvodů ★ CZECH/CONTINENTAL   A few years ago, this traditional pub was
modernized and supersized and it's lost some of its charm, but the food and service is
better, and the size of the place means it's usually possible to snag a table when other
places are full. The beer list features the Pilsner Urquell family, including the flagship
12-degree pilsner and Kozel's slightly sweetish dark. A mug of Pilsner Urquell costs 31Kč
and can be enjoyed with goulash or goose, and even trout or salmon.

Jilská 4, Prague 1. (℃ **224-219-999.** www.restauraceuvejvodu.cz. Main courses 139Kč–349Kč. AE, MC, V.
Sun–Thurs 10am–2am; Fri–Sat 10am–4am. Metro: Národní třída.

Exploring Prague

Most of Prague's main attractions are grouped in the city's core neighborhoods of Staré Město, Malá Strana, Hradčany, and Nové Město and are within comfortable walking distance of each other. For those that aren't, there are trams and the metro, which can usually get you to within a 5- to 10-minute walk from where you want to go.

As with any historic urban destination, the main sights are made up primarily of museums, churches, parks, and public squares. Most of the center has been protected as a UNESCO World Heritage site and it's no stretch to say that among European capitals, at least, Prague has the continent's best-preserved stock of buildings from the 14th to the 18th centuries.

You'll find exquisite examples from the history of European architecture—from Romanesque to Renaissance, from baroque to Art Nouveau to cubist—crammed side-by-side on twisting narrow streets. Seen from Charles Bridge, this jumble of architecture thrusts from the hills and hugs the riverbanks, with little of the 20th century's own excesses obscuring the grandeur of the past millennium

But Prague is more than simply great architecture. The spires and pillars and columns and cherubs festooned onto nearly every building create a festive mood, regardless of the season. A good part of enjoyment is simply strolling around with no particular destination in mind and enjoying the carnival-like atmosphere. The thousands of other visitors who are here for the same reason, while occasionally a distraction, help to reinforce the feeling that something special is going on.

Once you are done drinking in the atmosphere, you are never far from a pub or club for drinking of another sort. Beer lovers will feel especially honored. Czech beer is arguably the best—and cheapest—in the world and no one will look askance if you pair a beer or two with a fine dinner, or indeed have one for breakfast.

1 PRAGUE CASTLE & CHARLES BRIDGE

The huge hilltop complex known collectively as **Prague Castle (Pražský hrad)** ★★★, on Hradčanské náměstí, encompasses dozens of houses, towers, churches, courtyards, and monuments. (It's described in detail in "Walking Tour 2: Prague Castle [Pražský Hrad]" in chapter 8; see also the map on p. 159.) A visit to the castle can easily take an entire day, depending on how thoroughly you explore it. Still, you can see the top sights—St. Vitus Cathedral, the Royal Palace, St. George's Basilica, the Powder Tower, and Golden Lane—in the space of a morning or an afternoon.

Although the individual attractions are closed, you can also explore the castle complex at night, as it's generally lit until midnight, or make a return trip to see the fine collection of 19th-century Czech art exhibited in St. George's Convent (discussed later). The complex is always guarded and is safe to wander at night, but keep to the lighted areas of the courtyards just to be sure.

Value **Saving Money on Entrance Fees**

Prague's museums, especially the Jewish Museum, the Castle complex, and the holdings of the National Gallery, are becoming more and expensive every year. Be sure to take advantage of discounted senior or student admission fees if you qualify. Also, many museums offer a heavily discounted "family" rate that normally covers two adults and at least one or two children. Another option, if you think you might be visiting a lot of museums, is to prepurchase a **Prague Card.** This pass is valid for 4 days and allows you to visit more than 50 top attractions in the city, including Prague Castle (but unfortunately not the sites within the Jewish Museum complex). The price is 790Kč for adults and 550Kč for students under 26. You can buy it at the PIS information centers at the Old Town Hall at Staroměstské nám. 1 or at Rytířská 31, Prague 1. For more information and the list of sights, go to www.praguecitycard.com.

If you're feeling particularly fit, you can walk up to the castle, or you can take metro line A to Malostranská and then ride tram no. 22 two stops north to "Pražský hrad."

TICKETS & CASTLE INFORMATION   Tickets are sold at **Prague Castle Information Centers** located in the second and third courtyards after you pass through the main gate from Hradčanské náměstí. The centers also sell useful hand-held audio guides (250Kč) to help you make sense of the sights and tickets for individual concerts and exhibits. The castle is located at Hradčanské náměstí, Hradčany, Prague 1 (✆ **224-373-368;** fax 224-310-896; www.hrad.cz). Admission to St. Vitus Cathedral and the grounds is free. Seeing the rest of the sights requires a combined-entry ticket. A full-price ticket gets you into the Old Royal Palace (including "The Story of Prague Castle" permanent exhibition), St. George's Basilica, the Powder Tower, Golden Lane, Daliborka Tower, and the Prague Castle Picture Gallery and costs 350Kč adults, 175Kč students. A cheaper ticket covers the Old Royal Palace, St. George's Basilica, Golden Lane, and Daliborka Tower and costs 250Kč adults, 125Kč students. Tickets are valid for 2 days. The castle is open daily 9am to 6pm (to 4pm Nov–Mar). Metro: Malostranská, then take tram no. 22 up the hill two stops.

TOURING ST. VITUS CATHEDRAL (CHRÁM SV. VÍTA) ★★★

St. Vitus Cathedral (Chrám sv. Víta), named for a wealthy 4th-century Sicilian martyr, isn't just the dominant part of the castle, it's the most important section historically. In April 1997, Pope John Paul II paid his third visit to Prague in 7 years, this time to honor the thousandth anniversary of the death of 10th-century Slavic evangelist St. Vojtěch. He conferred the saint's name on the cathedral along with St. Vitus's, but officially the Czech state calls it just St. Vitus.

Built over various phases beginning in A.D. 926 as the court church of the Přemyslid princes, the cathedral has long been the center of Prague's religious and political life. The key part of its Gothic construction took place in the 14th century under the direction of

EXPLORING PRAGUE

7

PRAGUE CASTLE & CHARLES BRIDGE

ATTRACTIONS

Alfons Mucha Museum 46
Bedřich Smetana Museum 43
Bertramka 20
Bethlehem Chapel 44
Charles Bridge (Karlův most) 42
Charles Square
  (Karlovo náměstí) 56
Church of Our Lady Victorious 15
Church of St. Nicholas
  Malá Strana (Lesser Town) 11
  Old Town Square 29
Dvořák Museum 57
Estates Theater 40
Franz Kafka Museum 13
Havel's Market 41
House at the Black
  Mother of God 39
Jan Palach Square
  (náměstí Jana Palacha) 27
Kampa 18
Kampa Gallery-Sovovy
  Mlýny 19
Kinský Palace 31
Labyrinth 17
Lennon Wall 16
Letná Park 22
Loreto Palace 1
Maisel Synagogue 28
Malá Strana Town Hall 12
Municipal House 32
Museum of the City
  of Prague 33
Můstek Metro Station 47
Národní Memorial 48
National Museum 53
National Technical Museum 23
National Theater 49
New Jewish Cemetery 54
Old Jewish Cemetery 25
Old-New Synagogue 25
Old Town Hall and
  Astronomical Clock 30
Old Town Square
  (Staroměstské náměstí) 37
Olšanské Cemeteries 54
Petřín Tower and Petřín Hill 17
Pinkas Synagogue 26
Powder Tower 36
Prague Castle (Pražský Hrad) 6
Rašín Embankment Building
  (Dancing Building) 55
Royal Garden 5
Royal Palace 8
St. Agnes Convent 24
St. George's Convent 9
St. Vitus Cathedral 7
Schwarzenberg Palace 2
State Jewish Museum 25
Štefánik Observatory 17
Šternberk Palace Art Museum 4
Strahov Monastery and Library 3
Týn Church 38

Veletržní Palác 21
Vrtbovská Garden 14
Vyšehrad 58
Waldstein Gardens 10
Wenceslas Square
  (Václavské náměstí) 50

INFORMATION

Castle Information Office 6
Čedok Office 45
PIS Office 30

TRANSPORTATION/MAIL

Florenc Bus Station 34
Main Post Office 51
Main Train Station 52
Masaryk Station 35

GERMANY   POLAND

★ Prague
THE CZECH REPUBLIC

AUSTRIA   SLOVAKIA

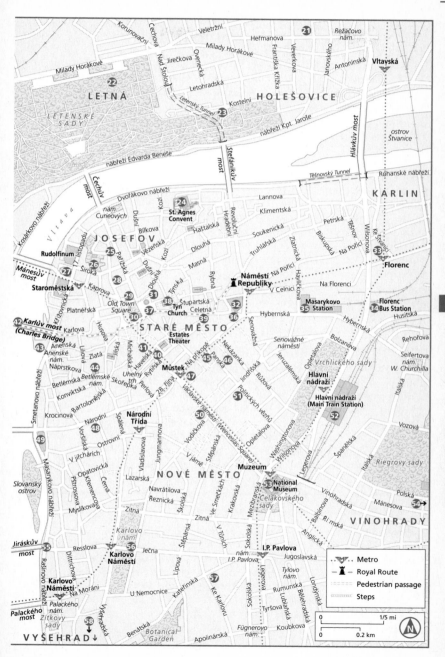

Metro

Royal Route

Pedestrian passage

Steps

0		1/5 mi
0	0.2 km	

Mathias of Arras and Peter Parléř of Gmünd. In the 18th and 19th centuries, subsequent baroque and neo-Gothic additions were made. The **Golden Portal** entrance from the third courtyard is no longer used; however, take a look above the arch. The 1370 mosaic *The Last Judgment* has been painstakingly restored with the help of computer-aided imagery provided by American art researchers.

As you enter the cathedral through the back entrance into the main aisle, the colored light streaming through the intricate **stained-glass windows** that rise to the Gothic ceiling above the high altar may dazzle you. Stained-glass windows painted by the Czech Republic's art nouveau master, Alfons Mucha, adorn the windows to your left above the third chapel from the entrance. The center windows, restored in the years after World War II, depict the Holy Trinity, with the Virgin Mary to the left and St. Wenceslas kneeling to the right.

Of the massive Gothic cathedral's 21 chapels, the **St. Wenceslas Chapel (Svatováclavská kaple)** ★★ stands out as one of Prague's few must-see, indoor sights. Midway toward the high altar on the right, it's encrusted with hundreds of pieces of jasper and amethyst and decorated with paintings from the 14th to the 16th centuries. The chapel sits atop the gravesite of Bohemia's patron saint, St. Wenceslas.

Just beyond this, the **Chapel of the Holy Rood (Kaple sv. Kříže)** leads to an underground **royal crypt.** In the early 1900s, the crypt was reconstructed, and the remains of the kings and their relatives were replaced in new sarcophagi. The center sarcophagus is the final resting place of Charles IV, the former emperor who died in 1378 and is the namesake of much of Prague. Charles's four wives are also buried here in one sarcophagus, and in front of them is George of Poděbrady, the last Bohemian king, who died in 1471. Unfortunately, the crypts were closed to visitors in 2009 after someone vandalized them, and it wasn't clear at press time if they would reopen for 2010.

CONTINUING THROUGH THE CASTLE COMPLEX

For more than 700 years, beginning in the 9th century, Bohemian kings and princes resided in the **Old Royal Palace (Starý královský palác)** ★★, located in the third courtyard of the castle grounds. Vaulted **Vladislav Hall (Vladislavský sál),** the interior's centerpiece, hosted coronations and is still used for special occasions of state such as inaugurations of presidents. The adjacent Diet was where kings and queens met with their advisers and where the Supreme Court was held. From a window in the Ludwig Wing, where the Bohemia Chancellery met, the Second Defenestration took place (see "Beware of Open Windows: The Czech Tradition of Defenestration," below). Since

---

(Tips) What's Going on Around Town?

Prague TV's website http://prague.tv is an excellent English-language resource for checking out what's happening around town. Other useful info sources include the **Prague Information Service's** website at www.pis.cz and the English-language newspaper *The Prague Post,* which is widely available on newsstands for 50Kč or online for free at www.praguepost.com. **Expats.cz** (www.expats.cz) runs an online bulletin board populated mainly by Prague's highly opinionated expat community. It's a good resource for taking the city's cultural pulse and gleaning hints on what to see and do.

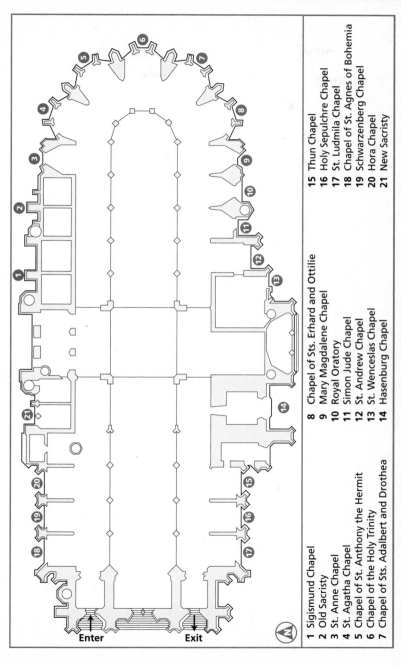

1 Sigismund Chapel
2 Old Sacristy
3 St. Anne Chapel
4 St. Agatha Chapel
5 Chapel of St. Anthony the Hermit
6 Chapel of the Holy Trinity
7 Chapel of Sts. Adalbert and Drothea

8 Chapel of Sts. Erhard and Ottilie
9 Mary Magdalene Chapel
10 Royal Oratory
11 Simon Jude Chapel
12 St. Andrew Chapel
13 St. Wenceslas Chapel
14 Hasenburg Chapel

15 Thun Chapel
16 Holy Sepulchre Chapel
17 St. Ludmila Chapel
18 Chapel of St. Agnes of Bohemia
19 Schwarzenberg Chapel
20 Hora Chapel
21 New Sacristy

Enter   Exit

Beware of Open Windows: The Czech Tradition of Defenestration

About 600 years before Prague's popular uprising brought down Communism, the Czech people began a long tradition of what might be considered a unique form of political protest—tossing people out of the window!

In 1402, Jan Hus, a lecturer from Prague University, became the leading voice in a growing condemnation of the Catholic Church. From a pulpit in Old Town's Bethlehem Chapel (later destroyed but reconstructed in the 1950s), Hus gained popular support for his claims that the omnipotent power of the mostly German-dominated clergy had to be contained. In 1414, he was invited to the Catholic ecclesiastical Council of Konstanz to explain his beliefs. Though the emperor had promised Hus safe conduct, on arriving he was promptly arrested, and a year later he was burned at the stake. The Protestant Hussite supporters declared him a martyr and rallied their calls for change around his death.

On July 30, 1419, a group of radical Hussites stormed the New Town Hall on Charles Square and demanded the release of other arrested proreform Hussites. After town councilors rejected the demand, the Hussites tossed them out of third-story windows, killing several. This became known as the First Defenestration, from the Latin for "out of the window." The incident sparked a 15-year battle known as the Hussite Wars, which ended in the defeat of the radical Protestants in 1434.

By the 17th century, the Austrian Catholics who came to power in Prague tolerated little dissent, but as Protestant Czechs became ever more wealthy,

2004, a new part of the permanent exhibition called **"The Story of Prague Castle"** has been presented within the Old Royal Palace. This project shows the transformation of the castle from the prehistoric period up to the present. For information and booking, contact ✆ **224-373-102** (www.pribeh-hradu.cz). It is open daily from 9am to 5pm and the 90-minute presentation costs 140Kč adults, 70Kč students. The castle's tour ticket includes admission to this exposition as well.

St. George's Basilica (Bazilika sv. Jiří) ★, adjacent to the Old Royal Palace, is Prague's oldest Romanesque structure, dating from the 10th century. It also houses Bohemia's first convent. No longer serving a religious function, the convent now contains the National Gallery's collection of 19th-century Czech art (see "Museums & Galleries," later in this chapter), which you should see on a separate visit if you have the time.

Inside the sparse and eerie basilica you will find relics of the castle's history along with a genealogy of those who have passed through it. If you look carefully at the outer towers, you'll notice that they're slightly different from each other: They have an Adam-and-Eve motif. The wider south tower represents Adam, while the narrower north tower is Eve.

Golden Lane (Zlatá ulička) and Daliborka Tower is a picturesque street of tiny 16th-century houses built into the castle fortifications. Once home to castle sharpshooters, the houses now contain small shops, galleries, and refreshment bars. In 1917, Franz they began criticizing the Habsburg monarchy. This bubbled over again on May 23, 1618, when a group of Protestant nobles entered Prague Castle, seized two pro-Habsburg Czechs and their secretary, and tossed them out of the eastern window of the rear room of the Chancellery—the Second Defenestration. In the Garden on the Ramparts below the Ludwig Wing, two obelisks mark where they landed. This act led, in part, to the conflict known as the Thirty Years' War, which ended again in victory in 1648 for the Catholics. The Habsburgs remained in power for another 270 years, ruling over Prague as a provincial capital until the democratic Czechoslovak state was born at the end of World War I.

A possible third defenestration occurred in 1948, with the tragic death of then-Foreign Minister Jan Masaryk in the wake of the Communist coup d'état that year. Masaryk, the son of the country's first president, either fell to his death or was pushed from a high window at the Foreign Ministry's Černín Palace (not far from Prague Castle). The mystery has never been cleared up, though Masaryk was fervently anti-Communist and most of the general public firmly believes the second scenario.

Though Prague's 1989 overthrow of the totalitarian Communist regime gained the name the Velvet Revolution for its nonviolent nature, scattered calls for another defenestration (some serious, some joking) were heard. Contemporary Czech politicians surely know to keep away from open windows.

Kafka is said to have lived briefly at no. 22; however, the debate continues as to whether Kafka actually took up residence or just worked in a small office there.

The **Prague Castle Picture Gallery (Obrazárna Pražského hradu)** displays European and Bohemian masterpieces, but few are from the original imperial collection, which was virtually destroyed during the Thirty Years' War. Of the works that have survived from the days of Emperors Rudolf II and Ferdinand III, the most celebrated is Hans von Aachen's *Portrait of a Girl* (1605–10), depicting the artist's daughter.

The **Powder Tower (Prašná věž, aka Mihulka)** forms part of the northern bastion of the castle complex just off the Golden Lane. Originally a gunpowder storehouse and a cannon tower, it was turned into a laboratory for the 17th-century alchemists serving the court of Emperor Rudolf II.

CROSSING THE VLTAVA: CHARLES BRIDGE

Dating from the 14th century, **Charles Bridge (Karlův most)** ★★★, Prague's most celebrated statue-studded structure, links Staré Město and Malá Strana. For most of its 600 years, the 510m-long (1,673-ft.) span has been a pedestrian promenade, though for centuries walkers had to share the concourse with horse-drawn vehicles and trolleys. These days, the bridge is filled to brimming with tourists, souvenir hawkers, portraitists, and the occasional busking musician in what feels like a 24/7 Mardi Gras celebration. In

Fun Facts **A Bridge Tale**

Why has Charles Bridge stood for so long? One great yarn through the ages has it that when stones for the bridge were being laid, the master builders mixed eggs into the mortar to strengthen the bond. At the time of the bridge's construction, one village allegedly tried to impress Emperor Charles IV by sending him carts filled with hard-boiled eggs. The gift may have been a welcome snack for the builders, but likely did little to strengthen the mortar.

2009, the crowding was made all the worse by the presence of scaffolding, as city authorities began a long-term project to clean and revitalize the bridge. Work is expected to continue into 2010. The bridge is still fully accessible, though the presence of modern construction equipment does mar the views somewhat.

The best times to stroll across the bridge are early morning and around sunset, when the crowds have thinned and the shadows are more mysterious. The 30 statues lining the bridge are explained in detail in "Walking Tour 1: Charles Bridge & Malá Strana (Lesser Town)," in chapter 8.

2 OTHER TOP SIGHTS

HRADČANY

Loreto Palace (Loreta) ★ Loreto Palace was named after the town of Loreto, Italy, where the dwelling of the Virgin Mary was said to have been brought by angels from Palestine in the 13th century. After the Roman Catholics defeated the Protestant Bohemians in 1620, the Loreto faction was chosen to lead the re-Catholicization of Bohemia. The Loreto legend holds that a cottage in which the Virgin Mary lived had been miraculously transferred from Nazareth to Loreto, an Italian city near Ancona. The Loreto Palace is an imitation of this cottage, and more than 50 copies have been constructed throughout the Czech lands.

The Loreto's facade is decorated with 18th-century statues of the writers of the Gospel— Matthew, Mark, Luke, and John—along with a lone female, St. Anne, mother of the Virgin Mary. Inside the **Church of the Nativity** are fully clothed remains of two Spanish saints, St. Felicissimus and St. Marcia. The wax masks on the skeletons' faces are particularly macabre.

Inside the **Chapel of Our Lady of Sorrows** is a painting of a bearded woman hanging on a cross. This is St. Starosta, or Vilgefortis, who, after taking a vow of virginity, was forced to marry the king of Sicily. It's said that God, taking pity on the woman, gave her facial hair to make her undesirable, after which her pagan father had her crucified. Thus, Starosta went into history as the saint of unhappily married women. The painting was created in the 1700s. Also on display is a portrait of St. Apolena (or Apollonia), a 3rd-century deacon who had her teeth knocked out as part of a torture for refusing to renounce Christianity. She's often represented in art by a gold tooth or pincer. As the patron saint of dentists, Apolena is sometimes referred to as the "saint of toothaches."

Loretánské nám. 7, Prague 1. ✆ **220-516-740.** www.loreta.cz. Admission 110Kč adults, 90Kč students, free for children under 6. Tues–Sun 9am–12:15pm and 1–4:30pm. Tram: 22 from Malostranská.

Strahov Monastery and Library (Strahovský klášter) ★　The second-oldest
monastery in Prague, Strahov was founded high above Malá Strana in 1143 by Vladislav
II. It's still home to Premonstratensian monks, a scholarly order closely related to the
Jesuits, and their dormitories and refectory are off-limits. What draws visitors are the
monastery's ornate libraries, holding more than 125,000 volumes. Over the centuries,
the monks have assembled one of the world's best collections of philosophical and theological texts, including illuminated (decorated with colored designs) manuscripts and
first editions.

The ceiling of the 1679 **Theological Hall** is a stunning example of baroque opulence,
with intricate leaf blanketing the walls and framing the 18th-century ceiling frescoes. The
rich wood-accented **Philosophical Library**'s 14m-high (46-ft.) ceiling is decorated with
a 1794 fresco entitled *The Struggle of Mankind to Know Real Wisdom,* by A. F. Maul-
bertsch, a Viennese master of rococo. Intricate woodwork frames the immense collection
of books. Ancient printing presses downstairs are also worth visiting, as are several altars
and the remains of St. Norbert, a 10th-century, German-born saint who founded the
Premonstratensian order. His bones were brought here in 1627, when he became one of
Bohemia's 10 patron saints. Paths leading through the monastery grounds take you to a
breathtaking overlook of the city.

Strahovské nádvoří 1, Prague 1. ⓒ **233-107-711.** www.strahovskyklaster.cz. Admission 80Kč adults,
50Kč students. Daily 9am–noon and 1–5pm. Tram: 22 from Malostranská metro station.

MALÁ STRANA (LESSER TOWN)
Church of St. Nicholas (Chrám sv. Mikuláše) ★★ **Moments**　This church is one
of the best examples of high baroque north of the Alps. However, K. I. Dientzenhofer's
1711 design didn't have the massive dome that now dominates the Lesser Town skyline
below Prague Castle. Dientzenhofer's son, Kryštof, added the 78m-high (256-ft.) dome
during additional work completed in 1752. Smog has played havoc with the exterior over
the years, yet the gilded interior is stunning. Gold-capped marble-veneered columns
frame altars packed with statuary and frescoes. A giant statue of the church's namesake
looks down from the high altar.

Malostranské nám. 1, Prague 1. ⓒ **257-534-215.** www.psalterium.cz. Admission 70Kč adults, 35Kč students. Concerts 500Kč. Daily 9am–5pm (4pm in winter); concerts are usually held at 5pm. Metro: Line A
to Malostranská.

STARÉ MĚSTO (OLD TOWN)
Estates' Theater (Stavovské divadlo)　Completed in 1783 by wealthy Count F.
A. Nostitz Rieneck, the neoclassical theater became an early symbol of the emerging high
Czech culture—with the Greek theme *Patriae et Musis* (the Fatherland and Music) etched
above its front columns. In 1799, the wealthy land barons who formed fiefdoms known
as The Estates gave the theater its current name.

Wolfgang Amadeus Mozart staged the premier of *Don Giovanni* here in 1787 because
he said that Vienna's conservative patrons didn't appreciate him or his passionate and
sometimes shocking work. They also wanted mostly German opera, but Praguers were
happy to stage the performance in Italian. "Praguers understand me," Mozart was quoted
as saying.

In 1834, Czech playwright J. K. Tyl staged a comedy called *Fidlovačka,* in which the
patriotic song "Kde domov můj?" ("Where Is My Home?") was a standout. It later
became the Czech national anthem. In the heady days at the end of World War II, in

A View with a Warning

It's worth climbing the Old Town Hall's tower for an excellent view over the red rooftops of Staroměstské náměstí and the surrounding area. But be warned: The steps are narrow, steep, and quite physically demanding, so the less courageous should take the elevator.

1945, the Estates' Theater was renamed Tyl Theater but when a total reconstruction of the building was completed in 1991 its previous name was reinstated.

Czech director Miloš Forman returned to his native country to film his Oscar-winning *Amadeus* (1984), shooting the scenes of Mozart in Prague with perfect authenticity at the Estates' Theater.

The theater doesn't offer daily tours, but tickets for performances—and the chance to sit in one of the many elegant private boxes—are usually available. Purchase tickets at the box office for the National Theater (discussed later). Tour events are occasionally scheduled, and individual tours for this and other major monuments can sometimes be arranged through **Prague Information Service** (ⓒ 221-714-444; www.pis.cz).

Ovocný trh 1, Prague 1. ⓒ 224-901-448. www.narodni-divadlo.cz. Metro: Line A or B to Můstek.

Old Town Hall (Staroměstská radnice) & Astronomical Clock (Orloj) ★★ (Kids)

Crowds congregate in front of Old Town Hall's Astronomical Clock *(Orloj)* to watch the glockenspiel spectacle that occurs hourly from 8am to 8pm. Built in 1410, the clock has long been an important symbol of Prague. According to legend, after the timepiece was remodeled at the end of the 15th century, clock artist Master Hanuš was blinded by the Municipal Council so that he couldn't repeat his fine work elsewhere. In retribution, Hanuš threw himself into the clock mechanism and promptly died. The clock remained out of kilter for almost a century.

It's not possible to determine the time of day from this timepiece; you have to look at the clock on the very top of Old Town Hall's tower for that. This astronomical clock, with all its hands and markings, is meant to mark the phases of the moon, the equinoxes, the seasons, the days, and numerous Christian holidays.

When the clock strikes the hour, a kind of politically incorrect medieval morality play begins. Two doors slide open and the statues of the Twelve Apostles glide by, while the 15th-century conception of the "evils" of life—a Death skeleton, a preening Vanity, a corrupt Turk, and an acquisitive Jew—shake and dance below. At the end of World War II, the horns and beard were removed from the moneybag-holding Jew, who's now politely referred to as Greed.

Staroměstské nám. 1/3, Prague 1. ⓒ **724-508-584.** www.pis.cz. Admission to tower 100Kč adults; 50Kč students, children under 10, and seniors. Mar–Oct Mon 11am–6pm, Tues–Sun 9am–6pm; Nov–Feb Mon 11am–5pm, Tues–Sun 9am–5pm. Metro: Line A to Staroměstská.

JOSEFOV

Within Josefov, you'll find the remnants of a once-vibrant community that for centuries was forced to fend for itself. Josefov served as the center of Jewish life in Prague from the 14th century to the end of the 19th century, when city authorities cleared the quarter to make way for new blocks of luxury apartment buildings (that are still standing). By that time, most of Prague's Jews had moved to other parts of town and Josefov had become a slum.

The Nazi occupation during World War II brought a violent end to much of Jewish life in Prague and around the Czech Republic. Of the more than 118,000 Jews living in the Czech lands of Bohemia and Moravia in 1939, only 30,000 survived to see the end of the war. Today, the Jewish community in the entire country comprises about 3,000 people, most of whom live in Prague.

It should be noted that the former Jewish ghetto is not a Holocaust site *per se*. By the time Nazis got here, most of the city's Jews had relocated to other, more affluent parts of Prague. Nevertheless, Josefov's synagogues can be seen as monuments to the survival of Judaism in central Europe, and the Old Jewish Cemetery, with generations buried upon one another, as an enduring symbol of the cohesion of Prague's ghetto. Prague's Jewish Quarter is described in detail in "Walking Tour 4: Josefov (Jewish Quarter)" in chapter 8.

The **Jewish Museum in Prague** (✆ **221-711-511;** www.jewishmuseum.cz) doesn't refer to one building, but rather the organization that manages the main sites of the former Jewish quarter. These include the **Old Jewish Cemetery,** the **Pinkas Synagogue,** the **Klaus Synagogue,** the **Maisel Synagogue,** the **Ceremonial Hall,** and the **Spanish Synagogue.** Each synagogue features a different exhibition on various aspects of Jewish customs and history. It's not possible to visit the sites individually; instead, you have to purchase a combined-entry ticket that allows access to all the main buildings. You'll find ticket counters selling the tickets inside the synagogues and at ticket windows around the quarter. Admission is 300Kč for adults, 200Kč for students, and free for children under 6. The museum's sites are open from April to October Sunday to Friday 9am to 6pm; and November to March Sunday to Friday 9am to 4:30pm. Note the museum is closed on Saturdays and Jewish holidays. Another synagogue, the **Old-New Synagogue** (see below), is considered separate from the Jewish Museum's main holdings and requires an additional admission ticket.

Old Jewish Cemetery (Starý židovský hřbitov) ★★

Just 1 block from the Old-New Synagogue, this is one of Europe's oldest Jewish burial grounds, dating from the mid–15th century. Because the local government of the time didn't allow Jews to bury their dead elsewhere, graves were dug deep enough to hold 12 bodies vertically, with each tombstone placed in front of the last. The result is one of the world's most crowded cemeteries: a 1-block area filled with tens of thousands of graves. Among the most famous persons buried here are the celebrated Rabbi Loew (Löw; 1520–1609), who created the legend of Golem (a giant clay "monster" to protect Prague's Jews); and banker Markus Mordechai Maisel (1528–1601), then the richest man in Prague and protector of the city's Jewish community during the reign of Rudolf II.

U Starého hřbitova; the entrance is from Široká 3. ✆ **221-711-511.** www.jewishmuseum.cz. Admission (combined entry to all of the Jewish Museum sites) 300Kč adults, 200Kč students, free for children under 6. Apr–Oct Sun–Fri 9am–6pm; Nov–Mar Sun–Fri 9am–4:30pm. Closed Sat and Jewish holidays. Metro: Line A to Staroměstská.

Impressions

Upon my word, if fate drove me to the furthest corner of the Earth, I could not otherwise but wander back after a while to ancient Vyšehrad and refresh my mind with the view.

—Karel Hynek Mácha, Czech poet (1810–36), buried at Vyšehrad Cemetery

(Moments) **The Art of Getting Lost**

Prague is popular—too popular, really—and you can find yourself in the middle of a special moment only to have it punctured by the grating voice of a tour guide or a boisterous group of traveling high school students. So my advice to visitors trying to get a peek into the real life of Czechs is simple: Get lost. Get really, really lost.

You won't stray too far, since "tourist Prague" encompasses a relatively small area. And you know the landmarks: the castle, the bridge, the river, Old Town Square. So leave the map behind.

My favorite times to get lost in Prague are early morning and late at night. One foggy morning, I woke up early, grabbed a coffee in the breakfast room of my Communist-era hotel, and headed out. I'm not sure which direction I went—left, I think. I strolled several blocks into unfamiliar territory. I found a wonderful bookshop where I picked up a Czech version of Maurice Sendak's *Where the Wild Things Are*. Then I ducked into an old camera shop in search of film. The shop carried not only the latest German and Japanese cameras but also fascinating, old eastern European cameras that looked to my American eyes like some discarded cosmonaut space garbage. Next, I discovered a little hut of a church that was dark and wonderful; two old Czech women dusted while I looked around. I'd love to tell you where these memorable places were, but you see, I was lost.

Another great way to get lost is to hop on a tram and let the driver take you where he's going. Get off when you see an intriguing neighborhood, if you're hungry, or if you have to use a restroom. Or, if you're adventurous, follow someone. For 40 minutes I trailed an elderly woman doing her shopping. Wow, did she get me lost! I followed her into a local food shop, not one of the big chains filled with processed foods and produce from Germany, but just a little shop. I bought some candy, which I still have—for me candy is the best kind of souvenir.

Late in the evening, as you wander aimlessly through Old Town, you'll half expect to see ghosts darting about. The lanterns along the uneven cobblestone streets don't really help you navigate; instead, I'm convinced that their function is to set a mysterious, quiet mood. That peacefulness is occasionally interrupted by the sounds of late-night revelers. You may be tempted to join them for a *pivo* (beer).

Roaming the streets of Prague is like unraveling a big ball of twine. When you get lost, you're likely to find something special, some experience that will make you feel "of" the place, rather than just passing through.

So remember where you are. Then get lost.

—*Bill Boedeker*

Old-New Synagogue (Staronová synagóga) ★ First called the New Synagogue to distinguish it from an even older one that no longer exists, the Old-New Synagogue, built around 1270, is Europe's oldest remaining Jewish house of worship. The faithful have prayed here continuously for more than 700 years, carrying on even after a massive 1389 pogrom in Josefov that killed over 3,000 Jews. Its use as a house of worship was interrupted only between 1941 and 1945 because of the Nazi occupation. The synagogue is also one of Prague's great Gothic buildings, built with vaulted ceilings and retro-fitted with Renaissance-era columns. It is not part of the Jewish Museum and requires a separate admission ticket that you can buy at the entrance to the synagogue.

Červená 2. (𝄐) **224-800-812.** www.synagogue.cz. Admission 200Kč adults, 140Kč students. (If part of the package for Jewish Museum, 490Kč adults, 330Kč students.) Free for children under 6. Jan–Mar Sun–Thurs 9:30am–4:30pm, Fri 9am–2pm; Apr–Oct Sun–Fri 9:30am–6pm; Nov–Dec Sun–Thurs 9:30am–5pm, Fri 9am–2pm. Closed Sat and Jewish holidays. Metro: Line A to Staroměstská.

ELSEWHERE IN PRAGUE

Vyšehrad ★   This sprawling rocky hilltop complex is the cradle of the Bohemian state. From this spot, legend has it, Princess Libuše looked out over the Vltava valley toward present-day Prague Castle and predicted the founding of a great kingdom and capital city. Ancient Vyšehrad castle, still standing, was the first seat of the first Czech kings in the Přemyslid dynasty before the dawn of the 10th century.

This was also the first Royal Route. Before the kings could take their seat at the more modern Prague Castle, they first had to pay homage to their predecessors at Vyšehrad and then follow the route to Hradčany for the coronation.

Today, the fortifications remain on the rocky cliffs, blocking out the increasing noise and confusion below. Within the confines of the citadel, lush lawns and gardens are crisscrossed by dozens of paths leading to historic buildings and cemeteries. Vyšehrad is still somewhat of a hidden treasure for picnics and romantic walks, and from here you'll see one of the most panoramic views of the city.

Vyšehrad Cemetery (Vyšehradský hřbitov) ★★ is the national cemetery within the ancient citadel on the east side of the Vltava. It's the final resting place of some 600 honored Czechs, including composers Antonín Dvořák and Bedřich Smetana and Art Nouveau painter Alfons Mucha. The complex of churches and gardens is a pleasant getaway from the city crush. The cemetery is on Soběslavova 1, Prague 2 (𝄐 **241-410-348;** www.praha-vysehrad.cz). To get here, take tram no. 3 or 16 from Karlovo náměstí to Výtoň south of New Town or take Metro line A (green) to Vyšehrad station and walk about 15 minutes.

3 MUSEUMS & GALLERIES

Many fine private art galleries showing contemporary work by Czech and other artists are in central Prague, within walking distance of Staroměstské náměstí. Although their primary interest is sales, most welcome browsing. See "Art Galleries" in chapter 9 for information on the city's top art galleries.

As for public museums and galleries, note that many museums are closed on Monday.

NATIONAL GALLERY SITES

The national collection of fine art is grouped for display in a series of venues known collectively as the **National Gallery (Národní Galerie).** Remember that this term refers to several locations, not just one gallery.

The National Gallery's holdings are eclectic and range from classic European masters at the **Šternberský palác** across from the main gate to Prague Castle to modern Czech and European works from the 20th and 21st centuries at the **Veletržní palác** in the neighborhood of Holešovice in Prague 7. Other important museums include a collection of 19th century Czech art at **St. George's Convent** in the Prague Castle complex and the extensive holdings of medieval and Gothic art at **St. Agnes Convent** near the river in Old Town.

The key Prague sites within the national gallery system are listed below.

Staré Město (Old Town)

St. Agnes Convent (Klášter sv. Anežky České) ★★ A complex of early Gothic buildings and churches dating from the 13th century, the convent, tucked in a quiet corner of Staré Město, began exhibiting much of the National Gallery's collection of medieval art in 2000. Once home to the Order of the Poor Clares, it was established in 1234 by St. Agnes of Bohemia, sister of Wenceslas I. The Blessed Agnes became St. Agnes when Pope John Paul II paid his first visit to Prague in 1990 for her canonization.

The most famous among the unique collection of Czech Gothic panel paintings are those by the Master of the Hohenfurth Altarpiece and the Master Theodoricus. The convent is at the end of Anežka, off Haštalské náměstí.

U Milosrdných 17, Prague 1. ✆ **224-810-628.** www.ngprague.cz. Admission 150Kč adults, 80Kč children. Tues–Sun 10am–6pm. Metro: Line A to Staroměstská.

Hradčany

St. George's Convent at Prague Castle (Klášter sv. Jiří na Pražském hradě) ★ The former convent at St. George's houses a fascinating collection of 19th-century Czech painting and sculpture that is especially strong on landscapes and pieces from the Czech national revival period. The collection shows the progression of the Czech lands from a largely agrarian province at the start of the century to a highly developed cultural and industrial space by the end.

Jiřské nám. 33. ✆ **257-531-644.** www.ngprague.cz. Admission 150Kč adults, 80Kč students, free for children under 6. Daily 10am–6pm. Metro: Line A to Malostranská plus tram no. 22.

Šternberk Palace (Šternberský palác) ★★ The jewel in the National Gallery crown, the gallery at Šternberk Palace, adjacent to the main gate of Prague Castle, displays a wide menu of European art throughout the ages. It features 5 centuries of everything from Orthodox icons to Renaissance oils by Dutch masters. Pieces by Rembrandt, El Greco, Goya, and Van Dyck are mixed among numerous pieces from Austrian imperial court painters. Exhibits such as Italian Renaissance bronzes rotate throughout the seasons.

Hradčanské nám. 15, Prague 1. ✆ **233-090-570.** www.ngprague.cz. Admission 150Kč adults, 80Kč students, free for children under 6. Tues–Sun 10am–6pm. Metro: Line A to Malostranská plus tram no. 22.

Outside of the Center

Veletržní palác (Museum of 20th- and 21st-Century Art) ★★ This 1928 Functionalist (Bauhaus-style) palace, built for trade fairs, was remodeled and reopened in 1995 to hold the bulk of the National Gallery's collection of 20th- and 21st-century works by Czech and other European artists. The highlights on three floors of exhibition

Purely Personal List of Five Can't-Miss Sights in Prague

Everyone has his or her own list of favorite things to see and do in Prague. After living here more than 15 years, I've included some of mine below. To avoid repetition, I'll assume that Old Town Square, Charles Bridge, Prague Castle, and the Old Jewish Cemetery are givens and there's no need to re-list them here. Contact and transport info for these can be found in the appropriate section of this chapter.

- **Veletržní palác.** The National Gallery's collection of 20th- and 21st-century art is a jaw-dropper. Forget the Klimts, Schieles, Picassos, and Rodins for a moment and head straight for the gallery of constructivist, functionalist, surrealist Czech art from 1900 to 1930. This was an especially fruitful period for Czech art, when it was at the vanguard of modern movements.

- **St. Agnes Convent.** I would have never guessed I had an interest in Gothic art, but this museum in a former convent is full of surprises. The 13th and 14th century paintings are filled with wit and humor and could easily have come off a post-Modern easel somewhere last week. The sculpture and statuary are ample evidence of Prague's preeminence in Europe in the Middle Ages.

- **The Palace Gardens (Palácové zahrady).** This series of four sculpted baroque gardens on the hill below Prague Castle is simply special, filled with hidden corners and lovely views. They're accessible from Valdštejnská street below or from Prague Castle above.

- **Vyšehrad cemetery.** I am sucker for celebrities, even dead ones. Dvořák, Smetana, Mucha, and the rest of the Czech pantheon are all laid to rest here in Prague's own version of Paris's Père-Lachaise. It's fun to poke around and look for familiar names, and the hilltop Vyšehrad setting is stunning.

- **Stromovka park.** This seemingly limitless preserve of walks and trails is perfect for cycling, rollerblading, or just strolling among the trees. This park is situated miles from the tourist throng but it's within easy walking distance of the river promenade and the zoo. Grab a pack lunch, a blanket, and a good book and take the afternoon off (as I like to do as often as I can).

—Mark Baker

space include paintings by Klimt, Munch, Schiele, and Picasso among other modern European masters, as well as a riveting display of Czech constructivist and surrealist works from the 1920s and '30s. The first floor features temporary exhibits from traveling shows. There's also a good gift shop on the ground floor.

Veletržní at Dukelských hrdinů 47, Prague 7. ℂ **224-301-111.** www.ngprague.cz. Admission 200Kč adults, 100Kč students. Free for children under 6. Tues–Sun 10am–6pm. Metro: Line C to Vltavská. Tram: 12, 14, or 17 to Strossmayerovo nám.

(Fun Facts) **Did You Know?**

- Charles University, central Europe's first postsecondary school, opened in Prague in 1348.
- Albert Einstein was a professor of physics in Prague from 1911 to 1912.
- The word *robot* was coined by Czech writer Karel Čapek and comes from a Slavic root meaning "to work."
- Contact lenses were invented by a Czech scientist.
- Baroness Bertha von Suttner, the first female recipient of the Nobel Peace Prize in 1905, was born in Prague and lived in the Kinský Palace on Old Town Square.
- Prague was a hotbed of early astronomy. The Danish astronomer Tycho Brahe and the German Johannes Kepler (who first discovered the laws of planetary motion) both worked on the court of Rudolf II. Christian Doppler, of "Doppler Shift" fame, taught in Prague and lived in a house not far from Old Town Square (not open to the public).
- The word *dollar* came from the Tolar coins used during the Austrian empire; the coins were minted in the western Bohemian town of Jáchymov from silver mined nearby.

OTHER MUSEUMS & GALLERIES
Malá Strana

Franz Kafka Museum   A long-term exhibition here presents first editions of Kafka's work, his letters, diaries, and manuscripts. This unique project, which was originally introduced in Barcelona in 1999, has been brought to the writer's birthplace and the city where he had strong ties. The exhibit is divided into two sections: The first, Existential Space, explains the huge influence of the city on Kafka's life and his writing. The second uses 3-D installations as well as good audiovisual technology to depict the author's "Imaginary Topography of Prague."

Hergetova Cihelna, Cihelná 2b, Prague 1. ⓒ **257-535-373.** www.kafkamuseum.cz. Admission 120Kč adults, 60Kč students. Daily 10am–6pm. Metro: Malostranská.

Museum Kampa–Sovovy mlýny ★   This building on Kampa Island served for most of its history, due to the location, as a mill. Throughout the centuries it was struck by floods, fires, and destructive wars. The premises underwent several transformations and reconstructions. In 2003, the Sovovy mlýny was opened as a museum of modern art by Czech-born American Meda Mládková and her foundation. She has been collecting works of Czech and central European artists since the 1950s. Her dream reached its pinnacle when she presented the permanent exhibition of František Kupka's drawings and Otto Gutfreund's sculptures.

U Sovových mlýnů 503/2, Prague 1. ⓒ **257-286-147.** www.museumkampa.cz. Admission 160Kč adults, 80Kč students, free for children under 6. Daily 10am–6pm. Metro: Malostranská.

Staré Město (Old Town)

Bedřich Smetana Museum (Muzeum B. Smetany)   Opened in 1936 (in what was the former Old Town waterworks) and jutting into the Vltava next to Charles Bridge, this museum pays tribute to the deepest traditions of Czech classical music and its most patriotic composer, Bedřich Smetana. The exhibits show scores, diaries, manuscripts, and gifts presented to the composer while he was the preeminent man of Prague music in the mid–19th century.

Novotného lávka 1, Prague 1. ℂ **222-220-082.** www.nm.cz. Admission 50Kč adults, 25Kč students and children. Wed–Mon 10am–noon and 12:30–5pm. Metro: Staroměstská. Tram: 17 or 18.

Nové Město (New Town)

Alfons Mucha Museum (Muzeum A. Muchy) ★   This museum opened in early 1998 near Wenceslas Square to honor the high priest of Art Nouveau, Alphonse (Alfons in Czech) Mucha. Though the Moravian-born, turn-of-the-20th-century master spent most of his creative years in Paris drawing luminaries like actress Sarah Bernhardt, Mucha's influence can still be seen throughout his home country. The new museum, around the corner from the Palace Hotel, combines examples of his graphic works, posters, and paintings, and highlights his influence in jewelry, fashion, and advertising. Those who remember the 1960s and 1970s will flash back to one of Mucha's most famous works, the sinuous goddess of Job rolling papers.

Panská 7, Prague 1. ℂ **221-451-333.** www.mucha.cz. Admission 120Kč adults, 60Kč students. Daily 10am–6pm. Metro: Můstek.

Dvořák Museum (Muzeum A. Dvořáka)   The country's best-known 19th-century Czech composer, Antonín Dvořák, lived here during his golden years. Built in 1712, the two-story rococo building, tucked away on a Nové Město side street, was Dvořák's home for 24 years until his death in 1901. In the 18th century when the building was erected, this part of Prague was frontier land. Czechs willing to open businesses so far from the center were called "Americans" for their pioneer spirit. This building came to be known as "America." Opened in 1932, the museum displays an extensive collection, including the composer's piano, spectacles, Cambridge cap and gown, photographs, and sculptures. Several rooms are furnished as they were around 1900. Upstairs, a small recital hall hosts chamber-music performances in high season.

Ke Karlovu 20, Prague 2. ℂ **224-918-013.** www.nm.cz. Admission 50Kč adults, 25Kč students, free for children under 6. Apr–Sept Tues–Sun 10am–1:30pm and 2–5:30pm; Oct–Mar 9:30am–1:30pm and 2–5pm. Metro: Line C to I. P. Pavlova.

National Museum (Národní muzeum) (Kids)   The National Museum, dominating upper Wenceslas Square (Václavské náměstí), looks so much like an important government building that it even fooled the Soviet soldiers, who fired on it during their 1968 invasion, thinking it was the seat of government. If you look closely at the columns you can still see bullet marks. This grandiose statement of nationalist purpose opened in 1893, as the national revival gained momentum. The exterior is rimmed with names of the great and good of the homeland (albeit with several foreign guests such as astronomer Johannes Kepler). Inside the grand hall on the first floor is the lapidarium with statues depicting the most important figures in Czech history, including the father of the republic, Tomáš Masaryk. Also on the first floor is an exhaustive collection of minerals, rocks, and meteorites from around the country.

The other floor's exhibits depict the ancient history of the Czech lands through zoological and paleontological displays. Throughout the prehistory exhibit are cases of human bones, preserved in soil just as they were found. Nearby, a huge model of a woolly mammoth is mounted next to the bones of the real thing, and half a dozen rooms are packed with more stuffed-and-mounted animals.

Václavské nám. 68, Prague 1. ✆ **224-497-111.** www.nm.cz. Admission 150Kč adults, 100Kč students, free for children under 6; free for everyone 1st Mon of each month. May–Sept daily 10am–6pm; Oct–Apr daily 9am–5pm. Closed 1st Tues each month. Metro: Line A or C to Muzeum station.

Elsewhere in Prague

Bertramka (W. A. Mozart Museum) ★   Mozart loved Prague, and when he visited, he usually stayed at this villa owned by the Dušek family. Now a museum, it contains displays of his written work and his harpsichord. There's also a lock of Mozart's hair, encased in a cube of glass. Much of the Bertramka villa was destroyed by fire in the 1870s, but Mozart's rooms, where he finished composing the opera *Don Giovanni,* were miraculously left untouched. Chamber concerts are often held here, usually starting at 5pm.

Mozartova 169, Prague 5. ✆ **257-318-461.** www.bertramka.com. Admission 110Kč adults, 50Kč students, free for children under 6. Concert tickets 390Kč adults, 250Kč students. Daily 9am–6pm (Nov–Mar 9:30am–4pm). Tram: 4, 6, 9, or 10 from Anděl metro station.

Museum of the City of Prague (Muzeum hlavního města Prahy) ★   Not just another warehouse of history where unearthed artifacts unwanted by others are chronologically stashed, this delightfully upbeat museum covers Prague's illustrious past with pleasant brevity. Sure, the museum holds the expected displays of medieval weaponry and shop signs, but the best exhibit in the neo-Renaissance building is an intricate miniature model of 18th-century Prague. It's fascinating to see Staré Město as it used to be and the Jewish Quarter before its late-19th-century face-lift. A reproduction of the original calendar face of the Old Town Hall astrological clock is also on display, as are a number of documents relating to Prague's Nazi occupation and the assassination of Nazi commander Reinhard Heydrich. The museum is 1 block north of the Florenc metro station.

Na Poříčí 52, Prague 8. ✆ **224-816-772.** www.muzeumprahy.cz. Admission 100Kč adults, 40Kč students, free for children under 6. Tues–Sun 9am–6pm (to 8pm 1st Thurs each month). Metro: Line B or C to Florenc.

National Technical Museum (Národní technické muzeum) Ⓚⁱᵈˢ   Czechs are justifiably proud of their long traditions in industry and technology. Before Communism, this was one of the world's most advanced industrialized countries. At the National Technical Museum, it's clear why. The depository holds nearly one million articles, although it can show only about 40,000 at a time. The array of machines, vehicles, instruments, and design documents is displayed in awesome detail. You can see the harbingers of radio and TV technology, the development of mechanization, and the golden age of rail service. (During the Austrian monarchy, velvet-lined cars were standard—only to be replaced by the frayed vinyl upholstery used by today's Czech Rail.)

Kostelní 42, Letná, Prague 7. ✆ **220-399-111.** www.ntm.cz. Note that the museum was closed as this book was being researched but was scheduled to reopen sometime in 2010. Tram: 1, 8, 25, or 26 from Hradčanská metro to Letenské náměstí.

4 CHURCHES & CEMETERIES

CHURCHES

Staré Město (Old Town)

Bethlehem Chapel (Betlémská kaple)   This is the site where, in the early 15th century, the firebrand Czech Protestant theologian Jan Hus raised the ire of the Catholic hierarchy with sermons critical of the establishment. He was burned at the stake as a heretic in 1415 at Konstanz in present-day Germany and became a martyr for the Czech Protestant and later nationalist cause. A memorial to Hus dominates the center of Old Town Square. The chapel was completed in 1394 and reconstructed in the early 1950s. In the main hall you can still see the original stone floors and the pulpit from where Hus preached; it's now used as a ceremonial hall for Czech national events.

Betlémské nám. 4, Prague 1. © **224-248-595.** Admission 50Kč adults, 30Kč students, free for children under 6. Apr–Oct daily 10am–6:30pm; Nov–Mar daily 10am–5:30pm. Metro: Line B to Národní třída.

Church of St. Nicholas (Kostel sv. Mikuláše)   At the site of a former Gothic church built by German merchants, this St. Nicholas church was designed in 1735 by the principal architect of Czech baroque, K. I. Dientzenhofer. He's the same Dientzen-hofer who designed Prague's other St. Nicholas Church, in Malá Strana (p. 117). This church isn't nearly as ornate, but has a more tumultuous history. The Catholic monastery was closed in 1787, and the church was handed over for use as a concert hall in 1865. The city's Russian Orthodox community began using it in 1871, but in 1920 management was handed to the Protestant Hussites. One notable piece inside is the 19th-century crystal chandelier with glass brought from the town of Harrachov. Concerts are still frequently held here; for details, see "Classical Music," in chapter 10.

Old Town Sq. at Pařížská, Prague 1. © **224-190-994.** Free admission, except for concerts. Daily 10am–4pm; Sun Mass at 10:30am, noon, and 3pm. Metro: Line A to Staroměstská.

Týn Church or the Church of Our Lady Before Týn (Kostel paní Marie před Týnem) ★   Huge, double square towers with multiple black steeples make this church Old Town Square's most distinctive landmark. The "Týn" was the fence marking the border of the central marketplace in the 13th century. The church's present configuration was completed mostly in the 1380s, and it became the main church of the Protestant Hussite movement in the 15th century (though the small Bethlehem Chapel in Old Town where Hus preached is the cradle of the Czech Protestant reformation). The original main entrance to the church is blocked from view when you look from Old Town Square because the Habsburg-backed patricians built in front of it with impunity.

Aside from the church's omnipresent lurch over the square and the peculiar way buildings were erected in front of it, it's well known as the final resting place of Danish astronomer Tycho Brahe, who died in 1601 while serving in the court of Austrian Emperor Rudolf II. Brahe's tombstone bearing his effigy as an explorer of many worlds is behind the church's main pulpit. The brilliant floodlights washing over the front of the church at night cast a mystical glow over the whole of Old Town Square.

Staroměstské nám. 14, Prague 1, entrance from Old Town Sq. below the red address marker 604. © **222-318-186.** Tues–Sat 10am–1pm and 3–5pm. Mass Wed–Fri 6pm; Sat 8am; Sun 9:30am and 9pm. Metro: Line A to Staroměstská.

The Art of Prague's Architecture

Prague's long history, combined with its good fortune in having avoided heavy war damage, makes it wonderful for architecture lovers. Along with the standard must-see castles and palaces comes a bountiful mixture of styles and periods. Buildings and monuments from the Middle Ages to the present are interspersed with one another throughout the city. For more on Prague's architecture, see chapter 2, "Prague & the Czech Republic in Depth," p. 9.

The best examples of Romanesque architecture are parts of **Prague Castle,** including St. George's Basilica. In Staré Město you'll see the best examples of the 3-century Gothic period: the **Convent of St. Agnes,** Na Františku; the **Old-New Synagogue,** Pařížská třída; **Old Town Hall** and the **Astronomical Clock,** Staroměstské náměstí; **Powder Tower,** Celetná ulice; and **Charles Bridge.** A few Renaissance buildings still stand, including **Golden Lane, Malá Strana Town Hall,** and **Pinkas Synagogue** (Široká ulice) in Staré Město.

Many of Prague's best-known structures are pure baroque and rococo, enduring styles that reigned in the 17th and 18th centuries. Buildings on Staroměstské náměstí and Nerudova Street date from this period, as does **St. Nicholas Church,** Malostranské náměstí, in Malá Strana, and the **Loreto Palace,** Loretánské náměstí, in Hradčany.

Renaissance styles made a comeback in the late 19th century. Two neo-Renaissance buildings in particular—the **National Theater,** Národní třída, and the **National Museum,** Václavské náměstí, both in Prague 1, have endured and are among Prague's most identifiable landmarks.

An exciting addition to the architectural lineup is the painstakingly refurbished 1911 Art Nouveau **Municipal House (Obecní dům)** ★★ at náměstí Republiky, Prague 1. Every opulent ceiling, sinuous light fixture, curling banister, etched-glass window, and inlaid ceramic wall creates the astonishing atmosphere of hope and accomplishment from the turn of the 20th century. This is Prague's outstanding monument to itself. The music salon, Smetana Hall (home to the Prague Symphony), has a gorgeous atrium roof with stained-glass windows. After World War I, with independence won, the democratic Czechoslovak Republic was declared here by the first National Council (parliament) in 1918. Daily guided tours are offered in the afternoons; see the information center inside for details and tickets.

Malá Strana (Lesser Town)

Church of Our Lady Victorious—Holy Child of Prague (Klášter Pražského jezulátka) This 1613 early baroque church of the Carmelite order is famous throughout Italy and other predominantly Catholic countries for the wax statue of infant Jesus displayed on an altar in the right wing of the church. The Holy Child of Prague was presented to the Carmelites by the Habsburg patron Polyxena of Lobkowicz in 1628 and is revered as a valuable Catholic relic from Spain. Copies of the "Bambino" are sold at the little museum in the church as well as on the Lesser Town streets, angering some of the faithful.

Other excellent examples of whimsical Art Nouveau architecture are the **Hotel Evropa,** on Václavské náměstí, and the main train station, **Hlavní nádraží,** on Wilsonova třída, both in Prague 1.

Prague's finest cubist design, the **House at the Black Mother of God (Dům U Černé Matky boží),** at Celetná and Ovocný trh in Old Town, is worth a look. The building is named for the statuette of the Virgin Mary on its well-restored exterior. It now houses a Museum of Cubism and modern art gallery. You'll also find a full cubist neighborhood of buildings directly under Vyšehrad Park near the right bank (Old Town side) of the Vltava.

The city's most unappealing structures are the socialist and Brutalist designs built from the mid-1960s until the end of Communism. Examples are the entrance and departure halls of **Hlavní nádraží,** Wilsonova třída, Prague 1; the **Máj department store** (now a Tesco), Národní třída 26, Prague 1; and the **Kotva department store,** náměstí Republiky, Prague 1.

However, the absolute worst are the prefabricated apartment buildings *(paneláky)* reached by taking metro line C to Chodov or Háje. Built in the 1970s, when buildings grew really huge and dense, each is eight or more stories tall. Today, half of Prague's residents live in *paneláky,* which rim the city.

One postrevolution development—the **Rašín Embankment Building** ★, Rašínovo nábřeží at Resslova, Prague 2—continues to fuel the debate about blending traditional architecture with progressive design. Known as the **Dancing Building,** it opened in 1996.

Codesigned by Canadian-born Frank Gehry, who planned Paris's controversial American Center and the Guggenheim Bilbao, the building's method of twisting concrete and steel together had never before been tried in Europe or elsewhere. An abstract Fred Astaire, dusting off his white tie and tails, embraces an eight-story ball-gowned Ginger Rogers for a twirl above the Vltava. The staggered design of the windows gives the structure motion when seen from afar. The only way to get the full effect is from across the river. The kicker is that the building is made out of prefabricated concrete, proving that the Communist *panelák* apartment houses could have been made more imaginatively. Ex-president Havel used to live next door in a modest apartment in the neoclassical building built and owned by his family.

Karmelitská 9, Prague 1. Museum of the Holy Child of Prague. ℭ **257-533-646.** Free admission. Mon–Sat 8:30am–6:30pm; Sun 9:30am–8pm. Metro: Line A to Malostranská.

CEMETERIES

New Jewish Cemetery (Nový židovský hřbitov)   Though it's neither as visually captivating nor as historically important as Prague's Old Jewish Cemetery (p. 119), the ivy-enveloped New Jewish Cemetery is popular because writer Franz Kafka is buried here. To find his grave, enter the cemetery and turn immediately to your right. Go along the wall about 90m (295 ft.) and look down in the first row of graves. There you'll find

Kafka's final resting place. If you don't have a yarmulke (skullcap), you must borrow one from the man in the small building at the entrance. He's quite happy to lend one, but don't forget to return it. If you only come to see Kafka, you may find yourself staying longer; the cemetery is a soothing and fascinating place.

Izraelská 1, Prague 3. © **272-241-893.** Apr–Sept Sun–Thurs 9am–5pm, Fri 9am–1pm; Oct–Mar Sun–Thurs 9am–4pm, Fri 9am–1pm. Metro: Line A to Želivského.

Olšanské Cemeteries (Olšanské hřbitovy) Olšanské hřbitovy is the burial ground of some of the city's most prominent former residents, including the first Communist president, Klement Gottwald, and Jan Palach, who set fire to himself in protest of the 1968 Soviet invasion. Olšanské hřbitovy is just on the other side of Jana Želivského Street from the New Jewish Cemetery.

Vinohradská St., Prague 3. Daily dawn–dusk. Metro: Line A to Flora or Želivského.

---

5 HISTORIC BUILDINGS & MONUMENTS

Education has always occupied an important place in Czech life. Professors at **Charles University**—the city's most prestigious and oldest university, founded in 1348—have been in the political and cultural vanguard, strongly influencing the everyday life of all citizens. During the last 50 years, the university has expanded into some of the city center's largest riverfront buildings, many of which are between Charles Bridge (Karlův most) and Čech's Bridge (Čechův most).

STARÉ MĚSTO (OLD TOWN)

Powder Tower (Prašná brána) Once part of Staré Město's system of fortifications, the Old Town Powder Tower (as opposed to the Powder Tower in Prague Castle) was built in 1475 as one of the walled city's major gateways. The 42m-tall (138-ft.) tower marks the beginning of the Royal Route, the traditional route along which medieval Bohemian monarchs paraded on their way to being crowned at Prague Castle. It also was the east gate to the Old Town on the road to Kutná Hora. The tower was severely damaged during the Prussian invasion of Prague in 1737.

The present-day name comes from the 18th century, when the development of Nové Město rendered this protective tower obsolete, and it began to serve as a gunpowder storehouse. Early in the 20th century, the tower was the daily meeting place of Franz Kafka and his writer friend Max Brod. On the tower's west side, facing Old Town, you'll see a statue of King Přemysl Otakar II, under which is a bawdy relief depicting a young woman slapping a man who's reaching under her skirt. The remains of the original construction are visible on the first floor above the ground.

Náměstí Republiky, gate to Celetná St., Prague 1. Admission 70Kč adults, 50Kč students, free for children under 6. Apr–Oct daily 10am–6pm. Metro: Line B to Náměstí Republiky.

NOVÉ MĚSTO (NEW TOWN)

Můstek Metro Station It's not the metro station itself, which is only about 30 years old, that warrants an entry here. But descend to Můstek's lower escalators and you'll see the illuminated stone remains of what was once a bridge that connected the fortifications of Prague's Old and New Towns. In Czech, *můstek* means "little bridge," but the ancient span isn't the only medieval remains that modern excavators discovered. Metro workers

had to be inoculated when they uncovered viable tuberculosis bacteria, which had lain
here dormant, encased in horse excrement, since the Middle Ages.

Na Příkopě, the pedestrian street above Můstek metro station, literally translates as "on the moat," a reminder that the street was built on top of a river that separated the walls of Staré Město and Nové Město. In 1760, it was filled in. The street follows the line of the old fortifications all the way down to the Gothic Powder Tower at náměstí Republiky.

Václavské nám. Prague 1. Metro: Line A.

National Theater (Národní divadlo) ★★ Lavishly constructed in the late Renaissance style of northern Italy, the gold-crowned National Theater, overlooking the Vltava, is one of Prague's most recognizable landmarks. Completed in 1881, the theater was built to nurture the Czech National Revival Movement—a drive to replace the dominant German culture with homegrown Czech works. To finance construction, small collection boxes with signs promoting the prosperity of a dignified national theater were installed in public places.

Almost immediately upon completion, the building was wrecked by fire and rebuilt, reopening in 1883 with the premiere of Bedřich Smetana's opera *Libuše.* The magnificent interior contains an allegorical sculpture about music and busts of Czech theatrical personalities created by some of the country's best-known artists. The motto *"Národ sobě"* ("A Nation to Itself") is written above the stage. Smetana conducted the theater's orchestra here until 1874, when deafness forced him to relinquish his post.

The theater offers guided tours by prior arrangement; tickets for performances are often available (see chapter 10) on the day of the show.

Národní třída 2, Prague 1. ☏ **224-901-506** (guided tours), or 224-901-448 (box office). www.narodni-divadlo.cz. Metro: Line B to Národní třída.

ELSEWHERE IN PRAGUE

Petřín Tower (Rozhledna) A one-third-scale copy of Paris's Eiffel Tower, Petřín Tower was constructed out of recycled railway track for the 1891 Prague Exhibition. It functioned as the city's primary telecommunications tower until the space-age Žižkovská věž (tower) opened across town. Those who climb the 59m (194 ft.) to the top are treated to striking views, particularly at night.

Petřínské sady, atop Petřín Hill, Prague 1. ☏ **257-320-112**. www.pis.cz. Admission 100Kč adults, 50Kč students, free for children under 6. Jan–Mar Sat–Sun 10am–5pm; Apr daily 10am–7pm; May–Sept daily 10am–10pm; Oct daily 10am–6pm; Nov–Dec Sat–Sun 10am–5pm. Tram: 12, 20, or 22 to Újezd, then ride the funicular to the top.

MODERN MEMORIALS

One of the city's most photographed attractions is the colorful graffiti-filled **Lennon Wall,** on Velkopřevorské náměstí. This quiet side street in Malá Strana's Kampa neighborhood near Charles Bridge is across from the French Embassy on the path leading from Kampa Park.

The wall is named after singer John Lennon, whose huge image is spray-painted on the wall's center. Following his 1980 death, Lennon became a hero of freedom, pacifism, and counterculture throughout eastern Europe, and this monument was born. During Communist rule, the wall's prodemocracy and other slogans were regularly whitewashed, only to be repainted by the faithful. When the new democratically elected government was installed in 1989, it's said that the French ambassador, whose stately offices are directly across from the wall, phoned Prague's mayor and asked that the city refrain from interfering with the monument. Today young locals and visitors continue to flock here, paying homage with flowers and candles. Lennon's picture has been repainted, larger and more angelic. It is now surrounded by graffiti more ridiculous than political.

The 1989 revolution against Communism is modestly remembered at the **Národní Memorial,** Národní 16, under the arches, midway between Václavské náměstí and the National Theater. A small bronze monument of peace-sign hands marks the spot where hundreds of protesting college students were beaten by riot police on the brutal, icy night of November 17, 1989.

6 HISTORIC SQUARES

The most celebrated square in the city, **Old Town Square (Staroměstské nám.)** ★★★, is surrounded by baroque buildings and packed with colorful craftspeople, cafes, and entertainers. In ancient days, the site was a major crossroads on central European merchant routes. In its center stands a memorial to Jan Hus, the 15th-century martyr who crusaded against Prague's German-dominated religious and political establishment. It was unveiled in 1915, on the 500th anniversary of Hus's execution. The monument's most compelling features are the dark asymmetry and fluidity of the figures. It has been in reconstruction since early 2007. Take metro line A to Staroměstská. The square and Staré Město are described in more detail in "Walking Tour 3" in chapter 8.

Officially dedicated in 1990, **Jan Palach Square (náměstí Jana Palacha),** formerly known as Red Army Square, is named for a 21-year-old philosophy student who set himself on fire on the National Museum steps to protest the 1968 Communist invasion. An estimated 800,000 Praguers attended his funeral march from Staroměstské náměstí to Olšanské Cemeteries (p. 130). To get to the square, take metro line A to Staroměstská at the Old Town foot of Mánesův Bridge. There is now a pleasant riverside park with benches. Charles University's philosophy department building is on this square; on the lower-left corner of the facade is a memorial to the martyred student: a replica of Palach's death mask.

One of the city's most historic squares, **Wenceslas Square (Václavské nám.)** ★★ was formerly the horse market (Koňský trh). The once muddy swath between the buildings played host to the country's equine auctioneers. The top of the square, where the National Museum now stands, was the outer wall of the New Town fortifications, bordering the Royal Vineyards. Unfortunately, the city's busiest highway now cuts the museum off from the rest of the square it dominates. Trolleys streamed up and down the square until the early 1980s. Today the 1km-long (½-mile) boulevard is lined with cinemas, shops, hotels, restaurants, and casinos.

The square was given its present name in 1848. The giant equestrian statue of St. Wenceslas on horseback surrounded by four other saints, including his grandmother, St. Ludmila, and St. Adalbert, the 10th-century bishop of Prague, was completed in 1912 by prominent city planner J. V. Myslbek, for whom the Myslbek shopping center on Na Příkopě was named. The statues' pedestal has become a popular platform for speakers. Actually, the square has thrice been the site of riots and revolutions—in 1848, 1968, and 1989. At the height of the Velvet Revolution, 250,000 to 300,000 Czechs filled the square during one demonstration. Take metro line A or B to Můstek.

Built by Charles IV in 1348, **Charles Square (Karlovo nám.)** once functioned as
Prague's primary cattle market. New Town's Town Hall (Novoměstská radnice), which
stands on the eastern side, was the site of Prague's First Defenestration—a violent protest
sparking the Hussite Wars in the 15th century (see "Beware of Open Windows: The
Czech Tradition of Defenestration," earlier in this chapter). Today, Charles Square is a
peaceful park in the center of the city, crisscrossed by tram lines and surrounded by buildings and shops. It is the largest square in town. To reach it, take metro line B to Karlovo
náměstí.

7 VÁCLAV HAVEL'S PRAGUE

Former Czech president Václav Havel's extraordinary life still acts as a magnet, drawing
to Prague those who are interested in understanding one of the most dominant factors
of recent history—the Cold War.

While it is easy to ascribe Havel's valiant struggle to pure altruism and a desperate
desire to end totalitarian rule in his homeland, many believe a more intimate force was
at work—his inextricable relationship to a beautiful, complex character—not his first
wife, Olga (to whom he addressed his famous letters from prison), but the city of Prague
itself.

To begin to understand Havel (and even close friends say they can't grasp the full
depth of his character), you must first try to see Prague in all its complex ironies. Even
during the darkest days of Communist rule, Havel remained faithful to the city of his
birth, although it would have been much easier to run away—as did many other dissidents and artists—to fame and fortune in the West.

Havel's family roots run deeply in Prague. He was reared in the city's grand palaces and
dingy theaters, and received his political education in Prague's smoky cafes and closely
observed living rooms.

Described below (and on the accompanying map on p. 134) are some of Havel's most
notable haunts both before and after 1989. Luckily for those who want to track his
footsteps, Havel's Prague is now somewhat more accessible (albeit heavily reconstructed
from the pre-revolutionary days)—and you won't have to worry about any StB (Communist-era secret agents) watching over your shoulder.

THE HAVEL FAMILY

Havel's father and namesake, a wealthy real estate developer and patron of Prague's newly
liberated, post–Habsburg Jazz Age, built the **Lucerna Palace** (entry from Štěpánská 61
or Vodičkova 36, Prague 1; metro: Můstek), in the 1920s. This fully enclosed complex
of arcades, theaters, cinemas, nightclubs, restaurants, and ballrooms became a popular
spot for the city's nouveau riche to congregate. The young Havel spent his earliest years
on the Lucerna's polished marble floors until the Communists expropriated his family's
holdings after the 1948 putsch. Soon thereafter, the glitter wore off this monument to
early Czech capitalism and the Lucerna lost its soul to party-sanctioned singalongs and
propaganda films.

After the fall of Communism and the mass return of nationalized property, the new
government gave the Lucerna back to the Havel estate. Unfortunately, this led to an ugly
family feud over the division of shares in the palace. Eventually the then-president and

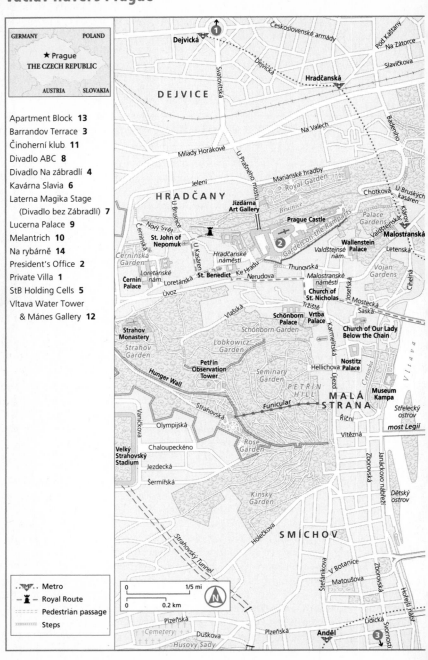

EXPLORING PRAGUE

7

VÁCLAV HAVEL'S PRAGUE

GERMANY   POLAND

★ Prague
THE CZECH REPUBLIC

AUSTRIA   SLOVAKIA

Metro

Royal Route

Pedestrian passage

Steps

0   1/5 mi

0   0.2 km

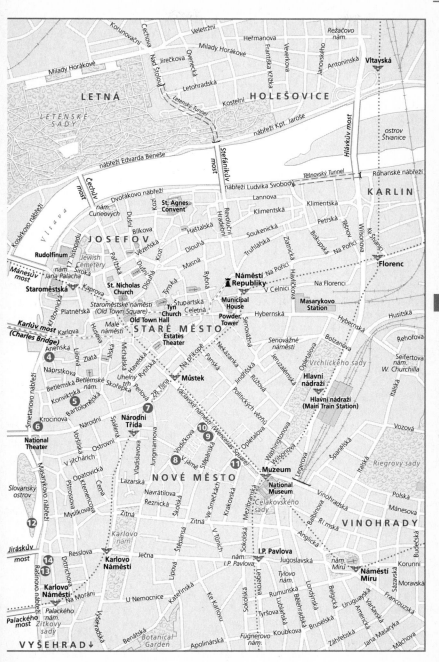

his second wife worked out a settlement with younger brother Ivan and his wife, but only after the battle became a daily feature in the tabloid press.

Today, the Lucerna is trying hard to regain its original grandeur. It's home to at least two excellent cafes, a trendy music club, a glittering ballroom, and a vintage cinema that still shows first-run movies. There's also a wacky statue descending from the ceiling by Czech artist David Černý depicting St. Wenceslas astride an upside-down horse—an ironic take on the country's obsession with its more glorious past.

To get to **Barrandov Terrace** you'll need to take one of the tourist boats from the center of Prague and head south on the Vltava (see details of boat tours later in this chapter). After about half an hour you will pass under the bridge of the superhighway at the southern edge of the city. About a mile farther, look to your right. You will see a creaking remnant of a once spectacular Art Deco resort tucked into the cliff. This is Barrandov Terrace, another heart-wrenching example of the elder Havel's grandiose plans destroyed by Communist-era squalor.

The flowing white balconies of the Barrandov Terrace were Prague's answer to 1920s Hollywood. Havel's uncle, Miloš Havel, commissioned Jazz Age architect Max Urban to build his dream—a top-notch riverside restaurant and cafe. It was meant to capture the glamour of the films produced at nearby Barrandov Studios, whose productions at the time rivaled Hollywood films in style and panache.

Sadly, Barrandov Terrace, like the Lucerna Palace, became a prime target of Communist expropriation, leading to its neglect and eventual closure. Unlike Lucerna, however, when the property was returned to the Havels after the 1989 revolution, its decay had gone past the point of no return and it was left to rot. Security fences prevent any close investigation on foot, but the view of the complex from the river is enough to make you ache for Prague's golden age of the First Republic.

THEATER & POLITICS

Divadlo ABC   Havel's first theater job was as a stagehand here in the late 1950s. This is one of the many intimate theaters in Prague where excitement was found in the spoken word rather than expensive visuals. Czech musicals and dry comedies are still performed here.

Vodičkova 28, Prague 1. 🕿 **224-215-943.** Tickets cost 90Kč–300Kč. Metro: Můstek.

Divadlo Na zábradlí   Havel became the resident playwright here in the early 1960s. It was on this stage that his play *The Garden Party* launched 25 years of subtly subversive dramas, which were to become the subtext of many dissident struggles during the Cold War. At present, dramas (for example, Chekhov's *Ivanov*) are on the program here every evening at 7pm. Performances are in Czech.

Anenské nám. 5, Prague 1. 🕿 **222-868-868.** Tickets run from 90Kč–250Kč. Metro: Staroměstská. Tram: 17 or 18.

Činoherní klub   After the early days of the revolution when Laterna Magika played a major role, the first attempts at forming a true political movement were made in this tiny club theater on a back street near Wenceslas Square. It is here that the Civic Forum (Občanské Fórum) movement took shape under Havel's understated leadership. This small theater, founded in the 1960s by a group of young and progressive actors and directors, has always been popular for its nonconventional performances. Talented Czech actors perform here nightly at 7:30pm.

Ve Smečkách 26, Prague 1. 🕿 **296-222-123.** Tickets cost 30Kč (standing) or 320Kč. Metro: Muzeum.

StB Holding Cells   Housed in a former convent, the StB Holding Cells were used by the StB (Communist secret police) to interrogate and hold political prisoners. Havel stayed in room P6 during one of his frequent visits between 1977 and 1989. After the revolution, the holding cells became a spartan but popular hostel with months-long waiting lists of tourists who wanted to stay in Havel's hovel. It's now a luxury hotel.

Bartolomějská 9, Prague 1. Metro: Národní třída.

Laterna Magika Stage (Divadlo bez Zábradlí)   This became Havel's "War Room," where he and a hearty band of artists and intellectuals plotted the peaceful overthrow of the government in late 1989. From this platform, Havel chaired 10 nights of debates among striking actors and artists on how best to rally the masses to their democratic cause. The resignation of the Politburo at the end of November 1989 set off rapturous celebrations in the theater. The remodeled place no longer reeks of cigarettes and stale beer nor, unfortunately, the aura of those heady November revolutionary days. Performances in Czech (mostly comedies by Czech and foreign playwrights) take place here every evening at 7pm.

Jungmannova 31, Prague 1. 𝄞 **224-946-436.** Tickets cost up to 300Kč. Metro: Můstek or Národní třída.

Melantrich   Midway up the right side of Wenceslas Square at no. 36 (now the British Marks & Spencer store), you will see a balcony jutting from the Melantrich publishing house. This is where, in late November 1989, Havel made his first appearances in front of the hundreds of thousands who were clamoring for his leadership in a peaceful coup d'état. His mumbling yet stoically defiant speeches solidified his position as the popular choice to guide Czechoslovakia out of the dark days. Soon, Alexander Dubček—leader of 1968's failed attempt to deliver "Socialism with a Human Face" which led to his banishment after the Warsaw Pact invasion—joined Havel along with blacklisted singers and artists to mark the beginning of the end of 4 decades of totalitarian rule.

Václavské nám. 36, Prague 1. Metro: Můstek.

Kavárna Slavia   Of all the Prague pubs, restaurants, and cafes that Havel patronized, this was his most recognized haunt (p. 104). Its reputation as the hangout of choice for Prague's dissidents and secret police became a staple in Western media accounts of life on this side of the iron curtain.

Smetanovo nábřeží 2, Prague 1. 𝄞 **224-218-493.** Metro: Národní třída.

Vltava Water Tower & Mánes Gallery   Jutting from the quay on the right (east) bank of the Vltava next to Jiráskův Bridge stands this brooding, dark, defunct water tower with a bulbous dome. Inside the dome, secret police agents spent days peering into Havel's meager top-floor flat on the opposite street corner. Havel has spoken often of the ways he used to taunt his hunters during his effective house arrests, and of the suffocation of knowing they were almost always there, watching his comings and goings and those of his guests.

Just below the tower stands an unspectacular building of white boxes, the art gallery and meeting hall **Mánes.** Havel calls this his favorite building in Prague. In a BBC documentary filmed several years after he became president, Havel described his love for this place of art right under his wardens' noses. The Mánes now shows many avant-garde artists who were taboo before the revolution.

Masarykovo nábřeží 250, Prague 1. 𝄞 **224-930-754.** www.galeriemanes.cz. Tues–Sun 10am–6pm. Tram: 17 or 21.

Apartment Block   While standing on the river side of the street from Jiráskův Bridge, look past the Frank Gehry–inspired Dancing Building. Next door you will find a discreet apartment block with a small tilted globe on its roof. The top-floor windows were the focus of secret agents' binoculars from the water tower across the way. This was Havel's base, his small, Bohemian bunker, from where he wrote his subversive essays and plotted his peaceful putsches. Until 1995 he and his first wife, Olga, lived as president and first lady in this relatively tiny place, refusing to accept the accommodations of state at Prague Castle. Later the couple bought a stylish villa in the high-rent district on the west side of town (financed by Havel's royalties and property). They chose to live in one of the castle's residences until the villa was reconstructed.

Rašínovo nábřeží 78, Prague 2. Metro: Karlovo nám. Tram: 17 or 21.

Na rybárně   At this fishmonger around the corner from his dissident-era apartment, Havel spent hours debating politics over a plate of trout and a bottle of tart Czech Frankovka wine. After the revolution, the back room became a shrine to visiting dignitaries and rock stars, who were treated to a down-market "state dinner" and then signed the wall in a bizarre piece of presidential protocol. It's still open and still a decent place to get a fish dinner. Among the famous autographs on the wall is Mick Jagger's, one of Havel's favorite rockers.

Gorazdova 17, Prague 2. Metro: Karlovo nám. Tram: 17 or 21.

THE PRESIDENTIAL YEARS

From the baroque balcony at the **President's Office** in Prague Castle (tram no. 22) that hovers over the courtyard opposite St. Vitus Cathedral in Prague Castle, Havel delivered a stirring inauguration speech following his first investiture on December 29, 1989. To a world transfixed by his unlikely journey from prison to presidential palace, he proclaimed the rebirth of "a humane republic that serves the individual and that therefore holds the hope that the individual will serve it in turn."

Havel's common man image was largely destroyed when he moved out of his modest riverside flat and into a **Private Villa** (Dělostřelecká 1, Prague 6; metro: Hradčanská, then tram no. 1, 8, or 18 to U Brusnice stop) in 1995. With this move, Havel returned to the tightly knit circle of wealthy Prague homeowners. Unfortunately, the high walls surrounding the villa make it nearly impossible to have the brief encounters with Havel frequently experienced by visitors to his old home.

---

8 PARKS & GARDENS

HRADČANY

The **Royal Garden (Královská zahrada)** ★ at Prague Castle, Prague 1, once the site of the sovereigns' vineyards, was founded in 1534. Dotted with lemon trees and surrounded by 16th-, 17th-, and 18th-century buildings, the park is consciously and conservatively laid out with abundant shrubbery and fountains. Entered from U Prašného mostu Street, north of the castle complex, it's open daily from 10am to 6pm in the summer season.

The castle's **Garden on the Ramparts (Zahrada na Valech)** ★ is on the city-side hill below the castle. Beyond beautifully groomed lawns and sparse shrubbery is a tranquil low-angle view of the castle above and the city below. Enter the garden from the south side of the castle complex, below Hradčanské náměstí. The garden is open daily from 10am to 6pm in the summer season.

In 2000, Prince Charles himself was present when the **Palace gardens (Palácové zahrady)** ★★ under Prague Castle toward Malá Strana were reopened after years of cleaning and reconstruction. The **Ledeburská, Malá and Velká Pálffyovská, Kolowratská,** and **Malá Fürstenberská** gardens are accessible from Valdštejnské nám. 3 (Ledeburský palác), or from Valdštejnská street, or from Garden on the Ramparts, Prague 1 (𝄐 **257-010-401;** www.palacovezahrady.cz). Admission is 79Kč for adults, 49Kč for students. Open April and October daily 10am to 6pm; May and September 9am to 7pm; June and July 9am to 9pm; and August 9am to 8pm.

MALÁ STRANA

Looming over Malá Strana, adjacent to Prague Castle, lush green **Petřín Hill (Petřínské sady)** is easily recognizable by the miniature replica of the Eiffel Tower that tops it (p. 131). Gardens and orchards bloom in spring and summer. Throughout the myriad monuments and churches are a mirror maze and an observatory (p. 141). The Hunger Wall, a decaying 6m-high (20-ft.) stone wall that runs up through Petřín to the grounds of Prague Castle, was commissioned by Charles IV in the 1360s as a medieval welfare project designed to provide jobs for Prague's starving poor. Take tram no. 12, 20, or 22 to Újezd and ride the funicular or start climbing.

On Petřín's steep slope, near Malostranské náměstí, is located **Vrtbovská zahrada** ★. Its entrance is through Karmelitská 25, Prague 1 (𝄐 **272-088-350;** www.vrtbovska.cz). This is often called the most beautiful terraced garden north of the Alps. It was built in the 18th century's baroque style by architect Kaňka, and Matyas Braun provided some of his sculptures. This very special site was totally neglected during the old regime (it partially served as a playground for a local nursery). The garden is open daily April to October from 10am to 6pm. Admission is 55Kč adults, 35Kč students. Take tram no. 12, 20, or 22 to Malostranské náměstí.

Near the foot of Charles Bridge in Malá Strana, **Kampa Park (Na Kampě)** ★ was named by Spanish soldiers who set up camp here after the Roman Catholics won the Battle of White Mountain in 1620. The park as it is today wasn't formed until the Nazi occupation, when the private gardens of three noble families were joined. It's a fine place for an inner-city picnic, though the lawns are packed in high season.

Part of the excitement of **Waldstein (Wallenstein) Gardens (Valdštejnská zahrada)** ★ at Letenská, Prague 1 (𝄐 **257-071-111**) is its location, behind a 9m (30-ft.) wall on the back streets of Malá Strana. Inside, elegant gravel paths dotted with classical bronze statues and gurgling fountains fan out in every direction. Laid out in the 17th century, the baroque park was the garden of Gen. Albrecht Waldstein (or Wallenstein; 1581– 1634), commander of the Roman Catholic armies during the Thirty Years' War. These gardens are the backyards of Waldstein's Palace—Prague's largest—which replaced 23 houses, three gardens, and the municipal brick kiln. It's now home to the Czech Senate. The gardens are open March to October, daily from 10am to 6pm.

ELSEWHERE IN PRAGUE

The plain on the hilltop across the Vltava north of Old Town is a densely tree-covered swath, maintained as a park since 1858. **Letná Park (Letenské sady)** ★ is easy to spot from Pařížská street in Old Town, just look north to see a giant metronome atop a hill. This spot once held the world's largest statue of Soviet dictator Josef Stalin, which was pulled down with much difficulty in 1962. Today, the park is a great spot for strolling and jogging, and the far eastern stretch holds arguably the city's nicest beer garden, with a drop-dead-gorgeous view of Old Town below. The garden is connected to two restaurants in a recently renewed, 19th-century, neo-Renaissance château (Letenský zámeček), where you can get a pub-style meal or formal dinner. Take tram no. 1, 8, 25, or 26 from Hradčanská metro station.

Farther to the north is the massive nature reserve **Stromovka** ★★ (metro: Nádraží Holešovice, then tram no. 5, 14, 15, or 17). Acres of densely tree-lined paths, mostly flat and paved, comprise a shaded set of corridors for long strolls, jogging, and even in-line skating.

Another favorite getaway is **Vyšehrad Park** ★ above the Vltava south of the city center. This 1,000-year-old citadel encloses a peaceful set of gardens, playgrounds, footpaths, and the national cemetery next to the twin-towered Church of Sts. Peter and Paul, reconstructed from 1885 to 1887. The park provides a fantastic wide-angle view of the whole city. Take metro line C to Vyšehrad or tram no. 3 or 16 to Výtoň. The park is open at all times.

If you have the time and want to spend the whole day relaxing in a natural setting, take tram no. 26 or bus no. 119 from Dejvická metro stop toward the airport to **Divoká Šárka** natural park ★ in Prague 6. In just 30 minutes you will find yourself in a forest full of paths, creeks, rocks, and waterfalls. Whether you like to just wander, jog, hike, or swim you will enjoy visiting this natural wonder, far off the tourist radar.

9 PRAGUE WITH KIDS

Traveling with children can be an exhausting experience if you don't plan ahead. Prague offers many options, including museums, theaters, cinemas, and parks with playgrounds. If your brood gets tired of walking, take a tram ride. The kids will quickly forget about sore legs. Also, the Vltava River offers the possibility of exploring the city from yet another angle. Below are some places to take your family to make visiting Prague more enjoyable.

ON HRADČANY

The Toy Museum (Muzeum hraček; ☏ 224-372-294), situated within the complex of Prague Castle, at Jiřská 6, is a place to come with your family to see and feel the nostalgia of the past. This is the world's second-largest exposition of toys, where you can find everything from pieces dating back to ancient Greece up to a collection of the most popular toys of our time. It is open daily from 9:30am to 5:30pm. Admission is 60Kč adults, 30Kč students (children 6–15), free for children under 6.

ON PETŘÍN HILL

Kids will enjoy the funicular ride to the top of Petřín Hill, capped by the **Petřín Tower,** a miniature replica of the Eiffel Tower. Once there, look for the **Labyrinth (Bludiště; ☏ 257-315-212; www.pis.cz)**, a mirror maze that you walk through. Like the tower replica, the Labyrinth was built for the 1891 Prague Exhibition, an expo that highlighted the beauty and accomplishments of Bohemia and Moravia.

Inside the Labyrinth is a gigantic painting/installation depicting the battle between Praguers and Swedes on the Charles Bridge in 1648, a commemoration of the fighting that ended the Thirty Years' War. In 1892, the building's other historic exhibits were replaced with mirrors, turning the Labyrinth into the fun house it is today. It's open April daily from 10am to 7pm; May to September daily from 10am to 10pm; October daily from 10am to 6pm; and November to March Saturday and Sunday from 10am to 5pm. Admission is 70Kč for adults and 50Kč for children above 10 years.

Also in the park is the **Štefánik Observatory** (℃ **257-320-540;** www.observatory.cz), built in 1930 expressly for public stargazing through a very big telescope. It is open April to August Tuesday to Friday from 2 to 7pm and 9 to 11pm, and Saturday and Sunday from 10am to noon, 2 to 7pm, and 9 to 11pm; September Tuesday to Friday 2 to 6pm and 8 to 10pm, Saturday and Sunday 10am to noon, 2 to 6pm, and 8 to 10pm; March and October Tuesday to Friday 7 to 9pm, Saturday and Sunday 10am to noon, 2 to 6pm, and 7 to 9pm; January, February, November, and December Tuesday to Friday 6 to 8pm, Saturday and Sunday 10am to noon and 2 to 8pm. Admission is 60Kč for adults and 40Kč for children.

The funicular departs from a small house in the park just above the middle of Újezd in Malá Strana; tram no. 12, 20 or 22 will take you to Újezd.

ELSEWHERE IN PRAGUE

Budding astronomers can try to catch the stars at the **Planetárium** in Stromovka Park, Královská obora, Prague 7 (℃ **220-999-001;** www.planetarium.cz). There are shows daily under the dark dome, including one in which highlighted constellations are set to music and another that displays that night sky. The shows are in Czech, but the sky is still fun to watch. To reach the planetarium, take tram no. 12, 14, 15, or 17 to Výstaviště and walk through the park to your left about 200m (600 ft.). Admission is from 50Kč to 150Kč. It's open Monday to Thursday from 8:30am to noon and from 1pm until the end of the last program at 8pm. Saturday and Sunday hours are from 9:30am to noon and from 1pm until the end of the evening program (8pm).

In the somewhat dilapidated **Výstaviště** fairgrounds adjacent to Stromovka Park is **Křižík's Fountain (Křižíkova fontána).** A massive system of water spigots spout tall and delicate streams of color-lit water in a spectacular light show set to recorded classical and popular music. Small children are especially fascinated. There's also a small amusement park on the fairgrounds. The water/music program (℃ **723-665-694;** www.krizikova fontana.cz) runs April to October from 7 to 11pm, and in the summer it's 8 to 11pm. Admission is 200Kč, free for children under 6. Take tram no. 12, 14, 15, or 17 to Výstaviště.

In the same complex—the Výstaviště fairgrounds—is located an attraction called **Sea World (Mořský svět;** ℃ **220-103-275;** www.morsky-svet.cz). This permanent exhibition of sea fish and animals as well as simulations of the underwater world appeals to children and adults. Sea World is open daily 10am to 7pm and tickets cost 240Kč adults, 145Kč children. Take tram no. 12, 14, 15, or 17 to Výstaviště.

If you are visiting Prague with kids, leaving the city center for a short trip makes for a good break. Try a trip to the **Prague Zoo,** which is situated in Prague 7-Trója, U Trojského zámku 120 (℃ **296-112-111;** www.zoopraha.cz). Take bus no. 112 from Nádraží Holešovice on the C line all the way to the zoo park. It is open April, May, September, October daily 9am to 6pm; June to August 9am to 7pm; March 9am to 5pm; January, February, November, and December 9am to 4pm. On weekends the place is packed with Praguers; it's better to plan the trip on a weekday. A family ticket for 1 day costs 450Kč for two adults and two children.

EXPLORING PRAGUE

7

PRAGUE WITH KIDS

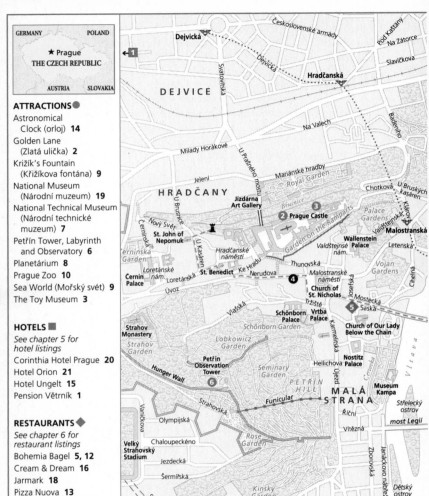

GERMANY   POLAND

★ Prague
THE CZECH REPUBLIC

AUSTRIA   SLOVAKIA

ATTRACTIONS●

Astronomical
Clock (orloj) **14**

Golden Lane
(Zlatá ulička) **2**

Križík's Fountain
(Křižíkova fontána) **9**

National Museum
(Národní muzeum) **19**

National Technical Museum
(Národní technické
muzeum) **7**

Petřín Tower, Labyrinth
and Observatory **6**

Planetárium **8**

Prague Zoo **10**

Sea World (Mořský svét) **9**

The Toy Museum **3**

HOTELS■
*See chapter 5 for
hotel listings*

Corinthia Hotel Prague **20**

Hotel Orion **21**

Hotel Ungelt **15**

Pension Větrník **1**

RESTAURANTS◆
*See chapter 6 for
restaurant listings*

Bohemia Bagel **5, 12**

Cream & Dream **16**

Jarmark **18**

Pizza Nuova **13**

Pizzeria Rugantino **11**

SHOPPING●
*See chapter 9 for
shopping listings*

Obchod loutkami **4**

Sparky's **17**

Metro
Royal Route
Pedestrian passage
Steps

0   1/5 mi
0   0.2 km

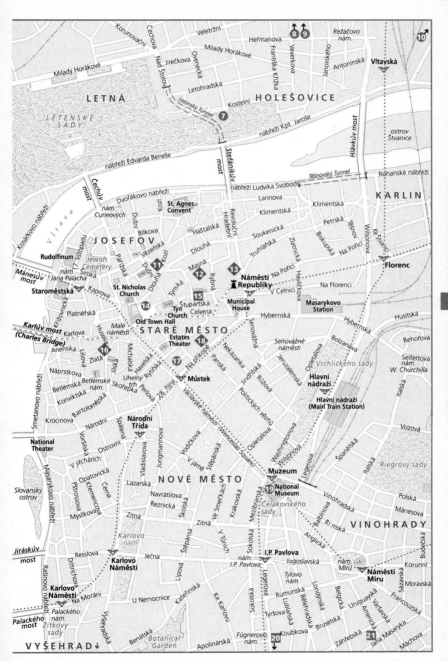

10 SIGHTSEEING OPTIONS

BUS TOURS

Prague streets can often become gridlocked, making any tour by car or bus frustrating. But if you want to take a guided English-language bus tour, among the best are those given by **Prague Sightseeing Tours,** Klimentská 52, Prague 1 (✆ **222-314-655;** www. pstours.cz). Its 3½-hour Grand City Tour leaves April to October, daily at 9:30am and 2pm (only 9:30am during winter), from the company's bus stop at náměstí Republiky. The tour costs 730Kč adults, 650Kč students, 380Kč children.

Better for the kids is the green, open-air, electric **Ekoexpres** (an electric bus in the shape of a train; ✆ **602-317-784;** www.ekoexpres.cz) that usually leaves every 30 minutes from behind the Jan Hus monument on Old Town Square. An hour's drive around the tourist areas of Old Town and up the hill to Prague Castle with a recorded narration in several languages costs 250Kč for adults and teenagers. Children up to age 12 travel free with their parents.

CRUISE-SHIP TOURS

Tourist cruise ships are the only commercial vessels allowed to pass through the city. This is an enjoyable, relaxing way to see Prague.

Evropská vodní doprava (✆ **224-810-030;** www.evd.cz), with a four-ship fleet, offers the most interesting sightseeing excursions. From April to October, several tours, including some serving decent inexpensive meals, disembark from Čechův, most at the northern turn of the Vltava, and sail past all the key riverside sights. A daily lunch tour with a smorgasbord and traditional Czech music leaves at noon, travels to the south end of the city, and returns by 2pm. The price, including meal, is 690Kč. A 1-hour tour, without meal, sails to Charles Bridge and back, leaving every hour from 10am to 6pm. It costs 220Kč. A 2-hour tour, without meal, leaves at 3pm and costs 350Kč. A dinner cruise to the south end of town leaves at 7pm and returns by 10pm. The price, including meal, is 790Kč for adults, 500Kč for children.

A competing service, **Jazzboat** (✆ **731-183-180;** www.jazzboat.cz), offers a similar nighttime dinner cruise along the river, but features a rotating menu of jazz music, including traditional, swing, blues, and Latin, on different nights of the week. The tours begin at 8pm nightly at pier no. 5 next to Čechův most (in front of the InterContinental Hotel) and last about 3 hours. The trip costs 590Kč adults, 300Kč students; the price includes a welcome drink but not dinner. Food is available onboard for around 360Kč per entree.

RENTING A ROWBOAT

Many people rent rowboats and paddleboats on the Vltava, which is free from commercial boat traffic. The remarkably romantic (if not sparkling clean) river slowly snakes through the middle of town and gleams beneath the city's spires.

You'll find boat rental outlets on Slovanský ostrov (Slavic Island). The docks are at the bottom of the steps on the small island opposite the National Theater. Both rowboats and paddleboats are on offer, and rates run about 80Kč per hour.

WALKING TOURS

Sylvia Wittmann's tour company, **Wittmann Tours,** Novotného lávka 5, Prague 1 (✆ **222-252-472;** www.wittmann-tours.com), offers daily walks around Prague's compact Jewish

> **⊙ Moments**   **An Old-Fashioned Tram Ride**
>
> Prague has had a system of tram lines since horses pulled the cars in the mid–18th century. The Communist-era tram cars aren't very attractive, and the new futuristic designs are built for efficiency rather than charm. You have to go back in time to have fun in a Prague tram, and you can, thanks to the Prague Transport Authority's (www.dpp.cz) **Historic Tram no. 91.**
>
> On weekends from March until November, the old-timer tram no. 91 clanks along a special circuit around town that takes it through major stops at Malostranské nám., Národní třída, Václavské nám., and many others. You are free to jump aboard and exit the tram at any stop you choose. Buy the ticket from the onboard conductor. Tickets cost 35Kč for adults and 20Kč for children under 10.

Quarter. A thousand years of history are discussed during the 3-hour stroll. From May to October, tours led by an English-speaking guide depart Sunday to Friday from Pařížská 28 at 10:30am and 2pm. From March 15 to April 30, and from November to December, tours depart at 10:30am. The tour's cost, including entrance fees to sights, is 880Kč for adults and 700Kč for students, free for children under 6 years. Wittmann Tours also offers a bus tour to the Terezín concentration camp costing 1,250Kč for adults, 1,100Kč for students, free for children under 10. The bus leaves from the same spot on Pařížská daily at 10am from May to October. March 15 through April, and November through December, the tour is available on Tuesday, Thursday, Saturday, and Sunday only. Make an advance reservation online or by calling the office. See chapter 11 for more on Terezín.

The group called **Prague Tours** (✆ **608-200-912** or 777-816-849) organizes guided walks around the city and visits of its main as well as lesser-known attractions. With them you will discover some of Prague's many secrets and mysteries. Groups leave throughout the day from a meeting point at the horse statue on Václavské náměstí (at no. 56; look for a guide holding a yellow umbrella); tickets are available on the spot from the guide. Each walk costs 400Kč per person. A special "All in One/Insider Tour" costs 600Kč per person. Ask about discounts for students and children.

It's not exactly a "walking tour," but tours on a Segway personal transporter have become increasingly popular in recent years. **Segway Tours** at Mostecká 4 (✆ **731-238-264;** www.segwayfun.eu) offers a series of guided Segway "walks" starting at around 1,500Kč per person for a tour of about 3 hours.

BY HORSE-DRAWN CARRIAGE

Each day dozens of *fiakry,* **horse-drawn carriages,** line up along the western side of Old Town Square to take visitors on a jaunt around the Old Town. It can be quite romantic, especially in the fall in the late afternoon or early evening, when there's a nip in the air and the coachman throws you a blanket to keep warm. Carriage rides don't come cheap, however. Negotiate the fare individually with the driver, but expect to pay around 1,000Kč for a 20- to 30-minute ride. It's customary to toss in a 10% tip for a personable driver.

BY VINTAGE AUTOMOBILE

Old-fashioned jalopies have become a familiar sight on the streets of Prague's Old Town and Malá Strana as more and more operators offer these popular antique car tours around town. You'll find most of the cars parked in and around Malé nám., near Old Town Square. **Prague Vintage Cars** (✆ 776-829-897; www.historytrip.cz) is a reliable operator and offers several types of tours starting at 1,100Kč per person for a ride around Old Town and a walking tour of Prague Castle.

BY PLANE

Točná Airport (✆ 241-773-454; www.aktocna.cz) organizes short charter sightseeing flights from a little airstrip on the edge of Prague. The days and times are negotiable, but you have to call 2 days ahead to set up a flight. For example, an 18-minute flight above Karlštejn Castle and back costs 2,000Kč per person. Each flight can carry up to three passengers.

Similarly, the **Prague Tourist Information Center** at Mostecká 4 (✆ 257-213-420; www.prague-information.eu) offers a series of helicopter tours, including one to Karlštejn Castle and back, from Točná airport. The cost is around 3,000Kč per person.

To get to Točná airport, take the metro line C to Kačerov station, then bus no. 205 to the last stop, Komořany, and walk 10 minutes through the forest.

BY BALLOON

Ballooning.CZ, Na Vrcholu 7, Prague 3 (✆ 222-783-995 or 607-517-535; www. ballooning.cz) offers an hour-long ride in a hot-air balloon for around 4,700Kč Monday to Friday or 5,200Kč on weekends. The takeoff is usually from Konopiště, about 40km (25 miles) south of Prague, so your trip there can be easily combined with a visit to Konopiště Castle.

---

11 STAYING ACTIVE

ACTIVITIES

BIKING Prague has a growing number of specially marked bike lanes, including a long and popular run that follows the Vltava River south of the center from the National Theater and another that starts around the Prague Zoo and follows the Vltava northward toward Germany. Two companies in central Prague specialize in rentals (and also give organized bike tours): **Praha Bike,** Dlouhá 24, Prague 1 (✆ 732-388-880; www.praha bike.cz); and **City Bike Prague,** Králodvorská 5, Prague 1 (✆ 776-180-284; www. citybike-prague.com).

GOLF Czechs are rediscovering golf on a tournament-caliber course with a world-class view at the **Prague Karlštejn Golf Club,** 30 minutes southwest of Prague. For details and directions, see chapter 11. You can improve your game during cold weather at the **Erpet Golf Center,** Strakonická 510, Prague 5 (✆ 296-373-111; www.erpet.cz). Opened in 1994, the renovated innards of a Communist-era sports hall now has an up-to-date setting of driving platforms, with pitching and putting greens on Astroturf and interactive video simulators. It's open daily from 8am to 11pm. Take metro line B to Smíchovské nádraží. The price is 300Kč per hour.

(Moments) The Prague International Marathon

"The narrow streets in the first 2 miles enforce a leisurely early pace, and the violinists on the Charles Bridge are the first live musicians along the way. After that, jazz, funk, samba, reggae and classical music groups help the runners as the miles begin to take their toll."

—George A. Hirsch, Publisher, *Runner's World*

The **Prague International Marathon (PIM),** Prague's premier annual civic-pride event, has grown by leaps and bounds since it was first run in 1995. The 42.2km (26.2-mile) race attracted just under 1,000 runners in its first year, but now the race traditionally brings in several thousand. That number combined with the **Fun Run,** a 4.2km (2.6-mile) race for families, totals about 40,000 people or more.

Many come to take advantage of the unique chance to run through Prague's cobblestone streets without having to dodge *Škodas* and trams. Others, especially nonrunners, love the festive atmosphere in Old Town Square, the music groups that line the race routes, and, of course, the great Czech beer that flows across the finish line.

The marathon route takes runners through the very heart of old Prague. The final stage of the race winds through the quirky streets of Old Town and eventually ends back at Old Town Square. Public transport on race day is free for participants who show their start number. A free massage and plenty of affordable *pivo* (beer) is available in the finish area, along with many other energy-restoring liquids.

For those who would like to give it a shot, the race takes place in mid-May, starting in Old Town Square (Staroměstské nám.). Marathoners can register for the race in person at the **PIM EXPO,** at Záhořanského 3, Prague 2, or in advance online at www.praguemarathon.com. The registration fee for the full marathon is about 1,750Kč; for family fun runs, the cost is about 300Kč.

HEALTH & FITNESS CLUBS   On the 25th floor of the Corinthia Hotel Prague, Kongresová 1, Prague 4, the **Apollo Day Spa** (© 261-191-111) provides weight machines, free weights, exercise bikes, step machines, a small pool (surrounded by glass with an expansive view of the city), a sauna, and a solarium. The modern facility also offers tanning beds, a whirlpool, and massages. A 1-day pass is 500Kč. The club is open Monday to Friday from 6:30am to 10pm and Saturday and Sunday from 7am to 10pm. Take metro line C to Vyšehrad.

World Class gym at Václavské nám. 22 (© 234-699-100) is a large health club in the city center, where you can try classes including aerobics, spinning, and yoga or work out in the gym for around 500Kč a day. It is open Monday to Friday 6am to 10:30pm, Saturday 7am to 10pm, Sunday 9am to 10pm.

The **Erpet Golf Center** (Fitness Center), Strakonická 510, Prague 5 (© 296-373-111; www.erpet.cz), has modern fitness machines, free weights, electronic rowers, and treadmills. There's also a relaxation center, with a dry sauna and a coed whirlpool that's usually open to the public. From May to September, the center is open Monday, Wednesday, Thursday and Sunday from 5pm to 10pm and costs 190Kč to enter. From October to April, the center is open daily from noon until 10pm and costs 390Kč. Take metro line B to Smíchovské nádraží.

JOGGING There are several nice runs near the center. One of the best is to head to **Letná** park, atop the hill across the Vltava from the InterContinental hotel. Here you'll find a peaceful loop that measures around 2km (1.2 miles). The best no-traffic, long-distance runs—flat, long, and mostly tree-lined—are found at **Stromovka** or **Divoká Šárka** parks (p. 140).

If you want to run through central Prague, use the traffic-restricted walking zones as often as you can. For an approximately 2.5km (1.5-mile) circuit, start at Můstek at the end of Wenceslas Square, run down Na Příkopě through the Powder Tower (Prašná brána) to Celetná Street all the way to Old Town Square, run around the Hus monument, run back to Železná Street past the Estates' Theater on to Rytířská Street, and run back to Můstek. This route is virtually free of cars, and your feet will be pounding the bricks. Try running in early morning or late evening when the streets aren't packed with crowds.

SWIMMING Summer doesn't last long in Prague, and when it arrives, many city dwellers are only too happy to cool off in one of the city's many pools. In addition to the hotel pools listed in chapter 5, there's the **Džbán Reservoir,** in the Divoká Šárka nature reserve, Prague 6. Džbán is fronted by a grassy "beach" that can—and often does—accommodate hundreds of bathers. There's a special section for nude swimming and sunbathing. To reach Šárka, take tram no. 26 from the Dejvická metro station. If you prefer a swimming pool or the weather doesn't cooperate, visit one of Prague's best aqua centers. The **Letňany Lagoon,** Tupolevova 665, Prague 9-Letňany (© **283-921-799;** www.letnanylagoon.cz), has a full-length pool as well as Jacuzzi and toboggan, which is a good fun for the whole family. You can also get a little refreshment and a drink while around the pool. The Lagoon is open Monday, Wednesday, and Friday 6 to 9am and noon to 10pm; Tuesday 7 to 9am and 4 to 10pm; Thursday 7 to 9am and noon to 10pm; Saturday and Sunday 9am to 10pm. Admission is 140Kč adults, 100Kč students. To get there take bus no. 140, 186, or 195 from metro line C Letňany station to the Tupolevova stop.

TENNIS At the **First Czech Lawn-Tennis Club Prague** at Štvanice Island (© **222-316-317;** www.cltk.cz), you can play on the courts where Martina Navrátilová and Ivan Lendl trained. The rental rate is from 360Kč to 720Kč per hour per covered court.

YOGA Yoga's popularity has been growing rapidly in Prague, and yoga classes are now on the menu at most fitness centers. One standout is **Lotus Center,** on Dlouhá 2, Prague 1 (© **774-421-097;** www.centrumlotus.cz), which offers classes in English for 80Kč to 120Kč.

SPECTATOR SPORTS

For information on games, tickets, and times for hockey and soccer games, check the *Prague Post* sports section. Buy tickets at stadium box offices or over team websites. The Ticket Portal website (www.ticketportal.cz) usually has a good selection of sports tickets, including booking for the Sparta Praha ice hockey team. To see the hockey team HC Slavia play, go to the website of Sazka arena (www.sazkaticket.cz), where the team plays its home matches.

ICE HOCKEY The main Czech professional hockey league, the 02 Extraliga, is one of the best in the world, and Czech stars are regularly drafted from here to play in the North American National Hockey League. Hockey season runs from mid-September until April, and taking in a match can be a real treat, especially for kids.

Prague has two professional teams that traditionally battle it out for national hockey supremacy. **HC Sparta Praha** plays its home matches at **Tesla Arena,** Za Elektrárnou 419, Prague 7 (𝒞 **266-727-443;** www.hcsparta.cz). Tickets are available from the stadium box office, open Monday to Friday 1–6pm, or over the Internet at www.ticketportal.cz. Tickets run from 110Kč to 240Kč. The stadium is part of the Výstaviště exhibition grounds. To find it, take metro line C to Holešovice and then tram no. 5, 14, 15, or 17 one stop to Výstaviště.

The second Prague-based team, **HC Slavia,** plays its home games at glamorous **Sazka Arena,** Ocelářská 460, Prague 9 (𝒞 **266-121-122;** www.hc-slavia.cz), the country's biggest and most modern indoor sports facility. In addition to hosting hockey matches, Sazka is a regular venue for rock concerts, wrestling matches and rodeos as well as other cultural and sporting events. Buy tickets at the Sazka box office starting from 10am on the day of the event or in advance over the Internet at www.sazkaticket.cz. Tickets run from 150Kč to 260Kč. To find the arena, take metro line B to the stop Českomoravská and it's a short walk from there.

SOCCER Soccer, or *fotbal* as it's called locally, is only slightly less popular than ice hockey. The Czechs traditionally rank among the world's best national teams. The main soccer league, the Gambrinus Liga, plays its games from late summer through November.

AC Sparta Praha, the top local soccer team, has a fanatical following, and games draw rowdy crowds to **Generali Arena** (or simply "Sparta stadium"), Milady Horákové 98, Prague 7 (𝒞 **296-111-400;** www.sparta.cz). Tickets for big matches often sell out long before game time, but seats are usually available up to the last moment for lesser matches. Buy the tickets at the stadium box office, open Monday to Friday 9am to noon, 1 to 5pm, or on game days 3 hours before kickoff. Tickets range from 100Kč to 360Kč for a domestic league game, higher for an international match. Take metro line A to Hradčanská and then take tram no. 1, 8, 25, or 26 to the Sparta stop.

Strolling Around Prague

Forget bus tours and taxis— walking is really the only way to explore Prague. Most of the oldest areas are walking zones with limited motor traffic. It's best to wear very comfortable, preferably flat, shoes. The crevices between the bricks in the street have been known to eat high heels. You might want to get in shape for all this walking before you leave home.

Below are some recommended routes, but don't worry about following the maps too closely—getting lost among the twisting narrow streets is also a wonderful way to discover Prague. Let the turns take you where they may; they usually lead to something memorable.

WALKING TOUR 1
CHARLES BRIDGE & MALÁ STRANA (LESSER TOWN)

START:	Old Town Bridge Tower (Staroměstská mostecká věž).
FINISH:	Church of St. Nicholas (Kostel sv. Mikuláše).
TIME:	About 3 to 4 hours.
BEST TIMES:	Early morning or around sunset, when crowds are thinner and the shadows most mysterious.
WORST TIME:	Midafternoon, when the bridge is packed.

Dating from the 14th century, Charles Bridge is Prague's most celebrated structure. As the primary link between Staré Město and the castle, it has always figured prominently in the city's commercial and military history. For most of its 650 years, the 510m-long (1,673-ft.) span has been a pedestrian promenade, as it is today.

The first sculpture, St. John of Nepomuk, was placed upon the bridge in 1683. It was such a hit that the church commissioned another 21 statues, which were created between 1698 and 1713. Since then the number has increased to 30. The locations of each statue are shown on the accompanying map. *Note:* As this book was being researched, city authorities had begun a long-term reconstruction project to repair damage to the bridge and to strengthen it. It is still crossable and beautiful, but the presence of scaffolding and work crews does detract from the setting somewhat. Work was expected to continue into 2010 but hopefully will be wrapped up by the time of your visit.

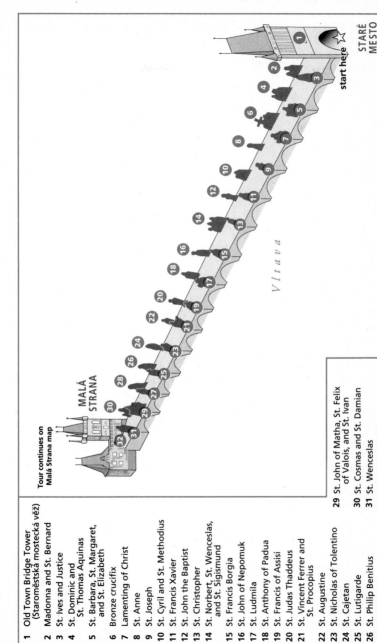

STARÉ
MESTO

start here

MALÁ
STRANA

**Tour continues on
Malá Strana map**

V l t a v a

1 Old Town Bridge Tower
   (Staroměstská mostecká věž)
2 Madonna and St. Bernard
3 St. Ives and Justice
4 St. Dominic and
   St. Thomas Aquinas
5 St. Barbara, St. Margaret,
   and St. Elizabeth
6 Bronze crucifix
7 Lamenting of Christ
8 St. Anne
9 St. Joseph
10 St. Cyril and St. Methodius
11 St. Francis Xavier
12 St. John the Baptist
13 St. Christopher
14 St. Norbert, St. Wenceslas,
   and St. Sigismund
15 St. Francis Borgia
16 St. John of Nepomuk
17 St. Ludmila
18 St. Anthony of Padua
19 St. Francis of Assisi
20 St. Judas Thaddeus
21 St. Vincent Ferrer and
   St. Procopius
22 St. Augustine
23 St. Nicholas of Tolentino
24 St. Cajetan
25 St. Lutigarde
26 St. Philip Benitius
27 St. Adalbert
28 St. Vitus
29 St. John of Matha, St. Felix
   of Valois, and St. Ivan
30 St. Cosmas and St. Damian
31 St. Wenceslas
32 Lesser Town Towers
   (Malostranské mostecké věže)

Tips Organized "Prague Tours"

Thematic walking tours are on the menu of a company called **Prague Tours.** It's run by experienced English-speaking guides who will help you discover Prague, its past and present, from different perspectives. To find out more about the tours, see p. 145 or call ℭ **608-200-912. Discover Prague** is another company that specializes in walking tours, including a 6-hour number they call their "ultimate walk." To contact them, call ℭ **777-812-278.**

As you stand in the shadow of the tower on the Old Town side of the bridge, first turn to your right, where you'll find an 1848 statue in tribute to Charles IV, who commissioned the bridge's construction between Prague's oldest quarters. Now walk toward the bridge entrance straight ahead, but first look up at the:

❶ Old Town Bridge Tower (Staroměstská mostecká věž)

This richly ornate 1357 design was made for Charles IV by Peter Parléř, the architect who drafted the Gothic plans for St. Vitus Cathedral. The original east side of the tower (facing the Old Town side) remains pristine, with coats of arms of the Bohemian king and Holy Roman Empire. Shields also depict each territory under the auspices of the Bohemian crown at that time.

Above the east-side arch, seated to the right of the standing statue of St. Vitus, is Charles himself, and on the left is a statue of his ill-fated son, Wenceslas IV (Václav IV), who lost the crown of the empire.

The tower's western side was severely damaged in a battle against invading Swedish troops in 1648. During the Thirty Years' War, the heads of 12 anti-Habsburg Protestants were hung for public viewing from iron baskets on the tower.

Climb to the top of the observation tower for postcard views of the bridge below.

As you pass through the archway, the first statue on the right is of the:

❷ Madonna

She is attending to a kneeling **St. Bernard,** flanked by cherubs. Like most of the statues on the bridge, this is a copy; the originals were removed to protect them from weather-related deterioration.

With your back to the Madonna statue, directly across the bridge is a statue of:

❸ St. Ives

He is the patron saint of lawyers and is depicted as promising to help a person who petitioned him. **Justice,** with a sword on his right, is also portrayed. If you see his outstretched hand holding a glass of beer, you'll know that Prague's law students have just completed their finals.

Cross back again and continue to do so after you view each statue.

❹ St. Dominic & St. Thomas Aquinas

These two figures are shown receiving a rosary from the hands of the Madonna. Below the Madonna are a cloud-enshrouded globe and a dog with a torch in its jaws, the symbol of the Dominican order.

❺ St. Barbara, St. Margaret & St. Elizabeth

These statues were sculpted by two brothers who worked under the watchful eye of their father, Jan Brokoff, who signed the work as a whole. Franz Kafka has written about the finely sculpted hands of St.

Barbara, the patron saint of miners, situated in the center of the monument. To art experts, however, the sculpture of St. Elizabeth (on the left) is the most artistically valuable figure in this group.

⑥ The Bronze Crucifix

Produced in Dresden, Germany, it was bought by the Prague magistrate and placed on Charles Bridge in 1657. The statue's gilded Hebrew inscription, which translates as "holy, holy, holy God," is believed to have been paid for with money extorted from an unknown Jew who had mocked a wooden crucifix that formerly stood on this site.

⑦ The Lamenting of Christ

This sculpture depicts Jesus lying in the Virgin Mary's lap, with St. John in the center and Mary Magdalene on the right. Executions were regularly held on this site during the Middle Ages.

⑧ St. Anne

The Virgin Mary's mother holds the baby Jesus as the child embraces the globe in this statue from 1707.

⑨ St. Joseph

This statue of Joseph with Jesus dates from 1854 and was put here to replace another that was destroyed by gunfire 6 years earlier by anti-Habsburg rioters.

⑩ St. Cyril & St. Methodius

These Catholic missionaries are credited with introducing Christianity to the Slavs.

⑪ St. Francis Xavier

One of the cofounders of the Jesuit order, he is depicted carrying four pagan princes on his shoulders—an Indian, a Tartar, a Chinese, and a Moor—symbolizing the cultures targeted for proselytizing. This is widely regarded as one of the most outstanding Czech baroque sculptural works.

⑫ St. John the Baptist

The saint is depicted here with a cross and a shell, symbols of baptism.

⑬ St. Christopher

The patron saint of raftsmen is shown carrying baby Jesus on his shoulder. The statue stands on the site of the original bridge watch-house, which collapsed into the river along with several soldiers during the Great Flood of 1784.

⑭ St. Norbert, St. Wenceslas & St. Sigismund

All three are patron saints of the Czech lands.

⑮ St. Francis Borgia

He was a Jesuit general and is depicted with two angels holding a painting of the Madonna. Look on the lower part of the sculpture's pedestal, where you'll see the three symbols of the saint's life: a helmet, a ducal crown, and a cardinal's hat.

⑯ St. John of Nepomuk

He was thrown to his death in chains from this bridge, and this, the oldest sculpture on the span, was placed here to commemorate him. The bronze figure, sporting a gold-leaf halo, was completed in 1683. The bridge's sole bronze statue, St. John is now green with age and worn from years of being touched for good luck. Just to the right of the statue along the top of the wall, you'll find a crossing marking the spot where he was allegedly tossed. Touch this too to ensure good fortune.

⑰ St. Ludmila

She points to a Bible from which St. Wenceslas is learning to read. In her left hand, St. Ludmila holds the veil with which she was suffocated. The statue's relief depicts the murder of St. Wenceslas.

⑱ St. Anthony of Padua

Dedicated in 1707, this statue depicts the preacher with baby Jesus and a lily. The relief is designed around a motif inspired by the saint's life.

⑲ St. Francis of Assisi

The first Roman Catholic martyr to be incorporated into the Bohemian liturgy, the contemplative saint is shown here between two angels.

⑳ St. Judas Thaddeus

He is depicted holding both the Gospel and the club with which he was fatally beaten.

㉑ St. Vincent Ferrer

He is shown boasting to **St. Procopius** of his many conversions: 8,000 Muslims and 25,000 Jews.

㉒ St. Augustine

Holding a burning heart and walking on "heretical" books, this statue of St. Augustine is a 1974 copy of a 1708 work. On the pedestal is the emblem of the Augustinians.

㉓ St. Nicholas of Tolentino

He is depicted as handing out bread to the poor. Behind him is a house with a Madonna, a mangle, and a lantern on its top-floor balcony. Walk quickly. Legend holds that if the lantern goes out while you pass by the statue, you'll die within the year.

㉔ St. Cajetan

The saint stands here in front of a column of cherubs while holding a sacred heart. Behind the statue, a triangle symbolizes the Holy Trinity.

㉕ St. Lutigarde

This figure was created in 1710 by 26-year-old M. B. Braun, and it is widely considered to be the most valuable sculpture on Charles Bridge. St. Lutigarde, a blind nun, is depicted here as able to see Christ on the cross, in order that she might kiss his wounds.

㉖ St. Philip Benitius

He was the general of the Servite order and is the only marble statue on the bridge. He's portrayed with a cross, a twig, and a book. The papal tiara lying at his feet is a symbol of the saint's refusal of the papal see in 1268.

㉗ St. Adalbert (1709)

The first bishop of Bohemia is blessing the Czech lands after returning from Rome.

㉘ St. Vitus

Attired as a Roman legionary, he stands on a rock between the lions to which he fell victim.

㉙ St. John of Matha, St. Felix of Valois & St. Ivan

This statue was commissioned for the Trinitarian order, which rescued Christians from Turkish captivity. In the huge rock is a prison, in front of which there's a dog and a Turk with a cat-o'-nine-tails guarding the imprisoned Christians. With money for their freedom, St. John is standing on the summit of the rock. St. Ivan is seated on the left, and St. Felix is loosening the bonds of the prisoners.

㉚ St. Cosmas & St. Damian

They are the patron saints of physicians and were known for dispensing free medical services to the poor. The statues, which were commissioned by Prague's medical faculty, are attired in gowns and hold containers of medicines.

㉛ St. Wenceslas

This statue was commissioned in 1858 by Prague's Klar Institute for the Blind.

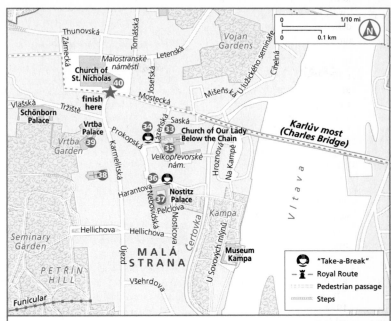

33 V lázních (In the Baths)
34 U zlatého jednorožce
   (At the Golden Unicorn)
35 Church of Our Lady Below the Chain
   (Kostel Panny Marie pod řetězem)

36 Maltézské náměstí (Maltese Square)
37 Nostitz Palace (Nostický palác)
38 Church of Our Lady Victorious
39 Vrtba Palace (Vrtbovský palác)
40 Church of St. Nicholas (Kostel sv. Mikuláše)

Follow the brick path toward the archway at the end of the bridge, but on your way, look up at the:

㉜ Lesser Town Towers (Malostranské mostecké věže)

The small tower on the left was built in the 12th century before Charles ever began construction on the bridge. It was a plain Romanesque structure, but Renaissance accents were added in the 16th century. The taller tower was built in the 15th century and completed the connection of the archway with the smaller tower built in the early 1400s.

After passing through the tower, you'll enter Mostecká Street. Take the first left to Lázeňská Street. At no. 6, on the left, you'll find a former hotel and bathhouse that now houses a small cafe:

㉝ V lázních (In the Baths)

This was a well-known stop for visitors to Prague in the 1800s. The pub and baths, which once hosted writer François-Rene de Chateaubriand, were in operation on this spot from the earliest periods of Lesser Town's existence.

Just up Lázeňská at no. 11, on the right side, is the former hotel:

❸ U zlatého jednorožce (At the Golden Unicorn)

This was another favored stop for honored guests, including Beethoven. A plaque on the front bears the composer's face. The hotel was originally built into the heavy walls that once ringed Malá Strana.

> ☕ **TAKE A BREAK**
> To the left of the Golden Unicorn you'll find a welcome respite from the tourist horde and the perfect spot for coffee or light lunch of salad or pasta. **Cukrkávalimonáda** (literally "sugarcoffeelemonade") at Lázeňská 7 has a comfy and countrified feel with wooden floorboards and a blackboard menu. The impossibly thick hot chocolate, perfect on a cold rainy day, is so rich it should be illegal. One cup is plenty for two. Main dishes run between 120Kč and 280Kč, coffee around 50Kč.

On the other side of the street, at the curve of Lázeňská, you come to the:

❸ Church of Our Lady Below the Chain (Kostel Panny Marie pod řetězem)

One of the best Romanesque designs in Prague, this church was built for the Order of the Maltese Knights, replacing the oldest church in Malá Strana after it burned in 1420. You can see remnants of the original inside the church courtyard.

After exiting the church back onto the street, go about 20 steps straight on Lázeňská to:

❸ Maltese Square (Maltézské náměstí)

On the first corner of the square is one of the city's most posh French restaurants packed into a former pub, U Malířů or "At the Painter's" (p. 92).

> ☕ **TAKE A BREAK**
> If **Cukrkávalimonáda** (see above) was full or you're in the mood for something more traditionally Czech, **Restaurace Vinárna U Vlada e (At the Governor's)** at no. 10 hits the spot. You can sit out front on the terrace and order coffee and dessert or a meal from a full Czech-style menu. Inside, on the left, is a more formal restaurant serving traditional Czech food. On the right is what used to be a horse stable, **The Konírna,** with vaulted ceilings, cozy and heavy wooden furniture, and a full menu of hearty Czech food. Main dishes cost between 180Kč and 600Kč, though daily lunch specials cut the cost substantially.

At one end of Maltézské náměstí you'll find the large:

❸ Nostitz Palace (Nostický palác)

This palace represents a grand, 17th-century, early baroque design attributed to Francesco Caratti. A Prague family that strongly supported the arts used to own it. Its ornate halls once housed a famed private art collection. The building now houses the Ministry of Culture, though you can still occasionally hear chamber concerts through its windows.

Facing Nostitz Palace, walk to the right and across Maltese Square (past the Mandarin Oriental Hotel) to find narrow Harantova Street (which was not signposted at the time of writing). Follow this a short way to Karmelitská Street. After crossing Karmelitská and walking to the right another 50m (150 ft.), you'll come to the:

❸ Church of Our Lady Victorious (Kostel Panny Marie Vítězné)

This is the home of the famed wax statue of the baby Jesus, the *Bambino di Praga,* seen as an important religious relic in Italy and other predominantly Catholic countries.

From the church entrance, continue up Karmelitská Street to see a complex of houses on the left side at no. 25, collectively known as:

㊴ Vrtba Palace (Vrtbovský palác)

In 1631, Sezima of Vrtba seized a pair of Renaissance houses and connected them to create his palace among the vineyards at the bottom of Petřín Hill. The lush, terraced gardens (Vrtbovská zahrada) surrounding this complex add to its beauty.

Proceed up Karmelitská, where you'll come finally to Malostranské náměstí. To the left, around the uphill side of the square, is the imposing dome of the:

㊵ Church of St. Nicholas (Kostel sv. Mikuláše)

This high-baroque gem was designed by K. I. Dientzenhofer and completed by his son in 1752. Relax among the statues and take in the marble-and-gilt interior (entry by paid admission only). The church often hosts excellent if expensive afternoon concerts. Buy tickets at the western entrance (on the side of the church facing Prague Castle). You can also climb the tower for views over Malá Strana and the Old Town in the distance.

WALKING TOUR 2	PRAGUE CASTLE (PRAŽSKÝ HRAD)

START:	The castle's front entrance, at Hradčanské náměstí.
FINISH:	Daliborka Tower.
TIME:	Allow approximately 2½ hours, not including rest stops.
BEST TIMES:	Weekdays from 9am to 5pm (to 4pm Nov–Mar).
WORST TIMES:	Weekends, when the crowds are thickest.

The history and development of Prague Castle and the city of Prague are inextricably entwined; it's impossible to envision one without the other. Popularly known as the "Hrad," Prague Castle dates to the second half of the 9th century, when the first Czech royal family, the Přemyslids, moved their seat of government here. Settlements on both sides of the Vltava developed under the protection of the fortified castle. Keep in mind as you are touring the castle that to enter most of the sites requires a combined-entry ticket that you can buy at one of two information centers in the castle courtyards. The good news is that entry into St. Vitus Cathedral is free, though the lines are often very long. It's possible to buy cheaper separate entry tickets to visit the Picture Gallery at Prague Castle and the National Gallery's Museum of 19th Century Czech Art in the Convent of St. George if you're not interested in visiting anything else. The Lobkowicz Palace's "Princely Collections," unfortunately, requires a separate entry ticket and is not included among the sites on the combined Prague Castle ticket.

Begin your tour from the castle's front entrance at Hradčanské náměstí. Walk through the imposing rococo gateway, topped by the colossal Battling Giants statues (1911 copies of 18th-c. granite works), to the:

❶ First Castle Courtyard (První hradní nádvoří)

An informal changing of the guard occurs here daily on the hour. It involves only five guards doing little more than some impressive heel clicking and rifle twirling.

Light It Up: The Rolling Stones Give Satisfaction

Are the lights flickering in Spanish Hall? If they are, someone might be playing with the remote control that operates the lighting.

In the summer of 1995, during the go-go '90s, the Rolling Stones played to a crowd of more than 100,000 people in their second Prague concert since the Velvet Revolution. After finishing, the Stones gave Václav Havel, then president and a big fan, a bright gift: They paid for a $32,000 overhaul of the lighting in four of the castle's grand halls, including the Spanish Hall and Vladislav Hall. The director and lighting designer of their record-breaking Voodoo Lounge Tour managed the project.

The result? Well, it's a somewhat more dignified spectacle than the raucous light show that was part of the mythical Voodoo Lounge Tour on stage. Mick Jagger, Keith Richards, Charlie Watts, and Ron Wood presented Havel with a remote control to operate the chandeliers and spotlights that now strategically cast their beams on baroque statues and tapestries.

The guards wore rather drab khaki outfits until 1989, when Václav Havel asked costume designer Theodor Pištěk, who costumed the actors in the film *Amadeus*, to redress them. Their smart blue outfits are reminiscent of those worn during the First Republic.

Directly ahead is the:

❷ Matthias Gateway (Matyášova brána)

Built in 1614 as a freestanding gate, it was later incorporated into the castle itself. The gateway bears the coats of arms of the various lands ruled by Emperor Matthias. Once you pass through it, you'll see a stairway on the right leading to the staterooms of the president of the republic. They're closed to the public.

The gateway leads into the Second Castle Courtyard (Druhé hradní nádvoří). Ahead, on the eastern side of the square, is the:

❸ Holy Rood Chapel (Kaple sv. Kříže)

Originally constructed in 1763, this chapel was redesigned in 1856. The chapel is noted for its high-altar sculpture and ceiling frescoes.

On the western side of the courtyard is the opulent:

❹ Spanish Hall (Španělský sál)

This hall was built in the late 16th century. During 1993 restorations, officials at the castle discovered a series of 18th-century *trompe l'oeil* murals that lay hidden behind the mirrors lining the hall's walls.

Adjoining the Spanish Hall is the:

❺ Rudolf Gallery (Rudolfova galerie)

This official reception hall once housed the art collections of Rudolf II. The last remodeling of this space—rococo-style stucco decorations—occurred in 1868.

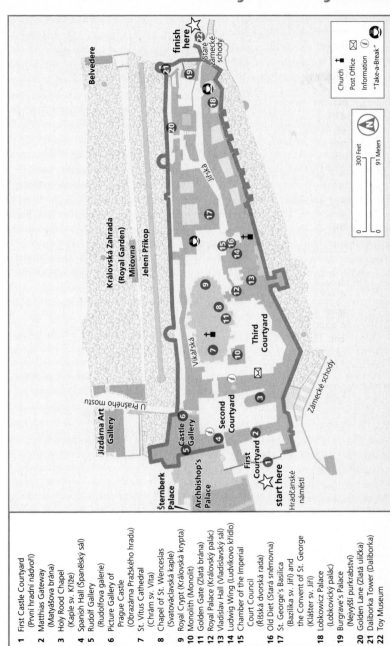

finish here

Belvedere

Královská Zahrada (Royal Garden)

Míčovna

Jelení Příkop

Staré zámecké schody

Church
Post Office
Information
"Take-a-Break"

0   300 Feet
0   91 Meters

Jizdárna Art Gallery

U Prašného mostu

Šternberk Palace

Archbishop's Palace

Second Courtyard

Vikářská

Jiřská

Third Courtyard

First Courtyard

start here

Hradčanské náměstí

Zámecké schody

1 First Castle Courtyard
  (První hradní nádvoří)
2 Matthias Gateway
  (Matyášova brána)
3 Holy Rood Chapel
  (Kaple sv. Kříže)
4 Spanish Hall (Španělský sál)
5 Rudolf Gallery
  (Rudolfova galerie)
6 Picture Gallery of
  Prague Castle
  (Obrazárna Pražského hradu)
7 St. Vitus Cathedral
  (Chrám sv. Víta)
8 Chapel of St. Wenceslas
  (Svatováclavská kaple)
9 Royal Crypt (Královská krypta)
10 Monolith (Monolit)
11 Golden Gate (Zlatá brána)
12 Royal Palace (Královský palác)
13 Vladislav Hall (Vladislavský sál)
14 Ludwig Wing (Ludvíkovo křídlo)
15 Chamber of the Imperial
   Court Council
   (Říšská dvorská rada)
16 Old Diet (Stará sněmovna)
17 St. George's Basilica
   (Bazilika sv. Jiří) and
   the Convent of St. George
   (Klášter sv. Jiří)
18 Lobkowicz Palace
   (Lobkovický palác)
19 Burgrave's Palace
   (Nejvyšší purkrabství)
20 Golden Lane (Zlatá ulička)
21 Daliborka Tower (Daliborka)
22 Toy Museum

On the northern side of the square is the:

⑥ Picture Gallery of Prague Castle (Obrazárna Pražského hradu)

Containing both European and Bohemian masterpieces, the gallery holds few works from the original imperial collection, which was virtually destroyed during the Thirty Years' War. Of the works that have survived from the days of Emperors Rudolf II and Ferdinand III, the most celebrated is Hans von Aachen's *Portrait of a Girl* (1605–10), depicting the artist's daughter.

A covered passageway leads to the Third Castle Courtyard (Třetí hradní nádvoří), dominated by the splendid:

⑦ St. Vitus Cathedral (Chrám sv. Víta)

Begun in 1334, under the watchful eye of Charles IV, Prague's most celebrated Gothic cathedral has undergone three serious reconstructions. The tower galleries date from 1562, the baroque onion roof was constructed in 1770, and the entire western part of the cathedral was begun in 1873. The whole thing was only finished in 1929.

Before you enter, notice the facade, decorated with statues of saints. The bronze doors are embellished with reliefs; those on the central door depict the construction history of the cathedral. The door on the left features representations from the lives of St. Adalbert (on the right) and St. Wenceslas (on the left).

Inside the cathedral's busy main body are several chapels, coats of arms of the city of Prague, a memorial to Bohemian casualties of World War I, and a Renaissance-era organ loft with an organ dating from 1757.

According to legend, St. Vitus died in Rome but was then transported by angels to a small town in southern Italy. Since his remains were brought here in 1355, Vitus, the patron saint of Prague, has remained among the most popular saints in the country. Numerous Czech Catholic churches have altars dedicated to him.

The most celebrated chapel, on your right, is the:

⑧ Chapel of St. Wenceslas (Svatováclavská kaple)

The chapel is built atop the saint's tomb. A multitude of polished semiprecious stones decorates the chapel's altar and walls. Other spaces are filled in with 14th-century murals depicting Christ's sufferings and the life of St. Wenceslas.

Below the church's main body is the:

⑨ Royal Crypt (Královská krypta)

The crypt contains the sarcophagi of kings Václav IV, George of Poděbrady, Rudolf II, and Charles IV and his four wives. The tomb was reconstructed in the early 1900s, and the remains of the royalty were placed in new encasements. Charles's four wives share the same sarcophagus. Visitor access to the crypts, unfortunately, was suspended in 2009 due to vandalism and it wasn't clear as this book was being researched when the crypts would reopen.

Exit the cathedral from the same door you entered and turn left into the courtyard, where you'll approach the:

⑩ Monolith (Monolit)

The marble obelisk measuring over 11m (36 ft.) tall is a memorial to the victims of World War I. Just behind it is an equestrian statue of St. George, a Gothic work produced in 1373.

Continue walking around the courtyard. In the southern wall of St. Vitus Cathedral, you'll see a ceremonial entrance known as the:

⑪ Golden Gate (Zlatá brána)

The tympanum over the doorway is decorated with a 14th-century mosaic, *The Last Judgment,* which has been carefully restored, bit by bit. The doorway's 1950s-era decorative grille is designed with zodiac figures.

An archway in the Third Castle Courtyard connects St. Vitus Cathedral with the:

⑫ Royal Palace (Královský palác)

Until the second half of the 16th century, this was the official residence of royalty. Inside, to the left, is the **Green Chamber (Zelená světnice),** where Charles IV presided over minor court sessions. A fresco of the court of Solomon is painted on the ceiling.

The adjacent room is:

⑬ Vladislav Hall (Vladislavský sál)

This ceremonial room has held coronation banquets, political assemblies, and knightly tournaments. Since 1934, elections of the president of the republic have taken place here below the exquisite 12m (39-ft.), rib-vaulted ceiling.

At the end of Vladislav Hall is a door giving access to the:

⑭ Ludwig Wing (Ludvíkovo křídlo)

In this wing, built in 1509, you'll find two rooms of the Chancellery of Bohemia (Česká kancelář), once the administrative body of the Land of the Crown of Bohemia. When the king was absent, Bohemia's nobles summoned assemblies here. On May 23, 1618, two hated governors and their secretary were thrown out of the eastern window of the rear room. This act, known as the Second Defenestration, marked the beginning of the Thirty Years' War (see the box "Beware of Open Windows: The Czech Tradition of Defenestration," in chapter 7).

A spiral staircase leads to the:

⑮ Chamber of the Imperial Court Council (Říšská dvorská rada)

The chamber met here during the reign of Rudolf II. In this room the 27 rebellious squires and burghers who fomented the defenestration were sentenced to death.

Their executions took place on June 21, 1621, in Staroměstské náměstí. All the portraits on the chamber walls are of Habsburgs. The eastern part of Vladislav Hall opens onto a terrace from which there's a lovely view of the castle gardens and the city.

Also located in the palace is the:

⑯ Old Diet (Stará sněmovna)

The Provincial Court once assembled here. It's interesting to notice the arrangement of the Diet's furniture, which is all centered on the royal throne. To the sovereign's right is the chair of the archbishop and benches for the prelates. Along the walls are seats for the federal officials; opposite the throne is a bench for the representatives of the Estates. By the window on the right is a gallery for the representatives of the royal towns. Portraits of the Habsburgs adorn the walls.

Stairs lead down to St. George's Square (náměstí Svatého Jiří), a courtyard at the eastern end of St. Vitus Cathedral. If the weather is nice, you might want to:

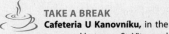

> **TAKE A BREAK**
> **Cafeteria U Kanovníku,** in the courtyard between St. Vitus and St. George's (náměstí Sv. Jiří 3), has a terrace garden with tables, where you can enjoy light fare and hot Czech food. They offer coffee for 60Kč and great chicken wraps for 120Kč daily from 10am to 5pm.

This square is dominated by:

⑰ St. George's Basilica (Bazilika sv. Jiří) & the Convent of St. George (Klášter sv. Jiří)

Benedictine nuns founded the convent in A.D. 973. In 1967, the convent's premises were acquired by the **National Gallery,** which now uses the buildings to display its interesting collection of 19th-century Czech art. See chapter 7 for complete information.

Leave the basilica and continue walking through the castle compound on Jiřská Street, the exit at the southeastern corner of St. George's Square. About 60m (197 ft.) ahead on your right (at no. 3) is the entrance to:

🔞 Lobkowicz Palace (Lobkovický palác)

This relatively recently reconstructed 16th-century manor now houses the "Princely Collections Exhibition," a gallery devoted exclusively to the Lobkowicz family collections, including some old masters paintings, original scores by Beethoven, and fine musical instruments. Note that entry to this museum requires a separate ticket and is not included on the combined Prague Castle entrance ticket.

TAKE A BREAK
Even if you don't decide to spring for the admittedly pricey admission to see the "Princely Collections," be sure to take a meal here inside the palace, which offers easily the best food and best views in the entire castle complex. You can have just a coffee and cake or a full Czech repast with all the goulash and dumplings you care to eat. In nice weather sit in the courtyard or, better, inside on the terrace overlooking Malá Strana. The views are as good as or even better than the food. It's open daily from 9am to 5pm.

Opposite Lobkowicz Palace is:

🔞 Burgrave's Palace (Nejvyšší purkrabství)

This 16th-century building, now considered the House of Czech Children, is used for cultural programs and exhibitions aimed toward children.

Walk up the steps to the left of Burgrave's Palace or, if these are closed, head back up in the direction of St. George's and take the first right to find tiny:

🔞 Golden Lane (Zlatá ulička)

This picturesque street of 16th-century houses built into the castle fortifications was once home to castle sharpshooters. The charm-filled lane now contains small shops, galleries, and refreshment bars. Franz Kafka supposedly lived at no. 22 for a brief time in 1917.

Turn right on Golden Lane and walk to the end, where you'll see:

🔞 Daliborka Tower (Daliborka)

This tower formed part of the castle's late Gothic fortifications dating from 1496. The tower's name comes from Squire Dalibor of Kozojedy, who in 1498 became the first unlucky soul to be imprisoned here. One Dalibor legend, immortalized in an opera by Czech composer Bedřich Smetana, has it that Dalibor learned to play the violin in prison and charmed the citizens of Prague who used to stand below the tower and listen to him play.

Turn right at Daliborka Tower, then left, and go through the passageway and down Jiřská Street. Here, at no. 6, you can visit the:

🔞 Toy Museum

Especially appreciated by children, this museum unsurprisingly holds a permanent exhibition of toys. Wooden and tin toys are on display here along with a collection of Barbie dolls.

Follow the main street downhill and walk through the lower castle gate to see a stunning panorama of Malá Strana and the Old Town across the river. From here you have two choices for reaching the Malostranská station on line A of Prague's metro. Make a right and follow the old castle steps (Staré zámecké schody) or bear slightly to the left for a more scenic journey through some restored vineyards and several more cafes and restaurants.

START:	Municipal House (Obecní dům), at náměstí Republiky.
FINISH:	Havel's Market (Havelský trh).
TIME:	Allow approximately 1 hour, not including any breaks or museum visits.
BEST TIMES:	Sunday to Thursday from 9am to 5pm and Friday from 9am to 2pm, when the museums and market are open.
WORST TIMES:	Weekend afternoons when the crowds are thickest, Monday when the museums are closed, and after 6pm when the market is closed.

Staré Město, founded in 1234, was the first of Prague's original five towns. Its establishment was the result of Prague's growing importance along central European trade routes. Staré Město's ancient streets, most meandering haphazardly around Staroměstské náměstí, are lined with many stately buildings, churches, shops, and theaters.

Although this tour is far from exhaustive, it takes you past some of Old Town's most important buildings and monuments. Go to náměstí Republiky 5, from the metro station of the same name. Begin at the:

❶ **Municipal House (Obecní dům)**

One of Prague's most photographed cultural and historical monuments, the Municipal House was built between 1906 and 1911 with money raised by Prague citizens. In the spring of 1997, it reopened after a long reconstruction, and historians say that it has been returned faithfully to its original grandeur.

From the beginning, this ornate Art Nouveau building has been an important Czech cultural symbol—the document granting independence to Czechoslovakia was signed here in 1918. The **Prague Symphony** performs in Smetana Hall, the building's most impressive room, with a gorgeous stained-glass ceiling. The detail of every decoration tells a story (see p. 128 for more information).

Inside you'll find a spacious period cafe, a French restaurant, and a Czech pub in the cellar with a fascinating ceramic still-life mural. Guided tours are offered most days (usually twice daily in the afternoon); buy tickets at the information center inside.

Facing the Municipal House main entrance, walk around to your left under the arch of the:

❷ **Powder Tower (Prašná brána, literally Powder Gate)**

Once part of Staré Město's system of fortifications, the Powder Tower was built in 1475 as one of the walled city's major gateways. After New Town was incorporated into the City of Prague, the walls separating Old Town from the new section became obsolete. So did the Powder Tower, which was recommissioned as a gunpowder storehouse. Climb to the top for a better view of where you're going.

The tower marks the beginning of the **Royal Route,** the traditional path along which medieval Bohemian monarchs paraded on their way to being crowned in Prague Castle's St. Vitus Cathedral.

Continue through the arch down Celetná Street (named after *calt,* a bread baked here in the Middle Ages) to the corner of Ovocný trh, where you'll find the:

❸ **House at the Black Mother of God (Dům U Černé Matky boží)**

At Celetná 34, this building is important for its cubist architectural style. Cubism, an angular artistic movement, was confined to painting and sculpture in France and most of Europe. As an architectural style, cubism is exclusive to Bohemia.

Constructed in 1912, this house features lots of jarring rectangular and triangular shapes that try to re-create in 3-D what cubism did for painting. The house is named for the Virgin Mary emblem on the corner of the building's second floor that was salvaged from the last building to stand on this site. There's also a small cubist museum to the left of the main entrance and around the corner is a sumptuous shop, Kubista, specializing in early Modern reproduction design and home furnishings.

With your back to the House of the Black Mother of God, cross Celetná and bear right to find a small passageway leading into Templová that begins just to the right of Celetná 27. Walk 2 short blocks, and turn left onto Jakubská. At the corner, on your right, you'll see:

❹ St. James's Church (Kostel sv. Jakuba)

Prague's second-longest church contains 21 altars. When you enter, look up just inside the church's front door. The object dangling from above is the shriveled arm of a 16th-century thief.

With your back to the entrance of St. James Church, cross the street and turn left to find the small Týn passageway that starts just to the left of Malá Štupartská 5. Walk through the pretty courtyard of the former custom's house, the Ungelt, continuing straight through the second gate and up a small alleyway to the Old Town Square. Keep the Ungelt in mind for a future shopping trip as there are some great stores here. As you reach Old Town Square, turn left to find the entrance (at Staroměstské náměstí 14) to the:

❺ Church of Our Lady Before Týn (Kostel paní Marie před Týnem)

This is one of the largest and prettiest of Prague's many churches. Famous for its twin spires that loom over nearby Staroměstské náměstí, the church was closely connected to the 14th-century Hussite movement for religious reform. After Roman Catholics crushed the reformers, many of the church's Hussite

symbols were removed, including statues, insignia, and the tower bells that were once known by Hussite nicknames. Note the tomb of Danish astronomer Tycho de Brahe (d. 1601), near the high altar.

Just in front of the church you can't miss the economic and spiritual heart of Prague's Old Town:

❻ Old Town Square (Staroměstské náměstí)

Surrounded by baroque buildings and packed with colorful cafes, craftspeople, and entertainers, Staroměstské náměstí looks the way an old European square is supposed to look.

This square has long been a focal point of Czech history and politics. Since the city's inception it has served as a meeting place for commerce, from the simple bartering of the Middle Ages to the privatization deals of the 1990s.

Old Town Square has also seen its share of political protest and punishment. Protestant Hussites rioted here in the 1400s. In 1621, the Catholic Habsburg rulers beheaded 27 Protestants here and hung some of the heads in baskets above Charles Bridge. A small white cross has been embedded in the square near the Old Town Hall for each of the beheaded.

In the 20th century, the square witnessed a whirlwind of political change. In 1918, the Czechs celebrated the founding of the new sovereign Republic of Czechoslovakia here. But then in 1939, the Nazis celebrated their occupation of the country on the same site. The Soviets then celebrated kicking the Nazis out of Prague in 1945. But in 1968 the Russians rolled their tanks through Prague again, this time as unwelcome invaders.

In February 1948, Communist party leader Klement Gottwald led a celebration in honor of the Communist seizure of

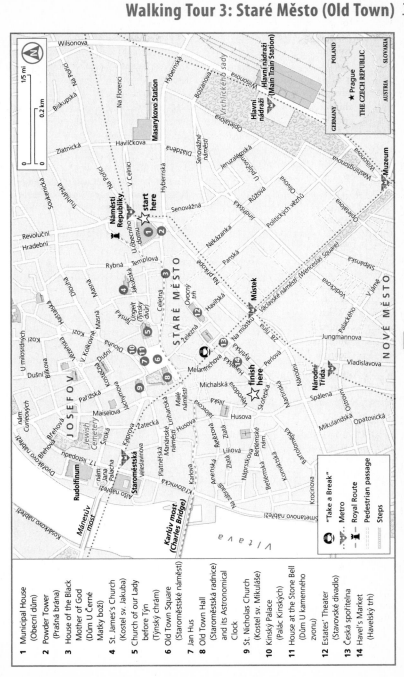

STROLLING AROUND PRAGUE

8

STARÉ MĚSTO (OLD TOWN)

1 Municipal House (Obecní dům)

2 Powder Tower (Prašná brána)

3 House of the Black Mother of God (Dům U Černé Matky boží)

4 St. James's Church (Kostel sv. Jakuba)

5 Church of our Lady before Týn (Týnský chrám)

6 Old Town Square (Staroměstské náměstí)

7 Jan Hus

8 Old Town Hall (Staroměstská radnice) and its Astronomical Clock

9 St. Nicholas Church (Kostel sv. Mikuláše)

10 Kinský Palace (Palác Kinských)

11 House at the Stone Bell (Dům U kamenného zvonu)

12 Estates' Theater (Stavovské divadlo)

13 Česká spořitelna

14 Havel's Market (Havelský trh)

power. No wonder the Czechs chose nearby Wenceslas Square to celebrate the return of their government in 1989.

To begin your walk around the square, go straight toward the massive black stone monument in the center (at present undergoing a renovation). Here you'll find the statue of:

❼ Jan Hus

Jan Hus was a fiery 15th-century preacher who challenged the Roman Catholic hierarchy and was burned at the stake for it. The statue's pedestal has been used as a soapbox by many a populist politician trying to gain points by associating himself with the ill-fated Protestant, although today you're more likely to find the international youth holding sway.

The struggle between the supporters of Hus, known as Hussites, set the stage for the religious wars that tore Bohemia apart in both the 15th and 17th centuries. The Hussite Church still lives today as the Protestant Czech Brethren, but since Communism its numbers have dwindled. Membership in the Catholic Church has also declined.

From here, turn around and walk left toward the clock tower.

❽ Old Town Hall (Staroměstská radnice)

Try to time your walk so you can pass the hall and its **Astronomical Clock** at the top of the hour. It's an understated show each hour where a mechanical parade of saints and sinners performs for the crowd watching below (p. 118). If you have time and your knees are up to it, try making the steep, narrow walk up to the top of the tower for a picturesque view of Old Town's red roofs.

Walking past the right side of the clock tower toward the northwest corner of the square, past the crosses on the ground marking spot of the public executions of 27 Czech noblemen in 1621, you'll come to:

❾ St. Nicholas Church (Kostel sv. Mikuláše)

This is the 1735 design of Prague's baroque master architect K. I. Dientzenhofer. The three-towered edifice isn't as beautiful or as ornate inside as his St. Nicholas Church in Lesser Town, but the crystal fixtures are worth a look. Like its namesake in Malá Strana, this church hosts expensive but high-quality concerts most afternoons. Tickets are sold at the door on the day of the performance.

From the front of the church, walk behind the back of the Hus monument, through the square, to the broad palace with the reddish roof and balcony in front. This is:

❿ Kinský Palace (Palác Kinských)

From the rococo balcony jutting from the palace's stucco facade, Communist leader Klement Gottwald declared the proletariat takeover of the Czechoslovak government in February 1948. Italian architect Lurago originally designed the building for Count Goltz. It was later taken over by the Habsburg Prince Rudolf Kinský in 1768. Aside from the dubious distinction of providing a balcony for Comrade Gottwald, the Kinský Palace is famous as the site of Franz Kafka's father's haberdashery on the ground floor as well as being the former home of Baroness Bertha von Suttner, a secretary to Alfred Nobel of peace prize fame and herself the first female recipient of the Nobel Peace Prize in 1905.

Next to this is the:

⓫ House at the Stone Bell (Dům U kamenného zvonu)

The medieval Gothic tower was built in the 14th century for the father of Charles IV, John of Luxembourg. These days it often hosts high-quality art exhibits.

From here, head back toward Old Town Hall, but then about midway to the tower, turn left toward the square's south end, and begin walking down Železná. Continue down this car-restricted walking zone about 300m (984 ft.); then, on the left you'll see the pale green:

⑫ Estates' Theater (Stavovské divadlo)

Mozart premiered his opera *Don Giovanni* in this late-18th-century grand hall. More recently, director Miloš Forman filmed many scenes in the story of the composer's life here.

Make sure to walk down Rytířská in front of the theater to get a full view of this beautifully restored building.

From the front of the theater, walk about 10 steps back up Železná and take the first left on Havelská.

TAKE A BREAK
At Havelská 27, you can stop for a tasty pasta, lasagna, tiramisu, or thick Italian espresso at **Kogo** (p. 98). There are tightly packed tables inside, but if the weather is nice, you can sit in the more comfortable archway. Hours are daily from 9am to 11pm. Salads and appetizers start at 180Kč, and you won't be disappointed by their homemade pasta (from around 200Kč).

Continue down Havelská. On the left you'll see:

⑬ Czech Savings Bank (Česká spořitelna)

After serving as the museum to late Communist party leader Klement Gottwald, the large neo-Renaissance building with statue inlays is once again a bank. The 1894 building was originally intended to be a bank, but after the 1948 coup it was seized by the government and turned into a repository for Communist propaganda. After the 1989 revolution, the building was returned to the bank, which restored the intricate friezes and frescoes depicting bankers' propaganda of early Czech capitalism. This is the largest Czech savings bank and worth a peek.

Your next destination is the popular street market that overtakes the remainder of Havelská Street. Simply continue on to:

⑭ Havel's Market (Havelský trh)

At this popular local meeting place, you'll find vegetables, fruit, drinks, soaps, toiletries, and an assortment of souvenirs. Prices here are generally lower than in most shops. Have fun browsing.

The nearest metro is Můstek, line A or B.

WALKING TOUR 4   **JOSEFOV (JEWISH QUARTER)**

START:	Lesser Square (Malé náměstí).
FINISH:	Restaurant Les Moules.
TIME:	Allow approximately 2 hours, not including rest stops or museum visits.
BEST TIMES:	Sunday to Friday from 9am to 5pm, when the cemetery and sights are open.
WORST TIME:	Saturday, the Sabbath, and Jewish holidays when everything is closed.

Josefov, Prague's former Jewish ghetto, lies within Staré Město. The wall that once surrounded the ghetto was almost entirely destroyed to make way for 19th-century structures. Prague was always considered one of Europe's great Jewish cities: Jews have been here since the end of the 10th century, and Prague traditionally was considered one of the centers of Jewish scholarship and learning.

Today, Prague's Jewish community numbers less than 3,000, and while few Jews live here these days, this is still the community's spiritual heart. Note that to enter most of the sites here, you'll need to buy a combined entry ticket (ticket windows and cashiers are located at points throughout the former ghetto). Admission to the Old-New Synagogue is not included and requires a separate (and expensive) ticket.

This tour may seem short, but the sights are highly detailed and provide much to ponder, so budget your time loosely. Start at:

❶ Lesser Square (Malé náměstí)

This square is adjacent to Staroměstské náměstí. Though it can't boast as much history as its larger companion, excavations have proven that Malé náměstí was a prime piece of real estate as far back as the 12th century. Archaeologists turned up bits of pottery, evidence of medieval pathways, and human bones from the late 1100s, when developers committed the medieval equivalent of paving over a cemetery to build a shopping mall. Today the square is home to Prague's branch of the Hard Rock Café chain, which only slightly diminishes the impact.

From Malé náměstí, walk north along the square to find U radnice. One block ahead, in the courtyard across from the Magistrate Building and tucked against St. Nicholas Church, you'll see:

❷ Franz Kafka's House

This building, on the site where the famous author was born, now houses a small gallery and shop to re-create the history of his life. But the best way to get a look Kafka's life is by visiting the Kafka Museum in Hergetova Cihelna (p. 124).

An unflattering cast-iron bust of Kafka, unveiled in 1965, sits just at the corner of Maiselova and U radnice. Walk straight ahead onto:

❸ Maiselova Street

This is one of the two main streets of the walled Jewish quarter, founded in 1254. As elsewhere in Europe, Prague's Jews were forced into ghettos. By the 16th century, Prague's 10,000 isolated Jews comprised 10% of the city's population.

The ban on Jews living outside the ghetto was lifted only in 1848. Eighty percent of the ghetto's Jews moved to other parts of the city, and living conditions on this street and those surrounding it seriously deteriorated. The authorities responded by razing the entire neighborhood, including numerous medieval houses and synagogues. The majority of the buildings here now date from the end of the 19th century; several on this street sport stunning Art Nouveau facades.

About halfway down the street, on your right, is the:

❹ Maisel Synagogue (Maiselova synagóga)

This neo-Gothic temple is built on a plot of land donated by Mordechai Maisel, a wealthy inhabitant of Prague's old Jewish quarter. The original synagogue was destroyed by fire in 1689 but was rebuilt. During the Nazi occupation of Prague, it was used to store furniture seized from the homes of deported Jews. Today, the building holds no religious services; it's home to the Jewish Museum's collection of silver ceremonial objects, books, and Torah covers confiscated from Bohemian synagogues by the Nazis during World War II. There's also a small but good gift shop.

Continue walking down Maiselova and turn left onto Široká to find the entrance to the Pinkas Synagogue and the Old Jewish Cemetery on the left side:

❺ Pinkas Synagogue (Pinkasova synagóga)

This is Prague's second-oldest Jewish house of worship. After World War II, the walls of the Pinkas Synagogue were painted with the names of more than

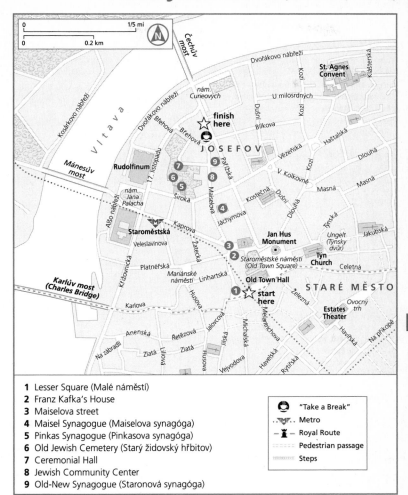

1 Lesser Square (Malé náměstí)
2 Franz Kafka's House
3 Maiselova street
4 Maisel Synagogue (Maiselova synagóga)
5 Pinkas Synagogue (Pinkasova synagóga)
6 Old Jewish Cemetery (Starý židovský hřbitov)
7 Ceremonial Hall
8 Jewish Community Center
9 Old-New Synagogue (Staronová synagóga)

"Take a Break"
Metro
Royal Route
Pedestrian passage
Steps

77,000 Czech Jews who perished in Nazi concentration camps. The Communist government subsequently erased the names, saying that the memorial was suffering from "moisture due to flooding." After the revolution, funds were raised to restore and maintain the commemoration.

Here too is another gripping reminder of the horrors of World War II. Displayed are the sketches by children who were held at the Terezín concentration camp west of Prague (see chapter 11). These drawings, which are simple, honest, and painful in their playful innocence, are of the horrific world where parents and other relatives were packed up and sent to die.

Next to the Pinkas Synagogue you'll find the entrance to the Old Jewish Cemetery. If you're not up for paying the (admittedly) steep combined entry fee to see the cemetery and the other sites, you can still sneak a peak at the Jewish cemetery through a small window off the street. To find the window, follow Široká street to ul. 17 listopadu, turn right and walk about 10m (30 ft.) beyond the entrance to the Museum of Applied Arts (ul. 17 listopadu 2). There you'll find a small opening in the fence on the right side.

6 Old Jewish Cemetery (Starý židovský hřbitov)

This is Europe's oldest Jewish burial ground, where the oldest grave dates from 1439. Because the local government of the time didn't allow Jews to bury their dead elsewhere, as many as 12 bodies were placed vertically, with each new tombstone placed in front of the last. Hence, the crowded little cemetery contains tens of thousands of graves.

Like other Jewish cemeteries around the world, many of the tombstones have small rocks and stones placed on them—a tradition said to date from the days when Jews were wandering in the desert. Passersby, it's believed, would add rocks to gravesites so as not to lose the deceased to the shifting sands. Along with stones, visitors often leave small notes of prayer in the cracks between tombstones.

Buried here is Rabbi Löw, who made from the mud of the Vltava River the legendary Golem, a clay "monster" to protect Prague's Jews. Golem was a one-eyed or three-eyed monster, depending on how you look at him. Legend has it that the rabbi would keep Golem around to protect the residents from the danger of mean-spirited Catholics outside the walls of the Jewish ghetto.

Löw's grave, in the most remote corner opposite the Ceremonial Hall, is one of the most popular in the cemetery; you'll see that well-wishers and the devout cram his tombstone with notes. Across the path from the rabbi is the grave of Mordechai Maisel, the 16th-century mayor of Josefov whose name was given to the nearby synagogue built during his term in office.

As you exit the cemetery on the left you'll pass the:

7 Ceremonial Hall

Inside the hall, rites for the dead were once held. Today it holds a part of the museum's permanent collection of Jewish customs and traditions, mostly relating to sickness and death.

Follow the street U Starého hřbitova back to Maiselova Street. Make a short right to find the Jewish Community Center at no. 18.

8 Jewish Community Center

This is an information and cultural center for local members of the Jewish community and their invited guests. It once was the Jewish Town Hall. Activities of interest to the community are posted here.

On the Community Center wall facing the Old-New Synagogue is a clock with a Hebrew-inscribed face. It turns left, counter to what's considered "clockwise."

Continue walking 1 block along Maiselova to find the small alley called Červená. You're now standing between two synagogues. On the right is the High Synagogue (Vysoká synagóga), closed to visitors. On your left is the:

9 Old-New Synagogue (Staronová synagóga)

Originally called the New Synagogue to distinguish it from an even older one that no longer exists, the Old-New Synagogue, built around 1270, is the oldest Jewish temple in Europe. The building has been prayed in continuously for more than 700 years, except from 1941 to 1945, during the Nazi occupation in World War II. The synagogue is also one of the largest Gothic buildings in Prague, built with vaulted ceilings and fitted with Renaissance-era columns.

Until a 19th-century planning effort raised the entire area about 3m (10 ft.), much of Josefov and Staré Město used to be flooded regularly by the Vltava. The Old-New Synagogue, however, has preserved its original floor, which you reach by going *down* a short set of stairs.

You can attend services here. Men and women customarily sit separately during services, though that's not always rigorously enforced.

At the end of Maiselova are a couple of decent refreshment options where you can have a meal and ponder the day:

WINDING DOWN

Les Moules, at Pařížská 19, is a fairly authentic Belgian tavern tossed down amid one of the fanciest parts of the Czech capital. There's good beer, mussels (of course), and a nice assortment of French-inspired hot and cold dishes. Mains run from 300Kč to 500Kč, but the daily lunch special offers better value. Around the corner, at Břechova 8, you'll find **Shelanu**, a small kosher deli (if you're more in the mood to keep the Jewish theme going). It's not exactly a deli in the New York sense, but has a refreshing mix of salads and sandwiches as well as pies and blintzes. Sandwiches run about 200Kč each. Open Sunday to Thursday 9am to 10pm, with shorter hours on Fridays and closed Saturdays. The casual atmosphere is better suited to a lunch or snack than an evening out.

Following Pařížská will lead you back to Staroměstské náměstí.

Prague Shopping

The rapid influx of visitors, wage growth, and a new consumer economy fueled by the shopping habits of the Czech nouveau riche have resulted in expensive boutiques and specialty shops burgeoning in Prague. Shopping malls now offer everything from designer baby clothes to Bruno Magli shoes. The selection of world-renowned labels is beginning to rival that of many western European cities, though shops tend to have a tiny inventory compared with the same outlets in Paris or London. Still, since labor and rent make operations cheaper here, you might find a bargain—particularly at sale time—for the same items offered at points farther west.

For those looking for a piece of Czech handiwork, you can find some of the world's best crystal and glass. Antiques shops and booksellers abound, and the selection of classical, trendy, and offbeat art is immense at the numerous private galleries. Throughout the city center you'll find quaint, obscure shops, some without phones or advertising.

1 THE SHOPPING SCENE

SHOPPING AREAS

The L-shaped half mile running from the middle of **Wenceslas Square** around the corner to the right on **Na Příkopě** and to the **Palladium Shopping Center** on **Náměstí Republiky** has become Prague's principal shopping hub. In this short distance you'll find several multilevel shopping gallerias, with foreign chains like **H&M, Next, Kenvelo, Pierre Cardin, Adidas,** and **Zara.** Between the centers is a wide array of boutiques and antiques shops.

The wide, tree-lined **Pařížská,** from Old Town Square to the Hotel Inter-Continental, has become Prague's answer to L.A.'s Rodeo Drive, filled with top-end luxury names like **Cartier, Hermes, Louis Vuitton, Hugo Boss,** and **Prada.** Along the streets running off of Pařížská, many of the best Czech designers have set up shop.

In the streets radiating off **Old Town Square,** particularly Celetná and Dlouhá, you'll find many of the city's best outlets for glass, porcelain, and jewelry. Indeed, Celetná has evolved into Prague's "glass alley."

Karlova, the street that connects the Old Town Square to Charles Bridge, is the place to go for cheap, throwaway souvenirs, like T-shirts, ball caps, and key chains. Many of the goods on offer here, such as faux "KGB" fur caps, Russian nesting dolls, and those ridiculously overpriced "Prague Drinking Team" sweatshirts, have little genuine relation to the city.

In **Malá Strana,** Nerudova street that climbs its way to the castle is filled with old book shops, art galleries, antique stores, and the usual gaggle of T-shirt and glass outlets.

Tips **How to Claim Your VAT Refund**

Recouping your tax money is easy; just follow these steps:

- When paying for your goods, ask the store for a Global Refund Cheque.
- Within 90 days of the date of purchase, present the voucher to a Czech Customs official to get a stamp. At the airport, the Customs Stamps official is located *before* Passport Control.
- Hand the stamp in *after* Passport Control to one of the Cash Refund Offices. Their staff will then refund your VAT, free of charge. Alternatively, you can use a direct crediting of a chosen credit card, or have a bank check sent to a chosen address.
- Be sure to give yourself plenty of time at the airport to handle all the formalities, including finding the offices and standing in line.

For more information, go to **www.globalrefund.com**.

HOURS & TAXES

Prague's centrally located shops rely on tourist business and keep fairly long hours. Most are open Monday to Friday from about 9am to 7pm and Saturday from 9am to 3pm, and sometimes much later. Many open on Sunday as well, though usually for a shorter time.

Prices for goods include the government's 19% value-added tax (VAT). All tourists carrying passports from outside the E.U., including Americans, Canadians, and Australians, can recoup much of this tax through VAT refund schemes. To make use of this concession, buy from stores displaying a TAX FREE sign. To qualify, the purchase price must exceed 2,000Kč, including the VAT, in 1 day in one store.

SHIPPING

Don't trust the post office when it comes to shipping valuable goods. If your package is larger than a breadbox, contact the international company **DHL** (Prague Airport; ☎ **220-300-111** or 840-103-000; www.dhl.cz). It charges around 1,960Kč for a 1-kilogram (2¼-lb.) parcel to the U.K. and 2,000Kč to the United States. You can use the DHL terminal at the Prague Airport, open Monday to Friday 8am to 6:45pm, or visit the Express Center at Václavské nám. 47 (the entrance is from Opletalova St.), open Monday to Friday 8am to 6:30pm and Saturday 9am to 3pm.

2 SHOPPING A TO Z

ANTIQUES

Antikvariát Pařížská ★ This is a musty market with valuable pieces of Czechoslovak history. Pictures, graphics, coins, medals, paper currency, and maps are on offer. Open daily from 10am to 6pm. Pařížská 8, Prague 1. ☎ **222-321-442.** Metro: Staroměstská.

Antique-Andrle Vladimír A wide selection of antique porcelain and ceramics, jewelry, and clocks distinguishes this shop. There's also a large selection of small antique

Antikvariát Pařížská **9**
Antique-Andrle Vladimír **21**
Art Deco Galerie **25**
Art Décoratif **24**
Artél **31**
Bat'a **45**
Big Ben Book Shop **19**
Boheme **17**
Bontonland Megastore **46**
Botanicus **26, 53**
Cartier **11**
Celetná Crystal **32**
Černá Růže **42**
Český Granát **16, 33**
Cristallino **29**
The Czech Museum
   of Fine Arts **22**
Dům hudebních nástrojů **48**
Dům Porcelánu Praha **56**
Dušák (Watchmaker
   and Goldsmith) **40**
Estée Lauder **28**
Galerie Art Praha **12**
Galerie Piva **2**
Globe Bookstore & Café **55**
Granát **15**
Halada **41**
Havel's Market **27**
Hermes **7**
H&M **51**
Hugo Boss **45**
Hunt Kastner Artworks **4**
Intersport **38**
Koruna Palace **47**
Kotva **20**
Kubista **30**
Moser **43, 23**
L'institute Guerlain **14**
Louis Vuitton **6**
Manu Faktura **24**
Obchod loutkami **1**
Obchodní Centrum Nový
   Smíchov **56**
Palác Flóra **58**
Palác Myslbek **39**
Palladium **35**
Prada **5**
Qubus **13**
Royal Jewelry-Zlatnictví **52**
Shakespeare & Sons **3**
Slovanský Dům **36**
Sparky's **37**
Tatiana **10**
Tesco **49**
Truhlář Marionety **17**
Ungelt Wine Shop **18**
Yves Rocher **54**
Zara **44**

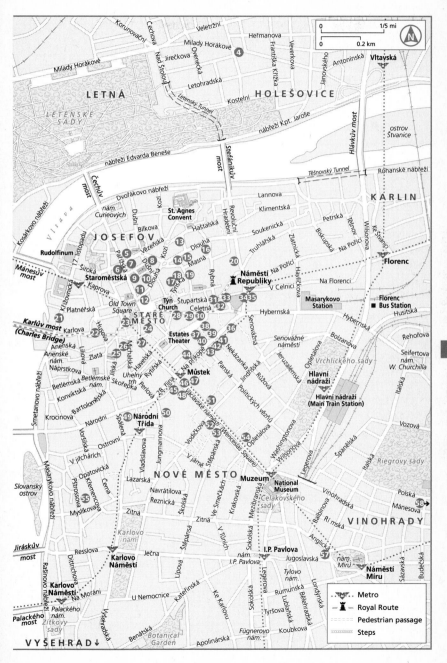

sculptures and other accessories. Open Monday to Saturday from 10am to 7pm and Sunday from 10am to 6pm. Křížovnická 1, Prague 1. © **222-311-625.** www.antiqueandrle.cz. Metro: Staroměstská.

Art Deco Galerie ★   This dandy store sells the trappings of Prague's golden age and is filled with colored perfume bottles and clothing from the 1920s and 1930s. Furniture and household items include Art Deco clocks and lamps. Open Monday to Friday from 2 to 7pm. Michalská 21, Prague 1. © **224-223-076.** Metro: Můstek.

Galerie Peron   This antiques shop is a bit unusual in that it specializes mostly in Czech modern art from the second half of the 20th century. Prices are on the high side, but the quality of the holdings is unmatched. Open Monday to Friday from 11am to 7pm, Saturday and Sunday from noon to 6pm. U Lužického semináře 12, Prague 1. © **257-533-507.** www.peron.cz. Metro: Malostranská.

ART GALLERIES

The Czech Museum of Fine Arts   This museum presents works of contemporary Czech and other Eastern European artists. Coffee-table books and catalogs with detailed descriptions in English and color reproductions usually accompany well-planned exhibitions. Open Tuesday to Sunday from 10am to 6pm. Husova 19 and 21, Prague 1. © **222-220-218.** www.cmvu.cz. Metro: Národní třída or Můstek.

Galerie Art Praha ★★   Unlike most of the shops in the vicinity of Old Town Square, this is a serious art gallery that offers innovative works from some of the best Czech and Slovak artists of the 20th century. Open daily from 10:30am to 6pm. Staroměstské nám. 20, Prague 1. © **224-211-087.** http://galerie-art-praha.cz. Metro: Staroměstská.

Hunt Kastner Artworks ★   This small, private gallery in the neighborhood behind Letná park features contemporary art from the best new Czech artists working in photography, painting, and video. Open Tuesday to Friday from 1pm to 6pm and Saturday from 2pm to 6pm. Kamenická 22, Prague 1. © **224-210-755.** www.huntkastner.com. Metro: Vltavská plus tram no. 1 or 25.

BOOKS

Big Ben Bookshop ★   Situated just opposite St. James Church in Old Town, Big Ben is a convivial spot to pick up Czech authors in translation, as well as a decent range

---

ⓘ Tips   Special Shopping Notes

In an effort to keep precious pieces of Czech heritage in the country, the government now requires export permits for a large range of objects, including glass and graphics over 50 years old, miniature art objects valued at more than 3,000Kč, and paintings valued at more than 30,000Kč. Most antiques shops provide export permits; ask for one if necessary.

In many shops, including supermarkets, customers are expected to bring their own bags. If you don't have one, ask for a taška; it'll cost about 5Kč.

(Value) Prague's Best Buys

Blood-red **garnets** are the official Czech national gem, and the ones that you can buy here are among the world's finest, as well as one of the country's top exports. Most garnets are mined near Teplice, about 63km (39 miles) northwest of Prague. There are at least five specific kinds. Bohemian garnets are the Pyrope type, an amalgam of calcium and magnesium that's almost always deep red. You can get a small necklace for as little as 700Kč or densely packed brooches or bracelets for more than 30,000Kč, depending on whether they're set in silver or gold. Be warned that fake garnets are common, so purchase your stones from a reputable shop like the ones recommended below.

Fine **crystal** has been produced in the Bohemian countryside since the 14th century. In the 17th and 18th centuries, it became the preferred glass of the world's elite, drawing royals and the rich to Karlovy Vary to buy straight from the source. The king of Siam made a fabled trip to this western Czech spa town in the 1930s just to choose place settings for his palace. Bohemian factories are responsible for artistic advances in gilding, cutting, and coloring. Today, the quality remains high, and you can still purchase contemporary glass for prices that are much lower than those in the West. See below for a list of Prague's most prominent glass retailers.

Antiques and **antiquarian books and prints** are widely available and are distinctive souvenirs, sold by specialist *antikvariáts*. For non-Czech speakers, the books will hold little appeal, but the real treasures here are old postcards, lithographs, and maps. These antiques shops are located throughout the city, but you'll find many in Old Town and Malá Strana.

Since beer is a little heavy to carry home and the local wine isn't worth it, take home a bottle of **Becherovka,** the nation's popular herbal liqueur from Karlovy Vary. You'll find the distinctive green decanter in shops around the city; it costs about 400 Kč per liter, but smaller sizes are widely available.

PRAGUE SHOPPING

9

SHOPPING A TO Z

of fiction and nonfiction. Also carries English magazines, newspapers, guidebooks, and a good selection of children's books. Open Monday to Friday from 9am to 6:30pm, Saturday 10am to 5pm, and Sunday from noon to 5pm. Malá Štupartská 5, Prague 1. © **224-826-565.** www.bigbenbookshop.com. Metro: Staroměstská.

Globe Bookstore and Cafe ★★   This beautiful bookshop in Nové Město is the current home of Prague's first English-language literary hangout (the original location was in Holešovice in Prague 7). There are lots of goodies on offer, including arguably the city's largest collection of English language literature and nonfiction (new and used). There's an adjacent large cafe, serving excellent espresso drinks and a great menu of soups, sandwiches, and small entrees. There are computers on hand to check e-mail, and the Wi-Fi is free. Open daily from 9:30am to 1am. Pštrossova 6, Prague 1. © **224-934-203.** www.globebookstore.cz. Metro: Národní třída.

Shakespeare & Sons ★   A veritable oasis of excellent English-language literature and nonfiction, including a wealth of Czech and other central European authors in translation. Though it's a tiny shop, you'll be tempted to browse for hours. The location is convenient, just off of Charles Bridge on the Malá Strana side. Open daily 11am to 7pm. U Lužického semináře, Prague 1. ✆ **257-531-894.** www.shakes.cz. Metro: Malostranská. Also at Krymská 12, Prague 10. ✆ 271-740-839. Metro: Náměstí Miru.

CRYSTAL & GLASS

Artěl ★★   American expat Karen Feldman has almost single-handedly revived interest in class Czech glass and stemware design from the 1920s and '30s. Her high-end reproductions are now sold around the world. This shop features her glass lines as well as funky, retro gifts, books, and found objects. Open daily 9am to 8pm April to December, 9am to 7pm January to March. Celetná 29 (entry from Rybná, Prague 1). ✆ **224-815-085.** www.artelglass.com. Metro: Náměstí Republiky.

Celetná Crystal ★   A wide selection of world-renowned Czech crystal, china, arts and crafts, garnets, and jewelry is displayed in a spacious three-floor showroom right in the heart of Prague. Open daily 10am to 10pm. Celetná 15, Prague 1. ✆ **222-324-022.** www. czechcrystal.com. Metro: Náměstí Republiky.

Cristallino ★   This store offers one of the largest assortments of Bohemia crystal and glass, as well as some porcelain and jewelry. Designs come from top Czech glassmakers and vary from classic patterns to modern glassware. Remember, if you're buying goods for more than 2,000Kč, ask for the Global Refund Cheque and get a stamp. Open daily 9am to 8pm April to December, 9am to 7pm January to March. Celetná 12, Prague 1. ✆ **224-225-173.** www.cristallino.cz. Metro: Náměstí Republiky.

Dům Porcelánu Prague ⟨ **Value** ⟩   Traditional Czech "onion" *(cibulák)* china is the calling card for this representative shop of the porcelain factory in Dubí near the German border. The folksy blue-on-bone cobalt onion patterns have become a familiar sight in country kitchens around the world. Open Monday to Friday from 9am to 7pm, Saturday from 9am to 5pm, and Sunday from 2 to 5pm. Jugoslávská 16, Prague 2. ✆ **221-505-320.** www.cibulak.cz. Metro: Náměstí Míru or I. P. Pavlova.

Moser ★★★   The Moser family began selling Bohemia's finest crystal in central Prague in 1857, drawing customers from around the world. Even the king of Siam made a special trip to the Karlovy Vary factory in the 1930s to pick his place settings. Soon after, the Nazis took over, and the Jewish Mosers fled. Following the war, the Communists seized the company but kept the Moser name. Surprisingly, the quality and reputation suffered little. The dark-wood showroom upstairs is well worth a look in. Open Monday to Friday from 9am to 8pm, Saturday and Sunday from 10am to 7pm. Na Příkopě 12, Prague 1. ✆ **224-211-293.** www.moser-glass.com. Metro: Náměstí Republiky.

DEPARTMENT STORES & SHOPPING MALLS

Černá Růže   This is primarily of interest for its faithfully restored, subdued 1920s Functionalist interior rather than an enticing mix of shops. Most of the stores here are second-rate clothing outlets and furniture stores, with the main exception being Moser's glamorous glass store on the second floor (see "Crystal & Glass," above). The center is open Monday to Friday 10am to 8pm, Saturday 10am to 7pm, and Sunday 11am to 7pm. Na Příkopě 12, Prague 1. ✆ **221-014-111.** www.cernaruze.cz. Metro: Můstek.

Koruna Palace   A small passage at the bottom of Wenceslas Square, Koruna Palace has an interesting mix of jewelry shops and clothing boutiques, plus the city's biggest music store, **Bontonland Megastore,** in the basement. Open Monday to Saturday from 9am to 8pm and Sunday from 10am to 8pm. Václavské nám. at Na Příkopě 1, Prague 1. ℂ 224-219-526. www.koruna-palace.cz. Metro: Můstek.

Kotva   Kotva at one time was the city's most prestigious department store. Now, with the giant Palladium shopping mall across the street, it feels more than ever like Communist-era anachronism. Still, it's a handy spot to grab everyday items like light bulbs, batteries, and shoelaces. The kiosks on the ground floor sell everything from wine and knives to watches and ground coffee. The mid-'70s Brutalism exterior is now a protected architectural monument. Open Monday to Friday from 9am to 8pm, Saturday from 10am to 7pm, and Sunday from 10am to 6pm. Náměstí Republiky 8, Prague 1. ℂ 224-801-111. www. od-kotva.cz. Metro: Náměstí Republiky.

Obchodní Centrum Nový Smíchov ★   This large Western-style shopping mall anchors the redevelopment of the once-derelict neighborhood of Smíchov around the Anděl metro stop. Nice mix of low- and high-end stores, including a larger branch of the Zara chain than you'll find in Old Town. There's a large food court and multiplex cinema on the top floor. Open daily 9am to 9pm (shops), 11am to 11pm (restaurants and entertainment). Plzeňská 8, Prague 5. ℂ 251-511-151. www.novysmichov.eu. Metro: Anděl.

Palác Flora ★   Similar to Obchodní Centrum Nový Smíchov (see above), this large shopping mall is in Vinohrady, just above the Flora metro station. Inside you will find a wide selection of shops, restaurants, and cafes and an entertainment center that includes Prague's only IMAX cinema. Open Monday to Saturday 9am to 9pm, Sunday 10am to 9pm. Vinohradská 149, Prague 3. ℂ 255-741-712. www.palacflora.cz. Metro: Flora.

Palác Myslbek   Clothing stores such as Sweden's **H&M** and Britain's **Next** are part of this atrium, as well as a number of smaller fashion names and a large sporting goods shop, **Intersport.** They're open Monday to Saturday from 9:30am to 7pm and Sunday from noon to 6pm. Na Příkopě 19-21, Prague 1. ℂ 224-835-000. www.myslbek.com. Metro: Můstek.

Palladium ★★   The city's largest and most prestigious shopping mall occupies a monumental historic building on náměstí Republiky that for centuries served as barracks for the city. Built into the original facade, five floors made of steel and glass entertain regiments of visitors in almost 200 shops and 30 restaurants. Among others, here you will find brands like Levi's, Marks & Spencer, Benetton, Guess, or Quicksilver. The food court is easily the city's best. Open daily 9am to 10pm (shops), 7am to 10pm (food store), 7am to 3am (restaurants and entertainment). Náměstí Republiky 1, Prague 1. ℂ 225-770-250. www.palladiumpraha.cz. Metro: Náměstí Republiky.

Slovanský dům ★   An attractive smaller shopping center with a few upscale names like Mexx that's chiefly prized for its handsome open-air courtyard, Kogo restaurant at the back, and multiplex cinema that shows nearly everything, including occasional Czech films in English or with English subtitles. Na Příkopě 22, Prague 1. ℂ 227-202-420. www. slovanskydum.com. Metro: Náměstí Republiky.

Tesco   U.K. retailer Tesco runs this midrange department store in the center of town, along busy Národní třída. It's a good place to find practical items, like extra socks or an umbrella, that you may have forgotten at home. The grocery store in the basement is arguably the best in the center of town. Open Monday to Friday from 8am to 9pm (food department from 7am), Saturday from 9am to 8pm (food department from 8am), and Sunday from 10am to 8pm (food department from 9am). Národní třída 26, Prague 1. ✆ **222-003-111.** Metro: Národní třída.

FASHION

Over the past few years, Prague has evolved into a decent place to buy clothing for both men and women. The area around **Wenceslas Square** and **Na Příkopě** features high-end mass market retailers like popular Spanish brand **Zara,** Na Příkopě 15, Prague 1 (✆ **224-239-860;** www.zara.com; metro: Můstek) and the ubiquitous **H&M** at Václavské nám. 19 (✆ **234-656-051),** among others. You'll find the more exclusive names along Pařížská, including **Cartier** (no. 2), **Hugo Boss** (no. 6, no. 28), **Hermes** (no. 12), **Louis Vuitton** (no. 13), and **Prada** (no. 16). Most stores along this stretch are open Monday to Friday from 9am to 7pm and on Saturdays and Sundays from 10am to 6pm.

Old Town is also home to the best Czech designers. Try **Boheme** at Dušní 8 (✆ **224-813-840;** www.boheme.cz) for stylish and well-made women's tops, dresses, and accessories. Boheme is open Monday to Friday from 11am to 7pm and Saturday from 11am to 5pm. **Tatiana** at Dušní 1 (✆ **224-813-723;** www.tatiana.cz) is less sensible, more elegant, and much more expensive. It's open Monday to Friday from 10am to 7pm and Saturday from 11am to 4pm.

GARNETS & JEWELRY

Dušák (Watchmaker and Goldsmith)   Dušák features Cartier, Gucci, Omega, Rado, and Certina chronographs and does repairs, too. Open Monday to Friday from 10am to 7pm, Saturday from 9am to 6pm, and Sunday from 1 to 6pm. Na Příkopě 17, Prague 1. ✆ **224-213-025.** www.dusak.cz. Metro: Můstek.

Granát ★   Authentic Czech garnets sourced from the original garnet veins in northern Bohemia are offered here. Prices are surprisingly reasonable; the settings, a mix of traditional and modern in both gold and silver. Open Monday to Friday from 10am to 6pm and Saturday from 10am to 1pm. Dlouhá 30, Prague 1. ✆ **222-315-612.** www.granat.eu. Metro: Staroměstská.

Halada ★   Beyond garnets, Halada has one of the best arrays of market-priced gold, silver, platinum, and fine gems in this city, which a little more than 2 decades ago used to ration wedding rings as a subsidized entitlement (no joke). Open Monday to Saturday from 9am to 7pm, Sunday 10am to 6pm. Na Příkopě 16, Prague 1. ✆ **224-218-643.** www. halada.cz. Metro: Můstek. Also at Pařížská 7, Prague 1. ✆ **222-311-868.** Metro: Staroměstská.

Royal Jewelry-Zlatnictví   The designs of the pendants and brooches sold here are some of the most unusual in the city. All items are set in 14- or 18-karat gold and range from 500Kč to about 50,000Kč and up. Open Monday to Saturday from 9am to 9pm and Sunday from 11am to 9pm. Václavské nám. 8, Prague 1. ✆ **224-222-404.** Metro: Můstek.

GIFTS & SOUVENIRS

Botanicus ★★ (Finds)   This chain of natural scent, soap, and herb shops is an amazing Anglo-Czech success story. Started by a British botanist and Czech partners on a farm northeast of Prague, Botanicus has found 101 ways to turn a plant into a sensuous gift and a lucrative trade. Open daily from 10am to 6:30pm. Týn 3 (Týnský dvůr), Prague 1. ✆ **234-767-446.** www.botanicus.cz. Metro: Staroměstská.

Manufaktura ★   Come here for one-stop shopping for authentic if eclectic Czech souvenirs, including wooden toys, natural soaps, regenerative salts, and ceramic figurines. Open daily from 10am to 6:30pm. Melantrichova 17, Prague 1. ☏ **221-632-480.** www. manufaktura.biz. Metro: Můstek.

HEALTH & BEAUTY

Prague has several studios where you can buy the best names in cosmetics as well as schedule an appointment for a facial or pedicure. **Estée Lauder,** Železná 18, Prague 1 (☏ **224-232-023;** metro: Můstek), is open Monday to Friday from 10am to 7pm and Saturday from 10am to 4pm. **Yves Rocher,** Václavské nám. 47, Prague 1 (☏ **221-625-570;** www.yvesrocher.cz; metro: Muzeum), is open Monday to Friday from 8:30am to 8pm and Saturday and Sunday from 10am to 6pm. **L'Institut Guerlain,** at Dlouhá 16, Prague 1 (☏ **227-195-330;** www.linstitut.cz; metro: Staroměstská), is open Monday to Friday 9am to 9pm, Saturday noon to 7pm.

HOME DECOR & DESIGN

Kubista ★★   Fans of Bauhaus and early Modern design will think they died and went to heaven here. The home furnishings, textiles, glassware, and jewelry mix originals and reproductions but everything here looks classy. Open daily from 10am to 8pm. Ovocný trh 19, Prague 1. ☏ **224-236-378.** www.kubista.cz. Metro: Náměstí Republiky.

Qubus ★   Qubus features funky retro furniture, lighting, and glass and furnishings with a distinctly contemporary feel from some of the best modern Czech designers. Open daily from 10am to 6pm. Rámová 3, Prague 1. ☏ **222-313-151.** www.qubus.cz. Metro: Staroměstská.

MUSIC

Bontonland Megastore   Selling everything from serious Bohemian classics to Beyoncé, the store is in the basement of the Koruna Palace, which is open Monday to Saturday from 9am to 8pm and Sunday from 10am to 7pm. Václavské nám. at Na Příkopě 1, Prague 1. ☏ **224-473-080.** www.bontonland.cz. Metro: Můstek.

MUSICAL INSTRUMENTS

Dům hudebních nástrojů (**Value**   You can buy all kinds of instruments here, from tiny harmonicas to a magnificent Petrof piano. Open Monday to Friday from 9am to 7pm, Saturday from 10am to 3pm. Jungmannovo nám. 17, Prague 1. ☏ **224-222-501.** www. guitarpark.cz. Metro: Můstek.

PHOTOGRAPHY

Jan Pazdera   Camera repairs and cheap darkroom equipment make this a Prague photo-snapper's favorite. The bulk of the selection is secondhand cameras, including Pentaxes and Russian Smenas. You can also find old telescopes, Carl Zeiss microscopes, light meters, and enlargers. Open Monday to Friday from 10am to 6pm. Vodičkova 28, pasáž ABC, Prague 1. ☏ **224-216-197.** Metro: Můstek.

SHOES

Baťa   Czechoslovakia's favorite footwear émigré, the late Tomáš Baťa, made his post-Communist return with a vengeance, taking a sizable chunk of the market long after the Nazis and then the Communists cut the original Moravian family factory to pieces. His

---

> **Value**   **An Open-Air Market**
>
> On the short, wide street perpendicular to Melantrichova, between Staroměstské náměstí and Václavské náměstí, Havel's Market (Havelský trh; no, not named after former president Václav Havel), Havelská ulice, Prague 1, features dozens of private vendors selling seasonal homegrown fruits and vegetables at decent prices for the city center. Other goods, including detergent, flowers, and cheap souvenirs, are also for sale. Open Monday to Friday from 8am to 6pm. Take metro line A or B to Můstek.

huge outlet on the site where his father started selling shoes earlier this century on Wenceslas Square has been remodeled for modern comfort. Baťa goods include travel bags, leather accessories, sports outfits, and top-line brands of athletic shoes. Open Monday to Friday from 9am to 9pm, Saturday from 9am to 8pm, and Sunday from 10am to 8pm. Václavské nám. 6, Prague 1. ✆ **221-088-472.** www.bata.cz. Metro: Můstek.

SPORTING GOODS

Intersport   With row upon row of clothes and equipment, Intersport is Prague's mega–sporting goods retailer. However, the prices aren't much better than what you'd find abroad, and the company's overzealous security staff forces you to park all your belongings in cubbyholes (you have to have correct change to use them). Open daily from 9:30am to 7pm. Palác Myslbek, Na Příkopě 19, Prague 1. ✆ **221-088-093.** www.intersport. cz. Metro: Můstek.

TOYS & PUPPETS

Obchod loutkami (**Kids**)   Although there are no ventriloquist dummies, many kinds of puppets are available here, including hand, glove, rod, and marionettes. Obchod loutkami isn't cheap, but its creations are expertly made and beautifully sculpted. Hundreds of characters from trolls to barmen are available in the store as well as online. Open daily from 10am to 8pm. Nerudova 47, Prague 1. ✆ **257-532-735.** www.marionettes.cz. Metro: Malostranská.

Sparky's ★★ (**Kids**)   This toy store in the center of the city is a welcoming spot for the whole family. The younger ones will find terrific souvenirs of Prague here. Open Monday to Saturday from 10am to 7pm, Sunday to 6pm. Havířská 2 (short street btw. Na Příkopě and the Estates' Theater), Prague 1. ✆ **224-239-309.** www.sparkys.cz. Metro: Můstek.

Truhlář Marionety ★★ (**Kids**)   With handmade wooden marionettes from timeless classic designs that date back to the Middle Ages, Truhlář Marionety is not cheap but worth every penny for an authentic souvenir. Open daily from 10am to 8pm. Týnskýdvůr 1, Prague 1. ✆ **224-895-437.** www.marionety.com Metro: Staroměstská.

WINE & BEER

Wine, beer, and Becherovka are sold in shops all over Prague, but one of the cheapest places to buy them is **Tesco** (see "Department Stores & Shopping Malls," above). Expect to pay about 300Kč for a medium bottle of Becherovka and 150Kč for six bottles of Budvar.

The **Ungelt Wine Shop** (© **224-895-449**), Týnský dvůr 5, Prague 1, offers a large
and high-quality selection of domestic and foreign wines. It's open daily 11am to 10pm.

You can find beer everywhere, but locating specialty beers from smaller brewers around the country can be a problem. **Galerie Piva** at Lázeňská 15, Prague 1, sells beer by the bottle from around the country, including Primátor's hard to find but worth the search 16-degree lager. Open daily 10am to 6pm.

Prague After Dark

For many Czechs, the best way to spend an evening is at the neighborhood pub, enjoying world-class beer and some boisterous conversation. These types of evenings are always open to visitors, of course, though the language may occasionally be an issue (at least at the start of the night before the beer kicks in).

If raucous beer nights are not your thing, Prague offers plenty of other diversions. The contemporary music scene is alive and kicking, and clubs all across town offer live acts or DJs playing rock, indie, techno, hip-hop, or whatever trend is popular at the moment. Prague has also developed into a popular stop for visiting international acts, both large and small. One recent summer night saw British new waver Morrissey, B. B. King, and U.S. rocker Joe Jackson all play separate gigs at venues across town. See the ticket agencies (see below) for shows that might be in town during your visit.

Jazz, too, has enjoyed a long tradition in the Czech lands from the early decades of the 20th century when American jazzmen were played on gramophones on imported vinyl. You'll find no fewer than six decent jazz clubs in the city center (listed later) and the quality of the playing is high.

Czechs are avid theatergoers and Prague for decades has enjoyed a vibrant drama scene (though with nearly all of the output in Czech, much of this sadly is inaccessible to visitors). Occasionally the National Theater will subtitle in English important works aimed at an international audiences, and theaters like Švandovo divadlo in Smíchov and Divadlo Archa in Nové Město sometimes stage English and American productions in their original language.

Opera is more accessible and Prague has at least two premier venues: the State Opera at the top of Wenceslas Square (Václavské nám.) and the National Theater. The former's repertoire is made up largely of Italian classics, while the latter frequently holds performances of works by national composers like Bedřich Smetana and Leoš Janáček. Both theaters are good value and tickets are often available at short notice, though the quality will vary from show to show.

Prague's longest-running entertainment tradition, of course, is classical music. Serious music lovers are best advised to take in a performance of the **Czech Philharmonic** at the Rudolfinum in Staré Město or the **Prague Symphony Orchestra** at the Obecní dům, near Náměstí Republiky. Another option is to see one of the many **chamber concerts** offered at churches and palaces around town. These can be very good, though ticket prices are often higher than for the Philharmonic and the quality may not be nearly as good.

If you're getting tired just reading about all of these entertainment possibilities, there's always the option of a good dinner followed by a quiet stroll over the Charles Bridge and through Malá Strana over ancient cobblestones and lit by mellow gas lamps.

TICKETS Cultural events are surprisingly affordable and accessible, and except for a few high-profile performances at the National Theater or the Prague Spring Music Festival, they rarely sell out. To check on schedules and secure tickets before arriving, surf the websites of the various venues you might want to visit. That will at least give you an idea of what's happening while you're here. Many venues now allow you to purchase tickets directly online with a credit card and pick them up at the box office once you get here.

You can also buy tickets ahead of your visit through the websites of major ticketing agencies, all of which have English-language pages and are geared up to serve incoming visitors. The major local agencies include **Ticketpro** (www.ticketpro.cz), **Bohemia Ticket** (www.bohemiaticket.cz), **Ticket Stream** (http://web.ticketstream.cz), and **Ticket Portal** (www.ticketportal.cz). These sites have the advantage of aggregating all of the events and highlighting the biggest shows that will be on during your visit. They also offer services that the individual box offices usually do not provide, such as delivering the tickets to your hotel room on arrival—though they levy a surcharge for the service.

Once in town, you have several options for sourcing tickets. The simplest and often cheapest option is to go directly to the venue box office. Most box offices hold normal working hours on weekdays and usually open again an hour or so before performances in the evenings. If you're intimidated by the language issue at the box office, simply write down what you want to see and the dates and number of tickets you need; the person behind the window will sort it out from there.

Another easy way to get tickets once you're in Prague is to visit one of the local ticket agency offices and buy the tickets in person. The man or woman behind the counter is likely to have a good idea of the biggest events happening on that day or in the coming days and provide good advice. Pay in cash or with a credit card. **Ticketpro** has several offices around town, including at **Prague Information Services** (© 221-714-444; www.pis.cz) offices at the Old Town Hall and at Rytířská 31. Ticketpro also sells tickets at Václavské nám. 38, Prague 1 (© 296-329-999), and through the helpful **Prague Tourist Center,** near the Můstek metro stop at Rytířská 12, Prague 1 (© 296-333-333), open daily from 9am to 8pm. **Bohemia Ticket** has offices at Na Příkopě 16, Prague 1 (© 224-215-031; www.bohemiaticket.cz) and is open Monday to Friday from 10am to 7pm, Saturday from 10am to 5pm, and Sunday from 10am to 3pm.

1 THE PERFORMING ARTS

Mozart reportedly shocked the Viennese when he once scoffed at his Austrian patrons, claiming that "Praguers understand me." His trips to the outpost in the Austrian Empire became the subject of music folklore. His defiant 1787 premiere of *Don Giovanni* is the high watermark in Prague's cultural history—not that there haven't been fine performances since. Czech composers Antonín Dvořák and Bedřich Smetana each moved the resurgent nation to tears in the 19th century, while Bohuslav Martinů and Leoš Janáček ushered in a new industrial-age sound to classical compositions in the first half of the 20th century. You can still hear many works in grand halls throughout Prague; they're worth a visit just to immerse yourself in the grandeur of the setting, let alone the musical accompaniment.

OPERA

Prague is a great opera town, though the standards don't quite reach New York, London, or Vienna levels. The good news is that opera here is much more affordable and tickets

PRAGUE AFTER DARK

10

THE PERFORMING ARTS

Agharta Jazz Centrum **20**
Baráčnická rychta **2**
Blues Sklep **30**
Bugsy's **14**
Chapeau Rouge **22**
Chez Marcel **19**
Church of St. Nicholas
 (Malá Strana) **1**
Church of St. Nicolas
 (Staré Město) **13**
Divadlo Archa **26**
Divadlo Ponel **40**
Duplex Club & Café **39**
Estates' Theater **21**
Fraktal **9**
Hapu **50**
Jáma **42**
JazzDock **5**
Karlovy Lázně **28**
Kino Aero **48**
Kino Suetozor **38**
Klementinum **12**
Klub Termix **51**
Kolkovna **16**
Laterna Magika **35**
Lávka **27**
Lucerna Music Bar **40**
Mecca **8**
Molly Malone's **17**
Municipal House
 (Smetana Hall) **24**
National Marionette
 Theater **11**
National Theater **34**
Nový Smíhov multiplex **6**
Palác Akropolis **52**
Palác Flóra **53**
Radost FX **45**
Reduta Jazz Club **37**
Rocky O'Reilly's **43**
Roxy **18**
Rudolfinum **10**
Saints Bar **54**
SaSaZu **9**
Slovanský Dům **23**
Sport Bar Praha **44**
State Opera House **47**
Švandovo Divadlo **4**
Theater on the Balustrade **29**
Tlustá Koala **25**
Tretter's **15**
U Fleků **41**
U Malého Glena **3**
U medvídků **36**
U staré paní **13**
U Vejvodů **29**
U zlatého tygra **28**
Valentino **55**
Vinohrady Theater **46**

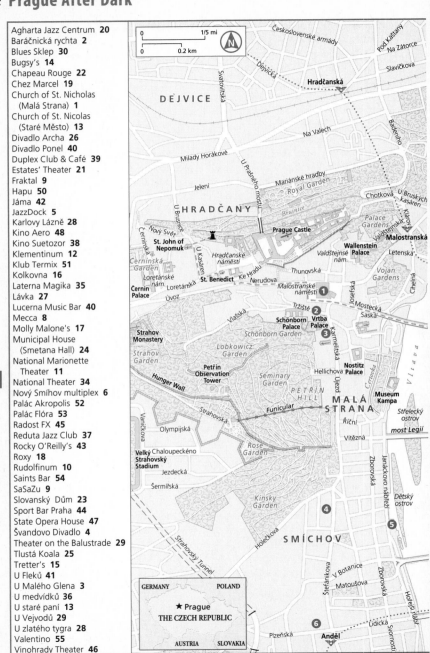

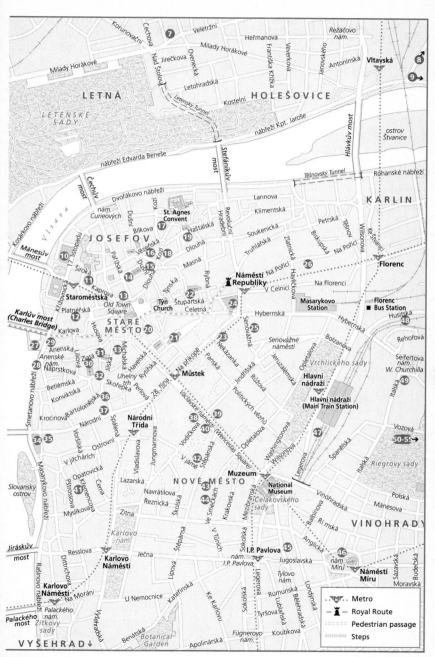

are usually easier to get. Prices at the State Opera, for example, range from 200Kč up to 1,150Kč for the best seat in the house.

Prague has three main venues for opera. The primary stage is the **Prague State Opera (Státní opera Praha),** at the top of Wenceslas Square, situated in a beautiful neo-Renaissance building blighted only by its unfortunate location across a major highway from the square. To find it, look to the left of the National Museum beside a modern building that used to house the headquarters of Prague-based Radio Free Europe.

The State Opera's repertoire is focused mainly on Italian classics, though a few Czech favorites are included each season. These are highly enjoyably performances, though local critics have been tough on the opera in recent years, calling its staging of Puccini's *Tosca,* for example, solid but staid and without sufficient emotion. Verdi's works like *La Traviata* and *Aïda* have also received mixed reviews.

The **National Theater (Národní divadlo)** is also a prime opera venue. This is home to the **National Opera,** and as you might expect the repertoire leans more toward home-grown productions such as Smetana's peppy *Prodaná nevěsta (The Bartered Bride)* or Janáček's inscrutable but interesting *Kát'a Kabanová.* The choreography is fun for the whole family, and explanations of the plot are provided in English. Once in a while, internationally acclaimed soloists stop by.

A third main venue, **The Estates' Theater (Stavovské divadlo)** ★, is wholly affiliated with the National Theater and as such mostly focuses on dramatic works performed in Czech. During some summers, however, private troupes put on performances of Mozart's *Don Giovanni* aimed primarily at tourists and these are worth looking out for. Other times of year, the theater occasionally stages wonderful and rare works of baroque opera.

See "Landmark Theaters & Concert Halls," below, for contact and ticketing details for the theaters discussed here.

CLASSICAL MUSIC

Prague is truly a great city for classical music, and a trip here is a rare chance to hear works by Czech composers such as Antonín Dvořák or Bedřich Smetana and other central Europeans performed in their natural setting.

The capital boasts three full orchestras and a virtual army of smaller chamber groups that perform regularly in churches and palaces around town. On any given day during the season (Sept–May) there may be as many as a dozen classical performances going on.

The high point of the classical music season is the annual **Prague Spring Music Festival** (www.festival.cz), which draws performers and music fans from around the world to Prague for 2 weeks from mid-May until the beginning of June. The main performances are held at the Art Nouveau **Smetana Hall** at the **Municipal House (Obecní dům;** see "Landmark Theaters & Concert Halls," below), though concerts are held at other venues around town. Tickets for festival concerts range from 400Kč to more than 3,000Kč and are available in advance through Ticketpro or in person at Hellichova 18, Prague 1 (© **257-310-414;** www.festival.cz).

The country's main orchestra, the **Czech Philharmonic** (www.ceskafilharmonie.cz), has an international reputation and performs at the stunning neo-Renaissance **Rudolfinum** in Staré Město. The Philharmonic has gone through some turbulent years in the recent past and as this book was being researched, it was currently without a conductor. Nevertheless, the performances are of a high standard and programs usually include at least one regional composer you're not likely to hear during a visit to your hometown

> ## (Tips) Dressing the Part
>
> Czechs generally are a casual live-and-let-live people. Ex-president Havel, who had collected an extensive official wardrobe, is etched in everyone's memory as the dissident playwright wearing old frayed sweaters. Journalists often show up for news conferences with the president or the prime minister in T-shirts. But if you plan on attending the opera or theater, **proper evening wear is highly recommended.** There may be no worse faux pas in Bohemia than dressing bohemian for a classical performance. For men: a dark suit or at least a coat and tie. For women: a midlength dress or pants.

symphony. Tickets range from around 400Kč to 600Kč for the best seats. For more on the venue and ticketing, see "Landmark Theaters & Concert Halls," below.

The Philharmonic's main rival, the **Prague Symphony Orchestra,** known locally by the initials **"FOK"** (www.fok.cz), has positioned itself as a fresher alternative, with a frequently livelier and more daring repertoire, and many more modern composers on the roster. The FOK performs regularly at the **Smetana Hall** of the **Municipal House (Obecní dům),** and this is where you'll find the company's box office and scheduling information.

The **Prague Radio Symphony Orchestra** is primarily a studio band but does make regular concert appearances. The group plays sufficiently good versions of classical and contemporary works in the Rudolfinum or Obecní dům.

Two solo Czech violinists to look out for when booking your tickets: the veteran virtuoso **Josef Suk,** a great-grandson of Dvořák, who still plays with crisp, if not exact, precision; and his flashier heir apparent, **Václav Hudeček,** who attacks every stanza with passion and bleeds through his bow.

CHURCH CONCERTS

In the years since the Velvet Revolution, Prague has developed a rapidly growing cottage industry of informal church concerts. Initially, these concerts were performed by music students and journeymen musicians as a way of picking up some spare cash. Nowadays, church concerts are big business and wherever you go, you're likely to see posters and flyers advertising the next extravaganza, featuring well-known and popular composers like Bach, Handel, Vivaldi and, naturally, Mozart.

Church concerts can be great when done well and a real treat, combining a lovely baroque setting with music that was composed precisely for that kind of setting. However, like many other things in Prague's tourist world, caveat emptor. Ticket prices for these informal church concerts have crept up so high in recent years, anywhere from 200Kč to 500Kč, that the more expensive concerts now cost as much as or more than a good seat at the Czech Philharmonic, and the quality of the playing is likely to be vastly inferior.

Be wary of touts, often dressed like Mozart and offering a menu of concerts, or aggressive promoters that seem more intent on getting you in the door than delivering a quality performance. The venues listed below can be counted on to hold concerts that provide good value for money.

PRAGUE AFTER DARK

10

THE PERFORMING ARTS

Because of its extravagant beauty, the **Chapel of Mirrors** ★ in the Klementinum, Mariánské náměstí 5, Prague 1 (✆ **222-220-879;** www.klementinum.com), is a favorite chamber concert venue. Almost every evening a classical concert highlights strings, winds, or the organ.

The Church of St. Nicholas (Kostel sv. Mikuláše), Staroměstské náměstí, Prague 1 (✆ **224-190-994**), is one of the city's finest baroque gems. Chamber concerts and organ recitals are popular here, usually starting in the late afternoon, and the acoustics are terrific. There's also a lot to look at: rich stucco decoration, sculptures of saints, and a crown crystal chandelier.

Prague's *other* **Church of St. Nicholas (Chrám sv. Mikuláše),** in Malá Strana, at Malostranské náměstí 1 (✆ **257-534-215;** www.psalterium.cz), is another beautiful baroque venue for early evening concerts. The music normally starts at 6pm and runs about 60 minutes. Admission costs 490Kč for adults, and 300Kč for students.

DANCE

Of all the musical arts in Prague, dance is the most accessible. From classical ballet to innovative modern dance, there are several options each week that demonstrate an enjoyable mix of grace, beauty, and athleticism. The **National Theater Ballet** troupe has seen most of its top talent go west, but it still has a deep roster as the country's premier troupe. Beyond the classical favorites at the venerable National Theater's main stage, the ballet's choreographer, Libor Vaculík, has come up with dance twists on films like *Some Like It Hot* and *Psycho* next door at the modern, comfortable theater-in-the-round, Nová scéna. Vaculík's works are popular, making this one of the most financially secure dance companies in Eastern Europe. Tickets range from 200Kč to 550Kč and are available from the National Theater box office (see below for details).

Divadlo Ponec ★, at Husitská 24a (✆ **222-721-531;** www.divadloponec.cz) in the outlying district of Žižkov, is home to more progressive modern dance and each year in June hosts the city's popular Tanec Praha modern dance festival. Performances are held most nights of the week and tickets cost around 200Kč. You can buy them through Ticketpro or at the theater box office (open Mon–Fri 5–8pm as well as 1 hr. before performances).

LANDMARK THEATERS & CONCERT HALLS

The Czech Philharmonic at Rudolfinum (Moments) Named for Habsburg Prince Rudolf, the beautifully restored Rudolfinum has been one of the city's premier concert venues since it opened in the 19th century. The Rudolfinum's Small Hall mostly presents chamber concerts, while the larger, more celebrated Dvořák Hall is home to the Czech Philharmonic. Though the acoustics aren't faultless, the grandeur of the hall makes a concert experience here worthwhile.

Alšovo nábřeží 12, Prague 1. ✆ 227-059-227 (box office open Mon–Fri 10am–6pm). www.ceskafilharmonie.cz. Metro: Staroměstská.

Estates' Theater (Stavovské divadlo) ★★ In a city full of spectacularly beautiful theaters, the massive pale-green Estates' still ranks as one of the most awesome. Built in 1783, the Estates' was home to the premiere of Mozart's *Don Giovanni,* which was conducted by the composer himself. The building, an example of the late baroque style, was reopened on the 200th anniversary of Mozart's death in 1991, after nearly 9 years of reconstruction. The theater hosts mainly dramas performed in Czech but occasionally has performances of Don Giovanni for tourists and also puts on very worthwhile baroque opera. Buy tickets at the National Theater box office (see below).

Ovocný trh 1, Prague 1. ✆ **224-901-448.** www.narodni-divadlo.cz. Metro: Line A or B to Můstek.

National Theater (Národní divadlo) ★★ This neo-Renaissance building overlooking the Vltava River was completed in 1881. The theater was built to nurture the Czech National Revival—a grassroots movement to replace the dominant German culture with that of native Czechs. To finance it, small collection boxes with signs promoting "the prosperity of a dignified national theater" were installed in public places. Almost immediately upon its completion, the building was wrecked by fire; it was rebuilt and opened in 1883 with the premiere of Bedřich Smetana's opera *Libuše*. The magnificent interior contains an allegorical sculpture about music and busts of Czech theatrical personalities as well as paintings created by Czech artists of the National Theater generation—Myslbek, Aleš, Hynais. Composer Bedřich Smetana conducted the theater's orchestra here until 1874, when deafness forced him to relinquish his post. Today, the theater plays host to a demanding repertoire of drama, opera, and ballet.

Národní 2, Prague 1. ✆ **224-901-448** (box office open daily 10am–6pm). www.narodni-divadlo.cz. Metro: Národní třída.

Prague Symphony Orchestra–Smetana Hall (Smetanova síň) ★★ Named for the popular composer and fervent Czech nationalist Bedřich Smetana (1824–84), Smetana Hall is an Art Nouveau gem. Since its reopening after the building's painstaking reconstruction, the ornate and purely exhilarating Smetana Hall has held a series of varied and top-notch musical events, and each May hosts the Prague Spring Music Festival.

In the Municipal House (Obecní dům), Náměstí Republiky 5, Prague 1. ✆ **222-002-336** (box office open Mon–Fri 10am–6pm). www.fok.cz. Metro: Náměstí Republiky.

State Opera House (Státní opera) ★ First called the "New German Theater" and then the "Smetana Theater," the State Opera was built in the 1880s for the purpose of staging Germanic music and drama. Based on a Viennese design, the Renaissance-style theater was rebuilt after suffering serious damage during the bombing of Prague in 1945. Over the years, the auditorium has hosted many great names, including Richard Wagner, Richard Strauss, and Gustav Mahler, whose Seventh Symphony premiered here. In addition to being home to the State Opera, the house stages other music and dance events. Buy tickets through Bohemia Ticket or at the theater box office.

Wilsonova 4, Prague 2. ✆ **224-227-266** (box office open Mon–Fri 10am–5:30pm; Sat–Sun 10am–noon and 1–5:30pm). www.opera.cz. Metro: Muzeum.

THEATERS

Drama has a long tradition in Czech life. Its enormous influence was reconfirmed during the revolutionary events of 1989, when theaters became the focal points and strategy rooms for the opposition.

Most of the city's theater offerings are in Czech, but a few English-language expatriate troupes have taken root and stage performances whenever they are ready—or not—at various locations. Check *The Prague Post* (on newsstands or at www.praguepost.com) for the latest listings.

Czech productions by local and translated authors are staged almost every night. The most highly respected theaters are the gorgeous **Vinohrady Theater (Divadlo na**

Vinohradech), Náměstí Míru 7, Prague 2 (℃ **224-257-601;** www.dnv-praha.cz), the former workplace of ex-president Václav Havel's wife, Dagmar, who made a final performance as Queen Kristina soon after becoming first lady. The **Theater on the Balustrade (Divadlo Na Zábradlí),** Anenské nám. 5, Prague 1 (℃ **222-868-868;** www.nazabradli. cz), is the place where Havel got his start as a playwright. Tickets, usually costing between 100Kč and 250Kč, should be bought in advance. Simultaneous translation into English is sometimes offered through earphones provided by the theaters, but the translator reads all parts from a script (usually without much dramatic verve). Ask when booking if translation is offered.

Two Prague theaters deserve special mention for their unusual commitment to performing dramatic works in their original language, including occasional English and American plays. They also both regularly schedule engaging concerts, performance-art pieces, and dance, and are worth checking out during your visit. **Divadlo Archa** ★★ is at Na Poříčí 26 in Nové Město, Prague 1 (℃ **221-716-333;** www.archatheatre.cz). The box office is open Monday to Friday from 10am to 6pm and performances usually start at 8pm.

The second theater, **Švandovo divadlo** ★★, at Štefánikova 57 in Smíchov, Prague 5 (℃ **257-318-666;** www.svandovodivadlo.cz), focuses on international dramatic works and dance and all performances in the main hall are subtitled in English. The box office is open Monday to Friday from 11am to 7pm, Saturday and Sunday 5 to 7pm.

Laterna Magika   This performance-art show based in the newer wing of the National Theater stages a range of multimedia productions, from a provocative, racy version of *Odysseus* to a choppy, inconsistent version of *Casanova,* but the stunning presence of the lead female lights up the stage. These are adult themes combining unique uses of dance, music, film, and light and can be very entertaining and easy to follow for audiences of any language.

Národní třída 4, Prague 1. ℃ **224-931-482.** www.laterna.cz. Box office open Mon–Sat from 10am–8pm. Tickets 680Kč; should be bought in advance. Metro: Národní třída.

National Marionette Theater (Národní divadlo marionet)   This is the best of Prague's handful of puppet theaters. The company's mainstay for years has been Mozart's *Don Giovanni.* It's entertaining, but you might want to bone up on the opera's storyline beforehand so that you have a better idea of what's going on.

Žatecká 1, Prague 1. ℃ **224-819-322.** www.mozart.cz. Tickets 590Kč. Metro: Staroměstská.

2 THE CLUB & MUSIC SCENE

The Velvet Revolution had its roots in the underground rock clubs that kept the youth tuned into something more than the monotones of the Communist Party during the gray 1970s and 1980s period known as "normalization." The Communists' persecution of the Czech garage band Plastic People of the Universe, named for a Frank Zappa refrain, motivated playwright Václav Havel and his friends to keep the human rights heat on the Politburo. As president, Havel paid homage to rock's part in the revolution and kept company with the likes of Zappa, Springsteen, Dylan, and the Stones—all of whom paid tribute to him as "the rock-'n'-roll president."

(Moments) Prague's Mysterious Nights

If you've never been here, Steven Soderbergh's 1991 film *Kafka* (widely available on DVD), starring Jeremy Irons, will give you a fine sense of the dark mystery trapped in the shadows cast over the palace walls and cobblestone streets throughout Old Town and Malá Strana. You'll never forget a slow stroll across Charles Bridge, with its dim lampposts (gas lamps are just being reinstalled here) cutting eerie silhouettes from the attendant statues. The artfully lit facades of Prague Castle hover above as if the whole massive complex is floating in the darkness. The domes and spires of the skyline leading up to Hradčany have more varied textures and contours than a Dutch master could ever have dreamed of painting. On warm evenings students singing with a guitar, or a violinist playing his heart out for a few koruny in his hat, create the bridge's ambient sound.

Evenings are also a fine time to walk through the castle courtyards; as the crowds disperse, a quiet solemnity falls over the city. From high atop the castle hill, you can see Prague sparkling below.

Across the river, the brightly lit belfries of Týn Church cast a spine-tingling glow on the rest of Old Town Square, and the mellow lamps around the Estates' Theater provide light for a memorable walk home after a performance.

Almost universally, the amps in clubs are turned up to absurd distortion. But while most wannabe bands playing Prague today lack the political edge of the pre-revolution days, some have kept their unique Slavic passion without slavishly copying international trends. Some bands to watch out for include hard rockers Kabát, the trendy folk band Čechomor, or pop acts like Kryštof, Chinaski, and Support Lesbiens.

ROCK & DANCE CLUBS

Duplex   Located in the heart of Wenceslas Square, this is one of Prague's more exclusive clubs. From the roof terrace, visitors enjoy a magnificent view of the city's very center. Prague's best DJs perform inside the club itself, where cool lighting and high-tech sound set the right atmosphere. Yes, it was here that Mick Jagger had his 60th birthday party during the Stones' fourth concert in Prague. Still, prices remain relatively reasonable for downtown. It's open daily 10:30pm to 3am (Fri–Sat until 5am).

Václavské nám. 21, Prague 1. (℃ **732-221-111.** www.duplex.cz. Admission 150Kč. Metro: Můstek.

Karlovy Lázně   This multilevel club has been around for several years and is getting a little long in the tooth, yet it still manages to draw huge lines out front after midnight of mostly university-age students clamoring to get inside to dance. The building consists of several floors of music, with each level having a different theme, with R&B on one level, disco on another, and so on. You get the idea. The club is open daily 9pm to 5am.

Smetanovo nábřeží 198 at Novotného lávka, Prague 1. (℃ **222-220-502.** www.karlovylazne.cz. Cover 150Kč. Metro: Staroměstská.

Klub Lávka   This classic late-night meat-market dance club has been around since shortly after the Velvet Revolution. It's actually a lot of fun if you're in the mood for it, and the crowd is a good mix of Czechs and visitors. The setting couldn't be lovelier, on a jetty that extends into the river just south of the Charles Bridge, with castle views to die for. For hard-core partyers the good news is that Klub Lávka is open late, and the music goes on until 5am.

Novotného lávka 1, Prague 1. ✆ **221-082-299.** www.lavka.cz. Cover 100Kč. Metro: Staroměstská.

Lucerna Music Bar ★   Big and a bit dingy, this Prague landmark in the belly of the downtown palace built by Václav Havel's father provides the best lineup of Czech garage bands, ex-underground acts, and an occasional reggae or blues gig. The drinks are still cheap for the city center. The crowd is mostly local and the biggest draws are the wildly popular '80s- and '90s-themed dance nights on Fridays and Saturdays. Open daily from 8pm to 3am, with live music usually beginning at 9pm.

Vodičkova 36, Prague 1. ✆ **224-217-108.** www.musicbar.cz. Cover 50Kč–150Kč. Metro: Můstek.

Mecca   For those who don't mind trekking into the depths of Prague 7 to be with some of the trendiest people in town, make your way to Mecca. You don't have to pray to the east to get in, but you'd better be one of the beautiful people, dressed well enough to get by the bouncers at the usually packed entrance. This converted warehouse in northeast Prague has been one of the most popular discos in town for several years now and shows no signs of letting up. Open Wednesday to Saturday 11am to 5am.

U Průhonu 3, Prague 7. ✆ **283-870-522.** www.mecca.cz. Cover 190Kč–290Kč, women enter free on Wed. Metro: Vltavská, then tram no. 1.

Palác Akropolis ★★   This reconverted cinema in Žižkov is Prague's premier venue for club-level live rock and world music acts. Brings in a surprisingly good roster of bands, including in recent years The Flaming Lips, the Strokes, and many more. The main concert hall, the old screening room, is makeshift and still feels kind of edgy after all these years. The back room doubles as a bar and a DJ room, with dancing going on into the wee hours long after the concert's over.

Kubelíkova 27, Prague 3. ✆ **296-330-911.** www.palacakropolis.cz. Cover 100Kč–250Kč, depending on the show. Metro: Jiřího z Poděbrad.

Radost FX   This was one of the first big dance clubs to open up after the Velvet Revolution and, surprisingly, it's still here and still going strong. The ground-floor vegetarian restaurant and café are mainstays of the neighborhood dining scene (p. 102), and the trendy downstairs club draws a mixed straight and gay crowd for themed dance nights. Open daily from 10pm to 5am.

Bělehradská 120, Prague 2. ✆ **224-254-776.** www.radostfx.cz. Cover 150Kč–250Kč. Metro: I. P. Pavlova.

Roxy   Another dance club and live music venue in a reconverted theater, Roxy pushes the boundaries of bizarre in its dark, stark dance hall down Dlouhá Street, near Old Town Square. Acid jazz, funk, techno, salsa, and reggae are among the tunes on the playlist. The list of acts, including The Hives, Asian Dub Foundation, and Franz Ferdinand, among others, is legendary. Bands usually hit the stage early because of noise restrictions, but the party goes on until the wee hours.

Dlouhá 33, Prague 1. ✆ **224-826-296.** www.roxy.cz. Cover 100Kč–250Kč. Metro: Staroměstská.

SaSaZu ★ This was far and away Prague's hottest club opening in 2009, bolstering Holešovice's claim to being the go-to district for nighttime fun. A cavernous dance club shares a name and space with an excellent Asian restaurant, meaning it's possible to slide right from dinner to the dance floor. Open daily from 11am to 3am.
Bubenské nábřeží 306, Prague 7. 🕐 **284-097-455.** www.sasazu.com. Cover from 150Kč–1,000Kč-plus, depending on the act. Metro: Vltavská, then tram no. 1, 25.

JAZZ

While Dixieland swing was huge in Prague during the 1920s and '30s, urban jazz really made its mark here during the 1960s, when those testing Communist authority flocked to the smoky caves and wore dark glasses. The chubby Czech songstress Vlasta Průchová grabbed a few hints from Ella Fitzgerald with her throaty voice and set the standard for Czech be-bop wannabes in the postwar period leading up to the Prague Spring. After defecting, her son Jan Hammer made it big in the United States with his computerized scores, among them the theme for the classic '80s TV hit *Miami Vice.*

Luckily, most of Prague's ensembles follow Vlasta's lead and not Jan's. There are several good venues for a cool evening with a traditional upright bass, piano, sax, and drum group or occasional shots of fusion and acid jazz. Probably the most publicized local gig of all time happened at the Reduta Jazz Club in 1994, when Bill Clinton showed up to play "Summertime" and "My Funny Valentine" for then-President Havel during a state visit.

U Malého Glena, listed under "Pubs," below, also offers jazz, fusion, and sometimes funk on most nights in its cellar. Try to go on a Sunday night, when they have a kind of local open-mic night and you never know who's going to show up. Some nights the best jazzmen in town turn up for an impromptu gig.

AghaRTA Jazz Centrum ★ Upscale by Czech standards, the AghaRTA regularly features some of the best music in town, from standard acoustic trios and quartets to Dixieland, funk, and fusion. Hot Line, the house band led by AghaRTA part-owner and drummer Michal Hejna, regularly takes the stage. Bands usually begin at 9pm, but try to come much earlier to snag one of the few places to sit. Open daily from 7pm to midnight. Železná 16, Prague 1. 🕐 **222-211-275.** www.agharta.cz. Cover 250Kč. Metro: Můstek.

Blues Sklep A relative and welcome newcomer to Prague's jazz scene, the Blue Sklep (Blues Cellar) focuses not surprisingly on the blues, bringing in bands and singers from around central Europe. Open daily from 7pm to 2:30am. Liliová 10, Prague 1. 🕐 **774-277-060.** http://bluessklep.cz. Cover 150Kč. Metro: Národní třída.

Jazz Dock ★★ One of the hottest openings in 2009 was this riverside jazz club in Smíchov bringing together a lineup of some of central Europe's best jazz, blues, and soul singers, along with good food and beautiful views out over the river. The club is big enough to give at least some of the tables good sightlines to the stage (unlike lots of other clubs in Prague); at the same time, it's small enough to be intimate. If you're looking for a romantic night of music and a view, this is your place. Concerts begin around 9pm. Open daily from 11am to 4am. Janáčkovo nábřeží 2, Prague 5. 🕐 **774-058-838.** Cover 150Kč. Metro: Anděl.

Reduta Jazz Club ★ Reduta has been around since the 1950s and still has a kind of welcoming retro feel, as if Charlie Parker or Miles himself might walk in at some point during the night. The club brings in basically the same mix of performers that the other clubs do, and standards here most nights are pretty high. The music usually starts around 9:30pm. Open daily from 9pm to midnight. Národní 20, Prague 1. ✆ **224-933-487**. www. redutajazzclub.cz. Cover 150Kč. Metro: Národní třída.

USP Jazz Lounge/U staré paní   Some of the best bands perform on this small stage downstairs from an overpriced pension in the middle of Old Town. The jazz is wonderfully close to most every table in this club, which is both visually pleasant and acoustically superior. Noted local jazzman Karel Růžička and his band play here frequently. Concerts begin at 9pm and usually last until midnight. Michalská 9, Prague 1. ✆ **732-606-094**. www. jazzlounge.cz. Cover 200Kč–300Kč. Metro: Můstek.

3 PUBS

Good pub brews and conversations are Prague's preferred late-evening entertainment. Unlike British, Irish, or German beer halls, a true Czech pub ignores accoutrements like cushy chairs and warm wooden paneling, and cuts straight to the chase—beer. While some Czech pubs do serve a hearty plate of food alongside the suds, it's the brew, uncommonly cheap at usually less than 35Kč a pint, that keeps people sitting for hours.

Foreign-theme pubs are popping up all over Prague, offering tastes ranging from Irish to Mexican. Still, it feels a bit like trying to sell Indian tea in China. Below are listed the best of the Czech brew stops followed by choices whose inspirations come from abroad.

CZECH PUBS

Baráčnická rychta   One of the nicest pubs in Malá Strana, the "Small Homeowners Association" (as the name translates) is away from the tourist throng on a small street just above the U.S. Embassy. It serves good food and Czech beer in a kind of old-time atmosphere. Open daily noon until 1am. Tržiště 23, Prague 1. ✆ **257-532-461**. www.baracnicka rychta.cz. Metro: Malostranská.

Kolkovna ★   Hard-core pub aficionados will claim this is not a true pub, since it's relatively free of smoke, has clean bathrooms, and serves excellent food, including both Czech classics and international dishes. On the other hand, no one will argue with the beer: Pilsner Urquell served from huge tanks brought in directly from the brewery to ensure freshness. It's a great spot to relax after a stroll through Old Town. Open daily from 11am to midnight. V kolkovně 8, Prague 1. ✆ **224-819-701**. www.kolkovna.cz. Metro: Staroměstská.

U Fleků ⟨**Overrated**⟩   It's hard to get too enthusiastic about U Fleků. Granted, the homemade beer, dark and sweetish, is some of the best in town and the place does date from 1459, but on most nights this pub is filled to brimming with tourists newly disgorged from buses waiting outside, and so ironically it's hard to get that feeling you're having an authentic experience. The food is decent but pricey for a pub; some nights there's music and you could be assessed a cover charge. Open daily from 9am to 11pm. Křemencova 11, Prague 2. ✆ **224-934-019**. www.ufleku.cz. Metro: Národní třída.

U medvídků (At the Little Bears) ★   This 5-century-old pub off Národní třída was the first in town to serve the original Budweiser, Budvar, on tap. It now serves its own microbrews, including some incredibly strong beers it calls "X-Beers." It also serves typical Czech pub food, including *cmunda,* potato pancakes topped with sauerkraut and cured meat. It's smoky inside, but still easier to breathe here than at most local pubs.

Tips **Není Pivo Jako Pivo: There's No Beer Like Beer**

This seemingly absurd local proverb makes sense when you first taste the golden nectar *(pivo)* from its source and realize that you've never really had *beer* before. While Czechs on the whole aren't religious, beer still elicits a piety unseen in many orthodox countries. The golden Pilsner variety that accounts for most of the beer consumed around the world was born here and has inspired some of the country's most popular fiction, films, poetry, and prayers.

For many Czechs, the corner beer hall *(hospoda* or *pivnice)* is a social and cultural center. Regulars in these smoke-encrusted caves drink beer as life-blood and seem ill at ease when a foreigner takes their favorite table or disrupts their daily routine. For those wanting to sample the rich, aromatic taste of Czech lagers without ingesting waves of nicotine, dozens of more ventilated pubs and restaurants have emerged since the Velvet Revolution. Alas, the suds in these often cost as much as five times more than those in the standard *hospoda.*

According to brewing industry studies, Czechs drink more beer per capita than any other people. The average Czech downs 320 pints of brew each year; the average American drinks about 190. Of course, a Czech *hospoda* regular will drink the year's average for a family of six. Pub regulars do not wonder why the Czech national anthem is a song that translates as "Where Is My Home?"

Several widely held Czech superstitions are connected with drinking beer. One says that you should never pour a different kind of beer in a mug holding the remnants of another brew. Bad luck is sure to follow. Some believe that the toast—usually *"Na zdraví!"* ("To your health!")—is negated if anyone fails to clink his or her mug with any of the others at your table and then fails to slam the mug on the table before taking the first chug. With beer such a cultural icon, it should come as no surprise that beer bellies, far from scorned or hidden, are actually a point of pride in many pubs. One popular Czech saying has it that "beer makes beautiful bodies" (well, it certainly makes for bigger ones). For more Czech beer lore, see chapter 2, p. 28.

PRAGUE AFTER DARK

10

PUBS

Open daily from 11:30am to 11pm. Na Perštýně 7, Prague 1. ℭ **224-211-916.** www.umedvidku. cz. Metro: Národní třída.

U Vejvodů   In the early years after the 1989 revolution, for many expats, U Vejvodů kept the spirit of a grimy student/workers pub alive in Old Town—dark, smoky, and noisy, with plenty of Pilsner beer flowing for just a couple of crowns. It was only a matter of time until this 15th-century building, "At the Duke's," became the subject of corporate interest for its space, history, and prime location. The brewers of Pilsner have moved in with row upon row of well-tended tables and booths among the alcoves and balconies, along with big-screen TVs showing the latest Czech sports triumph, and a wider range of cuisine beyond the pigs' knuckles and pickled eggs of yesteryear. Open Monday to Saturday 10am to 4am and Sunday 11am to 3am. Jilská 4, Prague 1. ℭ **224-219-999.** www.restauraceuvejvodu.cz. Metro: Národní třída.

U zlatého tygra (At the Golden Tiger)   One of the most Czech of the central city pubs, this was once the favorite watering hole of Václav Havel and one of his mentors, writer Bohumil Hrabal, who died in 1997. Particularly smoky and not especially visitor-friendly, this is a one-stop education in Czech pub culture. Pilsner Urquell is the house brew. Havel and former U.S. president Bill Clinton joined Hrabal for a traditional Czech pub evening here during Clinton's visit in 1994, much to the chagrin of the regulars. Open daily from 3pm to 11pm; try to arrive before 3pm to secure a table. Husova 17, Prague 1. © 222-221-111. www.uzlatehotygra.cz. Metro: Staroměstská or Můstek.

INTERNATIONAL PUBS

Jáma (The Hollow) ★   This place has been popular for several post-revolutionary years and draws an agreeable mix of Czech professionals as well as expats and visitors. It feels a lot like an American college pub; Czech and international food is served and Czech beer is on tap. There are excellent burgers, especially on Tuesdays, Jáma's official "burger day." Open daily from 11am to midnight. V Jámě 7, Prague 1. © 224-222-383. www.jamapub. cz. Metro: Můstek.

Molly Malone's   This comfy pub evokes the authentic warmth of an old country inn on a rainy Irish night. The farmhouse atmosphere is loaded with old-fashioned sewing-machine tables, velvet drapes, a roaring fireplace, and turn-of-the-20th-century skivvies hanging on a clothesline. There's plenty of boisterous laughter and Guinness on tap. Pub meals are served daily from 11am to 8pm. Open Sunday to Thursday from 11am to 1am and Friday and Saturday from 11am to 2am. U Obecního dvora 4, Prague 1. © 224-818-851. www.mollymalones.cz. Metro: Staroměstská.

Rocky O'Reilly's   Rocky's is one of the most popular of several Irish-themed bars around town, drawing in loads of British and Irish tourists on a Prague binge weekend, as well as some locals who enjoy the relaxed atmosphere and mix of Irish, English, and American food like burgers, salads, and sandwiches. Open daily from 10am to 2am. Štěpánská 32, Prague 1. © 222-231-060. www.rockyoreillys.cz. Metro: Můstek.

Tlustá Koala   The "Fat Koala" is a convivial pub that looks as if it might have stepped right out of the British Midlands. It's a great spot for an after-cinema beer or light meal if you've just seen something at the nearby Slovanský dům multiplex. Serves the Staropramen family of beers, which includes Stella Artois and Hoegaarden. There's a stand-up pub in the front room and lots of tables in the back. Open daily from noon to 2am. Senovážná 8, Prague 1. © 222-245-401. www.tlustakoala.cz. Metro: Náměstí Republiky.

U Malého Glena   Guinness is served on tap in this small Malá Strana haunt by the expat American called "Little Glen," who also owns the chain of Bohemia Bagel restaurants around town. This place has developed a firm clientele, with regular jazz nights performed in the microscopic-sized cellar. Sunday nights are open-jam nights; the lineup varies according to who feels like coming out that night, but can include some of the best players in town. Decent food—soups, salads, and burgers—are served until 1am. Open daily from 7:30pm to 3am. Karmelitská 23, Prague 1. © 257-531-717. www.malyglen.cz. Metro: Malostranská.

LATE-NIGHT BITES

Getting something to eat after normal restaurant hours is not that easy in Prague. Kitchen staffs seem to like to shut down early, especially on slow nights, meaning that at most places if you haven't put in a food order by 10pm, you might as well wait until breakfast. Most of the places mentioned above, including U Malého Glena and Rocky

O'Reilly's, will serve food until at least midnight. **Radost FX** (p. 102) in Vinohrady is the top late-dining choice, offering its vegetarian dishes, cocktails, and coffee drinks until at least 3am. If you get stuck, you'll find a bunch of late-night fast-food windows selling gyros, pizzas, and snacks throughout the night at the Národní třída tram stop next to Tesco in Nové Město.

4 THE BAR SCENE

Czechs still largely prefer the more intimate atmosphere of a pub to the colder, more businesslike mood of a typical bar, but nevertheless bars of all sorts, including honky-tonks, dives, and cocktail bars, continue to open up all over town. Some of the flashiest cocktail bars are located in Staré Město, near the Old Town Square.

Chapeau Rouge Hidden on a small Old Town back street, this loud and lively expat favorite has bars on several stories and a reckless, no-holds-barred vibe that draws huge crowds until well into the early morning hours. Also books live bands. Not for the faint-hearted. Open daily 11am to 3am. Jakubská 2, Prague 1. ℂ **222-316-328.** www.chapeau rouge.cz. Metro: Náměstí Republiky.

Fraktal This expat-friendly neighborhood joint is a good spot to seek out if you're traveling alone and want to pick up some new friends. Pull up a chair at the bar and order a Pilsner or sit down at a table in the backroom to have one of the better burgers in Prague or a surprisingly good steak. In nice weather you can sit out on the terrace, but be sure to arrive early to snag one of the few coveted tables. Open daily 11am to midnight. Šmeralová 1, Letná, Prague 7. ℂ **777-794-094.** www.fraktalbar.cz. Metro: Hradčanská plus tram no. 1, 8, 25, or 26 two stops to Letenské nám.

Hapu ★★ This is a cocktail bar with a difference. There's no flash and no attitude at this strictly neighborhood joint in Žižkov. The prices are lower here than at other cocktail places like Tretter's or Bugsy's, but the drinks are every bit as well made. Good for singles, since you can pull up a chair at the bar and chat up a cute barmaid or barman, whatever the case may be. Open daily 11am to 2am. Orlická 8, Žižkov, Prague 3. ℂ **222-720-158.** Metro: Flora.

Bugsy's This is similar to Tretter's New York Bar (see below) in that the bartenders are some of the best in town. If there's a difference, it's that this place feels quieter and less status conscious. Come for the great drinks and the chance to actually have a conversation. Open daily 7pm to 2am. Pařížská 10, Prague 1. ℂ **840-284-797.** www.bugsysbar.com. Metro: Staroměstská.

Tretter's New York Bar ★ This wildly popular cocktail bar, situated a couple of blocks from Old Town Square, is modeled loosely on a New York–style club circa 1930. The draws here are the very good cocktails and the flashy new-money crowd. Come early to get a table or try phoning to reserve in advance. On busy nights the guys who control the velvet rope outside enforce a dress code; play it safe and dress up a bit. Open daily 7pm to 2am. V kolkovně 3, Prague 1. ℂ **224-811-165.** www.tretters.cz. Metro: Staroměstská.

GAY & LESBIAN CLUBS
Prague's small gay and lesbian community is growing in its openness and choices for nightclubs and entertainment. See "Gay & Lesbian Travelers" in chapter 3 for information, or http://prague.gayguide.net.

The outlying residential district of Vinohrady has evolved into Prague's de facto gay district. While it's certainly no match for San Francisco's Castro or New York's West Village, the area does sport a number of clubs, cafes, and discos that are gay or gay friendly.

Klub Termix   This small basement in Vinohrady is one of the city's most popular gay discos and can get impossibly crowded on weekend evenings. Enter by ringing the buzzer and the doorman will let you in, but be sure to get there early in order to ensure entry. Open Monday to Saturday 8pm to 5am. Třebízského 4a, Prague 2. © **222-710-462.** www.club-termix.cz. Metro: Muzeum then tram no. 11 two stops.

Saints Bar ★   This relaxed bar on a quiet Vinohrady street is the place to go if big, loud discos are not your thing and you're more interested in kicking back and enjoying some friendly conversation. Open daily from 7pm to 4am. Polská 32, Prague 2. © **222-250-326.** Metro: Jiřího z Poděbrad.

Valentino ★   Another popular Vinohrady dance club that anchors a number of gay-friendly businesses, including the adjacent Celebrity Café, in the former Radio Palác building on Vinohradská street. This cavernous club spreads out on three floors and the giant dance room can accommodate a big crowd. The clientele is mixed, including lots of straight people who come for the music and the vibe. Open daily from 11am to 5am. Vinohradská 40, Prague 2. © **222-513-491.** www.club-valentino.cz. Metro: Muzeum then tram no. 11 two stops.

5 MOVIE THEATERS

The Czech Republic has an active domestic film industry and Czechs are avid moviegoers. The good news for visitors is that most Czech cinemas don't usually dub foreign films, meaning that American and English films are nearly always shown in their original language. The only exceptions generally are children's movies, where the kids are not expected to be able to read the subtitles.

The best places for first-run Hollywood blockbusters and the like are the multiplex cinemas at shopping centers around town. The best of these is arguably the Palace Cinemas complex at centrally located **Slovanský dům** ★, Na Příkopě 9/11, Prague 1 (© **840-200-240;** www.palacecinemas.cz), where around a dozen screens regularly show the best releases from Hollywood just as those movies are being released in the United States. Other good multiplexes with good transport connections to the center include **Palác Flóra,** Vinohradská 151, Prague 3 (© **255-741-002;** www.cinemacity.cz), near the Flora metro station, which has around 10 screens plus the city's only **IMAX** cinema, and the Palace Cinemas multiplex at the **Nový Smíchov shopping center,** Plzeňská 8, Prague 5 (© **840-200-240;** www.palacecinemas.cz), near the Anděl metro station.

Czech films are more problematic since they're usually screened exclusively in Czech, though some cinemas, including Slovanský dům (see above), occasionally show Czech films with English subtitles. **Kino Světozor** ★★ at Vodičkova 41, Prague 1 (© **224-946-824;** www.kinosvetozor.cz), across from the Lucerna Shopping Passage, is a classic art-house cinema showing a wide range of independent films from around the world, as well as Czech films subtitled in English. Another cinema gem, **Kino Aero** ★, at Biskupcová 31, Prague 3, in Žižkov (© **271-771-349;** www.kinoaero.cz), shows a similar collection of golden oldies, indies, and Czech movies, usually with English subtitles.

Prague is also home to a number of very interesting film festivals, including one of the largest urban international film festivals of its kind, **Febiofest** (www.febiofest.cz), in March and the ever-popular **One World** human rights film festival (www.jedensvet.cz) in March or April, which usually brings dozens of blockbuster documentaries to town. Most years in spring see the arrival of the **Days of European Film** festival (www.euro filmfest.cz), bringing the continent's best movies from the previous year to the city for a 2-week run. See the festival websites for dates and details.

PRAGUE AFTER DARK

10

MOVIE THEATERS

11

Day Trips from Prague

Venturing outside of Prague requires more patience and flexibility than you'll need within the city, due to the lack of tourist conveniences and scarcer use of English. For the adventurous, day trips to the surrounding countryside or longer excursions beyond can be surprising and rewarding. While Prague is well into its post-revolution reconstruction, many outlying provinces still groan under the decay of the former regime. But there are pockets of outstanding beauty, unique history, and eccentric pleasures that you can only experience by leaving the tourist bubble in the capital.

Prague has been blessed with golden spires, but the surrounding area is dotted with some of Europe's most **beautiful castles,** such as the majestic Karlštejn. Also spectacular are the impregnable Český Šternberk, the hunting lodge of Konopiště, and the interior of Křivoklát. The castle at Orlík overlooking the wide expanse of the Vltava may be the nicest of them all. As much as these sites testify to the country's beauty, there are also monuments that reflect its suffering. Witness the remains of the village of **Lidice,** which was leveled by the Nazis in a reprisal attack during World War II; and **Terezín** (*Theresienstadt* in German), the "model" Jewish ghetto, the so-called Paradise Ghetto, where a cruel trick duped the world and left tens of thousands to die. Also worth exploring is the medieval mining town of **Kutná Hora** (with the macabre "Bone Church" a mile away in Sedlec).

When you tire of touring castles, you can play a round of golf on a championship course in Karlštejn (or Mariánské Lázně if you have the time for a longer trip), sneak away to a cozy inn, or try the next generation of bungee jumping. You can also enjoy a glass of wine at the Renaissance Lobkowicz Château, the center of Czech winemaking in the most unlikely of places, **Mělník.**

---

1 TIPS FOR DAY-TRIPPING

All the destinations described below are easily accessible from Prague by car, train, or bus. Some may not have accommodations, so they are best visited within a day. Students and seniors (over 65) should always show ID cards and ask for discounts, which are sometimes available.

GETTING THERE

BY CAR A liter of gasoline costs about 30Kč, expensive by North American standards but cheaper than in western Europe. Gas stations are plentiful, and most are equipped with small convenience stores.

Except for main highways, which are a seemingly endless parade of construction sites, roads tend to be narrow and in need of repair. Add maniacal Czech drivers in BMWs and Mercedes fighting for the limited space alongside the Communist-era *Škodas,* and you may think that it's a better option to take the train. Especially at night, you should drive only on major roads. If you must use smaller roads, be careful. For details on car rentals, see chapter 3.

If you experience car trouble, major highways have emergency telephones from which you can call for assistance. There's also the **ÚAMK**, a 24-hour motor assistance club that provides service for a fee. They drive bright-yellow pickup trucks and can be summoned on main highways by using the SOS emergency phones located at the side of the road every kilometer or so. If you are not near one of these phones or are on a road that doesn't have them, you can contact ÚAMK at ✆ **1230**. This is a toll-free call.

BY TRAIN   Trains operated by the state-run **České dráhy** (Czech Rail; ✆ **840-112-113,** general train information for all stations; www.cd.cz) provide a good and less expensive alternative to driving. The fare is determined by how far you travel. A trip of 50km (31 miles) costs about 70Kč in second class and around 100Kč in first class. First class is not usually available, or needed, on shorter trips.

It's important to find out which Prague station your train departs from since not all trains leave from the main station, though all the major stations are on metro lines. Check when you buy your tickets. Trains heading to destinations in the north often depart from **Nádraží Holešovice,** Vrbenského ulice, Prague 7, above the Nádraží Holešovice metro stop on line C (red). Other northbound trains depart from

Masarykovo nádraží on Hybernská street, Prague 1, near Náměstí Republiky on metro line B (yellow). Local trains to the southeast, such as those heading to Karlštejn and Beroun, are commonly found at **Smíchovské nádraží,** Nádražní ulice, Prague 5, on metro line B (yellow). Many trains to eastern and southern Bohemia and Moravia leave from **Hlavní nádraží (Main Station),** Wilsonova 80, Prague 1, at the metro stop of the same name on metro line C (red) in the center.

BY BUS   The Czech bus system is a cacophonous mix of public and private bus companies, and finding the right bus can be a taxing ordeal. Nevertheless, because trains often follow circuitous routes (or train service may not be available at all to some destinations), buses can sometimes be a better option. Buses can get very crowded, however, so make sure that you buy your tickets early and arrive well before the bus is scheduled to depart so that you are sure to get a seat.

Prague's main bus station, **Central Bus Station—Florenc,** Křižíkova 5, Prague 8 (© **900-144-444** for bus connections information; www.florenc.cz), is above the Florenc metro stop on line C (red). Unfortunately, few employees speak English here, making it tricky for non-Czech speakers to obtain schedule information. To find your bus, you can try the large boards just next to the office where all buses are listed. They're in alphabetical order, but sometimes it's tough to find your destination since it may lie in the middle of a route to another place. The online timetable at **http://jizdnirady.idnes.cz** can be a real lifesaver and shows all bus connections and prices.

ORGANIZED DAY TOURS

Several companies operate day tours to popular destinations near Prague. Though most offer more or less the same services, it pays to shop around. Try the following agencies.

- **Martin Tour,** Štěpánská 61, Prague 1 (© **224-212-473;** www.martintour.cz), has been around for several years and offers a couple of worthy tours. The Karlštejn Castle tour is its best. The tour is offered Tuesday to Sunday, departing at 10am from Staroměstské náměstí. It takes 5 hours and is expedient because you don't wait around for the next general tour at the castle. A traditional Czech lunch at a nearby restaurant is included (diabetics, vegetarians, and babies can be accommodated). The tour with lunch costs 950Kč. The 5-hour trip to the country's Jewish memorial of Terezín costs 1,100Kč. The bus leaves five times a week at 9:30am from Staroměstské náměstí.
- **Čedok,** Na Příkopě 18, Prague 1 (© **221-447-242;** www.cedok.com/prague-excursions. aspx), in the heart of Prague, has its advantages. For one, it offers by far the widest array of tours outside of Prague. Čedok has been doing this so long that it has access to all the important sights as well as guides who speak several languages. Prices are

---

> (Tips)   **Finding Train & Bus Connections Online**
>
> You'll find a highly useful timetable showing both train and bus connections, as well as times, prices and departure stations, at **http://jizdnirady.idnes.cz** (note that you have to input city and destination names using their Czech spellings; i.e. "Praha" for Prague). Czech Rail has its own confusing website in English, German, and Czech at **www.cd.cz,** also showing departure times and stations as well as allowing you to reserve seats and book tickets online.

Tips   A Note on Tours

Though many good organized tours are offered, for the most part I'd recommend going it alone. This gives you the freedom to change plans at the last minute in order to get a little more of what you want, not just what the tours provide. Besides, you get a greater sense of accomplishment when you navigate on your own.

reasonable for what's offered. A day trip to Karlovy Vary, lunch, a swim at the Hotel Thermal outdoor pool, and a tour of the Moser glass factory costs 1,675Kč, while a journey to Karlštejn Castle and Château Konopiště, lunch and tour included, costs 1,950Kč.

- **Prague Sightseeing Tours,** Klimentská 52, Prague 1 (© **222-314-655;** www.pstours. cz), is another reputable firm with some excellent tours. The company offers a combination all-day tour of the castles Karlštejn and Konopiště on weekends that includes lunch. It's a good way to see both castles without the hassle of negotiating the train and bus stations. The price is 1,990Kč for adults and 1,700Kč for children.

2 KARLŠTEJN CASTLE ★★

29km (18 miles) SW of Prague

By far the most popular destination in the Czech Republic after Prague, Karlštejn Castle is an easy day trip for those interested in getting out of the city. Charles IV built this medieval castle from 1348 to 1357 to safeguard the crown jewels of the Holy Roman Empire. Although the castle had been changed over the years, with such additions as late Gothic staircases and bridges, renovators have removed these additions, restoring the castle to its original medieval state.

As you approach, little can prepare you for your first view: a spectacular Disney-like castle perched on a hill, surrounded by lush forests and vineyards. In its early days, the king's jewels housed within enhanced the castle's importance and reputation. Vandalism having forced several of its finest rooms to close, these days the castle is most spectacular from the outside. Unfortunately, many of the more interesting restored rooms are kept off-limits and open only for special guests.

ESSENTIALS

GETTING THERE   The best way to get to Karlštejn is by **train** (there's no bus service). Trains leave regularly from either Prague's Main Station (at the Hlavní nádraží metro stop on line C) or from Smíchovské nádraží, metro line B, and take about 40 minutes to reach Karlštejn. The one-way, second-class fare is 49Kč. It's a short, relaxing trip along the Berounka River. On the way you pass through Řevnice, Martina Navrátilová's birthplace. Keep your eyes open for your first glimpse of the majestic castle. Once you arrive at Karlštejn train station, it's a 20- to 30-minute hike up the road to the castle. While you're at the station, mark down the return times for trains to Prague to better plan your trip back.

You can also **drive** along one of two routes, both of which take 30 minutes. Here's the more scenic one: Leave Prague from the southwest along Highway 4 in the direction of Strakonice and take the Karlštejn cutoff, following the signs (and traffic!). The second, much less scenic route follows the main highway leading out of Prague from the west as if you were going to Plzeň. About 20 minutes down the road is the well-marked cutoff for Karlštejn. (You can tell you have missed the cutoff if you get to the town of Beroun. If that happens, take any exit and head back the other way; the signs to Karlštejn are also marked heading toward Prague.)

A trip to Karlštejn can easily be combined with a visit to Křivoklát (see below).

VISITOR INFORMATION   The ticket/castle information booth (© **311-681-370**) can help you, as can any of the restaurants or stores. The castle website at www.hradkarlstejn. cz is easy to navigate and has lots of useful information on the castle's history as well as tours and opening hours. You can also book tour tickets online.

ORGANIZED TOURS   All of the tour operators listed in "Organized Day Tours" above offer sightseeing trips to Karlštejn.

EXPLORING THE CASTLE

Since Karlštejn's beauty lies more in its facade and environs than in the castle itself, the 20- to 30-minute walk up the hill is, along with the view, one of the main features that makes the trip spectacular. It's an excursion well worth making if you can't get farther out of Prague to see some of the other castles. Seeing hordes of visitors coming, locals have discovered the value of fixing up the facades of their homes and opening small businesses (even if they have gone a little overboard on the number of outlets selling crystal!). Restaurants have improved tremendously. When you finally do reach the top, take some time to look out over the town and down the Well Tower.

To see the interior of the castle, you can choose from one of two tours. The 50-minute **Tour 1** will take you through the **Imperial Palace, Hall of Knights, Chapel of St. Nicholas, Royal Bedroom,** and **Audience Hall. Tour 2,** which lasts 70 minutes, offers a look at the **Holy Rood Chapel,** famous for the more than 2,000 precious and semiprecious inlaid gems adorning its walls; the **Chapel of St. Catherine,** Charles IV's own private oratory; the **Church of Our Lady;** and the **library.** Note that you need to make a reservation to visit the Holy Rood Chapel on Tour 2 (© **274-008-154;** fax 274-008-152; www.hradkarlstejn.cz). You can buy tickets and make reservations online.

The shorter Tour 1 costs 250Kč adults, 150Kč students, 20Kč children under 6. Tour 2 with the Holy Rood Chapel costs 300Kč adults, 200Kč students, free for children under 6. The castle is open Tuesday to Sunday: May, June, and September 9am to noon and 12:30 to 5pm; July and August 9am to noon and 12:30 to 6pm; April and October 9am to noon and 1 to 4pm; November, December, and March 9am to noon and 1 to 3pm; closed January and February.

ⓘ Tips   A Castle-Viewing Tip

Karlštejn is probably best seen from a distance, so take time to browse in the stores, enjoy the fresh air, and sit out on one of the restaurant patios or down by the riverside. Buy a bottle of the locally grown Karlštejn wine, a vintage started by King Charles IV, and admire the view.

ⓂMoments A Romantic Getaway

If the air and noise of Prague start to grate on your nerves, or if a quiet, romantic, overnight trip to a castle in the country sounds like the perfect getaway, head for the **Romantic Hotel Mlýn (Mill Hotel)** ★, 267 18 Karlštejn (ⓒ **311-744-411;** fax 311-744-444; www.hotelmlynkarlstejn.cz).

On the river's edge on the bank opposite the castle, the Mlýn is exactly what its name says—a mill. Converted into a hotel and recently reconstructed, this reasonably priced country inn takes you away from the hustle and bustle of traveling. Its 28 rooms are a little on the small side, but they're quaint and nicely decorated with rustic furniture. At the outdoor patio bar and very good restaurant, you can relax and enjoy the soothing sounds of the river. Service here is a cut above what it is at the other hotels in the area. If you are here for lunch or dinner when the outdoor grill has been fired up, take advantage of it. Use the hotel also as a base for bike and canoe trips along the river. The staff can help you with local tennis courts and reservations for a round of golf.

Rates average around 2,100Kč for a single and 2,600Kč for a double, though they fluctuate according to the season. Check the website for rates on the day you plan to travel. Credit cards are accepted. To get to the hotel, take the bridge across the river that leads to the train station and turn left at the first street. If you cross the rail tracks, you've gone too far.

TEE TIME: KARLŠTEJN'S CHAMPIONSHIP GOLF COURSE

Golfers may want to try their luck at the North American–designed **Prague Karlštejn Golf Club,** a course that hosted its first European PGA tour event 10 years ago. This challenging 27-hole, 10,523-yard course on the hill just across the river from the castle offers some pretty views. At the elevated tee on the second hole, you'll hit toward the castle. It's a breathtaking place to lose a ball. If you want a real challenge, see if you can match former Masters winner German Bernhard Langer's four-round total of 264 (24 under par).

Karlštejn is one of the few courses in the Czech Republic that really challenges a golfer's ability—narrow fairways, long roughs, and lightning-fast greens. Be prepared to walk uphill between holes. The course is open daily from 8am to sundown, and reservations for weekends should be made a couple of days in advance; call ⓒ **311-604-999** or go online to www.karlstejn-golf.cz. Be forewarned, however, it's not cheap, especially for visitors who may need to rent clubs and carts: greens fees are 2,000Kč for 18 holes Monday to Friday (slight discount if you tee off before 11am), and 3,000Kč Saturday, Sunday, and holidays. Motorized cart rentals are 1,300Kč per 18 holes, while a pull cart is 200Kč per round. Club rental is 1,000Kč per round.

To get here by car from Prague, take Hwy. 116 south through the castle town of Karlštejn. Once you cross the river and a set of train tracks, stay on the road, which veers right and goes up a hill. You'll see the golf course on the left and an entrance soon after. If you've taken the train, you can walk to the course through town, but be warned that it's an uphill hike. Take a taxi, which should cost 120Kč.

The **Restaurace Blanky z Valois** (© 608-021-075), on the main street heading up to the castle, serves pizzas and provide the only alternative to standard Czech fare in the area. Pizzas range from 90Kč to 180Kč. The restaurant is open daily from 11am to 10pm. The long wine list includes French and Italian vintages, but try and sample Karlštejn's own. This light, dry wine is surprisingly good considering it's not from Moravia, and it costs less than half the price of the imports.

Further along the main road, away from town and beyond the castle, you'll find the rustic inn **Pod Dračí skalou** ★ (© 311-681-177; www.poddraciskalou.eu). This is a great spot for a traditional pub lunch, including lots of dishes featuring wild game like boar, pheasant, and venison. Main courses are 150Kč to 250Kč. The restaurant is open Monday to Saturday 11am to 11pm, Sunday 11am to 8pm.

Restaurace U Janů (© 311-681-210), at the top of the village, is another good alternative. If it's hot out, take a seat on the welcoming shady terrace; if it's a chilly winter day, pull up a chair next to the fireplace inside. The menu is basic Czech. The venison specials make a nice change from the usual meat-and-dumpling meals. Main courses are up to 199Kč. It's open daily 9:30am to 10pm.

3 KŘIVOKLÁT ★

43km (27 miles) W of Prague

Less crowded and much less touristy than its neighbor upstream at Karlštejn, Křivoklát is the perfect destination for a lazy afternoon of touring. A royal castle mentioned as early as the 11th century, Křivoklát is set in the tranquil Berounka River Valley. The fortress was rebuilt several times over the years but retains its Gothic style. The royal family was among Křivoklát's frequent visitors, and during the Hussite Uprising, King Sigmund of Luxembourg hid his jewels here. The area surrounding the fortress is protected by UNESCO as a biosphere preservation area.

ESSENTIALS

GETTING THERE **Trains** run regularly from Prague's Smíchov station to the town of Beroun, where you must change to go on to Křivoklát. The trip takes 1¾ hours; the one-way, second-class fare is 98Kč. This is one of the nicer train rides in the Czech Republic, even though you have to change trains in Beroun. The train winds its way along the Berounka through some wooded areas near Prague.

If you're **driving,** leave Prague on the E50 expressway heading west toward Plzeň and exit at the Křivoklát cutoff. From there, follow Hwy. 116 as it snakes along the Berounka and turn left onto Hwy. 201, which eventually winds its way around to Křivoklát. The trip takes 45 minutes.

VISITOR INFORMATION There is no tourist information center, but the castle can provide information on the area. There is also an official website for the castle: www.krivoklat.cz.

ORGANIZED TOURS At the time of writing, none of the major sightseeing tour operators were offering dedicated tours to Křivoklát.

Tips A Sightseeing Tip

Křivoklát is near Karlštejn, so consider visiting both in 1 day if you drive or take the train. The contrast between the bustling Karlštejn and the sleepy Křivoklát is startling.

EXPLORING THE CASTLE

Often a castle tour fails to live up to expectations (Karlštejn comes to mind), but this is one of the best castle tours; it's almost a reverse of Karlštejn. Outside, Křivoklát pales in comparison to Karlštejn's beauty. But inside, Křivoklát blows its rival out of the water. Take time to study the intricate carvings at the altar in the **Royal Chapel.** They're not exactly angelic, as the angels are actually holding instruments of torture; Křivoklát was a prison for political criminals in the Middle Ages. The **Kings Hall,** a whopping 24m (79 ft.) long, is the second-longest secular hallway in the country after Prague's Vladislav Hall. In the **Knights Hall** you'll find a collection of fabulous late Gothic art. And the **Furstenberg Picture Gallery** is one of the country's largest castle libraries, with some 53,000 volumes on its shelves. Take that, Karlštejn!

Admission is 150Kč for adults and 105Kč for children. The castle is open to the public in March and November on Saturday and Sunday from 10am to 3pm. In October it's open Tuesday to Sunday from 10am to 4pm. In April, May, June, and September, hours are Tuesday to Sunday from 9am to 4pm. In July and August, hours are daily from 9am to 6pm. The tour runs about half an hour, and information in English is available.

WHERE TO STAY & DINE

Since Křivoklát is less touristy than Karlštejn, there aren't many restaurants here. Of the few that do exist, **Pension U Jelena,** at the bottom of the hill as you approach the castle, is your best bet. With six rooms, the pension can be used as an overnight stop if you want to spend a leisurely weekend hiking and biking between Křivoklát and Karlštejn. The restaurant specializes in game and main courses run from around 70Kč to 300Kč; American Express, MasterCard, and Visa are accepted.

For reservations at the hotel (you won't need them for the restaurant), call © **313-558-529** (fax 313-558-235; www.u-jelena.cz). Doubles cost 1,000Kč. If you don't want to stop here, you're better off eating down the road in Karlštejn or back in Prague.

4 KUTNÁ HORA ★

72km (45 miles) E of Prague

A medieval town that grew fantastically rich from the silver deposits beneath it, Kutná Hora is also a popular day trip from Prague. Small enough to be seen in a single day at a brisk pace, the town's ancient heart has decayed, which makes it hard to believe that this was once the second most important city in Bohemia. However, the town center is also mercifully free of the ugly, Communist-era buildings that plague many of the country's small towns. The historic center and Kutná Hora's main draw, St. Barbara's Cathedral, have been on the

UNESCO list for more than 10 years. Also, the macabre Bone Church (Kostnice), filled with human bones assembled in bizarre sculptures, is worth a visit.

ESSENTIALS

GETTING THERE The 50-minute **drive** from Prague is relatively easy. Take Vinohradská street, which runs due east from behind the National Museum at the top of Wenceslas Square, straight to Kutná Hora. Once out of the city, the road turns into Hwy. 333.

If you don't have a car, your best bet is to go by **bus,** which departs from Prague's Florenc Bus Station and takes about 1½ hours. It costs 70Kč. **Trains** take you to from Prague's Hlavní nádraží station to Kutná Hora in just over an hour for 97Kč.

VISITOR INFORMATION The **Information Center (Informační Středisko; ℂ 327-512-378;** www.kutnahora.cz), on Palackého nám. 377, provides the most comprehensive information service in town. Check to see if anything special such as a recital or an exhibition is showing. The office is open daily 9am to 6pm (Apr–Sept); Monday to Friday from 9am to 6pm and Saturday and Sunday from 10am to 4pm (Oct–Mar). The town has also posted very useful signs just about everywhere to help visitors get where they're going.

SEEING THE SIGHTS

The main attraction is the enormous **St. Barbara's Cathedral (Chrám sv. Barbory)** ★★ at the southwestern edge of town. In 1380, Peter Parléř began construction of the cathedral. The task was so great that it took several more Gothic masters, including Matthias Rejsek and Benedikt Rejt, close to 200 years to complete the project. From the outside, the cathedral's soaring arches, dozens of spires, and intricate designs raise expectations that the interior will be just as impressive—and you won't be disappointed.

On entering (you have to enter from the side, not the front), you'll see several richly decorated frescoes full of symbols denoting the town's two main industries of mining and minting. The ceiling vaulting, with floral patterns and coats of arms, has made many a jaw drop. Admission is 50Kč for adults and 30Kč for children. The cathedral is open from May until the end of September from Tuesday to Sunday from 9am to 5:30pm, and Monday from 10am to 4pm. From October until the end of April, it's open Tuesday to Sunday from 10am to 4pm.

When you leave the cathedral, head down statue-lined **Barborská Street,** where you'll pass the early baroque **Jesuit College,** built in the late 17th century by Giovanni Domenico Orsi. Farther down the road is the **Hrádek,** a 15th-century castle that now houses the **Czech Museum of Silver (Muzeum stříbra)** ★ (ℂ 327-512-159). If you take the tour of Hrádek, you'll actually tour one of the town's mine shafts. The tour begins in a small room filled with artifacts from the town's mining and minting industries. After a brief speech, it's time to don hard hats and work coats to tour the mine shaft. After a hike of about 270m (886 ft.), you'll descend into a narrow corridor of rock and dampness to spend about 15 minutes in the mines. Children like this part of the tour

Ⓣips Two Warnings

The Hrádek mine shaft can be a little claustrophobic (what mine isn't?). *Never* take your hard hat off (low, jagged ceilings can quickly bring about premature balding).

ATTRACTIONS ●
Czech Museum of Silver **4**
Italian Court (Vlašský Dvůr) **5**
Jesuit College **2**
St. Barbara's Cathedral (Chrám sv. Barbory) **1**
St. James's Church (Kostel sv. Jakuba) **6**

DINING ◆
Kometa **3**
Restaurant Café Harmonia **7**
U Kamenného Domu **8**

almost as much as they do the bone church. Admission is 130Kč for adults and 80Kč for children. The museum is open Tuesday to Sunday: April and October from 9am to 5pm; May, June, and September from 9am to 6pm; and July and August from 10am to 6pm. It's closed from November until the end of March.

Once you're back aboveground, go down the hill to **St. James's Church (Kostel sv. Jakuba)** and the **Italian Court (Vlašský Dvůr;** 𝄇 **327-512-873).** Even though the door is usually closed at St. James's, it's worth trying to open; perhaps you'll be able to glimpse the baroque paintings on the walls. More likely, though, you'll have to admire the church from the outside and then head on to the Italian Court.

Constructed in 1300 as a royal mint (what better way for a town to become rich than to print money?), the Italian Court derives its name from its original occupants, who were brought in from Florence to mint coins. The building houses a museum of coins made here between the 14th and 18th centuries, including the Czech groschen, the currency of choice in the Middle Ages. Another reason to take the tour is to see the ornate chapels, impressive in their details. Admission, including the tour, is 100Kč and 60Kč. It's open daily April to September from 9am to 6pm; October and March from 10am to 5pm; and November to February from 10am to 4pm.

(Kids) The Bone Church in Sedlec

A visit to Kutná Hora isn't complete without a trip to **Kostnice** ★★ (© **728-125-488;** www.kostnice.cz), the "Bone Church." It's located 1.6km (1 mile) down the road in Sedlec (within comfortable walking distance from the train station if you arrive by train). From the center of town, you can take a taxi or board a local bus on Masarykova Street.

From the outside, Kostnice looks like most other churches. But from the moment you enter the front door, you know that this is no ordinary church—all of the decorations are made from human bones. No kidding. František Rint, the church's interior decorator, created crosses of bone, columns of bone, chalices of bone, and even a coat of arms in bone for the Schwarzenberg family, which owned the church.

The obvious questions are: Where did the bones come from, and why were they used for decorations? The first question is easier to answer: The bones came from victims of the 14th-century plague and the 15th-century Hussite wars; both events killed thousands, who were buried in mass graves on the church's site. As the area developed, the bones were uncovered, and the local monks came up with this idea of how to put the bones to use.

Admission is 50Kč for adults and 30Kč for children. From April to September, the Bone Church is open daily from 8am to 6pm; October 9am to noon and 1 to 5pm; November to March 9am to noon and 1 to 4pm.

WHERE TO DINE

Surprisingly for the number of visitors it attracts, Kutná Hora has very few good restaurants. Still, you'll likely be hungry after a day of traveling and walking around, so these are some of the best of an admittedly average bunch:

One of the nice terraces is the **Restaurant Cafe Harmonia** (© **327-512-275**), Husova 105 (to the rear of St. James's Church), making it a convenient stop before a visit to the Bone Church. The salads are fresh and the soups are hot and hearty—something that isn't all too common in this town. Main courses are 70Kč to 180Kč; no credit cards are accepted. It's open daily from 10am to 11pm.

U Kamenného Domu (© **327-514-426**), Lierova 147 (2 blocks west of Palackého nám.), is very popular with the locals, serving hearty Czech specialties at bargain prices. There aren't any English menus, but don't be afraid to point at something you see on another table. The best bet here is the Czech staple meal of roasted pork, potato dumplings, and cabbage (109Kč), which will fill you up without the heavy cream sauce that seems to come on a lot of the other dishes. Main courses cost 69Kč to 180Kč. Credit cards are not accepted. The restaurant is open daily from 11am to 10pm.

Kometa (© **327-515-515**), Barborská 29, has decent Czech food and an excellent location just down from St. Barbara's Cathedral. A pretty facsimile of goulash and a reasonably priced *svíčkova* (braised beef with gravy and dumplings) at 95Kč help keep dining costs low. No credit cards are accepted. The restaurant is open daily from 11am to 11pm.

5 KONOPIŠTĚ ★

48km (30 miles) S of Prague

A 17th-century castle-turned-hunting-lodge built by the Habsburgs, Konopiště was the Club Med of its time. Here, the nobility relaxed amid the well-stocked hunting grounds surrounding the castle. In 1887, the castle became the property of Habsburg heir to the throne, Archduke Franz Ferdinand, who was particularly enamored of hunting until that fateful day in Sarajevo when he and his wife, Sophie, became the prey. It was Franz Ferdinand's assassination, after all, in 1914 that set off the Europe-wide conflagration of World War I.

If you're driving, you can see both Konopiště and Český Šternberk in 1 day (see directions on p. 214).

ESSENTIALS

GETTING THERE If you're **driving,** leave Prague on the D1 expressway heading south and exit at the Benešov cutoff. From there, turn right at the signs for Konopiště. *Watch out:* The turn sneaks up on you. The trip takes 45 minutes in average traffic. Note that the parking lot just outside the castle is your best bet, at 50Kč. There aren't any closer lots, and police are vigilant about ticketing or booting cars parked at the side of the road. The minimum fine is 1,000Kč.

If you don't have a car, the bus is the next-best option. Several **buses** run daily from a small commuter bus station at the **Roztyly** metro stop on metro line C (red) and let you off not far from the castle (tell the driver where you want to go) or go to nearby Benešov where you catch another bus to Konopiště. Purchase tickets at the Florenc bus station or directly from the driver. The 1-hour trip costs around 54Kč.

It's a little trickier to get here by **train** since the closest station is in nearby Benešov. The trip takes 50 minutes and costs 68Kč for a one-way, second-class fare. From Benešov you'll have to catch a local bus or taxi to the castle.

EXPLORING THE CASTLE & HUNTING GROUNDS

Since hunting on the grounds is no longer an option, Tour 1 at Konopiště will have to suffice. You'll know what I mean as soon as you begin the tour: Hundreds of antlers, bears, wild boars, and birds of prey practically jump off the walls, catching unsuspecting sweaters and dazzling children. The main hall is a testament to the archduke, who reportedly bagged tens of thousands of animals—only an estimated 1% of his total hunting collection is on display—and it still ranks as one of Europe's largest collections. Tour 1 also takes you through the castle's parlors, which have been restored with great attention to detail. Note the handcrafted wooden Italian cabinets with wonderfully detailed inlays and the collection of Meissen porcelain. Tour 1, lasting about 50 minutes, costs 200Kč for adults and 130Kč for children, and includes an English-speaking guide.

Tour 2 (for which you must buy tickets separately) is a little longer at 55 minutes and takes you through the weapons room, the chapel, and the party room, where only men were allowed. This tour is also 200Kč for adults and 130Kč for children, including a guide.

Tour 3 takes you through Ferdinand's private rooms. It lasts only about 10 minutes longer than the other tours and costs 300Kč for adults and 200Kč for children. While the third tour is interesting, unless you're a die-hard castle fan, it's not worth the money.

After exploring the castle's interior, wander around the manicured gardens where quails, pheasants, and peacocks roam freely. Children enjoy the moat, home to two bears who wander in circles for hours at a time. Down below the castle is a large pond where some people go swimming, though the water quality is questionable; I'd advise against it. Several large, open areas beg for a blanket, some sandwiches, and a nice bottle of red Frankovka wine. Picnicking is allowed, but stock up before coming since there's no place to get groceries near the castle.

The castle is open in April from Tuesday to Friday from 9am to noon and 1 to 3pm, Saturday and Sunday 9am to noon and 1 to 4pm; May to August Tuesday to Sunday from 9am to noon and 1 to 5pm; September Tuesday to Friday from 9am to noon and 1 to 4pm, Saturday and Sunday 9am to 5pm; October Tuesday to Friday from 9am to noon and 1 to 3pm, Saturday and Sunday 9am to 4pm; and November Saturday and Sunday from 9am to noon and 1 to 3pm. The castle grounds are open 24 hours year-round. For more information, visit www.zamek-konopiste.cz or call ✆ **317-721-366.**

WHERE TO STAY & DINE

Connections are not that great to Prague and if you have to stay the night, there's a decent motel just a short work from the castle. The **Amber Hotel Konopiště** (✆ **317-722-732**) resembles a mountain motor lodge. Rooms are on the small size, but very cute with rustic decor and well outfitted. The hotel has a small restaurant inside and a more comfortable, traditional grill restaurant, the **Stodola,** out front. Doubles (no singles) range from 1,500Kč to 1,700Kč. The Stodola restaurant is open daily from 6pm to 1am and accepts American Express, Diners Club, MasterCard, and Visa.

On the castle grounds, **Stará Myslivna** ★ (✆ **317-700-280;** www.staramyslivna. com) has recently undergone a thorough facelift and is by far the nicest place to eat within shouting distance. Not surprisingly, given the archduke's proclivities, the menu focuses on game, with several variations of pheasant, venison, and other forest animals, usually served in traditional Czech style with a sauce and dumplings. When the sun is out, sit outside on the terrace; in winter, there's usually a roaring fire in the fireplace. Main courses run from 140Kč to 240Kč; major credit cards are accepted. Open daily 10am to 10pm.

6 ČESKÝ ŠTERNBERK

48km (30 miles) SE of Prague

About 16km (10 miles) east of Benešov lies the menacing Český Šternberk castle, once one of Bohemia's most powerful fortifications. The structure was built in the Gothic style in the first half of the 13th century, during the reign of Wenceslas I. The Habsburgs put in some baroque additions and improved its defenses, leaving few Gothic elements in their wake.

ESSENTIALS

GETTING THERE If you're **driving,** leave Prague on the D1 expressway heading south and exit at the Český Šternberk cutoff. From there, follow Hwy. 111. It's a 55-minute drive. From Konopiště, take Hwy. 112 to Hwy. 111. It's a 25-minute drive.

A few **buses** run daily to and from Český Šternberk, but not from Prague's main Florenc station. Instead, you must take metro line C (red) south to the Roztyly stop. You

can buy tickets, costing 65Kč each way, at the Florenc station or from the bus driver at
Roztyly. The bus ride takes about 2 hours.

SEEING THE FORTRESS

This impressive fortress castle stands atop a hill, rising above the Sázava River. The
1-hour tour of Český Šternberk is worth taking. The enormous main hall and several
smaller salons, with fine baroque detailing, elaborate chandeliers, and period art, are
testaments to the wealth of the Šternberk family. After the tour, enjoy the grounds and
relax among the trees and babbling streams that surround the fortress before heading out.

Admission to the castle is 170Kč for adults and 110Kč for children, including a guided
tour in English. The fortress is open Tuesday to Sunday: June to August from 9am to
6pm, and May and September from 9am to 5pm. In April and October it's open only on
Saturday and Sunday from 9am to 5pm. The rest of the year, it's closed. For information,
call ✆ **317-855-101** or go to www.hradceskysternberk.cz.

WHERE TO DINE

Inside the castle, **Vinárna Český Šternberk** (✆ **317-855-168**) serves standard Czech
meat-and-potatoes meals, though the quality of food and service is reflected in the prices.
Main courses are 60Kč to 140Kč; no credit cards are accepted. Since the restaurant's
hours are the same as the castle's, you can't stop in for a quick bite to eat before the first
tour or after the last one.

---

7 MĚLNÍK

32km (20 miles) N of Prague

Bohemia isn't known as a winemaking region—this is beer country. Except, that is, for
the town of Mělník, where the Vltava and Labe (Elbe) rivers meet. While it's not quite
the Loire Valley, Mělník has a decidedly French bent, as the vineyards are stocked with
vines that originated in the Burgundy region.

Princess Ludmila began the tradition centuries before Bohemia passed through the
hands of the Romans and eventually King Charles IV. The center of Mělník winemaking
is the **Renaissance Lobkowicz Château,** owned since 1739 by the family of the same
name (except for a 40-year Communist-imposed interruption). The confluence of the
rivers provides a stunning backdrop to the château, where another French pastime—sitting on a terrace with a glass of Ludmila, Mělník's finest, as the afternoon sun slowly
fades—can be an art.

If you get a chance to visit in mid-September, check out the harvest festival, **Mělnické
Vinobraní** (www.melnicke-vinobrani.cz), for the latest vintages. Even if wine isn't your
cup of, well, wine, Mělník's historic center is worth a look, with its Gothic church of St.
Peter and St. Paul and its tower that provides a beautiful panorama of the area.

ESSENTIALS

GETTING THERE If you're **driving** from the north end of Prague, follow Hwy. 9,
which leads straight into Mělník. The trip takes 30 minutes.

Buses leave for Mělník from above the Nádraží Holešovice metro station in Prague
every hour or so. The trip takes about 40 minutes and costs 39Kč.

It's also possible to take a **boat** to Mělník down the Vltava river. The **Pražská paroplavební** company runs occasional all-day boat trips during the summer from the company's dock on the Vltava at Rašínovo nábřeží, Prague 1, just in front of the Dancing Building (see chapter 7, p. 129). This romantic and scenic tour takes about 6 hours (oneway); a round-trip ticket costs 490Kč adults, 250Kč students. Find out more on www.paroplavba.cz.

VISITOR INFORMATION   The information center is at náměstí Míru 11 (✆ **315-627-503;** www.melnik.cz), and is open from May to September daily 9am to 5pm, October to April Monday to Friday 9am to 5pm.

TOURING THE CHATEAU & TASTING THE WINE

Mělník's main attraction is the **Renaissance Lobkowicz Château** ★ (✆ **315-622-121;** www.lobkowicz-melnik.cz). The château is a mélange of styles, from its Renaissance balconies and *sgrafitti* (decoration made by cutting away parts of a surface layer—like plaster or clay—to expose a different-colored layer beneath) to its Gothic touches and baroque southern building. The tour showcases the Lobkowicz's fine taste; in the living quarters, you'll see a barrage of baroque furniture and 17th- and 18th-century paintings. A second tour lets you into the 13th-century wine cellar, where wine tastings regularly occur.

Admission to the château is 90Kč for adults and 70Kč for students, free for children under 12. The wine cellar tour is 40Kč, and wine tastings run from 90Kč for two wines to as much as 350Kč for VIP treatment. The château is open daily from 10am to 5pm.

WHERE TO DINE

The château has a decent restaurant, **Zámecká Restaurace** (✆ 315-622-121), with stunning views out over the valley. The menu is organized as a series of price fixe meals running from 250Kč to 300Kč, including soup, dessert, and coffee. The restaurant is open Tuesday to Sunday from 11am to 6pm.

---

8 TEREZÍN (THERESIENSTADT) ★★

48km (30 miles) NW of Prague

Noticing that northwest Bohemia was susceptible to Prussian attacks, Joseph II, the son of Austrian Empress Maria Teresa, decided to build **Terezín** to ward off further offensives. Two fortresses were built, but the Prussian army bypassed the area during the last Austro-Prussian conflict and in 1866 attacked Prague anyway. That spelled the end of Terezín's fortress charter, which was repealed in 1888. More than 50 years later, the fortifications were just what occupying Nazi forces needed.

> **(Tips) More Flood Damage**
>
> The town of Terezín and its memorial were badly struck by floods in August 2002. After a tremendous effort, the memorial has been reopened and is accessible to the public again.

Impressions

The most brutal thing was that they wanted to show a Terezín where there were nice healthy people. Each person was given a specific role to play. It was arranged beforehand down to the last detail, who would sit where and what they would say. Those people looking bad were not to appear at all. They [the Nazis] prepared Terezín so there weren't people looking ill, old, emaciated, or too many of them. They created the illusion of a self-governing normal town where ... people lived relatively decently.

—Anita Franková, survivor of Terezín

When people around the world talk of Nazi atrocities during World War II, the name Terezín (*Theresienstadt* in German) rarely comes up. At the so-called Paradise Ghetto, there were no gas chambers, no mass machine-gun executions, and no medical testing rooms. Terezín wasn't used to exterminate the Jews, Gypsies, homosexuals, and political prisoners it held. Rather, the occupying Nazi forces used it as a transit camp. About 140,000 people passed though Terezín's gates; more than half ended up at the death camps of Auschwitz and Treblinka.

Instead, Terezín will live in infamy for the cruel trick that SS chief Heinrich Himmler played on the world within its walls. On June 23, 1944, three foreign observers—two from the Red Cross—came to Terezín to find out if the rumors of Nazi atrocities were true. They left with the impression that all was well, duped by a well-planned "beautification" of the camp. The Germans carefully choreographed every detail of the visit. The observers saw children studying at staged schools that didn't exist, and store shelves, which had been specially set up, stocked with goods. So that the observers wouldn't think the camp was overcrowded, the Nazis transported some 7,500 of the camp's sick and elderly prisoners to Auschwitz. Children even ran up to an SS commandant just as the observers passed; the commandant handed the children cans of sardines to shouts of "What? Sardines again?" The trick worked so well that the Nazis made a film of the camp, *A Town Presented to the Jews from the Führer*, while it was still "self-governing."

Russian forces liberated Terezín on May 10, 1945, several days after Berlin had fallen to the Allies. Today, the camp stands as a memorial to the dead and a monument to human depravity.

ESSENTIALS

GETTING THERE If you're **driving,** Terezín lies just off the D-8 motorway that leads north out of Prague in the direction of Dresden and Berlin. Watch for the turnoff signs. It's a 45-minute drive.

Several **buses** leave daily from the small bus station above the **Nádraží Holešovice metro stop** (line C, red). The ride takes about an hour and costs 75Kč.

VISITOR INFORMATION The Museum of the Ghetto and the Small Fortress both have shops that stock reading material in several languages. Before heading out, you can read up on the area at the well-organized website www.pamatnik-terezin.cz.

ORGANIZED TOURS **Martin Tour,** Štěpánská 61, Prague 1 (© **224-212-473;** www.martintour.cz), offers a 5-hour bus trip to Terezín for 1,100Kč per person. The bus leaves five times a week at 9:30am from Staroměstské náměstí. See the website for more information and to book tickets.

The other travel agencies in Prague (listed earlier in this chapter under "Organized Day Tours") arrange their own guided tours to Terezín as well.

Wittmann Tours, Novotného lávka 5 Prague 1 (𝄢 **222-252-472;** www.wittmann-tours.com), specializes in Jewish legacy trips and offers a guided bus tour to the Terezín concentration camp that costs 1,250Kč for adults, 1,100Kč for students, free for children under 10. The bus leaves from Prague daily at 10am from May to October. March 15 through April, and November through December, the tour is available on Tuesday, Thursday, Saturday, and Sunday only. Make an advance reservation online or by calling the office. See chapter 7 for more information.

If you decide to go on your own and would like to have an English-speaking guide in the Jewish Memorial sites (it is included in the admission), you have to contact the company in writing before your departure. The e-mail address is pamatnik@pamatnik-terezin.cz.

SEEING THE CAMP

Terezín is a little hard to grasp at first. There are two main areas: the **Large Fortress** is essentially the town itself, the rectilinear streets laid out according to the best 18th-century military technology. Here was where the majority of ghetto residents lived during the Nazi occupation. You can walk around the still-drab streets and pay a visit the **Museum of the Ghetto,** which is headquartered in what was once the ghetto's school. The exhibits here chronicle the rise of Nazism and daily life in the camp. Admission to the museum is 160Kč for adults and 130Kč for children. It's open daily: November to March from 9am to 5:30pm and April to October from 9am to 6pm.

A 10-minute walk from the Large Fortress over the Ohře River brings you to the second main site, the **Small Fortress,** a smaller, more heavily fortified area that the Nazis used as a prison and torture zone for political prisoners. As you enter the main gate, the sign above, ARBEIT MACHT FREI (Work Sets One Free), sets a gloomy tone. You are free to walk through the prison barracks, execution grounds, workshops, and isolation cells. In front of the fortress's main entrance is the **National Cemetery (Národní hřbitov),** where the bodies exhumed from the mass graves were buried.

A combined ticket to enter both the **Ghetto Museum** and **Small Fortress** costs 200Kč for adults and 150Kč for children. The Small Fortress is open daily November to March 8am to 4:30pm and April to October 8am to 6pm. For more information or reservations for guided tours, call 𝄢 **416-782-225** (fax 416-782-300; www.pamatnik-terezin.cz).

WHERE TO DINE

It's understandable that there are few places to eat in Terezín. Indeed, you may not want to stay here much longer than you have to. However, inside the Large Fortress and the Museum is a decent inexpensive **buffet** with standard Czech fare.

---

9 LIDICE

32km (20 miles) NW of Prague

More than almost anywhere else in the world, two places in central Europe illustrate the destructive power of revenge: Dresden and Lidice. In 1942, when Czechoslovak

Impressions

I am returning, in the name of peace, 82 children to their native place as a warning symbol of the millions of murdered children in the senseless wars of mankind.
—Marie Uchytilová, in dedicating her 82 sculptures of children ages 1 to 16 removed by the Nazis from Lidice and executed at camps in Poland in 1942

paratroopers stationed in Britain assassinated SS Obergruppenführer Reinhard Heydrich, the highest-ranking officer in the Czech lands, the Nazis focused their anger on this tiny village. As Hitler's main leader in the newly claimed Nazi protectorate of Bohemia and Moravia, Heydrich had ruthlessly and systematically exterminated Jews and intellectuals, while coddling "ordinary" Czechs. The assassination of such a high-ranking official had to be dealt with severely. Why did Hitler choose Lidice? No one knows for sure, but this town was rumored to have accommodated the assassins, and someone had to pay.

When you get to Lidice, you'll see only a wooden cross and a green field where the town once stood. The Gestapo leveled the town and murdered its men. Women and children were taken to concentration camps, with less than half returning alive. In all, 348 of Lidice's 500 residents were killed. But in 1948, the Czech government, buffeted morally and financially by international outrage at this war crime, created a new town built on neighboring land. Today that town is beginning to get a little run-down, which often makes visitors feel even more melancholy.

ESSENTIALS

GETTING THERE If you're **driving,** take Hwy. 7 from the west side of Prague past the airport and head west onto Hwy. 551. It's a 20-minute drive.

Buses marked LIDICE-KLADNO depart for Lidice at the bus stops across the street from the Diplomat Hotel near the Dejvická metro station (last stop on the Green A line). Not all of the buses to Kladno stop in Lidice, so make sure you're on the right bus by confirming it with the driver. The ride takes about 25 minutes; it costs around 40Kč.

LEARNING ABOUT LIDICE

The **Lidice Memorial Museum** is a sobering monument to the town's martyred residents. In it are pictures of those killed, with descriptions of their fates. You can see a 20-minute English-language documentary on request; otherwise, a Czech version is usually running. There's also a 10-minute cassette that you can listen to as you walk around. Admission is 80Kč, and it's open daily: March from 9am to 5pm; April to October from 9am to 6pm; and November to February from 9am to 4pm. Call © **312-253-755** or go to www.lidice-memorial.cz for further information.

You're welcome to wander the field where the village once stood. Memorials in the "old" Lidice include a wooden cross marking the spot where the executed men were buried in a mass grave, and Lidice's old and new cemeteries (the old one was desecrated by the Nazis, who were looking for gold from the teeth of the dead).

Jumping into the Fourth Dimension

If you're looking for a not-so-cheap thrill or a vacation pick-me-up, Orlík could be the place for you. While most visitors come here for a peaceful walk in nature or a day at the beach, this attraction is of a different kind.

From high above the river on the Žd'ákovský Bridge, near another castle called Zvíkov, fearless men and women, tethered to two cords, jump off of the 50m-high (164-ft.) structure to reach the "fourth dimension." The 4-D jumping is supposed to be better than traditional bungee jumping because it allows you to fall farther before the two cords that tether you start to break your fall.

Many thrill-seekers—an average of 60 people a day—have taken the plunge, from an 11-year-old to a 60-year-old man. Each jump costs 900Kč. Weather permitting, you can try it June to September, from 11am to 5pm on Saturday and Sunday. The bridge is on the main highway leading out of town to the southeast (Hwy. 23). For more information, go to www.bungee.cz.

10 ORLÍK

70km (43 miles) S of Prague

Castles closer to Prague like Karlštejn and Konopiště get all the attention, but it is worthwhile to take the time to visit **Orlík Castle** ★. Set among forests that line the Vltava where it swells from the Orlík Dam, the castle never disappoints. It was built in the 13th century but has burned down several times, only to rise from the ashes with new additions and extensions. Inherited by the Schwarzenberg family in 1719 upon the death of Maria Ernestina, a member of the Habsburg dynasty, the castle was set high up on a hill, overlooking a once-vibrant trade route. It stayed that way until 1962, when water trapped by the Orlík Dam downriver flooded thousands of acres of land, bringing the water level up to the castle's lower walls.

Returned to the Schwarzenberg family in 1992, the castle retains its splendor, while the surrounding area has become one of the most popular lake resorts in the Czech Republic. Orlík is also one of the nicest swimming areas in the country and therefore is a very popular vacation destination for camping.

ESSENTIALS

GETTING THERE By car, this is an easy 1-hour **drive** from Prague. Take Hwy. 4 heading southwest out of the city. Turn right on Hwy. 19 and then right again into Orlík.

Buses headed to **Orlík** leave from the bus stop **Na Knížecí** at the Smíchovské nádraží station. Most buses will require a change, usually in Písek, but be sure to ask the driver. The 2-hour trip will cost around 90Kč each way.

VISITOR INFORMATION There's no real information center in this tiny town, but if you go to the castle gift shop, you can get some basic information.

EXPLORING THE CASTLE

Castle tours explain the history of the Schwarzenberg family and take you through a fine collection of artifacts celebrating the victory over Napoleon at the Battle of Leipzig in 1815. Keep an eye out for the hand-carved wooden ceiling that took more than 4 years to complete. Admission, including a guided tour in English, is 150Kč for adults and 80Kč for children. Hours are Tuesday to Sunday: June to August, from 9am to 6pm; May and September, from 9am to 5pm; and April and October, from 9am to 4pm. For more information call © 382-275-101 or go to www.schwarzenberg.cz/orlik.

WHERE TO DINE

Behind the castle gift shop, the **Restaurace U Toryka** ★, U zámku 116 (© 382-275-181; www.utoryka.cz), surprises you with its high-quality Czech offerings, including a spicy house goulash, though the portions could be a little bigger. Main courses are 90Kč to 240Kč; no credit cards are accepted. It's open daily from 10am to 8pm.

12

The Best of Bohemia

Of the two regions that make up the Czech Republic, the better known is the westernmost one, Bohemia. It is the land that gave Europe its favorite catchall term for free spirit: "Bohemian." Despite being beaten into submission by successive Austrian, German, and Soviet hegemony, that spirit has lived on. In the 14th century, the region's capital, Prague, was the seat of the Holy Roman Empire under Charles IV. So Bohemians maintain their collective historical memory that they too, at least briefly, ruled the world. Even under the domination of the Austrians, Bohemia's industrial base was world-class, and in the peace between the two world wars of the 20th century, independent Bohemia, especially Prague, created some of the greatest wealth on earth.

Much was lost in the destruction of World War II and the 4 decades of Communism that followed. The good news is that Bohemia is slowly returning to its earlier prominence, leaving behind its reputation as a satellite in the former Eastern Bloc and forging a more familiar role as a crossroads at the heart of Europe.

1 EXPLORING BOHEMIA

Though Bohemia was never divided historically, there are clear-cut distinctions in the region's geography that make going from town to town easier if you "divide" it into sections. After exploring Prague and central Bohemia, decide which area you'd like to see first and then plan accordingly.

WESTERN BOHEMIA

Home to the country's spa towns, western Bohemia is one of the few places where a full-blown tourist infrastructure was already in place by the time of the Velvet Revolution in 1989. Its main towns—**Karlovy Vary (Carlsbad), Mariánské Lázně (Marienbad),** and to a lesser extent, **Plzeň**—offer a wide array of accommodations, restaurants, and services to meet every visitor's needs and means.

A relatively inexpensive network of trains and buses covers the region, allowing travel between towns and to and from Prague with a minimum of fuss. West Bohemia is generally rougher terrain, so only serious bikers should consider seeing the area on two wheels.

SOUTHERN BOHEMIA

Once the religious hotbed of the country, south Bohemia was a focal point of the Hussite wars that eventually ravaged many of its towns and villages. Though the days of war took their toll, the region still features fine examples of architecture from every era. Southern Bohemia is also home to the Czech Republic's second-largest castle at **Český Krumlov,** a UNESCO-protected site that dazzles with its Disney-like qualities no matter how many times you visit.

There are two good approaches for exploring south Bohemia. If you're traveling by train or bus from Prague, make **Tábor** your first stop. It's on a main route, so the arrangements

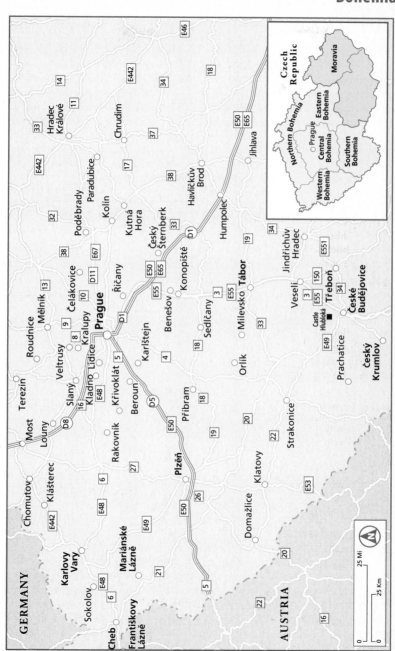

are easy. Then continue heading south, hooking up with **Třeboň, České Budějovice,** and **Český Krumlov.** If time is of the essence, you may want to set up camp in the area's main city, České Budějovice, and make several day trips, since nothing is that far away (Tábor, the farthest town, is 60km/37 miles away).

For those who have more time, consider a bike tour. These days, with the possibility of attack from Austria far diminished, south Bohemia is a much quieter setting with a less rugged terrain than west Bohemia. Biking here is much more feasible, and you'll find dozens of quaint towns dotting the countryside. **Central European Adventures,** Jáchymova 4, Prague 1 (✆ **222-328-879;** http://cea51.tripod.com), can arrange superb tours that include bike rentals, guides (English-speaking), transportation, and even canoe trips through southern Bohemia at a fraction of what it would cost if you arranged the same trip from home. Another organizer, the Czech-based **Greenways Travel Club** (✆ **519-511-572;** www.gtc.cz), organizes several Bohemian bike trips, including along the popular Prague-Vienna trail that runs straight through southern Bohemia

---

2 KARLOVY VARY (CARLSBAD) ★

120km (75 miles) W of Prague

The discovery of Karlovy Vary (Carlsbad) by Charles IV reads like a 14th-century episode of the old hit TV show *The Beverly Hillbillies.* According to local lore, the king was out huntin' for some food when up from the ground came a-bubblin' *water* (though discovered by his dogs and not an errant gunshot). Knowing a good thing when he saw it, Charles immediately set to work building a small castle in the area, naming the town that evolved around it Karlovy Vary, which translates as "Charles's Boiling Place." The first spa buildings were built in 1522, and before long, notables like Albrecht of Wallenstein, Peter the Great, and later Bach, Beethoven, Freud, and Marx all came to Karlovy Vary for a holiday retreat.

After World War II, Eastern Bloc travelers (following in the footsteps of Marx, no doubt) discovered the town, and Karlovy Vary became a destination for the proletariat. On doctors' orders, most workers would enjoy regular stays of 2 or 3 weeks, letting the mineral waters ranging from 110°F (43°C) to 162°F (72°C) from the town's 12 springs heal their tired and broken bodies. Even now, a large number of spa guests are here on doctor's orders and many of the "resorts" you see, in fact, are upscale hospitals.

Most of the 40-plus years of Communist neglect have been erased as a barrage of renovations continues to restore the spa's former glory. Gone is the statue of Russian cosmonaut Yuri Gagarin. Gone are almost all the fading, crumbling building facades that used to line both sides of the river. In their places stand restored buildings, cherubs, caryatids, and more.

Today, some 150,000 people, both traditional clientele and newer patrons, travel to the spa resort every year to sip, bathe, and frolic, though most enjoy the "13th spring" (actually a hearty herb-and-mineral liqueur called Becherovka) as much as—if not more than—the 12 nonalcoholic versions. Czechs will tell you that all have medical benefits. In a historical irony, the Russians have re-discovered Karlovy Vary in droves, so don't be surprised to hear Russian on the streets much more frequently than English, German, or Czech.

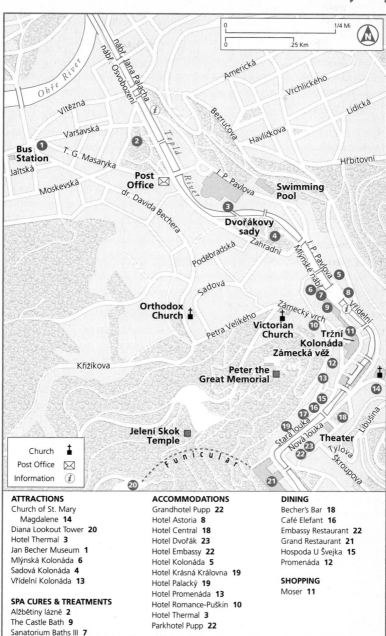

ATTRACTIONS
Church of St. Mary
  Magdalene **14**
Diana Lookout Tower **20**
Hotel Thermal **3**
Jan Becher Museum **1**
Mlýnská Kolonáda **6**
Sadová Kolonáda **4**
Vřídelní Kolonáda **13**

SPA CURES & TREATMENTS
Alžbětiny lázně **2**
The Castle Bath **9**
Sanatorium Baths III **7**

ACCOMMODATIONS
Grandhotel Pupp **22**
Hotel Astoria **8**
Hotel Central **18**
Hotel Dvořák **23**
Hotel Embassy **22**
Hotel Kolonáda **5**
Hotel Krásná Královna **19**
Hotel Palacký **19**
Hotel Promenáda **13**
Hotel Romance-Puškin **10**
Hotel Thermal **3**
Parkhotel Pupp **22**

DINING
Becher's Bar **18**
Café Elefant **16**
Embassy Restaurant **22**
Grand Restaurant **21**
Hospoda U Švejka **15**
Promenáda **12**

SHOPPING
Moser **11**

GETTING THERE At all costs, *avoid the train from Prague,* which takes more than 4 hours on a circuitous route. If you're arriving from another direction, Karlovy Vary's main train station is connected to the town center by bus no. 12 or 13.

Taking a bus to Karlovy Vary is much more convenient. Frequent express **buses** travel from Prague's Florenc bus station in 2¼ hours at a cost of about 140Kč. One of the best bus lines offering the trip is **Student Agency** (✆ **800-100-300;** www.studentagency.cz), which runs hourly buses to Karlovy Vary from Florenc bus station, and even shows a film during the trip. For information on train and bus timetables, go to www.jizdnirady.cz.

From Karlovy Vary's Dolní nádraží (bus station) take a 10-minute walk or the local bus no. 4 into Karlovy Vary's spa center. Note that you must have a ticket to board local transport. You can buy tickets for 16Kč at the bus station stop, or from the bus driver, which will then cost you 20Kč.

The nearly 2-hour **drive** from Prague to Karlovy Vary can be very busy and dangerous due to undisciplined Czech drivers. If you're going by car, take Hwy. E48 from the western end of Prague and follow it straight through to Karlovy Vary. This two-lane highway widens in a few spots to let cars pass slow-moving vehicles on hills. The spa area is closed to private vehicles, so you'll have to leave the car in one of several parking lots surrounding the area and walk from there.

VISITOR INFORMATION **Infocentrum města Karlovy Vary** is located near the main Mlýnská Kolonáda, at Mlýnské nabřeží 5 (✆ **355-321-176**). It's open Monday to Friday from 9am to 7pm and Saturday and Sunday from 10am to 6pm. It has a window at the terminal of the **Dolní (lower) nádraží** bus and train station, Západní ulice (✆ **353-232-838**). These are the official town's information centers, which will answer your questions and help you with accommodations, getting tickets for entertainment in the city, and so on. Be sure to pick up *Promenáda* magazine, a comprehensive collection of events with a small map of the town center. Alternatively, you'll find information on www.karlovyvary.cz.

SPECIAL EVENTS The **Karlovy Vary International Film Festival** is the place to see and be seen. Each summer (in early July), the country's film stars, celebrities, and wealthy folks, supported by a cast of international stars like Sharon Stone, Robert Redford, and Morgan Freeman, can be spotted taking part in one of Europe's biggest film festivals. Nine venues screen more than 300 films during the 10-day festival. If you think you might want to attend, book accommodations well in advance, and note that the prices for rooms and meals are correspondingly higher during the festival. Go to www.iffkv.cz for more information.

Karlovy Vary plays host to several other events, including a **jazz festival** and **beer Olympiad** in May, a **Dvořák singing contest** in June, a **Summer Music Festival** in August, and a **Dvořák Autumn Music Festival** in September and October.

For details on the festivals, contact the information center listed above.

 Tips **A Driving Warning**

Be warned that drivers on Hwy. E48 between Prague and Karlovy Vary are often reckless. Please take extra care when driving.

ORIENTATION Karlovy Vary is shaped like a T, with the Teplá River running along the stem of the resort and the Ohře River at the top of the T. Most of the major streets are pedestrian promenades lining both sides of the Teplá.

EXPLORING KARLOVY VARY

The town's slow pace and pedestrian promenades, lined with turn-of-the-20th-century Art Nouveau buildings, turn strolling into an art form. Nighttime walks take on an even more mystical feel as the sewers, the river, and the many major cracks in the roads emit steam from the hot springs running underneath.

Avoid Karlovy Vary's "New Town," which happens to be conveniently left off most tourist maps. Its only real attractions are a McDonald's and a couple of ATMs (which you can also find in the historic center).

If you're traveling here by train or bus, a good place to start your exploration is the **Hotel Thermal,** I. P. Pavlova 11 (© **359-001-111**), at the northern end of the Old Town's center. Built in the 1970s, it exemplifies how obtrusive Communist architecture could be. Nestled between the town's eastern hills and the Ohře River, the glass, steel, and concrete Thermal sticks out like a sore thumb amid the rest of the town's 19th-century architecture. Nonetheless, you'll find three important places at the Thermal: the only centrally located outdoor public pool; an upper terrace boasting a truly spectacular view of the town; and Karlovy Vary's largest theater, which holds many of the film festival's premier events. Take it all in. But since the Hotel Thermal is not that pleasing to the eye, it's best to keep walking so you won't remember too much of it.

As you enter the heart of the town on the river's west side, you'll see the ornate white wrought-iron gazebo named **Sadová Kolonáda** adorning the beautifully manicured park, **Dvořákovy Sady.** Continue to follow the river, and about 100m (328 ft.) later you'll encounter the **Mlýnská Kolonáda.** This long, covered walkway houses several Karlovy Vary springs, which you can sample free 24 hours a day. Each spring has a plaque beside it describing its mineral elements and temperature. Bring your own cup or buy one just about anywhere (see the box "Spa Cures & Treatments," below) to sip the waters, since most are too hot to drink from with your hands. When you hit the river bend, you'll see the majestic **Church of St. Mary Magdalene** perched atop a hill, overlooking the **Vřídlo,** the hottest spring. Built in 1736, the church is the work of Kilián Ignác Dientzenhofer, who also created two of Prague's more notable churches—both named St. Nicholas.

Housing Vřídlo, which blasts water some 15m (49 ft.) into the air, is the glass building where a statue of Soviet cosmonaut Yuri Gagarin once stood. (Gagarin's statue has since made a safe landing at the Karlovy Vary Airport, where it greets the waves of Russian visitors who flood the town.) Now called the **Vřídelní Kolonáda,** the structure, built in 1974, houses several hot springs that you can sample for free daily from 6am to 7pm. There are also public restrooms, open daily 6am to 6pm and costing 10Kč.

Heading away from the Vřídelní Kolonáda are Stará and Nová Louka streets, which line either side of the river. Along **Stará (Old) Louka** are several fine cafes and glass and crystal shops. **Nová (New) Louka** is lined with many hotels and the historic town's main theater, built in 1886, which houses paintings by notable artists like Klimt and has just finished a major renovation project that has restored the theater to its original splendor.

Both streets lead eventually to the **Grandhotel Pupp,** Mírové nám. 2 (© **353-109-111**). The Pupp's main entrance and building several years ago underwent extensive renovations that more or less erased the effects of 40 years of state ownership under

Communism (under the former regime, the hotel's name was actually "Moskva-Pupp" just to remind everyone who was actually calling the shots). Regardless of capitalism or Communism, the Pupp remains what it always was: the grande dame of hotels in central Europe. Once catering to nobility from all over Europe, the Pupp still houses one of the town's finest restaurants, the Grand (see below), while its grounds are a favorite with the hiking crowd.

If you still have the energy, atop the hill behind the Pupp stands the **Diana Lookout Tower** (*C* **353-222-872**). Footpaths lead to the tower through the forests and eventually spit you out at the base of the tower, as if to say, "Ha, the trip is only half over." The five-story climb up the tower tests your stamina, but the view of the town is more than worth it. For those who aren't up to the climb up the hill, a cable car runs up the hill every 15 minutes June to September daily from 9:15am to 6:45pm; February, March, November, and December 9:15am to 4:45pm; April, May, and October 9:15am to 5:45pm; for 40Kč one-way, 70Kč round-trip.

And if you have some time left at the end of your stay, visit the **Jan Becher Museum,** T. G. Masaryka 57 (*C* **359-578-142;** www.becherovka.cz), to find out about the history of the town's secret: the formula for Becherovka. This herbal liquor is a sought-after souvenir, and you will get to taste it here. The museum is open daily 9am to 5pm; admission is 100Kč adults, 50Kč students.

SHOPPING

Crystal and porcelain are Karlovy Vary's other claims to fame. Dozens of shops throughout town sell everything from plates to chandeliers.

Ludvík Moser founded his first glassware shop in 1857 and became one of this country's foremost names in glass. You can visit and take a 30-minute tour of the **Moser Factory,** kapitána Jaroše 19 (*C* **353-416-132;** www.moser-glass.com; bus no. 1, 10, or 22), just west of the town center. Its glass museum is open daily 9am to 5pm, and tours run daily 9am to 3pm. There's also a **Moser Store,** on Tržiště 7 (*C* **353-235-303**), right in the heart of New Town; it's open daily from 10am to 7pm (Sat–Sun until 6pm). Dozens of other smaller shops also sell the famed glass and are as easy to find in the Old Town as spring water.

If you're looking for something a little cheaper, try a box of *Oplatky,* thin round wafer cookies on sale throughout the spa area. The fillings range from vanilla to chocolate to nut and occasionally coffee—just don't try to wash them down with a mug of spa water!

WHERE TO STAY

Private rooms used to be the best places to stay in Karlovy Vary with regard to quality and price. But this is changing as more and more hotels renovate and raise standards—as well as prices. Private accommodations can still provide better value, but they take a little extra work. If you want to arrange a room, try the **Infocentrum** (see above). Expect to pay about 1,500Kč for a double.

Some of the town's major spa hotels accommodate only those who are paying for complete treatment, unless for some reason their occupancy rates are particularly low. The hotels I've listed below accept guests for stays of any length.

Parking is a problem for nearly all of the hotels, aside from the bigger properties like the Grandhotel Pupp and the Thermal, which have their own paid parking lots. You're best advised to leave your car in one of the paid lots just outside the immediate spa area and walk (or take a taxi) to your hotel.

Very Expensive

Grandhotel Pupp ★   The Pupp, built in 1701, is one of Europe's oldest grand hotels. Its public areas boast the expected splendor and charm, as do the renovated guest rooms. The best ones tend to be those facing the town center and are located on the upper floors; these have good views and sturdy wooden furniture. Some rooms have amenities such as air-conditioning, television, minibar, and safe, though not all do. The Grand has as grand a dining room as you'll find, with the food to match (see "Where to Dine," below). The hotel also has a stylish casino (open midnight–4am). The rack rates are high, but check the website for occasional deals.

Mírové nám. 2, 360 91, Karlovy Vary. ℂ **353-109-111.** Fax 353-226-032. www.pupp.cz. 111 units. 7,750Kč double deluxe; from 11,250Kč suite. Rates include breakfast. AE, DC, MC, V. Valet parking. **Amenities:** 4 restaurants; bar; cafe; golf course; health club; pool; room service; tennis courts; casino. *In room:* TV, hair dryer, minibar.

Expensive

Hotel Central   Located next to the theater, this hotel certainly is central. A recent face-lift has restored the hotel to its 1920s splendor, though it's probably not worth the relatively expensive price tag for rooms that aren't overly spacious, but only adequate. Those on the upper floors provide great views of the Vřídelní Kolonáda.

Divadelní nám. 17, 360 01 Karlovy Vary. ℂ **353-182-630.** Fax 353-182-631. www.interhotel-central.cz. 87 units. 4,400Kč double; 5,100Kč suite. AE, MC, V. **Amenities:** Restaurant; Internet; pool; treatment center. *In room:* TV, minibar.

Moderate

Hotel Dvořák ★   As part of the Vienna International hotel chain, the Dvořák has improved immensely over the several years, especially in terms of service. This hotel is within sight of the Pupp, but it's less expensive. The Pupp may have the history and elegance, but the Dvořák has the facilities. The rooms are spacious, with elegant decor and medium-size bathrooms with lots of marble. The staff is very attentive. Business travelers will appreciate the hotel's business facilities.

Nová Louka 11, 360 21 Karlovy Vary. ℂ **353-102-111.** Fax 353-102-119. www.hotel-dvorak.cz. 126 units. 3,375Kč double. AE, DC, MC, V. **Amenities:** Restaurant; fitness center; indoor pool; sauna. *In room:* TV, hair dryer, minibar.

Hotel Embassy ★   On the riverbank across from the Pupp, the Embassy has well-appointed rooms, many with an early-20th-century motif. Set in a historic house, the rooms are medium-size with medium-size bathrooms. The staff here really helps make this hotel worthy of consideration, as does the proximity to the pub, which serves some of the best goulash and beer in the city.

Nová Louka 21, 360 01 Karlovy Vary. ℂ **353-221-161.** Fax 353-223-146. www.embassy.cz. 20 units. 3,130Kč double; 3,990Kč suite. AE, MC, V. **Amenities:** Pub; lobby bar; indoor golf; pool table. *In room:* TV, minibar.

Hotel Kolonáda   The Kolonáda, with its lovely facade, was formed by a merger of the Otava and Patria hotels. As the name suggests, it's across from the Mlýnská Kolonáda. The hotel's interior is modern and renovated, as are the rooms, the best of which overlook the Kolonáda.

I. P. Pavlova 8, 360 01 Karlovy Vary. ℂ **353-345-555.** Fax 353-347-828. www.kolonada.cz. 162 units. 3,185Kč double; 3,788Kč suite. AE, MC, V. **Amenities:** 2 restaurants; bar; cafe; relaxation center w/pool; mountain-bike rental; Internet. *In room:* TV, fridge, minibar, hair dryer.

Spa Cures & Treatments

Most visitors to Karlovy Vary come for a spa treatment, a therapy that lasts 1 to 3 weeks. After consulting with a spa physician, you're given a specific regimen of activities that may include mineral baths, massages, waxings, mudpacks, electrotherapy, and pure oxygen inhalation. After spending the morning at a spa or sanatorium, you're usually directed to walk the paths of the town's surrounding forest.

The common denominator of all the cures is an ample daily dose of hot mineral water, which bubbles up from 12 springs. This water definitely has a distinct odor and taste. You'll see people chugging it down, but it doesn't necessarily taste very good. Some thermal springs actually taste and smell like rotten eggs. You may want to take a small sip at first. Do keep in mind that the waters are used to treat internal disorders, so the minerals may cleanse the body thoroughly—in other words, they can cause diarrhea.

You'll also notice that almost everyone in town seems to be carrying "the cup." This funny-looking cup is basically a mug with a built-in straw running through the handle. Young and old alike parade around with their mugs, filling and refilling them at each thermal water tap. You can buy these mugs everywhere for as little as 60Kč or as much as 230Kč; they make a quirky souvenir. **But be warned:** None of the mugs can make the warmer hot springs taste any better.

The minimum spa treatment lasts 1 week and must be arranged in advance. A spa treatment package traditionally includes room, full board, and complete therapy regimen; the cost varies from about 900Kč to 2,500Kč per person per day, depending on season and facilities. Rates are highest from May to September and

Hotel Krásná Královna (the Beautiful Queen Hotel)   A fresh property with a familiar face has emerged in the spa zone. The original accents of this 18th-century guesthouse have been revived with fresh colors, classic furniture, and fine accessories. This family-run hotel is again offering comfort and a cozy atmosphere as well as access to spa amenities in the town.

Stará Louka 335/48, Karlovy Vary. © **353-852-611.** Fax 353-852-612. www.krasnakralovna.cz. 21 units. 3,200Kč double; 4,100Kč suite. AE, MC, V. **Amenities:** Restaurant. *In room:* TV, hair dryer, minibar.

Hotel Palacký Ⓥalue   This is one of the better deals in town. The hotel is ideally situated on the west side of the river so it gets sun almost all day. The rooms, with their mostly bare walls and low beds, seem huge, especially the ones with a river view. The staff can seem more like furniture than people who help guests, but that's a small price to pay for the relatively good value.

Stará Louka 40, 360 01 Karlovy Vary. © **353-222-544.** Fax 353-223-561. www.hotelpalacky.cz. 20 units. 2,250Kč–2,730Kč double. AE, MC, V. **Amenities:** Restaurant. *In room:* TV, fridge, hair dryer.

Hotel Promenáda   Next door to the Romance-Puškin is the Promenáda. This hotel faces the Kolonáda and has a beautiful view of the old center of the town. Rooms on the lower floors are more spacious than those on the upper levels, but all have an elegant decor highlighted with wrought-iron bed frames and large windows.

lowest from November to February. Nearly all of the hotels in town will provide spa and health treatments, so ask when you book your room. Most will happily arrange a treatment if they don't provide them directly.

If you're coming for just a day or two, you can experience the waters on an "outpatient" basis. The largest therapeutic complex in town (and in the Czech Republic) is the **Alžbětiny Lázně-Lázně V,** Smetanovy sady 1145/1 (© **353-304-211;** www.spa5.cz). On its menu are more than 60 kinds of treatments, including water cures, massages, a hot-air bath, a steam bath, a whirlpool, and a pearl bath, as well as use of their swimming pool. You can choose packages of different procedures that run between 340Kč for an anti-cellulite beer bath to 980Kč for a hot stone massage. It's open Monday to Friday 8am to 3pm for spa treatments; the pool is open Monday to Friday 9am to noon and 1 to 9pm, Saturday 9am to 9pm, and Sunday 9am to 6pm.

The **Sanatorium Baths III,** Mlýnské nábřeží 7 (© **353-225-641**), welcomes day-trippers with mineral baths, massages, saunas, and a cold pool. It's open Monday to Friday 7am to 2pm for spa treatments; the swimming pool and sauna are open Monday to Friday 3 to 6pm and Saturday 1 to 5pm.

The Castle Spa (Zámecké Lázně), Zámecký vrch 1; (© **353-225-502;** http://carlsbad-plaza.com), is a relatively new (and fancy) spa and wellness house located in a reconstructed site at the foot of the Castle Tower (Zámecká věž) in the old city center. You can make reservations over the website and see a menu of treatments, including both those that require a medical exam and those that don't. The latter include massages, and various baths and aroma treatments.

Tržiště 31, 360 01 Karlovy Vary. © **363-225-648.** Fax 353-229-708. www.hotel-promenada.cz. 16 units. 3,200Kč–3,700Kč double. AE, MC, V. **Amenities:** Restaurant; cafe. *In room:* TV, minibar.

Hotel Thermal   What better way to experience what it was like to stay in Karlovy Vary under Communism? Built in the 1970s, Hotel Thermal towers above the town, rising like a steel-and-glass phoenix from the steam of the river's spas. But because of its size—and the cinema on its ground floor—it becomes a hub during the film festival. All kidding aside, the Thermal also qualifies as a possible place to stay because of its location, services, and size. Don't expect anything exciting, but do take a picture of yourself in the *Star Trek* seats in the lobby bar. While the reception area is still very much a throwback to the 1970s, the guest rooms have been tastefully refurbished and the bathrooms refitted in a modern style.

I. P. Pavlova 11, 360 01 Karlovy Vary. © **359-001-111.** Fax 359-002-603. www.thermal.cz. 273 units. 3,100Kč double. AE, MC, V. **Amenities:** 2 restaurants; bar; heated outdoor pool; cinema. *In room:* TV.

Inexpensive

Hotel Astoria   In the heart of the historic town, the restored Astoria mainly caters to spa guests but, unlike many of its competitors, it is big enough to usually have several rooms available for nontreatment visitors. The staff can be a little gruff at times, but the rooms are big, with satellite TV an added bonus. The restaurant serves standard Czech fare, with a lot of vegetable dishes as well, though I'd recommend trying one of the other places in town for a less bland experience.

Vřídelní 92, 360 01 Karlovy Vary. ℂ **353-335-111.** Fax 353-224-368. www.astoria-spa.cz. 100 units. 2,250Kč double. AE, MC, V. **Amenities:** Restaurant. *In room:* TV, fridge.

Hotel Romance-Puškin   This place has now been renamed, but for years it's carried the name of the great Russian poet we know as Pushkin. The hotel occupies an intricately ornamented 19th-century Art Nouveau building that has been renovated. It has a terrific location, close to the springs. The rooms are rather basic, but they're comfortable enough. Ask for one that has a balcony facing St. Mary Magdalene Church and enjoy one of the nicest views in the Old Town.

Tržiště 37, 360 90 Karlovy Vary. ℂ **353-222-646.** Fax 353-224-134. www.hotelromance.cz. 37 units. 2,000Kč–2,940Kč double. AE, MC, V. **Amenities:** Restaurant; room service. *In room:* TV, hair dryer, minibar.

WHERE TO DINE

Expensive

Embassy Restaurant ★★ CZECH/CONTINENTAL   On the ground floor of the Embassy Hotel, this is one of the oldest and best restaurants in town. It offers an intimate dining room with historic interior. If you visit in winter, get a table next to the original hearth. In summer, sit on the bridge outside the front door. Here you'll find many traditional Czech dishes with slight twists that make them interesting. The grilled loin of pork covered with a light, creamy green pepper sauce makes a nice change from the regular roast pork served by most Czech restaurants. The spicy goulash is more reminiscent of Hungary's piquant flavors than blander Czech fare. The warm strawberries and peppercorns dessert is much better than it sounds.

Nová Louka 21. ℂ **353-221-161.** Reservations recommended. Soups 70Kč; main courses 220Kč–600Kč. AE, MC, V. Daily 11am–11pm.

Grand Restaurant CONTINENTAL   It's no surprise that the Grandhotel Pupp has the nicest dining room in town: an elegant space with tall ceilings, huge mirrors, and glistening chandeliers. A large menu features equally large portions of salmon, chicken, veal, pork, turkey, and beef in a variety of heavy and heavier sauces. Even the mouthwatering trout with mushrooms is smothered in butter sauce.

In the Grandhotel Pupp, Mírové nám. 2. ℂ **353-109-646.** Reservations recommended. Soups 80Kč; main courses 290Kč–750Kč. AE, MC, V. Daily noon–3pm and 6–11pm.

Promenáda ★ CZECH/CONTINENTAL   This cozy, intimate spot may not be as elegant as the Grand Restaurant, but the cooking is more adventurous. Across from the Vřídelní Kolonáda, the Promenáda offers a wide menu with generous portions. The daily menu usually includes well-prepared wild game, but the mixed grill for two and the chateaubriand, both flambéed at the table, are the chef's best dishes. The wine list features a large selection of wines from around Europe, but don't neglect the Czech wines. An order of crêpes suzette, big enough to satisfy two, rounds out a wonderful meal.

Tržiště 31. ℂ **353-225-648.** Reservations highly recommended. Soups 70Kč; appetizers 90Kč–320Kč; main courses 290Kč–750Kč. AE, MC, V. Daily noon–11pm.

Moderate

Becher's Bar CONTINENTAL   A renovation plan in the mid-1990s gave birth to this slightly upscale cocktail lounge—basically the town's one and only cocktail bar—that calls out for Tom Jones (or his Czech equivalent, Karel Gott) to pick up a microphone and begin crooning and gyrating. The menu is part roadhouse, part pub, and overall a pleasant change from the regular heavy meals offered around town. Plus, it's the only place around open this late, with live music most nights to boot.

In the Grandhotel Pupp, Mírové nám. 2. ⓒ **353-109-483.** Appetizers and light meals 140Kč–250Kč. AE, MC, V. Daily 7pm–4am.

Hospoda U Švejka CZECH   This addition to the pub scene plays on the tried-and-true touristy *Good Soldier Švejk* theme. Luckily, the tourist trap goes no further, and once inside, you find a refreshingly nonsmoky though thoroughly Czech atmosphere. Locals and tourists alike rub elbows while throwing back some fine lager for 69Kč per half liter, and standard pub favorites such as goulash and beef tenderloin in cream sauce.

Stará Louka 10. ⓒ **353-232-276.** Soups 55Kč ($3); appetizers 69Kč–109Kč; main courses 159Kč–319Kč. AE, MC, V. Daily 11am–10pm.

Inexpensive

Cafe Elefant COFFEE/DESSERT   Who needs to travel all the way to Vienna? Since this is a cafe in the true sense of the word, all you'll find are coffee, tea, alcoholic and nonalcoholic drinks, desserts, and enough ambience to satisfy the hordes of Germans who flock to this landmark. (Be prepared to hear more Russian or German than Czech, as this is a see-and-be-seen haunt for foreigners.) The Elefant is widely known for its Belle Epoque style and is famous for its freshly baked cakes. Its many outdoor tables overlook the pedestrian promenade.

Stará Louka 32. ⓒ **353-223-406.** Cakes and desserts 50Kč–120Kč. AE, MC, V. Daily 10am–10pm.

3 MARIÁNSKÉ LÁZNĚ (MARIENBAD)

46km (29 miles) SW of Karlovy Vary, 160km (100 miles) W of Prague

When Thomas Alva Edison visited Mariánské Lázně in the late 1800s, he reportedly declared, "There is no more beautiful spa in all the world." Mark Twain, who also stopped by, was slightly more critical. He acknowledged the beauty of the architecture, but in typical Twain style decried what he saw as a "health factory."

Mariánské Lázně now stands in the shadow of the Czech Republic's most famous spa town, Karlovy Vary, but it wasn't always that way. First noted in 1528 by Bohemian historians, the town's mineral waters gained prominence at the end of the 18th and beginning of the 19th century. Nestled among forested hills and packed with romantic and elegant pastel hotels and spa houses, the town, commonly known by its German name, Marienbad, has played host to such luminaries as Goethe (this is where his love for Ulrike von Levetzow took root), Chopin, Strauss, Wagner, Freud, and Kafka (in addition to Edison and Twain). England's Edward VII found the spa resort so enchanting that he visited several times and even commissioned the building of the country's first golf club.

ESSENTIALS

GETTING THERE   There are several express trains from Prague's main station for 238Kč (trip time: 2 hr., 50 min.). Mariánské Lázně train station, Nádražní nám. 292, is south of the town center; take bus no. 5 into town. If getting here from Karlovy Vary, there are about eight trains daily; the trip takes 1 hour and 40 minutes and the fare is 55Kč. For timetables, go to www.jizdnirady.cz.

The **bus** from Prague takes about 3 hours and often requires a change in Plzeň. It costs about 180Kč. The Mariánské Lázně bus station is adjacent to the train station on Nádražní náměstí; take bus no. 5 into town.

Driving from Prague, take Hwy. E50 through Plzeň to Stříbro—about 22km (14 miles) past Plzeň—and head northwest on Hwy. 21. The clearly marked route can take up to 2 hours. Parking is not generally a problem as there's paid street parking on the main drag, Hlavní třída.

VISITOR INFORMATION   Along the main strip lies the **Infocentrum,** Hlavní 47, 353 01, Mariánské Lázně (☏ **354-622-474**). In addition to dispensing advice, the staff sells maps and concert tickets and can arrange accommodations in hotels and private homes. It's open daily 9am to noon and 1 to 6pm, closed on Sundays in January and February. For information and tips about what's going on, go to www.marianskelazne.cz.

SPECIAL EVENTS   One of the few places in central Europe not to claim Mozart as one of its sons, Mariánské Lázně has instead chosen to honor one of its frequent visitors, Chopin, with a yearly festival devoted entirely to the Polish composer. The **Chopin Festival** usually runs for 8 to 10 days near the end of August. Musicians and directors from all over the world gather to play and listen to concerts and recitals. In addition, several local art galleries hold special exhibits. Tickets range from 180Kč to 1,500Kč.

Each June, the town plays host to a **classical music festival** with many of the Czech Republic's finest musicians, as well as those from around the world. For more details or ticket reservations for either event, contact **Infocentrum** (see "Visitor Information," above).

Patriotic Americans can show up on **July 4** for a little down-home fun, including a parade and other flag-waving special events commemorating the town's liberation by U.S. soldiers in World War II.

Sports-minded travelers can play one of the country's best golf courses and see how you measure up to the likes of Seve Ballesteros, Bernhard Langer, and Sam Torrance, who all played here at the first European PGA tour event, the Czech Open.

ORIENTATION   Mariánské Lázně is laid out around **Hlavní třída,** the main street. A plethora of hotels, restaurants, travel agencies, and stores fronts this street. **Lázeňská Kolonáda,** a long, covered block beginning at the northern end of Hlavní třída, contains six of the resort's eight major springs.

TAKING THE WATERS

When you walk through the town, it's almost impossible to miss eye-catching **Lázeňská Kolonáda,** just off Skalníkovy sady. From Hlavní třída, walk east on Vrchlického ulice. Recently restored to its former glory, this colonnade of cast iron and glass is adorned with ceiling frescoes and Corinthian columns. It was built in 1889 and connects half a dozen major springs in the town center; this is the focal point of those partaking in the ritual. Bring a cup to fill or, if you want to fit in with the thousands of guests who are serious about their spa water, buy one of the porcelain mugs with a built-in straw that are offered just about everywhere. Keep in mind that the waters are used to treat internal disorders, so the minerals may act to cleanse the body thoroughly by causing diarrhea. You can wander the Kolonáda any time; water is distributed daily from 6am to noon and 4 to 6pm.

Located just next to the colonnade is the modern landmark of the city. A pool surrounding a flower sculpture of stainless steel and stone is known as **"The Singing Fountain"** and contains a set of 250 water jets. At the top of every odd hour, between 7am and 9pm, and at 10pm, these jets spray in sync to music by different composers.

The Spa Treatment

For a relaxing mineral bubble bath or massage, make reservations through the **Marienbad Kur & Spa Hotels Information Service,** Masarykova 22, 353 29 (*© **354-655-501;** www.marienbad.cz). Also ask at your hotel, as most provide spa treatments and massages or can arrange them. Treatments begin at 350Kč and go north in a hurry from there. The city's main website (www.marianske lazne.cz) contains an excellent description in English of the various springs, as well as the treatments and cures available at the spa.

LEARNING ABOUT THE CITY'S PAST

There's not much town history, since Mariánské Lázně officially came into existence only in 1808. But engaging brevity is what makes the two-story **City Museum (Městské Muzeum),** Goetheovo nám. 11 (*© **354-622-740**), worth recommending. Chronologically arranged displays include photos and documents of famous visitors. Goethe slept here, in the upstairs rooms in 1823, when he was 74 years old. If you ask nicely, the museum guards will play an English-language tape that describes the contents of each room. You can also request to see the museum's English-language film about the town. Admission is 60Kč and it is open Tuesday to Sunday from 9:30am to 5:30pm.

HIKING OR GOLFING

If the thought of a spa treatment doesn't appeal, you can take a relaxing walk through the woods. The surrounding forest, **Slavkovský les (Slavkov Forest),** has about 70km (43 miles) of marked footpaths and trails through the gentle hills that abound in the area.

If you're a die-hard golfer or just looking for a little exercise, the **Royal Golf Club of Mariánské Lázně** (*© **354-624-300;** www.golfml.cz), a 6,135-yard, par-72 championship course, lies on the edge of town. The club takes pay-as-you-play golfers, with a fully equipped pro shop that rents clubs. Greens fees are 1,500Kč to 1,700Kč and club rental is 500Kč. Reservations are recommended on weekends.

WHERE TO STAY

The main strip along Hlavní třída is lined with incredibly grand-looking hotels, many with rooms facing the Kolonáda. But don't be deceived by appearances. Many of the hotels are far more impressive on the outside than they are on the inside. Most of the hotels, in fact, are filled with spa patients and have an atmosphere more akin to an upscale hospital.

The best bet is simply to stroll along Hlavní třída and shop around for a room. You'll likely end up with a better deal.

Also, don't be confused by the room rates. Many of the hotels have complicated pricing menus that include spa treatments and board that you may not want or need. To add to the confusion, many properties break with Czech tradition and list prices per person (not per room). Ask the receptionist for an all-in price before agreeing to take the room.

There is paid parking on the street along Hlavní, and most of the hotels will have their own paid lots.

Grandhotel Pacifik After a renovation of the building, this hotel has become one of the top establishments on the main strip. Alas, the guest rooms are outfitted with sterile though decent furniture. Ask for a room that faces the street. The restaurant and cafe have also been redone, much for the better. All are now bright and cheery, pleasant for a quick coffee or drink.

Mírové nám. 84, 353 29 Mariánské Lázně. ℭ **354-651-111.** Fax 354-651-200. www.marienbad.cz. 109 units. 3,750Kč double; 4,800Kč suite. AE, V. **Amenities:** Restaurant; treatment center. *In room:* A/C, TV, hair dryer, minibar.

Hotel Villa Butterfly ★ One of the many hotels on the main street to be spruced up and expanded, the Butterfly has upgraded to 94 bright and spacious rooms. In fact, from the front hall to the fitness room and even all the way to its new underground parking, the Butterfly has really taken off. An English-speaking staff and a good selection of foreign-language newspapers at the reception area are added bonuses. The Fontaine is one of the town's largest restaurants yet remains a quiet place to eat top-rate Czech and international cuisine. The hotel offers guests Internet access.

Hlavní třída 655, 353 01 Mariánské Lázně. ℭ **354-654-111.** Fax 354-654-200. www.marienbad.cz. 96 units. 3,000Kč double; 4,320Kč suite. Rates include breakfast. AE, DC, MC, V. **Amenities:** 2 restaurants; bar; cafe; wellness center; conference center. *In room:* A/C, TV, hair dryer, minibar.

Parkhotel Golf ★ One of the more luxurious hotels in town, the Golf isn't actually in town but across from the golf course about 3km (2 miles) down the road leading to Karlovy Vary. This hotel is busy, so reservations are recommended. The English-speaking staff delivers on their pledge to cater to every wish. The rooms are bright and spacious, and there's an excellent restaurant and terrace on the first floor. Not surprisingly, given the hotel's name, the staff can help arrange a quick 18 holes across the street. The hotel has also opened its own spa center to pamper guests a little more.

Zádub 580, 353 01 Mariánské Lázně. ℭ **354-622-651.** Fax 354-622-655. www.parkhotel-golf.cz. 27 units. 3,800Kč double; 4,900Kč suite. Rates include breakfast. AE, DC, MC, V. **Amenities:** Restaurant; bar; fitness center; golf course; pool; room service; spa center; sauna; tennis courts. *In room:* TV, hair dryer, minibar.

Moderate

Hotel Bohemia ★ In the middle of the action on Hlavní, the Bohemia has several rooms with balconies that overlook the Kolonáda. It has been recently remodeled and improved, rooms tend to be a little larger, and for those looking for location, you can't get more central.

Hlavní třída 100, 353 01 Mariánské Lázně. ℭ **354-610-111.** Fax 354-610-555. www.orea.cz/bohemia. 76 units. 2,800Kč–3,820Kč double. AE, DC, MC, V. **Amenities:** Restaurant; cafe; treatment center. *In room:* TV, minibar.

Hotel Excelsior Across from the Nové Lázně (New Bath), the Excelsior has benefited inside and out from a face-lift. Several rooms have 19th-century period furnishings and ornate balconies overlooking the park that leads up to the Kolonáda. There are two restaurants, including the Churchill, one of the best watering holes on the strip. The hotel staff is also more attentive than those at some other hotels in town.

Hlavní třída 121, 353 01 Mariánské Lázně. ℭ **354-697-111.** Fax 354-625-346. www.hotelexcelsior.cz. 64 units. 3,400Kč double. AE, DC, MC, V. **Amenities:** 2 restaurants; Internet; spa and health treatments. *In room:* TV, hair dryer, minibar.

(Kids) Family Fun

If you're looking for a weekend break with the family and want to have an enjoyable experience outdoors, book a weekend at the modest **Koliba** ★, Dusíkova 592 (© **354-625-169**). In the summer, dozens of miles of wooded trails are open for hiking and biking. Be careful, though, because many of the paths lead through the golf course, and while golf is becoming more popular in the Czech Republic, the skill level is still such that you need to beware of errant balls. In the winter, try out the mini–ski hill. Two tows at the foot of the hotel take you up a 150m (492-ft.) hill perfect for anyone learning to ski. There are also dozens of kilometers of cross-country ski trails through the local forests that are always in top condition. A 1-day ski-pass costs about 300Kč.

The après-ski atmosphere of the lodge, with its giant fireplace and numerous tables, provides the perfect respite from a hectic week. At night the flames of the open grill roasting all different sorts of game will ease the pain of all those bumps and bruises. In the summer, the trails are ideal for hiking.

OREA Hotel Palace Zvon ★ The recently renovated 1920s Palace is a beautiful Art Nouveau hotel about 90m (300 ft.) from the Kolonáda. The rooms are extremely comfortable, with high ceilings and large bay windows lending an airy effect. In addition to a good Bohemian restaurant with a lovely terrace, the hotel contains a cafe, a wine room, and a snack bar.

Hlavní třída 68, 353 01 Mariánské Lázně. © **354-686-111.** Fax 354-686-222. www.orea.cz/palace-zvon. 126 units. 2,600Kč double; 3,600Kč suite. AE, DC, MC, V. **Amenities:** Restaurant; bar; cafe; wine room; spa and health treatments. *In room:* TV, hair dryer, minibar.

Inexpensive

Hotel Koliba ★ (Value) Away from the main strip but still only a 7-minute walk from the Kolonáda, the Koliba is a rustic hunting lodge set in the hills on Dusíkova, the road leading to the golf course and Karlovy Vary. The rooms are warm and inviting, with the wooden furnishings giving the hotel the feel of a country cottage.

Dusíkova 592, 353 01 Mariánské Lázně. © **354-625-169.** Fax 354-626-310. http://koliba.xercom.cz. 15 units. 1,800Kč double Sun–Thurs; 1,960Kč double Fri–Sat. AE, MC, V. **Amenities:** Restaurant/bar; bike rental, ski lift. *In room:* TV, minibar.

Residence Omega (Finds) (Kids) Walk through the passage from the main street and before you know it, you'll be standing at one of the more recently built accommodation options in town. The Omega is slightly different from the hotels that line the street in that it is several apartments that have been connected to form a hotel. Inside you find very bright, sunny rooms with small living areas and kitchenettes, as well as spotless bathrooms. This is a great find for families, as the hotel is cheap but big enough to allow kids their own living space.

Hlavní třída 36a, 353 01 Mariánské Lázně. ©/fax **354-601-300.** 6 units. 1,600Kč–1,800Kč double apt. AE, MC, V. *In room:* TV, minibar.

Moderate

Churchill Club Restaurant ★ CZECH Don't let the name fool you—the food is traditional Czech, not British, with few surprises. A lively bar with a good selection of local and imported beer makes the Churchill one of the few fun places to be after dark in this quiet town. Try the Winston steak platter if you're really hungry.

Hlavní třída 121. © **354-622-705.** Soups 35Kč; main courses 80Kč–520Kč. AE, MC, V. Daily 11am–11pm.

Koliba ★ CZECH Like the hotel it occupies, the Koliba Restaurant is a shrine to the outdoors. The dining room has a hearty, rustic atmosphere that goes perfectly with the restaurant's strength: wild game. Check the daily menu to see what's new, or choose from the wide assortment of specialties *na roštu* (from the grill), including wild boar and venison. The Koliba also has an excellent selection of Moravian wines that you can order with your meal or at its wine bar.

Dusíkova 592. © **354-625-169.** Reservations recommended. Soups 35Kč; main courses 119Kč–425Kč. MC, V. Daily 11:30am–10pm.

Restaurant Fontaine CZECH/INTERNATIONAL The Fontaine is one of the more formal gastronomical experiences you will find in town. The dining room is very large but remains quiet, though it's a little too well lit. Bow-tied waiters serve traditional Bohemian specialties like succulent roast duck, broiled trout, and chateaubriand, as well as some inventive variations. Try the duck in oranges for an interesting mix of sweet and sour.

In the Villa Butterfly, Hlavní třída 655. © **354-654-111.** Soups 45Kč; main courses 90Kč–410Kč. AE, DC, MC, V. Daily noon–2:30pm and 6:30–10pm.

Inexpensive

Classic Cafe/Restaurant CZECH A nice place to stop for a light bite, the Classic offers a large assortment of good fresh salads. This open, airy cafe/restaurant has one of the friendliest staffs in town, though a few more tables out front would be welcome. It also brews a mean espresso.

Hlavní třída 131. No phone. Salads 45Kč–145Kč; main courses 69Kč–219Kč. AE, DC, MC, V. Daily 9am–11pm cafe, 11am–11pm restaurant.

4 PLZEŇ (PILSEN)

88km (55 miles) SW of Prague

"Zde se narodilo pivo." The phrase ("the birthplace of beer") greets you at almost every turn in Plzeň. And they aren't kidding. Some 400 years ago, a group of men formed Plzeň's first beer-drinking guild, and today beer is probably the only reason you'll want to stop at this otherwise industrial town. Unfortunately for the town, its prosperity and architecture were ravaged during World War II, and few buildings were left untouched. The main square, Náměstí Republiky, is worth a look, but after that there's not much to see.

ESSENTIALS

GETTING THERE It's more comfortable taking the train to Plzeň than the bus. A fast **train** from Prague whisks travelers to Plzeň in just under 2 hours without you having to witness the mayhem caused by Czech drivers. Trains between the two cities are just as

(Fun Facts) Plzeň's Claim to Fame

Founded in 1295 by Václav II, Plzeň was and remains western Bohemia's administrative center. King Václav's real gift to the town, however, wasn't making it an administrative nerve center but granting it brewing rights. More than 200 microbreweries popped up, one in almost every street-corner basement. Realizing that the brews they were drinking had become mostly plonk by the late 1830s, rebellious beer drinkers demanded quality, forcing the brewers to try harder. "Give us what we want in Plzeň, good and cheap beer!" became the battle cry. In 1842, the brewers combined their expertise to produce a superior brew through what became known as the Pilsner brewing method. If you don't believe it, look in your refrigerator. Most likely, the best beer in there has written somewhere on its label "Pilsner brewed."

plentiful and fit almost every schedule. The train costs 147Kč second class. To get from the train station to town, walk out the main entrance and take Americká Street across the river; turn right onto Jungmannova, which leads to the main square.

The **bus** trip from Prague takes 1½ hours, and it tends to be cramped. It costs 90Kč one-way. If you do take the bus, head back into town along Husova to get to the square.

Thanks to the government's highway-building scheme, Plzeň has moved closer to Prague—or at least it seems that way. A once treacherous 2-hour **drive** on a narrow two-lane highway has been replaced by an easy 45-minute cruise on the Hwy. D5, which leaves Prague from the west. Once you get to Plzeň, dump your car in a paid parking lot or use pay parking on the street.

VISITOR INFORMATION   Trying to be as visitor-friendly as possible, the **City Information Center Plzeň,** náměstí Republiky 41, 301 16 Plzeň (© **378-035-330;** fax 378-035-332; www.icpilsen.cz or www.plzen.eu), is packed with literature to answer your questions. It is open daily 9am to 6pm.

SPECIAL EVENTS   If you're an American or speak English, being in Plzeň in early May is quite an experience. Unlike most of the rest of the country, which was liberated from the Nazis by the Soviet Red Army, Plzeň was liberated by U.S. troops. Soldiers under the command of Gen. George S. Patton took the city on the morning of May 6, 1945. The city still marks the liberation with a big festival in the first week of May, when Czechs drive around in old U.S. army jeeps, everyone seems to be dressed up like a GI, and the city goes on a 5-day bender.

In mid-August the city hosts a modest music festival called **Jazz on the Streets,** highlighted with several concerts by top-name Czech musicians.

Anxious to capitalize on its beer heritage and always happy to celebrate, Plzeň has started its own Oktoberfest, called **Pivní slavnosti (Beer fest),** which takes place in the end of September and beginning of October.

For more details on festivities for all events, contact the **City Information Center Plzeň** (see above).

ORIENTATION   Plzeň's old core is centered on náměstí Republiky. All of the sights, including the brewery, are no more than a 10-minute walk from here.

A trip to the **Plzeňské Pivovary** (**Pilsner Breweries;** $\textcircled{C}$ **377-062-888;** www.prazdroj.cz/
en), at U Prazdroje 7 will interest anyone who wants to learn more about the brewing
process. The "brewery" actually comprises several breweries, pumping out brands like
Pilsner Urquell and Gambrinus, the most widely consumed beer in the Czech Republic.
The brewery has responded to the high demand for tours with a menu of sightseeing
options that includes no less than two different brewery tours, a brewing museum, and
a presentation called "Brewing—A Successful Czech Industry" (a full list is included on
the brewery website at www.prazdroj.cz/en). Most visitors will be content with simply
the 1-hour main tour and possibly a quick look in at the Beer Museum down the street
(see below). Brewery tours in English are held daily at 12:45pm, 2:15pm, and 4:15pm.
Tickets, which include an English-speaking guide and entry to the Beer Museum, cost
250Kč for adults and 130Kč for students and seniors. And, *yes,* the tour does include a
beer tasting.

If you didn't get your fill of beer facts at the brewery, the **Pivovarské muzeum** (**Beer
Museum;** $\textcircled{C}$ **377-235-574;** www.prazdroj.cz/en) is 1 block away on Veleslavínova 6.
Inside this former 15th-century house, you'll learn everything you wanted to know about
beer but were afraid to ask. In the first room, once a 19th-century pub, the guard winds
up an old German polyphone music box from 1887 that plays the sweet, scratchy strains
of Strauss's *Blue Danube.* Subsequent rooms display a collection of pub artifacts, brewing
equipment, and mugs. Most displays have English captions, but ask for a more detailed
museum description in English when you enter. Entry to the museum is included with
the brewery tour ticket, but it's also possible to skip the beer tour and buy a ticket just
for the museum (but who would want to do that?). Separate entry into the museum costs
90Kč for adults and 60Kč for children. The museum is open daily from April to December from 10am to 6pm (to 5pm Jan–Mar).

The Beer Museum is also the starting point for an unrelated (to brewing, that is) tour,
though they still give you a glass of beer to drink. Here you'll find the entrance to the
Pilsen Historical Underground ($\textcircled{C}$ **377-235-574;** www.plzenskepodzemi.cz), a series
of subterranean passages that was built starting in the 14th century to protect residents
of the medieval city from attack as well as other purposes. Tours of the underground cost
90Kč for adults and 60Kč for children and seniors. Daily English-language tours are
conducted at 1pm.

EXPLORING PLZEŇ

Filled with more knowledge than you may want about the brewing process, proceed to
the main square to see what's hopping elsewhere in town. Dominating the center of the
square is the Gothic **Cathedral of St. Bartholomew,** with the tallest steeple in the Czech
Republic at 100m (328 ft.). A beautiful marble Madonna graces the main altar. The
church is open daily from about 7am to 8pm.

You'll see Italian flair in the first four floors of the 16th-century **Town Hall** and in the
sgrafitti (etchings) adorning its facade. Later on, more floors were added, as well as a
tower, gables, and brass flags, making the building appear as though another had fallen
on top of it. The Town Hall ($\textcircled{C}$ **378-032-550**) is open Monday to Friday from 8am to
6pm, Saturday from 9am to 1pm. In front of the Town Hall, a **memorial** built in 1681
commemorates victims of the plague.

Just west of the square on Sady pětatřicátníků lie the shattered dreams of the several
thousand Jews who once called Plzeň home. The **Great Synagogue,** the third largest in the

world, was built in the late 19th century. A painstaking restoration project has brought back this shrine's beauty and is a must-see to take in some of the history that makes the Czech Republic so fascinating. The synagogue is now used to host photo and art exhibits.

WHERE TO STAY

The **City Information Center** (see "Visitor Information," above) can provide a list of private rooms and low-cost pensions around town. Expect to pay about 600Kč per person for this kind of accommodation. Most of the hotels offer paid on-site parking.

Hotel Central ★   As you look around the historically beautiful Old Town square, one thing stands out: the Hotel Central. This rather sterile building is across from St. Bartholomew's Church. The surly staff notwithstanding, the hotel's a solid choice and surprisingly quiet despite its central location. The rooms have been recently remodeled and all look fresh. Ask for one of the rooms facing east; they have a nice view of the church as the sun rises. The hotel's restaurant and cafe are both smoke free.

Náměstí Republiky 33, 301 00 Plzeň. ✆ **377-226-757.** Fax 377-226-064. www.central-hotel.cz. 77 units. 2,200Kč–2,800Kč double. AE, MC, V. **Amenities:** Restaurant; cafe; bar; exercise room; sauna; solarium. *In room:* TV, minibar.

Hotel Continental ★ (Value)   The old-time Continental recalls the period from the two world wars, when Pilsen was a boomtown. It languished under the Communists but is slowly finding new life. The owners have worked hard to update many of the rooms, giving them funky names like the "John Malkovich" suite (110), after the U.S. actor, or the "Gérard Depardieu" (313), where the French actor stayed during the filming of the movie *Victor Hugo.* Ask to see several rooms, since they're all different. Not all of them are that nice, but the hotel is still great value.

Zbrojnická 8, 305 34 Plzeň. ✆ **377-235-292.** Fax 377-221-746. www.hotelcontinental.cz. 55 units. 1,720Kč double; 2,500Kč suite. AE, MC, V. **Amenities:** Restaurant; bar; casino. *In room:* TV.

Hotel Slovan (Value)   An elegant turn-of-the-20th-century staircase graces the entrance foyer to this venerable hotel. But after that, the rooms descend into the same 1970s-modern decor that, hard as it is to believe, was once in fashion. Nonetheless, as one of the cheapest places in the city, the clean and quiet rooms remain very good value. The city's main square is only about 2 blocks north.

Smetanovy sady 1, 301 37 Plzeň. ✆ **377-227-256.** Fax 377-227-012. http://hotelslovan.pilsen.cz. 96 units. 1,600Kč double. AE, MC, V. **Amenities:** Restaurant; bar. *In room:* TV.

Pension K   About a block from the Old Town square, this 18th-century home has been converted into a nice pension with a relaxing atmosphere. All rooms are comfortable and have washroom facilities and satellite TV.

Bezručova 13, 305 34 Plzeň. ✆/fax **377-329-683.** 13 units. 1,400Kč double. No credit cards. *In room:* TV, no phone.

WHERE TO DINE

Grill Restaurant 106.1 CZECH/CONTINENTAL   Near náměstí Republiky, this small restaurant named after a local radio station excels at grilled meats and poultry. Appetizers like mozzarella slices with tomatoes and olive oil stand out in this city devoted to the beer culture. The fondues are a little pricey but not a bad alternative if you have someone to share with.

Bezručova 20, Plzeň. ✆ **377-222-371.** Soups 35Kč; main courses 90Kč–270Kč. MC, V. Mon–Sat 11am–midnight.

Restaurace Na Spilce ★ CZECH The Na Spilce looks like a 600-seat tourist trap, but the food is quite good and reasonably priced. The standard *řízky* (schnitzels), goulash, and *svíčková na smetaně* (pork tenderloin in cream sauce) are hearty and complement the beer that flows from the brewery. If you've got a big appetite or just can't decide, try the *Plzeňská bašta,* with ample servings of roasted pork, smoked pork, sausage, sauerkraut, and two kinds of dumplings.

U Prazdroje 7 (just inside the brewery gates). ℂ **377-062-755.** Soups 35Kč; main courses 70Kč–230Kč. AE, MC, V. Sun–Thurs 11am–10pm; Fri–Sat 11am–11pm.

Restaurace Žumbera CZECH A real pub that attracts mainly Czechs, Žumbera has food that's a cut above that of its competitors (of which there are many). If you can't decide, try the *Žumberská mísa,* which is piled high with roast pork, smoked meat, spinach, cabbage, and several types of dumplings.

Bezručova 14. ℂ **377-322-436.** Soups 35Kč; main courses 72Kč–160Kč. MC, V. Mon–Thurs 9am–10pm; Fri–Sat 9am–midnight; Sun 9am–7pm.

Šenk Na Parkánu ★ CZECH This is part of the Beer Museum and is meant to evoke an old-fashioned tap room, where you can try various types of beer direct from the brewery, including hard-to-find varieties like unfiltered and unpasteurized yeast lager and other concoctions that are likely to attract *pivophiles.* The menu here is limited pretty much to beer snacks and small items.

Veleslavínova 4. ℂ **377-324-485.** No credit cards. Sun–Thurs 11am–10pm; Fri–Sat 11am–1am.

U Salzmannů CZECH This oldest pub in Plzeň, dating from 1637, has been renovated to reincarnate a previous *Jugendstil* rendition of the building. The beer is fresh, but the food is a little disappointing in its standard appearance and taste—you would expect a little flair, given the edifice. However, if you want to stay near the main square and don't want to make the long walk back across the river and up the hill to the brewery pubs, this pub will fulfill your needs admirably.

Pražská 8. ℂ **377-235-855.** www.usalzmannu.cz. Soups 35Kč; main courses 90Kč–195Kč. AE, MC, V. Daily 10am–11pm.

---

5 CHEB (EGER) & FRANTIŠKOVY LÁZNĚ

168km (103 miles) W of Prague, 40km (25 miles) SW of Karlovy Vary

Few people who travel through Cheb—most on their way across the border to Germany—actually stop and take a look around. From the outside, that's understandable, but it's too bad, since the center of Cheb is one of the more architecturally interesting places in west Bohemia. Its history is fascinating as well.

A former stronghold for the Holy Roman Empire on its eastern flank, Eger, as it was then known, became part of Bohemia in 1322. Cheb stayed under Bohemian rule until it was forcibly handed over to Germany as part of the 1938 Munich Pact. Soon after the end of World War II, it was returned to Czech hands, when most of the area's native Germans, known as Sudeten Germans, were expelled for their open encouragement of the invading Nazi army. You can see this bilingual, bicultural heritage in the main square, which could be mistaken for being on either side of the border if it weren't for the Czech writing on windows. These days, the Germans have returned as tourists (regrettably, many indulge in the town's thriving sex trade—although it's been cleaned up in recent years, you may still see a woman standing incongruously next to a bus stop wearing nothing but a bathing suit). Still, Cheb is worth exploring for its mélange of architectural styles, the eerie Jewish Quarter, Špalíček, and the enormous Romanesque Chebský Hrad (Cheb Castle).

Only about 20 minutes up the road from Cheb is the smallest of the three major Bohemian spa towns, **Františkovy Lázně.** Though it pales in comparison to Karlovy Vary and Mariánské Lázně, Františkovy Lázně has taken great strides in the past few years to erase the decline it experienced under Communism. There's not much to see save for the **Spa Museum,** which holds an interesting display of bathing artifacts, but it's a quieter place to spend the night than Cheb. Listed below are places to stay and dine in both Cheb and Františkovy Lázně.

ESSENTIALS

GETTING THERE   Cheb is located on the E48, one of the main highways leading to Germany. If you're **driving** from Prague, take the same route you would to Karlovy Vary, which eventually brings you to Cheb. The drive takes about 2 hours.

To get to Františkovy Lázně from Cheb by car, take Hwy. E49. The trip takes about 20 minutes.

Express **trains** heading due west from Prague usually stop in Cheb, as do several trains daily from Karlovy Vary. Cheb is on a main train route of the Czech Republic, so it's easy to catch international connections here. The train from Prague takes around 4 hours and costs 356Kč second class.

While it's a long bus ride (around 4 hr.), several buses do make the trip daily to Cheb from Prague's Florenc bus station. The price is around 250Kč.

VISITOR INFORMATION   You'll find maps, guidebooks, and lodging at the **Tourist Information Centre,** Jateční 476/2 (© **354-440-302;** fax 354-440-330; www.tic. mestocheb.cz).

ORIENTATION   At the center of the Old Town lies the triangular náměstí Krále Jiřího z Poděbrad. Most of the main sights you'll want to see lie either directly on the square or on one of the many streets leading off it.

EXPLORING CHEB

The main square, **náměstí Krále Jiřího z Poděbrad,** attracts most of the attention and is a good place to begin a stroll of the Old Town. Though it has been overrun with tourist shops and cafes that serve mediocre German fare, the square still shines with Gothic burgher houses and the baroque **Old Town Hall (Stará radnice).** At its south end, the **statue of Kašna Roland,** built in 1591 and a former symbol of capital punishment, reminds people of the strength wielded by justice. At the other end of the square stands the **Kašna Herkules,** a monument to the town's former strength and power. Next to it is a cluster of 11 timber houses, called **Špalíček.** These used to be owned by Jews in the early 14th century, but a fervently anti-Semitic clergy in the area incited such hatred that the Jews were forced up Židská ulice (Jews St.) and into an alleyway called ulička Zavražděných (Murder Victim's Lane), where they were unceremoniously slaughtered in 1350.

Across from Špalíček is the **Cheb Museum** (© **354-422-246**), where another murder took place almost 300 years later—that of Albrecht von Wallenstein in 1634. On the upper level, a display vividly depicts the assassination. The museum's first floor displays many 20th-century paintings, from which you can trace the town's slow demise. Admission is

50Kč. From May through October, the museum is open Tuesday to Sunday from 9am to 5pm, and from November through April, Wednesday to Sunday 9am to 5pm.

The Old Town is also packed with churches. The most interesting is **St. Nicholas,** around the corner from the museum. It's a hodgepodge of architectural styles: Its Romanesque heritage is reflected in the tower windows, while a Gothic portal and baroque interior round out the renovations over the years. The church is open daily from 9am to 6pm.

TOURING CHEB CASTLE

An excellent example of Romanesque architecture in the northeast part of the Old Town is **Cheb Castle.** Overlooking the Elbe River, the castle, built in the late 12th century, is one of central Europe's largest Romanesque structures.

The castle's main draws are its **Chapel of Sts. Erhart and Uršula** and the **Černá věž (Black Tower).** The two-tiered, early Gothic chapel has a somber first floor where the proletariat would congregate, while the emperor and his family went to the much cheerier and brighter second floor with its Gothic windows.

Across the courtyard from the chapel stands the **Černá věž (Black Tower).** From its 18m-high (59-ft.) lookout, you'll have the best views of the town. The tower seems dusty and smeared with pollution; its color is black because the blocks from which it is made are lava rocks taken from the nearby Komorní Hůrka volcano (now dormant).

There are no tours of the castle and the English text provided at the entrance does little to inform you. Admission is 50Kč. The castle and tower are open to the public from early April through October from Tuesday to Sunday 9am to 5pm.

WHERE TO STAY

In Cheb

Hotel Hvězda (Hotel Star) Overlooking the rather noisy main square, the Hvězda is one of the few stars of the Cheb hotel universe. The rooms are small, but most overlook the square, and the staff tries to make your stay comfortable. If you can't stay in Františkovy Lázně and don't want to drive farther, this is a decent choice.

Náměstí Krále Jiřího z Poděbrad 4-6, 350 02 Cheb. ℂ **354-422-549.** Fax 354-422-546. www.hotel-hvezda.cz. 40 units. 1,050Kč double. AE, MC, V. *In room:* TV.

In Františkovy Lázně

Hotel Tři Lilie (Three Lilies Hotel) The four-star Three Lilies is worth the extra money since it's one of the only luxury hotels in the area. Cheb needs a nice hotel like this. At night, you can relax, blocking out noise in your spotless, spacious room that's outfitted with satellite television. The staff is very attentive and can arrange spa treatments, massages, and other health services.

Národní 3, 351 01 Františkovy Lázně. ℂ **354-208-900.** Fax 354-208-905. www.franzensbad.cz. 32 units. 2,700Kč double; 4,860Kč suite. AE, MC, V. **Amenities:** Restaurant/bar; cafe; spa treatments. *In room:* TV, minibar.

WHERE TO DINE

In Cheb

There are lots of restaurants and cafes on the central square, Náměstí Krále Jiřího z Poděbrad. The best advice would be to walk around and check menus to see something you like. Some of the better places are listed below.

Kavárna Špalíček CZECH This kavárna is better for a coffee stop than for a full meal. You can enjoy great people-watching from the terrace, but Špalíček's real charm lies inside the building, which sits like an island in the middle of the square. This special place is a piece of living history.

Náměstí Krále Jiřího z Poděbrad. ⊘ **354-422-568.** Soups 40Kč; main courses 90Kč–240Kč. No credit cards. Daily 10am–10pm.

Restaurace Fortuna CZECH If you're craving a *schnitzel*, this is as good a place as any. Most Czech specialties are served, and the goulash's slightly piquant sauce is a pleasant surprise. It's one of the only restaurants open late, and a terrace right on the main square lends to its appeal.

Náměstí Krále Jiřího z Poděbrad 28. ⊘ **354-422-110.** Soups 30Kč; main courses 119Kč–189Kč. No credit cards. Daily 10am–10pm.

U Koček CZECH Another decent option for goulash, pork cutlets, *svíčková,* fried cheese, and some interesting chicken dishes, the best of which is probably the chicken with mushrooms. The prices here seem to be slightly lower than the competition, so it's a good choice if you're on a tight budget.

Kamenná 1. ⊘ **354-422-170.** Main courses 98Kč–189Kč. No credit cards. Daily 10am–10pm.

In Františkovy Lázně

Hotel Tři Lilie (Three Lilies Hotel) CZECH/CONTINENTAL Just as its hotel is the cream of the local crop, so too is the Three Lilies restaurant. Though the service fails to keep pace with the upscale appearance, this restaurant does very well with creative game dishes that combine Czech basics and European flair.

Národní třída 3. ⊘ **354-208-900.** Main courses 130Kč–520Kč. AE, MC, V. Daily 7am–9pm.

6 ČESKÉ BUDĚJOVICE

147km (91 miles) S of Prague

This fortress town was born in 1265, when Otakar II decided that the intersection of the Vltava and Malše rivers would be the site of a bastion to protect the approaches to southern Bohemia. Although Otakar was killed at the battle of the Moravian Field in 1278 and the town was subsequently ravaged by the rival Vítkovic family, the construction of České Budějovice continued, eventually taking the shape originally envisaged.

In the 15th century, the Hussite revolution swept across southern Bohemia, with one exception—České Budějovice, which, with its largely Catholic population, remained true to the king. Passing the loyalty test with flying colors, it developed into one of Bohemia's wealthiest and most important towns, reaching its pinnacle in the 16th century. This rise made České Budějovice an architecturally stunning place. As the town prospered, older Gothic buildings took on a Renaissance look. A new town hall was built and the flourishing old market (Masné Krámy) was rebuilt. Towering above it all was a new 72m-tall (236-ft.) turret, the Black Tower. Sadly, the Thirty Years' War (1618–48) and a major fire in 1641 ravaged most of the town, leaving few buildings unscathed. But the Habsburg Empire came to the town's rescue in the 18th century, building baroque-style edifices that stand to this day.

Today, České Budějovice, the hometown of the original Budweiser brand beer, is now more a bastion for the beer drinker than a protector of Bohemia. But its slow pace, relaxed atmosphere, and interesting architecture make it a worthy stop, especially as a base for exploring southern Bohemia or for those heading on to Austria.

ESSENTIALS

GETTING THERE If you're **driving,** leave Prague to the south via the main D1 expressway and take the cutoff for Hwy. E55, which runs straight to České Budějovice. The trip takes about 1½ hours.

Daily express **trains** from Prague make the trip to České Budějovice in about 2½ hours. The fare is 320Kč first class or 213Kč second class. Several express **buses** run from Prague's Roztyly station (on the metro's C line) each day and take 3 hours; tickets cost 152Kč.

VISITOR INFORMATION **Tourist Infocentrum,** náměstí Přemysla Otakara II. 2 (© **386-801-413;** www.c-budejovice.cz), provides maps and guidebooks and finds lodging. It is open Monday to Friday 8:30am to 6pm, Saturday until 5pm, and Sunday 10am to 4pm. In winter it is open Monday and Wednesday 9am to 5pm; Tuesday, Thursday, Friday 9am to 4pm; and Saturday 9am to 1pm.

SPECIAL EVENTS Each August, České Budějovice hosts the largest **International Agricultural Show** in the country (www.vcb.cz).

If you're passing through in the late fall or winter and want to see Czechs at their most emotional, head out to a match of the **Czech Extraliga hockey** league at the hockey arena on ulice F. A. Gerstnera 8/7, where the local team, HC Mountfield, does battle. Arguably some of the best hockey in the world is played in the Czech Republic, which you can see for a fraction of the price—from 100Kč to 180Kč—you'd pay to see players of a similar caliber in the North American National Hockey League. The games are rarely sold out. The box office (© **386-352-705;** www.hokejcb.cz) opens 1 hour before the game. The local newspapers, tourist information center, and posters pasted around the town will tell you what time the next match is.

ORIENTATION České Budějovice's circular Staré Město (Old Town) centers around the Czech Republic's largest cobblestone square, náměstí Přemysla Otakara II.

EXPLORING THE TOWN

You can comfortably see České Budějovice in a day. At its center is one of central Europe's largest squares, the cobblestone **náměstí Přemysla Otakara II**—it may actually be too large, as many of the buildings tend to get lost in all the open space. The square contains the ornate **Fountain of Sampson,** an 18th-century water well that was once the town's principal water supply, plus a mishmash of baroque and Renaissance buildings. On the southwest corner is the **Town Hall,** an elegant baroque structure built by Martinelli between 1727 and 1730. On top of the Town Hall, the larger-than-life statues by Dietrich represent the civic virtues: justice, bravery, wisdom, and diligence.

One block northwest of the square is the **Černá věž (Black Tower),** which you can see from almost every point in the city. Consequently, its 360 steps are worth the climb to get a bird's-eye view in all directions. The most famous symbol of České Budějovice, this 70m-tall (236-ft.) 16th-century tower was built as a belfry for the adjacent **St. Nicholas Church.** This 13th-century church, one of the town's most important sights, was a bastion of Roman Catholicism during the 15th-century Hussite rebellion. You shouldn't miss the church's flamboyant, white-and-cream, 17th-century baroque interior.

The tower is open Tuesday to Sunday (daily July–Aug) from 10am to 6pm; admission is 20Kč. The church is open daily from 9am to 6pm.

TOURING A BEER SHRINE

On the town's northern edge sits a shrine to those who pray to the gods of the amber nectar. This is where **Budějovický Budvar,** Karolíny Světlé 4 (© **387-705-111**), the original brewer of Budweiser beer, has its one and only factory. Established in 1895, Budvar draws on more than 700 years of the area's brewing tradition to produce one of the world's best beers.

One trolley bus—no. 2—and bus no. 8 stop by the brewery; this is how the brewery ensures that its workers and visitors reach the plant safely each day. You can also hop a cab from the town square for about 150Kč.

The brewery offers 1-hour guided tours in Czech, English, and German at 2pm from Monday to Friday in season (Apr–Oct) and Tuesday to Friday at 2pm during the rest of the year. Normally, it's okay just to show up, but to be sure call ahead to the **Budvar Visitors' Centre** at the brewery (© **387-705-341;** http://budweiser-budvar.cz) to reserve a place. Tours cost 100Kč.

Once you're inside the brewery, the smell may cause flashbacks to some of the wilder frat parties you've attended. This is a traditional brew, and not much has changed at the brewery over the past hundred years or so. The room where everything moves along conveyer belts and goes from dirty old bottles to boxed cartons is fascinating.

WHERE TO STAY

Several agencies can locate reasonably priced private rooms. Expect to pay about 700Kč per person, in cash. The **Tourist Infocentrum,** náměstí Přemysla Otakara II. 2 (© **386-801-413**), can point you toward a wide selection of conveniently located rooms and pensions.

Grandhotel Zvon Location is everything to the city's most elegant hotel, which occupies several historic buildings on the main square. In fact, pretty soon the hotel and its accompanying businesses will occupy nearly a quarter of the addresses in the area. The upper-floor rooms have been thoroughly renovated and tend to be more expensive, though the views from all the front rooms can't be topped. Try to avoid the smaller rooms, usually reserved for tour groups. One of the biggest changes here in recent years has been the staff, which appears to be learning that guests deserve respect and quality treatment.

Náměstí Přemysla Otakara II. 28, 370 01 České Budějovice. © **381-601-601.** Fax 381-601-605. www. hotel-zvon.cz. 75 units. 2,800Kč–5,000Kč double. AE, DC, MC, V. **Amenities:** Restaurant; cafe; bar; Internet. *In room:* TV, minibar.

Hotel Bohemia ★ The Bohemia really isn't a hotel but a small pension in the city center, as you'll discover when you walk into the lobby and think that you've stepped into someone's house. The staff make you feel like one of the family, with their attentive service, and the rooms are pleasant despite being a little small.

Hradební 20, 370 01 České Budějovice. © **386-360-691.** Fax 386-116-116. www.bohemiacb.cz. 18 units. 1,790Kč double. AE, MC, V. **Amenities:** Restaurant. *In room:* TV, minibar.

Hotel Gomel Not known for its ambience, the 18-floor Gomel has a straightforward approach and offers comfortable, clean rooms with either a tub or a shower and few other frills. Views from the upper floors can't be beat; ask for one that faces into town. Still relatively rare for this part of the country, some of the rooms have air-conditioning. Located just off the main road entering the city from the north, the Gomel is hard to miss—it's the tallest building around—and is only a few minutes' walk from the historic Old Town.

Pražská 14, 370 04 České Budějovice. ✆ **389-102-111.** Fax 389-102-333. www.cpihotels.cz. 204 units. 2,400Kč double; 3,900Kč suite. Rates include breakfast. AE, DC, MC, V. **Amenities:** Restaurant; bar; casino. *In room:* TV, hair dryer, minibar.

Hotel Malý Pivovar (Small Brewery) ★★   Around the corner from the Zvon, this renovated 16th-century microbrewery combines the charms of a B&B with the amenities of a modern hotel. The kind of management found here is a rarity in the Czech tourism industry: They work hard to help out. The rooms are bright and cheery, with antique-style wooden furniture and exposed wooden ceiling beams providing a farmhouse feeling in the center of town. It's definitely worth consideration if being directly on the square (you're only 30m/98 ft. from it) isn't a priority. This is also one of the best places to arrange a trip to the brewery.

Ulice Karla IV. 8–10, 370 01 České Budějovice. ✆ **386-360-471.** Fax 386-360-474. www.malypivovar.cz. 29 units. 2,760Kč double; 3,200Kč suite. Rates include breakfast. AE, DC, MC, V. **Amenities:** Restaurant/ pub; wine bar. *In room:* TV, minibar.

Hotel U Solné brány   Another of the growing numbers of conveniently located hotels just off the main square, U Solné brány is one of the products of post-Communism: a bright renovated hotel with friendly management. It almost feels like a pension. Most rooms have balconies, making a cold Budvar from the minibar almost mandatory in the early evening or as a nightcap.

Radniční ul. 11, 370 01 České Budějovice. ✆ **386-354-121.** Fax 386-354-120. www.hotelusolnebrany.cz. 11 units. 1,990Kč double; 2,290Kč suite. Rates include breakfast. AE, MC, V. **Amenities:** Restaurant. *In room:* TV, minibar.

WHERE TO DINE

Masné Krámy (Meat Shops) ★★ CZECH   If you've pledged not to go to any "tourist traps," rationalize going to this one by reminding yourself that it's also a historic building dating from the 14th century. Just northwest of náměstí Přemysla Otakara II, labyrinthine Masné Krámy occupies a series of drinking rooms on either side of a long hall and is a must for any serious pub-goer. The inexpensive and filling food is pure Bohemia, including several pork, duck, and trout dishes. Come for the boisterous atmosphere or for what's possibly the best goulash in the Czech Republic.

Krajinská 29. ✆ **387-201-301.** www.masne-kramy.cz. Main courses 120Kč–270Kč. AE, MC, V. Mon–Thurs 10:30am–11pm; Fri–Sat 10:30am–midnight; Sun 10:30am–9pm.

Potrefená husa CZECH/INTERNATIONAL   This addition to the list of local restaurants is owned by Budvar's competitor, the Prague brewery Staropramen. In its modern interior, which is divided into a bar, restaurant, and large terrace with a pleasant view of the river, there is a good selection of pasta, meat dishes, and salads at reasonable prices. The barbecue ribs are very popular, and so is the Czech potato soup served in a bread bowl.

Česká 66. ✆ **387-420-560.** Main courses 89Kč–295Kč. AE, MC, V. Mon 11am–midnight; Tues–Thurs 11am–1am; Fri 11am–1:30am; Sat noon–1:30am; Sun noon–midnight.

12

Keeping Up with the Schwarzenbergs: Visiting a 141-Room English Castle

Only 8km (5 miles) north of České Budějovice lies **Hluboká nad Vltavou** ★ (© 387-843-911; www.zamek-hluboka.eu). Built in the 13th century, this castle has undergone many face-lifts over the years, but none that left as lasting an impression as those ordered by the Schwarzenberg family. As a sign of the region's growing wealth and importance in the mid–19th century, the Schwarzenbergs remodeled the 141-room castle in the neo-Gothic style of England's Windsor Castle. No expense was spared in the quest for opulence. The Schwarzenbergs removed the impressive wooden ceiling from their residence at Český Krumlov and reinstalled it in the large dining room. Other rooms are equally garish in their appointments, making a guided tour worth the time, even though only about a third of the rooms are open to the public.

The castle is open daily May to August from 9am to 5pm (last tour at 4pm); April, September, and October on Tuesday to Sunday from 9am to 4:30pm (last tour at 3pm). There is a lunch break between noon and 12:30pm. Tours in English cost 220Kč adults, 150Kč students.

To complete the experience, the **Alšova Jihoeská Galerie (Art Gallery of South Bohemia;** © 387-967-041) in the Castle's riding hall at Hluboká, houses the second-largest art collection in Bohemia, including many interesting Gothic sculptures from the area, and Dutch painters from the 16th to 18th centuries. It is open daily May to September from 9am to 6pm.

The castle's distance from České Budějovice is short enough to make it a pleasant bike trip from the city or a quick stop either on the way to or from Prague, Třeboň, or Tábor. The town's information center (see below) can help with bike rentals.

If you're driving to Hluboká from České Budějovice, take Highway E49 north and then Hwy. 105 just after leaving the outskirts of České Budějovice. For cyclists or drivers who prefer a slower, more scenic route, take the road that runs behind the brewery; it passes through the village of Obora.

The town's **Information Center** at Zborovská 80 (© **387-966-164;** www. hluboka.cz) will provide you with maps, souvenirs, and answers to your questions.

U královské pečeti (At the Royal Seal) ★ CZECH   This typical Czech-style pub serves up hearty food at reasonable prices. It offers a tasty goulash as well as *svíčková* or game dishes. Located in the popular Hotel Malý Pivovar, this is a very good choice for authentic Czech food.

In the Hotel Malý Pivovar, ulice Karla IV. 8–10. © **386-360-471.** Soups 40Kč; main courses 80Kč–290Kč. AE, DC, MC, V. Daily 10am–11pm.

7 ČESKÝ KRUMLOV ★★★

19km (12 miles) SW of České Budějovice

If you have time on your visit to the Czech Republic for only one excursion, seriously consider making it **Český Krumlov.** One of Bohemia's prettiest towns, Krumlov is a living gallery of elegant Renaissance-era buildings housing charming cafes, pubs, restaurants, shops, and galleries. In 1992, UNESCO named Český Krumlov a World Heritage Site for its historical importance and physical beauty.

Bustling since medieval times, the town, after centuries of embellishment, is exquisitely beautiful. In 1302, the Rožmberk family inherited the castle and moved in, using it as their main residence for nearly 300 years. You'll feel that time has stopped as you look from the Lazebnický Bridge and see the waters of the Vltava below snaking past the castle's gray stone. At night, by the castle lights, the view becomes even more dramatic.

Few dared change the appearance of Český Krumlov over the years, not even the Schwarzenbergs, who had a flair for opulence. At the turn of the 19th century, several facades of houses in the town's outer section were built, as were inner courtyards. Thankfully, economic stagnation in the area under Communism meant little money for "development," so no glass-and-steel edifices (the Hotel Thermal in Karlovy Vary comes to mind) jut out to spoil the architectural beauty. Instead, a medieval sense reigns supreme, now augmented by the many festivals and renovations that keep the town's spirit alive.

ESSENTIALS

GETTING THERE   From České Budějovice, it's about a 45-minute **drive** to Krumlov, depending on traffic. Take Hwy. 3 from the south of České Budějovice and turn onto Hwy. 159. The roads are clearly marked, with several signs directing traffic to the town. From Prague, it's a 2- to 3-hour drive down Hwy. 3 through Tábor. Once you reach Krumlov, you'll have to stow the car in one of several numbered paid parking lots around town. Choose **parking lot no. 2,** and follow the road all the way to the end; this puts you within 5 to 10 minutes' walk of the historic square.

The only way to reach Český Krumlov **by train** from Prague is via České Budějovice, a slow ride that deposits you at a station relatively far from the town center (trip time: 3 hr., 50 min.). Several trains leave daily from Prague's Hlavní nádraží; the fare is 250Kč. If you are already in České Budějovice and you want to make a trip to Krumlov, several trains connect these two cities throughout the day. The trip takes about an hour and costs 50Kč. For timetables, go to **www.jizdnirady.cz.**

The nearly 3-hour **bus** ride from Prague sometimes involves a transfer in České Budějovice. The fare is 136Kč, and the bus station in Český Krumlov is a 10-minute walk from the town's main square.

VISITOR INFORMATION   Right on the main square, the **Information Centrum,** náměstí Svornosti 2, 381 01 Český Krumlov (✆ **380-704-622;** fax 380-704-619; www. ckrumlov.info), provides a complete array of services, from booking accommodations to reserving tickets for events, as well as a phone and Internet service. It's open daily June through September from 9am to 7pm; in April, May, and October from 9am to 6pm; and from November to March from 9am to 5pm.

Be warned that the municipal hall is in the same building, and it's crowded with weddings on weekends. If someone holds out a hat, throw some change into it, take a

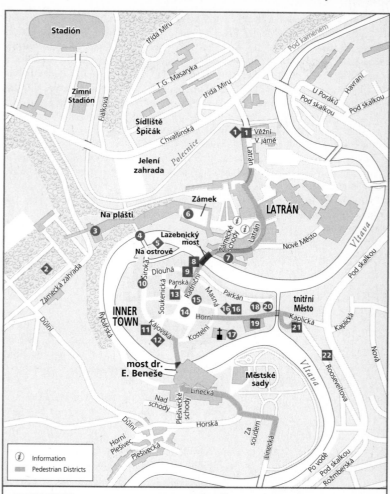

ATTRACTIONS ●

Český Krumlov Chateau **6**
　Most Na Plášti **4**
　Gardens **3**
　Theater **20**
Egon Schiele Foundation/
　Egon Schiele Centrum **10**
Former hospital and
　church of St. Jošt **7**
Náměstí Svornosti **14**
Okresní Muzeum **18**
Radnice (Town Hall) **15**
St. Vitus Cathedral **17**

ACCOMMODATIONS ■

Hotel Dvořák **8**
Hotel Konvice **16**
Hotel Růže **19**
Hotýlek & Hospoda u
　malého Vítka **9**
Pension Anna **22**
Pension Barbakán **21**
Pension Marie **11**
Pension Na louži **12**
Pension Ve Věži **1**
Zlatý Anděl **13**

DINING ◆

Hospoda Na louži **12**
Kavárna **16**
Krčma Markéta **2**
Krumlovský Mlýn **1**
Restaurace Na Ostrově **12**

ⓘ　Information
▬　Pedestrian Districts

traditional shot of liquor from them, and say *"Blahopřeji!"* ("Congratulations!") to every-one in the room.

SPECIAL EVENTS After being banned during Communism, the **Slavnosti pětilisté růže (Festival of the Five-Petaled Rose)** has made a triumphant comeback. It's held each year during the summer solstice. Residents of Český Krumlov dress up in Renaissance costume and parade through the streets. Afterward, the streets become a stage for chess games with people dressed as pieces, music, plays, and even duels "to the death."

Český Krumlov also plays host to the **International Music Festival** every July and August, attracting performers from all over the world. Performances are held in nine spectacular venues. Tickets and details are available over the festival website (www.festival krumlov.cz) or through **Ticketstream** (www.ticketstream.cz) or the event organizer in Prague: **Auviex**, at Perlitová 1820, Prague 4 (© **241-445-404**; www.auviex.cz).

Though much quieter in the winter, the town comes alive on **New Year's Eve** when its spectacular setting is lit up by midnight fireworks shot from a hill next to the center of town. Hotels and pensions fill up quickly, so reservations are recommended. Most res-taurants and hotels have a special dinner/dancing deal that is also recommended to ensure you have a place to party when you return from watching the fireworks.

ORIENTATION Surrounded by a circular sweep of the Vltava River, Český Krumlov is easy to negotiate. The main square, **náměstí Svornosti,** is at the very center of the Inner Town. The bridge that spans the Vltava a few blocks away leads to a rocky hill and the Latrán area, above which is the castle, **Český Krumlov Château.**

STROLLING THROUGH ČESKÝ KRUMLOV

Bring a good pair of walking shoes and be prepared to wear them out. Český Krumlov's hills and alleyways cry out for hours of exploration, but if you push the pace you can see everything in 1 day. No cars, thank goodness, are allowed in the historic town, and the cobblestones keep most other vehicles at bay. The town is split into two parts—the **Inner Town** and **Latrán,** which houses the castle. They're best tackled separately, so you won't have to crisscross the bridges several times.

Begin your walk at the **Okresní Muzeum (Regional Museum;** © **380-711-674)** at the top of Horní ulice 152. Once a Jesuit seminary, the three-story museum now con-tains artifacts and displays relating to Český Krumlov's 1,000-year history. The highlight of this mass of folk art, clothing, furniture, and statues is a giant model of the town that offers a bird's-eye view of the buildings. Admission is 60Kč. The museum is open May to September, daily 10am to 5pm (until 6pm July–Aug); in October to December and March to April, it's open Tuesday to Friday 9am to 4pm, and Saturday and Sunday 1 to 4pm.

Across the street is the **Hotel Růže (Rose),** Horní 154 (© **380-772-100;** www.hotel ruze.cz), which was once a Jesuit student house. Built in the late 16th century, the hotel and the prelature next to it show the development of architecture—Gothic, Renaissance, and rococo influences are all present. If you're not staying at the hotel, don't be afraid to walk around and even ask questions at the reception desk.

Continue down the street to the impressive late-Gothic **St. Vitus Cathedral.** The church is open daily from 9am to 5pm.

As you continue down the street, you'll come to **náměstí Svornosti.** Few buildings here show any character, making the main square of such an impressive town a little disappointing. The **Radnice (Town Hall),** at náměstí Svornosti 1, is one of the few exceptions. Open daily from 9am to 6pm, its Gothic arcades and Renaissance vault inside are exceptionally beautiful in this otherwise run-down area. From the square, streets fan out in all directions. Take some time to wander through them.

When you get closer to the river, you still can see the high-water marks on some of the quirky bank-side houses, which were devastated by the floods of 2002. Most of the places have taken the opportunity to make a fresh start after massive reconstruction. **Krumlovský Mlýn (The Krumlov Mill)**, Široká 80 (*C* **736-634-460**; www.krumlovskymlyn. cz), is a combination restaurant, gallery, antiques shop, and exhibition space. For an additional treat, stroll through the exhibition of historical motorcycles. Open daily 10am to 10pm.

One of Český Krumlov's most famous residents was Austrian-born artist Egon Schiele. He was a bit of an eccentric who on more than one occasion raised the ire of the town's residents (many found his use of young women as nude models distressing), and his stay was cut short when the locals' patience ran out. But the town readopted the artist in 1993, setting up the **Egon Schiele Art Centrum** in Inner Town, Široká 70–72, 381 01, Český Krumlov (*C* **380-704-011**; www.schieleartcentrum.cz). It documents his life and work, housing a permanent selection of his paintings as well as exhibitions of other 20th-century artists. Admission is 120Kč; hours are daily from 10am to 6pm.

After you see the museum, cut down Panenská ulice to Soukenická 39 and stop in at **Galerie u rytíře Kryštofa**, Panenská 6, where you can try on the latest in body armor! This place is like the wardrobe room at a theater, and almost everything is for sale. It's open Monday to Saturday from 10am to 6pm, Sunday from 1 to 6pm.

For a different perspective on the town, take the stairs from the **Městské divadlo (Town Theater)** on Horní ulice down to the riverfront and rent a rowboat from **Maleček Boat Rentals** (*C* **380-712-508**; www.malecek.cz) at 400Kč for an hour-long trip.

You might want to grab a light lunch at one of the many cafes in Inner Town before crossing the river. As you cross the bridge and head toward the castle, you'll see immediately to your right the former **hospital and church of St. Jošt.** Founded at the beginning of the 14th century, it has since been turned into apartments. Feel free to snoop around, but don't enter the building.

EXPLORING THE CHÂTEAU

Reputedly the second-largest castle in Bohemia (after Prague Castle), **Český Krumlov Château** was constructed in the 13th century as part of a private estate. Throughout the ages, it has been passed on to a variety of private owners, including the Rožmberk family, Bohemia's largest landholders, and the Schwarzenbergs, the Bohemian equivalent of the Hilton family. Perched high atop a rocky hill, the château is open only from April to October, exclusively by guided tours.

Follow the path for the long climb up to the **castle.** Greeting you is a round 12th-century **tower**—painstakingly renovated, with its Renaissance balcony. You'll pass over the moat, now occupied by two brown bears. Next is the **Dolní Hrad (Lower Castle)** and then the **Horní Hrad (Upper Castle).**

There are three main guided tours, plus separate entries to the Castle Tower and the Lapidarium. If you don't have the money or time for one of the tours, you're free to walk around the grounds, though most of the interiors will be inaccessible. Tour 1 begins in the rococo **Chapel of St. George,** and continues through the portrait-packed **Renaissance Rooms,** and the **Schwarzenberg Baroque Suite,** outfitted with ornate furnishings that include Flemish wall tapestries, European paintings, and also the extravagant 17th-century **Golden Carriage.** Tour 2 includes the **Schwarzenberg portrait gallery** as well as their 19th-century suite. Tour 3 presents the Castle's fascinating **Baroque Theater,** though at more than $20 a ticket, sadly, this is priced more for real theater aficionados than the general public. Tours last about 1 hour and depart frequently. Most are in Czech or German, however. If you want an English-language tour, arrange it ahead of time (© **380-704-711;** www.castle.ckrumlov.cz). The guided tours in English cost 240Kč adults, 140Kč students (Tour 1); 180Kč adults, 100Kč students (Tour 2); 380Kč adults, and 220Kč students (Tour 3). The tickets are sold separately. The castle hours are from Tuesday to Sunday: June to August 9am to 6pm; April, May, September, and October 9am to 5pm. The last entrance is 1 hour before closing.

Once past the main castle building, you can see one of the more stunning views of Český Krumlov from **Most Na Plášti,** a walkway that doubles as a belvedere to the Inner Town. Even farther up the hill lie the castle's riding school and gardens.

WHERE TO STAY

With the rise of free enterprise after the fall of Communism, many hotels have sprouted up or are getting a "new" old look. PENSION and ZIMMER FREI signs line the streets and offer some of the best values in town. For a comprehensive list of area hotels and help with bookings, call or write to the Information Centrum listed above in "Visitor Information."

Very Expensive

Hotel Růže (Rose Hotel)   Once a Jesuit seminary, this stunning Italian Renaissance building has been converted into a well-appointed hotel. Comfortable in a big-city kind of way, it's packed with amenities and is one of the top places to stay in Český Krumlov (though prices have risen considerably in recent years and it's not clear it's still really worth this much money). For families or large groups, the larger suites (while still *very* expensive for what you get) have eight beds and at least provide better value.

Horní 154, 381 01 Český Krumlov. © **380-772-100.** Fax 380-713-146. www.hotelruze.cz. 71 units. 5,800Kč double; 7,300Kč suite. Rates include breakfast. AE, MC, V. **Amenities:** Restaurant; bar; health club; pool. *In room:* TV, hair dryer, minibar.

Expensive

Hotel Dvořák ★   The location of the Hotel Dvořák, right next to the bridge, could not be better. Add to that the views are spectacular and the service top-notch. Rooms are thoughtfully decorated, bright, and airy. The terrace restaurant out front is a perfect pit stop for coffee and a rest on your promenade through town.

Radniční 101, 381 01 Český Krumlov. ℂ **380-711-020.** Fax 380-711-024. www.krumlovhotels.cz. 22 units. 2,500Kč double; 3,800Kč suite. Rates include breakfast. AE, MC, V. **Amenities:** Restaurant; bar; sauna. *In room:* TV, minibar.

Zlatý Anděl (Golden Angel) ★ The Golden Angel has emerged from a chrysalis with new wings. After a long reconstruction and renovation of its rooms, including new furniture, the Golden Angel has shed its Communist furnishings for more stylish fittings right down to the marble bathrooms. Think about getting a suite rather than a regular room, since a couple of them are loft apartments that are much more open. A small pub adds to the fact that this is now the best place on the square.

Náměstí Svornosti 10–11, 381 01 Český Krumlov. ℂ **380-712-310.** Fax 380-712-927. www.hotelzlaty andel.cz. 40 units. 2,000Kč–2,900Kč double; 2,300Kč–4,000Kč suite. Rates include breakfast. AE, MC, V. **Amenities:** Restaurant; bar; terrace. *In room:* TV, minibar.

Moderate

Hotel Konvice ★★ The rooms at the Konvice are on the small side and have rustic furniture. The real lure here is the view. Ask for a room with a view out the back—as you gaze at the river and the castle on the opposite bank, you'll wonder why anyone would choose to stay anywhere else.

Horní ul. 144. 381 01 Český Krumlov. ℂ **380-711-611.** Fax 380-711-327. www.boehmerwaldhotels.de. 10 units. 1,500Kč double; 3,500Kč suite with castle view. Rates include breakfast. AE, MC, V. **Amenities:** Restaurant. *In room:* TV.

Hotýlek & Hospoda u malého Vítka ★ Here's another impossibly cute hotel in Český Krumlov. This one occupies a Renaissance-era house just a few doors up from the bridge that's been remodeled top to bottom by a skilled wood carver. Each of the rooms is snug and clean and has been named after popular Czech cartoon characters. The breakfast downstairs is plentiful and the little tavern serves excellent Czech specialties.

Radniční 27, 381 01 Český Krumlov. ℂ/fax **380-711-925.** www.vitekhotel.cz. 20 units. 1,500Kč double; 2,500Kč triple. Rates include breakfast. AE, MC, V. **Amenities:** Restaurant; bar. *In room:* TV.

Pension Barbakán After a change in management, the Barbakán, across from the theater, has spruced itself up, inside and out. The new owners have redone the inside of the pension completely, putting new bathrooms in all the units and generally keeping the premises spotless. Take breakfast out on the back garden's terrace on warm summer mornings and watch the goings-on below at the riverbank.

Horní 26, 381 01 Český Krumlov. ℂ/fax **380-717-017.** www.barbakan.cz. 8 units. 1,990Kč double; 2,490Kč triple. Rates include breakfast. AE, MC, V. **Amenities:** Restaurant; bar. *In room:* TV.

Inexpensive

Pension Anna ★ **Kids** Along "pension alley," this is a comfortable and rustic place. What makes the pension a favorite are the friendly management and homey feeling you get as you walk up to your room. Forget hotels—this is the kind of place where you can relax. The owners even let you buy drinks and snacks at the bar downstairs and take them to your room. The suites, with four beds and a living room, are great for families and groups.

Rooseveltova 41, 381 01 Český Krumlov. ℂ/fax **380-711-692.** www.pensionanna.euweb.cz. 8 units. 1,250Kč double; 1,550Kč suite. Rates include breakfast. No credit cards. **Amenities:** Bar. *In room:* TV.

(Moments) A Renaissance Pub Endures

Most visitors don't venture far enough into the castle grounds to experience this place during the day or night. That's their loss, for one of the finest dining experiences in the Czech Republic is offered at **Krčma Markéta,** Zámek 62 ((℃ **775-155-504**).

To get here, walk all the way up the hill through the castle, past the Horní Hrad (Upper Castle) and past the Zámecké divadlo (Castle Theater). Walk through the raised walkway and into the Zámecká zahrada (Castle Garden), where you'll eventually find this Renaissance pub.

When you go inside, you'll feel as if you've left this century. A relatively recent change in ownership has brought in "modern" conveniences like real sets of plates as opposed to the original wooden blocks on which food used to be served; and there is even a menu now, but the atmosphere is still wonderfully unique. Take a peek at the fire to see what's roasting; usually there're a wide variety of meats, including succulent pork cutlets, rabbit, chickens, and pork knees, a Czech delicacy. Before the night is over, you'll probably find yourself talking to someone else at the pub's large wooden tables.

Krčma Markéta is open year round, Tuesday to Sunday from 11am to 9pm, and main courses cost 120Kč to 250Kč.

Pension Marie   The facade of this pension, next door to Na louži (see below), has been completely restored. Inside, however, the plain furniture fails to rival the charm of its neighbor. On the plus side, the beds are longer than what you'll find at pensions nearby.

Kájovská 67, 381 01 Český Krumlov. (℃/fax **380-711-138.** www.ckrumlov.info. 6 units. 1,390Kč double; 2,540Kč suite. No credit cards. **Amenities:** Cafe. *In room:* TV.

Pension Na louži ★   Smack-dab in the heart of the Inner Town, the small Na louži, decorated with early-20th-century wooden furniture, is a charming change from many of the bigger, bland rooms found in nearby hotels. If the person at reception starts mentioning names without apparent reason, don't worry; it's not a language problem. Management has given the rooms human names instead of numbers. The only drawback is that the beds (maybe the people for whom the rooms were named were all short) can be a little on the short side.

Kájovská 66, 381 01 Český Krumlov. (℃/fax **380-711-280.** www.nalouzi.cz. 7 units. 1,500Kč double; 1,800Kč triple; 2,300Kč suite. No credit cards. **Amenities:** Restaurant/bar.

Pension Ve Věži (In the Tower) ★ (Finds)   A private pension in a renovated medieval tower just a 5-minute walk from the castle, Ve Věži is one of the most magnificent places to stay in town. It's not the accommodations themselves that are so grand; none have a bathroom and all are sparsely decorated. What's wonderful is the ancient ambience. Reservations are recommended.

Pivovarská 28, 381 01 Český Krumlov. (℃ **721-523-030.** www.pensionvezi.cz. 4 units (all with shared bathroom). 1,200Kč double. Rates include breakfast. No credit cards.

Moderate

Konvice ★ CZECH   If weather permits, eat outside overlooking the river at the Kavárna. Try the boned chicken breast smothered in cheese or any of the steaks and salads. Portions are big and the view is spectacular.

In the Hotel Konvice, Horní ul. 144. 🕐 **380-711-611.** Main courses 115Kč–340Kč. AE, MC, V. Daily 8am–10pm.

Krumlovský mlýn CZECH   This restored mill house, whose history dates from the 16th century, is a restaurant, antiques shop, and exhibition in one. Large wooden tables and benches are part of the thematic restaurant on the ground floor, where a traditional Czech menu is served. The terrace on the bank of the Vltava River above the water channel here is a terrific place to sit in the summer.

Široká 80. 🕐 **736-634-461.** www.krumlovskymlyn.cz. Main courses 180Kč–425Kč. No credit cards. Daily 10am–10pm.

Restaurace Na Ostrově (On the Island) CZECH   In the shadow of the castle and, as the name implies, on an island, this restaurant is best on a sunny day when the terrace overflows with flowers, hearty Czech food (including plenty of chicken and fish), and lots of beer. The staff is very friendly, which helps with your patience since usually only two waiters work each shift, making service on the slow side. A great place to relax and enjoy the view.

Na ostrově 171. 🕐 **380-711-326.** Main courses 139Kč–399Kč. No credit cards. Daily 10am–10pm.

Inexpensive

Hospoda Na louži CZECH   The large wooden tables encourage you to get to know your neighbors at this Inner Town pub, located in a 15th-century house. The atmosphere is fun and the food above average. If no table is available, stand and have a drink; tables turn over pretty quickly, and the staff is accommodating. In summer, the terrace seats only six, so dash over if a seat empties. Be sure to save space for homemade fruit dumplings for dessert.

Kájovská 66. 🕐 **380-711-280.** Main courses about 100Kč. No credit cards. Mon–Sat 10am–11pm; Sun 10am–10pm.

---

8 TŘEBOŇ ★

24km (15 miles) E of České Budějovice

Just a 30-minute bus ride east of České Budějovice, Třeboň is a diamond in the rough, a walled city that time, war, and disaster have failed to destroy. Surrounded by forests and ponds, the town slowly grew from the 12th to the mid–14th century, when four of the Rožmberk brothers (also known as the Rosenbergs) took over, making Třeboň a home away from home (their official residence was down the road in Český Krumlov). Třeboň quickly flourished, attaining key brewing and salt customs rights. Adding to the town's coffers were more than 5,000 fishponds built by fish master Štěpánek Netolický and his successor, Mikuláš Rathard.

Though war and fires in the 17th and 18th centuries razed most of the town's historic Renaissance architecture, a slow rebuilding process eventually restored nearly every square foot of the walled town to its original state. Under Communism, Třeboň was awarded spa rights, which kept money flowing in and buildings in good repair.

The town is not as breathtaking as Krumlov, but Třeboň hasn't been completely over-run by tourists who trample everything in their wake. Instead, Třeboň exists with or without visitors. Český Krumlov is great, but if you have time and want to chill out for a day, consider Třeboň. Třeboň is the best small town in which to overnight when you're traveling in the region or just looking for some peace and quiet.

The 4-day festival "Okolo Třeboně" takes place here in the beginning of July annually. You can experience several street happenings, sport and fun competitions, and listen to Czech folk music performed on stages in the city center and the nearby park. This mul-tigenre event always turns out to be a long party with its unforgettable atmosphere. Check the exact dates at the information center and also ask about the historic Knight Tournament, which, if it occurs, can be a lot of fun, too. Unfortunately, there's no set date for it and it isn't an annual event.

ESSENTIALS

GETTING THERE   **Buses** leave from the České Budějovice bus station every hour or so. The trip lasts 30 to 40 minutes and the fare is about 30Kč.

By **train** from Prague the journey usually requires a change in Veselí nad Lužnicí. The train takes 2½ hours; the second-class fare is 192Kč. Trains and buses also regularly leave for Třeboň from Jindřichův Hradec and Tábor.

Driving from Prague, take Hwy. E55 through Tábor and turn left onto Hwy. 150 just past the town of Veselí nad Lužnicí. The trip takes at least 1½ hours. From České Budějovice, take Hwy. E551 east to Třeboň.

VISITOR INFORMATION   **Informační Středisko** is in the heart of the Old Town at Masarykovo nám. 103, 379 01 Třeboň (℃ **384-721-169;** fax 384-721-356; www. trebon-mesto.cz). The staff members are excellent and speak several languages, notably German. They provide maps, guidebooks, and information on tours and lodging. Open Monday to Friday from 9am to 5pm.

ORIENTATION   There are only three ways to penetrate Třeboň's Old Town walls, short of pole vaulting. To the east is **Hradecká brána (Castle Gate);** on the southern edge of town lies **Svinenská brána;** and to the west is **Budějovická brána.** Once you're inside any of these gates, the six or so streets that comprise the Old Town can be easily navigated.

EXPLORING TŘEBOŇ

City officials, quick to notice that helping visitors helps them, have placed signs guiding visitors to almost every nook and cranny of the center. Since the walled city is relatively small, there's no wrong place to begin a tour, but I prefer to start at the southern gate by the **Svinenská brána,** the oldest of the town's three gates, for reasons that'll become immediately apparent. Just outside the gate and to the right stands the **Regent Brewery,** founded in 1379. Locals will tell you that their brew is every bit as good as Budvar, and they're not lying. On entering Old Town, continue straight through Žižkovo náměstí and you'll arrive at **Masarykovo náměstí,** where the beautifully colored Renaissance facades look as though they were built yesterday.

To the left lies the entrance to Třeboň's showpiece, **Zámek Třeboň (Třeboň Castle;** ℃ **384-721-193).** The castle's history is similar to the history of the town. The original Gothic castle was destroyed by fire and reconstructed several times, most recently in

1611. Rather ordinary looking from the outside, it has splendidly decorated rooms that provide a terrific backdrop to the 16th-century furnishings. An exhibition on pond-building fascinates most children. A large part of the castle now houses regional archives. Admission is 100Kč. April, May, September, and October hours are Tuesday to Sunday from 9 to 11:40am and 12:45 to 4pm. June through August, it's open from 9 to 11:40am and 12:45 to 5:15pm.

Walk out the castle gate and straight along Březanova Street to the **Augustinian monastery** and the 14th-century **St. Giles Church** next to it. Inside the church are replicas of some of the finest Gothic works in central Europe; the originals have been moved to the National Gallery in Prague. The church and monastery are open Monday to Saturday from 9am to 7pm and Sunday from 9am to 6pm.

To the south of the Old Town lies **Rybník Svět,** a large pond that locals flock to on hot afternoons. Several locations around the pond rent windsurfers, bikes, and other outdoor equipment with which to enjoy the surrounding areas. On the southeast shore of the pond is **Schwarzenberská hrobka (Schwarzenberg Mausoleum).** Built in 1877, this neo-Gothic chapel and crypt is the resting place for most members of the Schwarzenberg family.

WHERE TO STAY

Bílý Koníček (White Horse) ★ (**Value**)   Across from the Zlatá Hvězda, this place has plain but tidy rooms and a friendly staff. However, the rooms tend to be a little noisy because the hotel is on the road that cars take through town. For the most part, though, the streets are pretty quiet, and the restaurant downstairs is a good bet for a quick bite.

Masarykovo nám. 97, 379 01 Třeboň. (**©**/fax **384-721-213.** www.hotelbilykonicek.cz. 23 units. 1,000Kč double. MC, V. **Amenities:** Restaurant/bar. *In room:* TV.

Hotel Bohemia & Hotel Regent   These two hotels share everything, from a parking lot to a receptionist. If you don't want to stay in the center of town, either one is a good choice. Located down by the "beach" area, their Communist-era functional look is out of place. However, the rooms are clean and affordable, and the tennis courts and proximity to the pond are a plus.

U Světa 750, 379 01 Třeboň. (**©** **384-721-394.** Fax 384-721-396. www.bohemia-regent.cz. 84 units. 1,590Kč–2,200Kč double; 1,950Kč–2,900Kč suite. AE, MC, V. **Amenities:** 2 restaurants; cafe; bar; miniature golf course. *In room:* TV, minibar.

Hotel Zlatá Hvězda   Despite having rather spartan rooms, the Zlatá Hvězda is the most upscale hotel in town, and its location on Masarykovo náměstí can't be beat. An added plus is that the friendly staff can help arrange brewery tours, fishing permits, horseback riding, bike rentals, and several other outdoor activities. The reception will sometimes cut rates on slow nights.

Masarykovo nám. 107, 379 01 Třeboň. (**©** **384-757-111.** Fax 384-757-300. www.zhvezda.cz. 48 units. 2,900Kč double; 4,300Kč suite. Rates include buffet breakfast. AE, DC, MC, V. **Amenities:** 2 restaurants; spa; bowling alley. *In room:* TV, fridge, hair dryer.

Pension Siesta   If all the pensions in the Czech Republic showed up for a contest to see which was friendliest, this one might win. Just outside and to the right of the Hradecká brána, the Siesta is a small but quiet and clean alternative to the hotels on the square. What makes it special are Petr Matějů and his wife, who go out of their way to

THE BEST OF BOHEMIA

12

TŘEBOŇ

Finds   A Farm Stay

With the collapse of Communism and the system of collective farming that went along with it, many farms were returned to their original owners in a state of disrepair. But slowly, some are being restored to the prosperity they enjoyed before World War II. One such farm, **Holenský Dvůr** ★, Ratiboř 52, region Jindřichův Hradec (② **384-382-376;** fax 384-383-445; www.holenskydvur.cz), is a recently refinished farm offering a comfortable stay surrounded by early European rural charm. Set among the gently rolling hills and fishponds of south Bohemia near Třeboň, this pension is a relaxing alternative to the hustle and bustle of more touristed spots such as Český Krumlov or Karlovy Vary. You can rent a mountain bike or go on horseback and tour the countryside, or hike through the meadows.

The pension's 10 rooms and 2 apartments are bright, clean, and refreshingly well appointed, with some of the cleanest and most spacious bathrooms in the country. The owners recently came through on their promise of an indoor pool.

Rooms rates are calculated per person, per night, with the rates excluding board, ranging from 390Kč per person in winter, spring and fall to 450Kč in July and August. To get here, take the E55 highway south out of Prague toward České Budějovice. About 19km (12 miles) south of Tábor, head east on Rte. 23 toward Jindřichův Hradec to Kardašova Řečice.

take care of their guests. The pension also has a pleasant terrace in front by the stream, where you can enjoy an afternoon drink and snack.

Hradební 26, 379 01 Třeboň. ②/fax **384-724-831.** www.pensionsiesta.cz. 7 units. 1,080Kč double. No credit cards. *In room:* TV.

WHERE TO DINE

Bílý Koníček CZECH   Located in the hotel of the same name, Bílý Koníček has a standard Czech menu of meat, dumplings, and potato dishes that are reasonably priced. In summer, its terrace is a great place to sit and cool off; the building's shadow keeps you out of the direct sunlight. The beer from just down the road is always fresh and cold.

Masarykovo nám. 97. ② **384-721-213.** Main courses 108Kč–216Kč. V. Sun–Thurs 9am–10pm; Fri–Sat 9am–midnight.

Pizzeria Macondo PIZZA   If you're tired of fish and can't face another dumpling, Macondo makes decent affordable pizzas that are filling. They seem to have traded the ketchup, which is customary in much of the country, for real tomato sauce, resulting in a definite turn for the better. The salads are also fresh, and the beverage menu features probably the town's widest selection of cocktails.

Zámek 112. ② **384-724-880.** Pizzas 90Kč–140Kč. No credit cards. Daily 11am–10pm (9pm on Sun).

9 TÁBOR

88km (55 miles) S of Prague, 59km (37 miles) N of České Budějovice

The center of the Hussite movement following religious leader Jan Hus's execution in Prague, Tábor was officially founded in 1420 and named by the Hussites after the biblical Mount Tábor. Forsaking their property, the Hussites came here to receive Christ on his return to earth. The group of soldiers leading Tábor, some 15,000 in all, felt that they had been commanded by God to break the power of the Catholics at that time. Legendary warrior Jan Žižka led the Taborites, as this sect of Hussites was known. Time and time again, Žižka rallied his troops to defeat the papal forces, until he was struck down in battle in 1424. For 10 more years the Hussites battled on, but their loss at Lipany signaled the end of the uprising, and an agreement was reached with Emperor Sigmund of Luxembourg of the Holy Roman Empire. Later, the town submitted to the leadership of Bohemia's Jiří z Poděbrad (George of Poděbrad) and blossomed economically, creating the wealth needed to construct the Renaissance buildings now found in the historic Old Town.

ESSENTIALS

GETTING THERE   If you're **driving,** leave Prague by Highway D1 and turn off at the E55 exit (signs BENEŠOV, ČESKÉ BUDĚJOVICE). Hwy. E55 runs straight into the city of Tábor. It's a 1-hour drive. Once you're in Tábor, parking can be a problem. Try to snag a paid spot along the street as you approach the center.

Tábor is about 90 minutes by express **train** from Prague or close to an hour from České Budějovice. The train station has a baggage check, and you can get to the center of town by taking bus no. 11, 14, or 31. From Prague, the fare is 210Kč first class, 134Kč second class.

The **bus** trip to Tábor lasts about 1½ hours from Prague and costs 84Kč. To get to the center, it's about a 20-minute walk; go through the park and then bear right at its farthest corner to walk along třída 9. května into town.

VISITOR INFORMATION   Next to the Hussite Museum, **Infocentrum města Tábor,** Žižkovo nám. 2, 390 01, Tábor (© **381-486-230;** fax 381-486-239; www.tabor.cz), is stocked with information of all types: from maps, film, and postcards to advice about lodging, restaurants, and the best place for ice cream. The center's staff has volumes of pamphlets, phone numbers, and good advice. It's open May to September, Monday to Friday from 8:30am to 7pm, Saturday and Sunday from 9am to 4pm; and October to April, Monday to Friday from 9am to 4pm.

SPECIAL EVENTS   In September, the **Táborská Setkání (Tábor Meeting)** takes place. Each year, representatives from towns worldwide named after Mount Tábor congregate for some medieval fun—parades, music, and jousting. The 4-day event even reenacts the historic battle of Tábor, with brilliantly clad warriors fighting one another "to the death." For more details on the Tábor Meeting and summer cultural events, see **www.tabor. cz**, or contact **Infocentrum města Tábor** (see "Visitor Information," above).

ORIENTATION   Staré město (Old Town) is situated around Žižkovo náměstí, site of the town church and the Hussite Museum. Medieval walls surround the entire Old Town core. The Kotnov Castle, now one of the town's museums, is at the southwest corner. Outside the historic town, there's little to see in Tábor besides factories and the ubiquitous *paneláky* (apartment buildings) that ring most every big Czech town and city.

Fun Facts   An A-Maze-ing City

If you get confused by roads that twist, turn, and then end as you leave the square, the Taborites have caught you exactly as planned—the town was designed to hold off would-be attackers with its maze of streets.

EXPLORING TÁBOR

Most of the city's sights are on or around **Žižkovo náměstí.** On the square's west side is the **Museum of the Hussite Movement** (© 381-254-286, www.husitskemuzeum.cz). The late-Gothic former town hall now chronicles the movement that put Tábor on the map and in the history books. In front of the building lie stone tables where Hussite ministers gave daily communion. Leading from the museum's entrance, twisting and turning 650m (2,133 ft.) underneath the square, is a labyrinth of **tunnels** dating from the 15th century. After visiting the museum, take one of the guided tours that snakes through the underground maze, which has housed everything from beer kegs to women imprisoned for such dastardly things as quarreling with men. The tunnels also doubled as a way to sneak under enemy guards if the town ever fell, allowing Hussite soldiers to launch an attack from behind. Note that the museum was closed in 2009 for reconstruction but was expected to reopen in 2010. Before reconstruction, admission to the museum was 80Kč and to the tunnels 60Kč. Opening hours for both are April to October daily 8:30am to 5pm, and November to March Monday to Friday 8:30am to 5pm.

When you emerge from the tunnels, you'll be on the opposite side of the square, facing the **Church of Transfiguration of Our Lord** (© 381-251-226), with its vaulted impressive stained-glass windows and Gothic wooden altar. Climb the tower for one of the best views of the town. Open daily from 10am to 5pm May through August, and Saturday and Sunday 10am to 5pm in September and October. Admission is 25Kč.

You can pay homage to the Hussite military mastermind Jan Žižka at his **statue** next to the church. For a wondrous avenue of Renaissance buildings, stroll down **Pražská ulice,** off the southeast corner of the square. From here you can turn down Divadelní and head along the Lužnice River toward **Kotnov Castle** (© 381-252-788). If your feet aren't up to the walk, you can take a more direct route to Kotnov by heading straight down Klokotská ulice, which runs away from the square next to the Hussite Museum.

A 14th-century castle that forms the southwest corner of the town wall, **Kotnov Castle** is most recognizable for its round **tower,** with another great view of the town. Inside the castle is a well-organized collection on the Middle Ages, with old farming tools, armor, weapons, uniforms, and other artifacts. Admission is 40Kč, and it's open April to September daily from 8:30am to 5pm.

WHERE TO STAY

The number of quality hotels in Tábor continues to grow; still there are several good privately run pensions in town and this is a good place to experience going "local." Expect to pay about 800Kč per person. The information center next to the town hall at Žižkovo nám. 2 can provide a list of recommendations or call and book a room for you (see "Visitor Information," on previous page). Many of the hotels will not have on-site parking but rather offer access to a nearby paid garage or lot.

Hotel Nautilus ★★ Easily the most stylish and comfortable hotel in town, though slightly pricier than most of the other places nearby. The owners have taken a former run-down townhouse on the square and transformed into a lovely four-star boutique hotel, complete with original artwork and eye-catching design touches that extend from the lobby to the light and airy rooms. Even if you don't stay here, stop by for a meal, the nicest place on the square to eat. The presidential suite is priced as a honeymoon-only affair.

Žižkovo nám. 20. května 617, 390 02 Tábor. ℂ **380-900-900.** Fax 380-900-999. www.hotelnautilus.cz. 22 units. 2,800Kč double; 7,800Kč presidential suite. AE, MC, V. **Amenities:** Restaurant. *In room:* TV.

OREA Hotel Dvořák ★ Located in a recently reconstructed historic building of Tábor brewery, which is part of the Kotnov Castle complex, this addition to the list of hotels in Tábor is a good choice not only for families but for business travelers as well. The colorful interior design is inviting, and the rooms are a good size with comfortable beds.

Hradební 3037, 390 01 Tábor. ℂ **381-207-211.** www.orea.cz. 72 units. 2,880Kč double; 3,600Kč suite. AE, MC, V. **Amenities:** Restaurant; bar; pool; room service; sauna. *In room:* TV, hair dryer, minibar.

Pension 189 Karel Bican This atmospheric, family run pension is just a short walk from the central square. Book well in advance or ring the buzzer and hope for the best, as this place tends to fill up fast. The rooms are furnished in traditional style and are cute and quiet Some have modest efficiency kitchens. There's a pleasant garden and terrace and the owners rent bikes.

Hradební 189/16, 39001 Tábor. ℂ **381-252-109.** Fax 381-254-109. 5 units. 1,500Kč double. AE, MC, V. **Amenities:** Sauna, bike rental. *In room:* TV.

WHERE TO DINE

Bowling Club CZECH Yes, really. There's a bowling alley here, too. The pub upstairs serves good Czech food and beer all day, and since there's not too much to do in town at night, you may want to go bowling downstairs. Don't worry, they serve beer downstairs as well—you can't have one without the other.

Třída 9. května 678. ℂ **381-498-308.** Soups 40Kč; main courses 79Kč–280Kč. No credit cards. Mon–Thurs 3pm–2am; Fri 3pm–3am; Sat 2pm–3am; Sun 2pm–midnight.

Restaurace Beseda CZECH Beseda is a good place to stop after you slink through the tunnels and climb the tower at the Church of Transfiguration of Our Lord. You've probably seen this menu in just about every town so far, but the food is above average if not new. Their *svíčková* (sirloin in a cream sauce with dumplings) is a favorite. On hot summer days, the patio is great for people-watching while drinking a cold Budvar.

Žižkovo nám. 5. ℂ **381-253-723.** Main courses 70Kč–260Kč. No credit cards. Daily 10am–10pm.

The Best of Moravia

While Bohemia is the traditional home of a beer-favoring populace and the seat of Czech industrial muscle, the less-visited kingdom of Moravia to the south and east has spawned a people more attuned to the farmland and the potent wines it creates. For 1,000 years Moravians have watched as the wealth of their Czech brethren has been put on display in numerous palaces and factories, but Moravians have plenty of their own accomplishments to be proud of.

The provincial capital of Brno is the home of modern genetics, the place where a curious monk named Gregor Mendel discovered the building blocks of life in his monastic garden 150 years ago. It is also the birthplace of one of the most famous novelists of the latter half of the 20th century, Milan Kundera. The Czechs' own favorite author, Bohumil Hrabal, coincidentally, was born here as well. While Brno is definitely in Prague's shadow when it comes to historic architecture, it is home to some of the country's finest early modern and Functionalist buildings built in the 1920s and '30s. And it is to Brno, the country's second-largest city, where Czech industry comes to show its wares on the national exhibition grounds.

Smaller towns maintain their real Moravian character, with lively song and dance and colorful traditional costumes that seem to have fallen by the wayside in Bohemia. Even the food is a little different: The bland goulash in Prague becomes a little spicier in Moravia, owing to the Hungarian influence that has seeped in from neighboring Slovakia.

Here, winemaking is taken as seriously as it is in most other European grape-growing regions. Many wine bars throughout Moravia serve the village's best straight from the cask, usually alongside traditional smoked meats. While the Bohemians have the sweet taste of Becherovka to sip at meals, Moravians have the sharp taste of *slivovice* (plum spirits) to cleanse the palate (sometimes for hours on end if it's *domácí*—home-brewed).

Having seen its fair share of history, Moravia conjures up a different image than Bohemia: Here, too, castles and picture-perfect town squares exist. But the friendly people and slower lifestyle set Moravia apart.

1 BRNO: THE REGION'S CAPITAL

224km (139 miles) SE of Prague, 128km (79 miles) N of Vienna

An industrial city with an industrial-strength image as "boring," Brno suffers the fate of many second cities around the world—no respect. Sure, as you approach from the highway, the sight of dozens of concrete apartment buildings may give you second thoughts. But bear with the Communist-inspired urban sprawl—the bad rap is undeserved. In fact, Brno is a vibrant and interesting city with a panache all its own.

Since Brno came of age in the 19th century on the back of its textile industry, the city's architecture, for the most part, lacks the traditional Gothic, Renaissance, and baroque elements that are part of the fabric of cities like Prague. But spend a day or two here, and

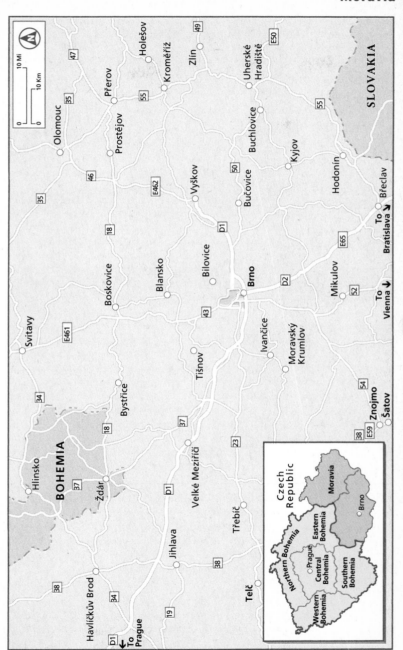

the beauty of the old city center will become apparent. Empire and neoclassical buildings abound. For fans of early modern architecture, Brno is an unexpected delight. In the 1920s and '30s, the city was a leading center of Functionalist design. The high point of any tour is the Villa Tugendhat, a masterpiece by Mies van der Rohe, one of the giants of modern architecture.

Quirky sights like the Brno Dragon and the Wagon Wheel add character. Špilberk Castle and the Gothic cathedral of Saints Peter and Paul give historical perspective. And lush streets and parks make aimless wandering a pleasure.

ESSENTIALS

GETTING THERE **Driving** to Brno from Prague is simple but a bit nerve-wracking. The main country's main freeway, the D1 (also called the E50), in theory, whisks you the 200km (120 miles) from Prague to the center of Brno in around 2 hours, but traffic can be heavy and road-construction delays are frequent. Be especially careful in winter when icy roads make the drive particularly treacherous.

If you're not a fan of white-knuckle driving, **train** travel between Prague and Brno is much more relaxing and takes just 2¾ hours. Special high-speed Pendolino trains (www. pendolino.cz) cut the journey to about 2½ hours. **Trains** leave approximately once every half-hour during the day and hourly in the evenings. Any train heading to Budapest and Bratislava and the majority of Vienna-bound trains will stop in Brno. Most trains depart from Hlavní nádraží (Main Station), though many also leave from nádraží Holešovice. Second-class express fare is around 300Kč. Brno is an excellent jumping-on spot for onward trains to Bratislava (1 hour), Budapest (4 hr.), and Vienna (2 hr.).

Brno's aging train station is long overdue for a thorough face-lift, and there's even talk of shutting down the station altogether and moving it to another location. The good news is that it's within easy walk of the center of the city, at the foot of the main pedestrian walk, Masarykova ulice. To reach the center from the train station, follow the signs to "centrum," first descending into a confusing passageway of shops and kiosks and then climbing the stairs on the other side, which brings you into the old town.

Buses are as convenient as trains and have the added advantage of being cheaper. Most buses depart from Prague's Florenc station to Brno every hour. The trip takes 2½ hours and costs around 140Kč. Reservations are recommended during peak hours. Buses will either drop you at the city's main bus station (located behind the train station) or in front of the Grandhotel Brno (see later). **Student Agency** (✆ **800-100-300**), which in spite of the name sells tickets to travelers of any age, is the leading local operator for buses to Brno and back to Prague.

VISITOR INFORMATION The **Turistické Informační Centrum** (Tourist Information Center/TIC; ✆ **542-211-090;** www.brno.cz or www.ticbrno.cz; Radnická 8; open 9am–5pm Mon–Sat, 9am–3pm Sun) is situated in the Old Town Hall. The English-speaking staff hand out free maps with excellent walking tours already sketched out. The staff can also advise on hotels but usually will not book rooms. There are also two computers on hand for checking e-mail. The tourist office has branches at Nádražní 8 (✆ **542-221-450;** open Mon–Fri 9am–1pm, 1:30–5pm), across from the main train station, and at the Exhibition Grounds, Hall E (open during fair times).

SPECIAL EVENTS Usually when the words *special events* and Brno are mentioned in the same sentence, the phrase *trade fair* isn't too far behind. Many fairs held at Brno's

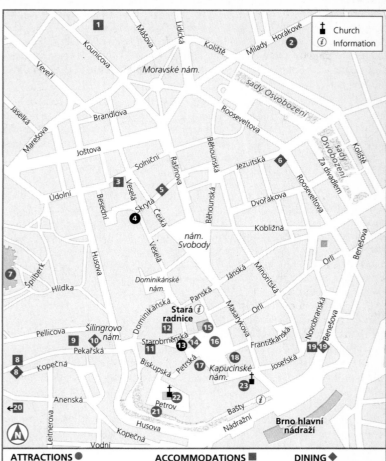

THE BEST OF MORAVIA

13

BRNO: THE REGION'S CAPITAL

ATTRACTIONS ●
Cathedral of Saints Peter
   and Paul **22**
Denisovy Sady **21**
Kapucínský Klášter
   (Capuchin Monastery) **23**
Kostel Nalezení
   svatého Kříže **23**
Moravian Regional
   Museum **17**
Old Town Hall **15**
Parnas Fountain **16**
Reduta Divadlo **18**
Špilberk Castle
   (Brno City Museum) **7**
Villa Tugendhat **2**
Zelný trh (Cabbage Market) **16**

ACCOMMODATIONS ■
Comsa Brno Palace **11**
Grandhotel Brno **19**
Holiday Inn **8**
Hotel Brno **20**
Hotel Continental **1**
Hotel Pod Špilberkem **9**
Hotel Royal Ricc **12**
Hotel Santander **20**
Hotel Slavia **3**
Hotel Orea Vroněž **8**

DINING ◆
Brabander **10**
Pivnice Hotel
   Pegas **5**
Špalíček **14**
U Královny Elišky **8**
Zahradní
   Restaurace **19**
Zemanova Kavárna **6**

SHOPPING ●
Antikvaríat Alfa **4**
Velký Špalíček **13**

BVV exhibition grounds are world-class displays of technology, industrial machinery, and even well-groomed pets.

Brno celebrates music as well, hosting the **Janáček Music Festival** each June and the **Brno International Music Festival (Moravský Podzim)** in September and October. However, probably the most attended event occurs each August when the **Motorcycle Grand Prix** tour rolls into town to tackle the Brno Circuit. For details on all events and a list of fairs at the BVV fairgrounds, contact **Informační Centrum** (see "Visitor Information," above) or go to **www.brno.cz**.

ORIENTATION Brno is a large rambling city, but most sights are concentrated in its inner core. At the center is **náměstí Svobody (Freedom Square)**, connected to the train station by Masarykova ulice. Just west of Masarykova is **Zelný trh (Cabbage Market)**, the largest square in town. Cars can't pass through the Old Town, but tram no. 4 barrels through with little regard for the pedestrians in its way.

The city is small enough for walking. All hotels, restaurants, and sights are close to each other, so you will likely not have to use public transportation. The only exception is for those staying at the Holiday Inn or Voronež.

If you need information on public transportation, the Tourist Information Office can provide a good map. Brno has a comprehensive network of trams and buses (www.dpmb. cz). Tickets range in price from 14Kč for 10 minutes of travel on one tram or bus without any transfers, to 18Kč for 15 minutes including transfers and 22Kč for 60 minutes with transfers. You can buy tickets at kiosks and tobacconists, or from yellow ticketing machines at some stops. You can also buy 30Kč tickets from the drivers allowing for 60 minutes of traveling including transfers. Be sure to validate your ticket on entering the tram or bus.

STROLLING AROUND BRNO

The Old Town holds most of the attractions you'll want to see, so it's probably best to start at the former seat of government, the Old Town Hall on Radnická 8. To get there, walk from the train station along Masarykovo and make a left at Orlí Street; if you're coming from náměstí Svobody, head toward the train station and turn right on either Panská or Orlí.

Brno's oldest secular building, from the 13th century, the **Old Town Hall** is a hodge-podge of styles—Gothic, Renaissance, and baroque elements melding together, demonstrating Brno's development through the ages. Almost everything in the building has a story or legend attached to it, beginning with the front door and its crooked Gothic portal. Designed by Anton Pilgram, who lists Vienna's vaunted St. Stephen's Church on his résumé, the door was completed in 1510. Town officials supposedly reneged on their original payment offer, and a furious Pilgram took revenge by bending the turret above the Statue of Justice.

On the second floor, a modest collection of armor, coins, and photos is displayed in the same room where town councilors met from the 13th century right up until 1935. Climb the stairs of the tower for an interesting, if not beautiful, city view; smokestacks and modern buildings battle for attention.

Before you leave Old Town Hall, examine two of Brno's most beloved attractions—the **Brno Dragon** and the **Wagon Wheel.** The "dragon" hanging from the ceiling is actually not a dragon, but an alligator given to the city by Archprince Matayás in 1608. Here also stands the Wagon Wheel, a testament to Brno's industrious image. Local lore has it that a carpenter named Jiří Birek from nearby Lednice wagered with locals that he could chop down a tree, fashion a wheel from it, and roll it the 40km (25 miles) to Brno all in a single day. Well, he managed to do it, but the townspeople, certain that one man couldn't do so much in 1 day, decided that Birek must have had assistance from the devil. With this mindset, they refused to ever buy his works again.

Just south of the Old Town Hall is **Zelný trh (Cabbage Market),** a farmers' market since the 13th century. You can still buy a head or two of the leafy vegetable at the market today as entrepreneurs sell their wares under the gaze of **Hercules,** depicted in the **Parnas Fountain** in the square's center. The fountain used to be a vital part of the market; quick-thinking fishermen let their carp swim and relax in the fountain until the fish were chosen for someone's dinner.

At the southern corner of **Zelný trh** lies the 17th-century **Reduta Divadlo,** a former home of Mozart. Another block closer to the train station, on Kapucínské náměstí, is the **Kostel Nalezení svatého Kříže (Church of the Sacred Cross)** and the **Kapucínský Klášter ★★ (Capuchin Monastery; ✆ 542-213-232).**

The Capuchin Monastery is best known for its fascinating (if gruesome) crypts, which along with Kutná Hora's Bone Church count among the most ghoulish sights in the Czech Republic. Kids will either love or be terrified by (parental discretion advised) the mummified remains of dozens of former monks and Austrian noblemen lying on the floor in their final repose. The basement's special ventilation helps maintain the corpses in their original state. The noblemen paid large sums of money to be interred here in the hope that proximity to the monks might improve their prospects in the afterlife. The monastery is open May to September Monday to Saturday from 9am to noon and 2 to 4:30pm and Sunday from 11 to 11:45am and 2 to 4:30pm (Feb–Apr and Oct–Dec closed on Mon; closed Jan).

Dominating **Zelný trh** at its southwest corner is the **Moravian Regional Museum,** Zelný trh 8, Brno (✆ 542-321-205; www.mzm.cz), housed in the Dietrichstein Palace. Completed in 1620, the palace was used by Russian Marshal Kutuzov to prepare for the battle of Austerlitz. These days, the museum displays a wide array of stuffed birds and wild game, as well as art, coins, and temporary exhibits. Admission is 30Kč adults, and 15Kč students and children. It's open Tuesday to Saturday from 9am to 5pm.

From the museum, head up Petrská Street to the **Cathedral of Saints Peter and Paul.** Perched atop a hill overlooking the city, the cathedral was built in the late 12th and early 13th centuries. In 1743, it was rebuilt in a baroque style, only to be re-Gothicized just before World War I. The resulting melding of styles gives the cathedral a unique character. The cathedral is open Monday to Wednesday and Friday and Saturday from 6:30am to 6pm, Thursday from 6:30am to 7:30pm, and Sunday from 8:30am to 6pm.

Take a break at **Denisovy sady,** the park behind the cathedral, and prepare to climb the hill to get to Špilberk Castle. If you're not up for it, tram nos. 6, 9, 14, and 17 go near the castle, but you'll still have a short but strenuous walk from there. If you want to walk all the way, head along Biskupská, where **interesting houses** provide a nice foreground to the bustling city. Make a left on Starobrněnská to Husova and then left on to Pellicova. At Pellicova 11 is a fine example of František Uherka's cubist architectural vision.

But the real reason for this climb is **Špilberk Castle ★★.** If there's one building in the Czech Republic that's ready to be overrun by visitors, it's Špilberk—and it's had practice. It was built in the 13th century, and the Hussites controlled the castle in the

What Time Is It?

If you tour the cathedral in the late morning, you may think that you've switched time zones. Don't worry: The cathedral bells strike noon an hour early in remembrance of a quick-thinking bell ringer who, seeing that the city was on the verge of attack by the Swedes during the Thirty Years' War, found out that the army was planning to take the city by noon. If not successful by then, Swedish commander General Torstenson is said to have decided the attack would be called off and the army would beat a hasty retreat. The bell ringer, sensing that the town couldn't repel the Swedes, rang the cathedral bells an hour early at 11am, before the army could attack. True to his word, Torstenson packed up and went home.

15th century. The Prussians saw the castle's position as an excellent lookout when they occupied it in the early 17th century. It was a fearsome prison during the Habsburg occupation in the 18th and 19th centuries. The Nazis converted it into a barracks and prison for holding and torturing Czech political prisoners during World War II.

At Špilberk's **Brno City Museum** ★ (© **542-123-611;** www.spilberk.cz), you can see several permanent exhibitions such as "Prison of Nations" or "History of Brno" and others. Admission to all exhibitions, casemates, and the lookout tower is 160Kč adults, 90Kč students. It's open Tuesday to Sunday from 9am to 6pm May to September, and October and April from 9am to 5pm; and Wednesday to Sunday 10am to 5pm November to March.

MORE TO SEE & DO

MUSEUMS At first glance, this sleek villa looks like just another stylish modern home, but many count the **Villa Tugendhat** ★★, Černopolní 45 (© **545-212-118;** www. tugendhat-villa.cz; admission Kč120 adult and 60Kč child; open 10am–6pm Wed–Sun) among noted modern architect Mies van der Rohe's best works. Mies broke new ground here in the late 1920s with—among other things—a fully open floor plan and huge wall-sized windows at the back. He used expensive woods and marbles, rather than ostentatious decoration, to give the house its character. Visits are only allowed with a guided tour that must be arranged in advance. The tourist office can help with this, or call the number above or visit the web site. The villa may or may not be open to the public during your trip, since the city has been threatening for several years to close it down to carry out long delayed renovations. To visit, take tram no. 3, 5, or 11 from the center to the Dětská nemocnice (Children's Hospital) stop.

SHOPPING Once back in the city center, take some time for a quick meal and browse along the **pedestrian shopping zone,** which unfolds between náměstí Svobody and the train station. Prices for goods are often cheaper here than in Prague, so you may find a better deal for the crystal vase or pair of earrings you were thinking of buying. Brno has several large shopping malls; the most impressive one in the center is the **Velký Špalíček** shopping center (Dominikánská 5; © **543-237-385;** www.velkyspalicek.cz) that starts at the top of the Zelný trh (Cabbage market). For rare maps, lithographs, and posters, plus an unusual selection of autographed photos of Czech superstars, including one of crooner Karel Gott (p. 24), the country's answer to Tom Jones, peek in at **Antikvariát Alfa** (Veselá 39; ✆ **542-211-947;** open Mon–Fri 10am–6pm, Sat 10am–1pm).

SOCCER Sports fans can partake in a Sunday ritual as dear to Czechs as football is to Americans by taking the 20-minute walk north from the main square to Brno stadium, where first league **soccer team 1. FC Brno** plays its home games. Grab a beer and a sausage and cheer along. Tickets, beginning at around 80Kč, are always plentiful and can be bought at the stadium on game day.

WHERE TO STAY

Brno's bread and butter are regular trade fairs held at the exhibition grounds outside the center. Try to avoid arriving during a major fair (usually in May and Sept), when hotels raise rates 50% or more. The organizer carries a fair schedule on its website (www.bvv.cz).

Expensive

Comsa Brno Palace ★★★ Brno's newest luxury hotel occupies a stunningly restored 19th-century town palace, within easy walking distance of the Špilberk Castle or the city center. The four-story atrium will take your breath away. The rooms maintain the same high standard, artfully blending old-world charm and modern convenience.

Šilingrovo nám. 2, 602 00 Brno. ✆ **532-156-777.** Fax 532 156 711. www.comsabrnopalace.com. 119 units. 3,500Kč–4,500Kč double. AE, DC, MC, V. Valet parking (387Kč]). **Amenities:** Bar; concierge; fitness center. In room: TV, hair dryer, Internet, minibar.

Holiday Inn ★ Yes, that's right. The best surprise is no surprise—even in Brno. The very modern Holiday Inn Brno, on the fairgrounds, caters mainly to the trade-fair crowd, so be warned that prices may jump steeply when events are scheduled. Everything, from the rooms to the restaurant to the bars, looks eerily similar to their counterparts in other Holiday Inns around the world. Still, the beds are more comfortable than most, and the rooms are spotless, with large writing desks and showers that have no problems with water pressure. The staff is very friendly and speaks English.

Křížkovského 20, 603 00 Brno. ✆ **543-122-111.** Fax 543-246-990. 201 units. www.ichotelsgroup.com. 3,120Kč double; 3,600Kč suite. AE, DC, MC, V. Parking (400Kč per day). **Amenities:** Restaurant; bar; Internet; pool. In room: TV, hair dryer, minibar.

Hotel Royal Ricc ★★ A small, quiet inn set just off the Cabbage Market, the Ricc is part of the Romantic Hotel chain. Though the soft pink facade of the building isn't very impressive, the attention to detail inside the building combines the rustic feel of a bed-and-breakfast with the service of a top-quality hotel. Rooms vary in size, but all are decorated with antiques that give a warm, welcome feeling lacking in most competing hotels. Make sure to look up, since many rooms have beautifully restored ceilings with intricate artwork. There are sitting rooms, a wine bar, and a restaurant as well that all live up to the surroundings. Paid parking and high Wi-Fi fees, though, add significantly to the room price.

Starobrněnská 10, 602 00 Brno. ✆ **542-219-262.** Fax 542-219-265. www.romantichotels.cz. 30 units. 3,600Kč double; 6,000Kč suite. AE, MC, V. Parking (390Kč per day). **Amenities:** 2 restaurants; wine bar; Internet (400Kč). In room: TV, hair dryer, minibar.

Grandhotel Brno ★   Since it was taken over by the Austria Hotels International chain in the mid-1990s, the Grandhotel has lived up to its name. Its rooms are spacious and well appointed, though some rooms located at the front get a little noisy due to the major street running past with its never-ending stream of trams; ask for a room that has windows facing north, away from the commotion. The rack rate puts this hotel in the expensive category, but the daily rate posted on the hotel's website can push this hotel into the moderate range. The location right from the train station is especially convenient if you're arriving by train.

Benešova 18–20, 657 83 Brno. © **542-518-111.** Fax 542-210-345. www.austria-hotels.at/grand-hotel-brno. 105 units. 2,875Kč double; 3,400Kč suite. AE, DC, MC, V. Parking 150Kč. **Amenities:** 2 restaurants; nightclub; room service; casino. *In room:* TV, A/C, hair dryer, Internet, minibar.

Hotel Continental ★★   This high-rise Communist-era hotel is trying to capitalize on its funky '60s design, and fans of Jetsons'-style futurism will feel right at home. The rooms on the top floor, outfitted with flat-screen TVs and high-end toiletries, have gotten a full design makeover and are as hip as anything you're likely to find in Prague, or New York's East Village for that matter. The very helpful staff is approachable for advice on how to reach the sights. The Continental is north of the city center, so you'll get some cleaner air and a nice short walk into the center.

Kounicova 6, 662 21 Brno. © **541-519-111.** Fax 541-211-203. www.continentalbrno.cz. 230 units. 1,875Kč–2,500Kč double. AE, DC, MC, V. Parking. **Amenities:** Restaurant; bar; concierge. *In room:* A/C, TV, hair dryer, Internet, minibar.

Hotel OREA Voroněž   The Voroněž has added conference rooms and a pool and renovated its restaurants. But for all the new glitz, it still is basically a Czech *panelák* (housing complex) dressed up as a hotel trying hard to shed its Communist-era image—and furniture. It's across from the fairgrounds, making it convenient for those here on business. In many of the medium-size rooms, 1970s Naugahyde furnishings have been replaced with light pastel-and-wood beds, desks, and chairs, and these redone rooms make the grade. Except during the busiest times, you can always find a room here.

Křížkovského 47, 603 73 Brno. © **543-141-111.** Fax 543-212-002. www.orea.cz. 368 units. From 2,100Kč double; 3,000Kč suite. AE, DC, MC, V. **Amenities:** Restaurant; bar; fitness room; Internet; pool. *In room:* TV, minibar.

Hotel Slavia   This is a big, refurbished 19th-century hotel with a wisp of lingering Communist-era neglect about it. Nevertheless, it's the best location for the money in Brno, just off the main square. Rooms are spartan, with bland furniture, but clean. The rooms are not uniformly sized, so take a look at a couple before choosing.

Solniční 15, 662 16 Brno. © **542-321-249.** Fax 542-211-769. www.slaviabrno.cz. 82 units. From 2,290Kč double. AE, DC, MC, V. Parking (150Kč per day). **Amenities:** Restaurant; cafe. *In room:* TV, Wi-Fi, minibar.

Inexpensive

Hotel Brno   Once a run-down dive, the Brno has been given a face-lift and a new lease on life. The Communist-era rooms, while small and sparsely furnished, have been freshened up. Near the city center, the hotel even has its own tennis courts, but its main attraction is as a quiet place to lay down your head at the right price.

Horní 19, 639 00 Brno. © **543-214-046.** Fax 543-215-308. www.hotelbrno.cz. 90 units. 1,290Kč double. AE, DC, MC, V. **Amenities:** Restaurant. *In room:* TV.

Hotel pod Špilberkem ★ This is a small, family run hotel with an excellent loca- tion, within easy walking distance of the center and Špilberk castle. The name means "under the Špilberk," and indeed several rooms, while plainly furnished, at least have views up toward the castle. Though the street is busy, the rooms are set back. There's off-street parking, but watch the narrow doorway into the parking courtyard.

Pekařská 10, 602 00 Brno. ✆ **543-235-003.** Fax 543-235-066. www.hotelpodspilberkem.cz. 25 units. 1,900Kč double. MC, V. **Amenities:** Restaurant; Internet. *In room:* TV.

Hotel Santander ★★ Hotels in trade-fair towns are anonymous places, so it's a nice surprise to be greeted by name when you arrive at this family-owned villa on the western edge of town. The rooms are large and clean, if a bit sterile. Ask for no. 7, a rustic double with its own private entrance to a lovely back garden. The breakfast buffet, included in the room rate, is the best in town.

Pisárecká 6, 603 00 Brno. ✆ **547-220-233.** Fax 543-220-375. www.hotelsantander.cz. 15 units. 1,600Kč double. AE, DC, MC, V. *In room:* TV.

WHERE TO DINE

Expensive

U Kastelána ★★ CZECH/CONTINENTAL Prague residents tend to scoff at the suggestion that the best restaurant in the country may not be in the capital, but here in Brno. Since opening its doors a few years ago beside a nondescript shopping center, U Kastelána has been winning awards and garnering the attention of Czech foodies with creative dishes like its signature rabbit cassoulet and monkfish served in a spicy sausage emulsion. Start off your meal to remember with veal carpaccio or "corn cappuccino" soup, which is a sweet corn soup spiced with chili oil. While prices for evening meals can climb pretty high, the daily luncheon specials make this an affordable treat.

Kotlařská 51a. ✆ **541-213-497.** Reservations recommended. Main courses 260Kč–530Kč. AE, DC, MC, V. Mon–Sat noon–midnight; Sun noon–10pm.

U Královny Elišky CZECH If you're searching for the quintessential Moravian experience, look no further. Nestled in the back wall of the castle where the stables used to be, this never-ending maze of cellars and alcoves oozes Moravian charm. Browse through a menu loaded with pork, chicken, fish, and beef dishes as a Gypsy band wanders the premises. An extensive wine list complements the wide variety of meals. *One warning:* The appetizers on the tray wheeled to your table can cost up to 360Kč each, so don't hesitate to ask how much your choice will run.

Mendlovo nám. 1. ✆ **543-212-578.** Main courses 200Kč–480Kč. AE, MC, V. Tues–Sat 9pm–midnight.

Moderate

Brabander ★★ CZECH Here you'll find fancy dining, but not so fancy that you can't relax. The menu carries excellent international dishes, like grilled salmon glazed with soy sauce, at reasonable prices for the quality of the cooking. There's dining on two levels; opt for upstairs, which is larger and more convivial.

Pekařská 4. ✆ **543-215-250.** Reservations recommended. Main courses 180Kč–300Kč. AE, DC, MC, V. Mon–Sat noon–midnight; Sun noon–10pm.

Zahradní Restaurace Le Grand (Garden Restaurant Le Grand) CZECH/ INTERNATIONAL When you enter this restaurant, you might expect the prices to be higher than they are. The setting is first-rate, with fountains and lots of plants and nonintrusive background music. This used to be one of eastern Europe's finest Chinese restaurants, but now the menu features Czech and international dishes. Try the Moravian plate piled with pork, duck, smoked meat, sauerkraut, and two kinds of dumplings.

In the Grandhotel Brno, Benešova 18. ℭ **542-518-111.** Reservations recommended. Main courses 150Kč–400Kč. AE, DC, MC, V. Daily 11:30am–2pm and 5:30–10:30pm.

Inexpensive

Pivnice Hotel Pegas ★ CZECH   This central microbrewery is a regular spot for visiting British stag parties (courtesy of Ryanair), but don't let that put you off. Sample the wheat beer—a rarity in the barley-only Czech Republic. The tables are usually fully booked by 8pm, so go early to get a spot. This is also an in-house hotel with clean rooms at decent prices.

Jakubská 4. ℭ **542-210-104.** Main courses 90Kč–160Kč. AE, V, MC. Daily 9am–midnight.

Špalíček ★ CZECH   A rustic, traditional Czech pub situated just off a main square, the "Cabbage Market" serves local specialties like roast pork and dumplings, along with very passable mugs of Brno's home beer, Starobrno. It offers a daily lunch special with soup and main course for 79Kč. Sit out on the terrace in nice weather.

Zelný trh 12. ℭ **542-211-526.** Main courses 100Kč–150Kč. No credit cards. Mon–Sat 10am–11pm.

Zemanova Kavárna ★★ CZECH   This fully restored 1920s-era Functionalist cafe now has a multipurpose role as highly stylized cultural center, atmospheric restaurant, and, naturally, a cafe. Stop in for the excellent-value lunch specials, where soup and a very well done traditional main like roast pork or schnitzel runs around 79Kč. The black and white photos on the wall complete the fun period-piece feel.

Jezuitská 6. ℭ **542-218-096.** Main courses 100Kč–150Kč. AE, DC, MC, V. Mon–Sat 10am–11pm.

BRNO AFTER DARK

While it may lack Prague's energy, Brno still has plenty to offer at night. A strong cultural program dominates, with a local theater and symphony offering world-class entertainment. Go to www.brno.cz to find out what's going on at major venues, or visit the Informační Centrum (see earlier in this chapter) to get tickets.

For the young at heart, the **Metro Music Bar** (Poštovská 6, Alfa-Pasáž; ℭ **515-533-452;** www.metromusic.cz; daily 6pm–3am) is the place to dance. The program changes daily from live bands to DJs and back. Otherwise, make like a Czech and go to any number of local pubs, which are located on nearly every street corner. Start out at the **Pivnice Pegas** (Jakubská 4; ℭ **542-210-104**) for microbrews just off the main square, and from there just wander the streets. You'll go no more than 2 minutes in any direction before another pub tempts you.

2 TELČ ★

149km (92 miles) SE of Prague, 86km (53 miles) W of Brno

As you go through towns while traveling in Moravia, you may be tempted to pass up Telč, dismissing it as yet another "small town with a nice square." Don't. Those who make the trip to Telč strike gold. Telč is one of the few towns in Europe that can boast of not being reconstructed since its original edifices were built. It now enjoys the honor of being a United Nations (UNESCO) World Heritage Site. Its uniformly built houses and castle give it an almost too-perfect look, as though no one ever really lived here.

Due to its small size, you can explore Telč in a just a few hours. Those traveling by car to Brno or Vienna should stop here on the way. I recommend spending the night to admire the **illuminated castle and square,** especially if there's an evening recital or concert at the castle. You can also combine a stop here with a visit to Znojmo (see below).

ESSENTIALS

GETTING THERE Located about halfway between České Budějovice and Brno, Telč can be reached by taking Hwy. 23. **Driving** from Prague, take Hwy. D1 in the direction of Brno and exit at Jihlava, where you pick up Hwy. 38 after going through the town. Then head west on Hwy. 23. You can leave your car in one of three large parking lots at the town's northern and southern gates. It's a 2-hour drive from Prague.

Train connections to Telč aren't great, so be patient. First-class fare from Prague costs 310Kč, and second-class fare is 250Kč. The town lies on the Havlíčkův Brod, Kostelec u Jihlavy line, where you'll have to change in Kostelec u Jihlavy. Once you get there, you'll find several trains departing daily to Telč. The train station offers storage, though its hours aren't the most dependable. Figure on a journey time of 4 to 5 hours if you are lucky.

Better than the train is the more direct route by **bus,** costing 142Kč. Buses leave from Prague's Florenc bus station four times a day, and take about 3 hours. The castle and town square are a 10-minute walk from the bus station. To get to town, exit through the station's back entrance, turn right on Tyršova, and then turn left on Rudnerova. Follow this street as it bears left, and turn right at the second small alley. This will guide you to the main square.

VISITOR INFORMATION Since UNESCO gave its backing to Telč in 1992, services for visitors have blossomed, and none more so than the information center on the main square. At the **Informační Středisko,** náměstí Zachariáše z Hradce 10 (© **567-112-407;** www.telc-etc.cz or www.telcsko.cz; info@telc-etc.cz), you'll find bountiful information on accommodations, cultural events, guided tours, and even hunting; brochures are in Czech, German, and English. The staff is eager to arrange reservations. Open April Monday to Friday 8am to noon and 1 to 5pm, Saturday and Sunday 10am to noon and 1 to 4pm; May and September Monday to Friday 8am to 5pm, Saturday and Sunday 10am to 5pm; June to August Monday to Friday 8am to 6pm, Saturday and Sunday 10am to 6pm; October Monday to Friday 8am to noon and 1 to 5pm, Saturday and Sunday 10am to noon and 1 to 4pm; November to April Monday and Wednesday 8am to noon and 1 to 5pm, Tuesday and Thursday 8am to noon and 1 to 4pm, and Friday 8am to noon and 1 to 3pm.

SPECIAL EVENTS The **Prázdniny v Telči (Holidays in Telč),** a season of concerts, recitals, and fairs, runs from the end of July to the middle of August. For details, contact the **Informační Středisko** (see "Visitor Information," above) or www.prazdninyvtelci.cz.

ORIENTATION Telč's historic center is shaped like a trapezoid and is surrounded by lakes on three sides. At the center is a very large square named after the town's former owner, Zachariáš z Hradce.

Start with a tour of **Telč Château** (© 567-243-943; www.zamek-telc.cz) at the northwest end of the main square. Zacharias of Neuhaus, whose name now graces the main square, was so enamored of the Renaissance style rampant in Italy that in 1553 he commissioned Antonio Vlach, and later Baldassare Maggi de Ronio, to rebuild the château, originally a 14th-century Gothic structure. This castle's exterior, however, cannot prepare you for its interior—hall after hall of lavish rooms with spectacular ceilings.

Highlights inside the château include the **Africa Hall,** with rhino heads, tiger skins, and other exotica from expeditions accumulated by Karel Podstatky, a relative of the castle's last owner, in the early 1900s. The **Banquet Hall**'s *sgrafitti* seems to mock those who overindulge, and the **Marble Hall of Knights** features a wood ceiling decorated with bas-reliefs from 1570, plus a fine collection of armor. In the **Golden Hall,** where balls and ceremonies once took place, 30 octagonal coffers with mythological scenes stare down at you from the ceiling.

A 1-hour guided tour of the castle halls in Czech costs 100Kč adults, 60Kč students, free for children under 6. To see the residences, take the additional 45-minute tour, which costs 80Kč. The fee for an English-language guide is an additional 100Kč per person. The castle is open Tuesday to Sunday: May to September from 9am to noon and 1 to 5pm; October and April from 9am to noon and 1 to 4pm; the castle is closed November to March.

Next to the castle is the **Church of St. James (Kostel sv. Jakuba),** its walls adorned with late-15th-century paintings. Next to St. James is the baroque **Jesuit Church of the Name of Jesus.**

After strolling the castle grounds, head back to the main square, where a sea of soft pastel facades awaits. If you find yourself wondering how the entire square can be so uniform, you're not alone. After rebuilding the castle, Zacharias realized that the rest of the place looked, well, out of place. To rectify the situation, he promptly rebuilt the facade of each building on the square, though Gothic columns belie what once was. Of particular note is the building referred to as **House 15,** where a round oriel and *sgrafitti* portraying the crucifixion, Saul and David, Christopher, and faith and justice jut onto the street corner. And watching over it all are the cherubs on the Marian column, built in 1718.

WHERE TO STAY

If you haven't arranged lodging ahead of time, head straight to the information center in the main square, where the staff has a complete list of what's available. For hotels, expect to pay upwards of 1,400Kč for a double.

Private accommodations are also available, and for the most part, these rooms are comparable to hotel rooms (if not better and less expensive), though there are far fewer amenities. The information center staff will call and arrange for you to meet the room's owner so you can check out the place. Several rooms located directly on the square are available. Rates will be about 500Kč per person. On slow days, owners will usually negotiate a better price.

Hotel Celerin   Located in a small corner of the square, the Celerin is a little hard to find, but worth the effort. The rooms themselves are only average, but the real selling point is the view out over the square of the front rooms. By all means try to get a room with a view. Looking out over the square at night when it's bathed in light will remind you why this town is a UNESCO treasure. Travelers with disabilities will find the staff here helpful, and some rooms are fully accessible.

Náměstí Zachariáše z Hradce 43, 588 56 Telč. ℭ **567-243-477.** Fax 567-213-581. www.hotelcelerin.cz. 12 units. 1,600Kč double. Rates include continental breakfast. AE, DC, MC, V. **Amenities:** Restaurant; bar. *In room:* TV, fridge.

Hotel Černý Orel (Black Eagle Hotel)   On the main square overlooking the Marian column, the Black Owl is a favorite among visitors. The room has a lingering old-fashioned feel and the rooms are a bit faded but clean. Ask for a view of the square; the staff will usually accommodate this request if a room is available. A lively restaurant downstairs serves good Czech fare.

Náměstí Zachariáše z Hradce 7, 588 56 Telč. ℭ **567-243-222.** Fax 567-243-221. www.ucernehoorla.eu. 33 units (5 rooms without toilet). 1,800Kč double. AE, MC, V. **Amenities:** Restaurant. *In room:* TV.

Hotel Telč   Just off the main square, the Telč has rooms that feel spacious because of their high ceilings. The park next to it adds to the effect and provides a sense of being out in the country, a good choice if you've had enough of staying in noisy city centers. Rooms facing the street are brighter but louder than those to the rear. The all-wood furnishings add some ambience, but the bathrooms are cramped.

Na Můstku 37, 588 56 Telč. ℭ **567-243-109.** Fax 567-223-887. www.hoteltelc.cz. 10 units. 1,550Kč–1,840Kč double. AE, DC, MC, V. **Amenities:** Restaurant. *In room:* TV, minibar.

WHERE TO DINE

Švejk CZECH   With very good Czech staples like goulash and roast pork, this is the place to go if The Black Eagle is too crowded. Sit on the terrace in the summer with a commanding sweep over the entire square. The location, just around the corner from Telč Château, is convenient for a hearty after-tour lunch.

Náměstí Zachariáše z Hradce 1. ℭ **567-213-151.** Main courses 90Kč–180Kč. No credit cards. Daily 10am–midnight.

U Černého Orla (At the Black Eagle) ★ CZECH   If it looks as though every visitor in town is trying to get in here, it's because they are. The Black Eagle is worth the effort. This is one of the few restaurants in Telč that can be trusted to serve good food consistently. Crowd in at any free space and enjoy a wide range of Czech meals. The hearty soups are especially welcome on days when the sun isn't shining. When it is, get a table on the terrace out front—though the service, which is quick if you're inside, usually slows down considerably.

Náměstí Zachariáše z Hradce 7. ℭ **567-243-222.** Reservations recommended. Main courses 80Kč–190Kč. AE, MC, V. June–Sept daily 7am–10pm; Oct–May Tues–Sun 7am–10pm.

---

3   ZNOJMO

190km (118 miles) SE of Prague, 64km (40 miles) S of Brno

Most travelers blow through Znojmo, the wine and pickle capital of the Czech Republic, at about 97kmph (60 mph), tired of getting caught behind trucks and buses en route to Vienna. But it wasn't always that way.

Znojmo was settled as far back as the 7th century, and the town gained prominence in the 9th century, when the Great Moravian Empire took control. In the 11th and 12th centuries, Prince Břetislav I constructed a fortress here; in 1226, the town was granted rights (including collecting taxes and making wine) by the king—even before the Moravian capital of Brno. Znojmo's position on the border made it a natural location as a trading center, and Czech kings always ensured that the town was taken care of, using it as a lookout over the Austrian frontier. Alas, the original town hall was destroyed during World War II, and the Communist-inspired sprawl that followed has taken away some of Znojmo's character. But the old center remains vibrant, with many religious buildings still intact. The Town Hall's 70m-tall (230-ft.) tower lets you take in a view of the city and surrounding area—both old and new.

These days Znojmo is enjoying a rebirth as a regional hiking and cycling center, and trails fan out all along the border region with Austria. For maps and suggestions, ask at Informační Středisko (see below).

And why is Znojmo considered the pickle capital of the Czech Republic? Simply because the **pickles** taste so good. They're made from the best cucumbers the country has to offer. And when put into a spicy sauce, as they are in *Znojemský guláš*, these sweet-and-sour pickles really taste great. You'll get pickle fever, too, I promise. When you do, and want to buy some, you'll notice just how many shops proudly display the Znojmo pickle.

And then there's the **wine.** If you're looking for the region's best vintages, try **Frankovka** (a smooth, full-bodied red) or **Ryzlink** (a light, dry white), with the Znojemské (from Znojmo) or Mikulov labels. These good wines are available almost everywhere; a liter costs no more than 150Kč. Wine bars often serve the best vintages straight from the cask. You can also fill up—with both wine and fuel—at some gas stations.

To best enjoy the town's wine and pickles, you should spend at least a few hours here, or overnight if you've got some time. Znojmo's location on the Prague–Vienna route makes it a natural place to stop. An added bonus is its proximity to Telč—you can see both in 1 day if you want.

ESSENTIALS

GETTING THERE Znojmo is most easily reached by **car** and is especially convenient for those heading to or from Vienna or Telč. Take Hwy. D1 from Prague and exit at Hwy. 38 in the direction of Jihlava. As you enter the town you're already on the right highway, so just pass by the town center and follow the signs. From Prague, the trip should take about 2½ hours.

Several **trains** to Znojmo leave Brno throughout the day, though some require a quick change in Hrušovany. The ride takes about 2 hours and costs 117Kč. From Prague, the complete trip takes at least 5 hours via Brno and costs 670Kč.

Several **bus** from Prague's Florenc station make the daily run to Znojmo in about 3 hours. The one-way fare is around 200Kč. From Brno, the trip is much quicker (around an hour) and costs about 65Kč one-way. Almost as many buses run between the two places as do trains.

VISITOR INFORMATION In the center of Znojmo, **Informační Středisko** at Obroková 10, Znojmo (© **515-222-552;** www.znojmocity.cz), can help with accommodations, maps, and directions. Ask what's on in town, and they can book tickets for you on the spot. The office is open May, June, and September on Monday to Saturday from 9am to 1pm and 1:30 to 5pm; July and August daily 8am to 8pm; and October to April on Monday to Friday from 9am to 1pm and 1:30 to 5pm, Saturday from 8am to 12:30pm.

SPECIAL EVENTS   In late August and early September, residents of Znojmo celebrate their vintages at the **Znojmo Wine Festival.** Taste wine, eat pickles, and listen to traditional Moravian music late into the night, which is normally tranquil on other nights. For details, contact **Informační Středisko** (see "Visitor Information," above).

ORIENTATION   Znojmo's main square is **Masarykovo náměstí,** and pretty much everything you'll want to see is on or near it. **Zelenářská Street,** which runs off the square's northwest corner, leads to the castle and St. Nicholas Church.

STROLLING THROUGH ZNOJMO

A walking tour of Znojmo takes about 2 to 3 hours. Begin at **Masaryk Square,** where the **Art House (Dům umění; ☎ 515-226-503)** holds a small collection of coins, plus temporary exhibitions. It is open Tuesday to Saturday from 9am to 6pm. Admission is 20Kč. The southern end of the square is one of the few historic areas that hasn't been maintained well; the dilapidated **Capuchin Monastery (Kapucínský klášter)** and **Church of St. John the Baptist** show few signs that they were once focal points of the town.

Impossible to miss is the **Town Hall Tower (☎ 515-216-297),** the only remaining piece of what was once referred to as Moravia's prettiest town hall. The actual town hall met misfortune during World War II, but the late-Gothic 70m-high (230-ft.) tower still stands guard. For 25Kč, you can climb up to the lookout, which offers a picturesque view of the castle and the Dyje River. Try not to let the nondescript department store that occupies the spot where the town hall once stood wreck the picture. The tower is open May to September, Monday to Friday 9am to 1pm and 2 to 6pm, Saturday and Sunday 9am to 1pm and 2 to 5pm; April, Monday to Friday from 9am to 1pm and 2 to 6pm, Saturday 9am to 1pm; and October to March, Monday to Friday 9am to 6pm, Saturday 9am to noon.

Follow the small alleyway called **Kramářská** to **Slepičí trh** (the former Hen Market) to find the entrance to the **Znojemské podzemí (Znojmo Underground)** ★★ where almost 30km (19 miles) of tunnels used to store everything from pickles to munitions. If there's a tour just leaving or a few people waiting, arrange to join them, since the tours (which are in Czech only, though English-language pamphlets are provided) are given only to groups of more than six. Admission is 50Kč adults, 30Kč students. The Underground is open May, June and September, daily 9am to 4pm; April, Monday to Saturday 10am to 4pm; July and August, daily 9am to 8pm; and October, Saturday only, 10am to 4pm. For reservations call ☎ 515-221-342.

Head back 1 block west to Zelenářská ulice and follow it away from the square to Malá Mikulášská ulice, which leads to the Gothic **St. Nicholas Church** and behind it the bi-level **St. Wenceslas Chapel.** The church is supposed to be open only for services and the occasional concert, but check the door just in case.

Farther on, you'll come to the 11th-century **Rotunda sv. Kateřiny** ★, one of the oldest and best examples of Romanesque architecture still standing in the Czech Republic. Inside are painstakingly restored frescoes of the Přemyslid rulers dating back to the mid–12th century.

The Painted Cellar of the Šatov Vineyard

Wine, art, and history aficionados unite! The **Painted Cellar of Šatov,** one of the region's most prolific vineyards, awaits. But this isn't an ordinary tour of a vineyard or just a historic place—it's both.

The town of Šatov lies just before the Austrian border, about 10km (6 miles) south of Znojmo. So close is Šatov to the border that it was once part of Austria. The town and its surrounding vineyards have long produced some of the country's finest Moravian wines. The excellent soil conditions and Continental climate make it perfectly suited for grapes.

You'll find several cellars here (most of them associated with the Znovín winery—see below), and during late autumn Moravian hospitality opens the doors to just about anyone who knocks, but few cellars can rival the splendor of the painted cellar.

The cellar was most likely carved out in the late 19th century for reasons still a mystery today, but it took its current form when a one-armed man named Max Appeltauer descended into the tunnels and began his work there in 1934. As you enter the cellar and go down about 18m (59 ft.), a musty odor envelops you and you wonder how Appeltauer could have spent so much time here. But as you look around the 20m (66-ft.) tunnel, you'll be thankful he did. Not an artist by trade, Appeltauer set to carving and then painting into the sandstone walls an **eclectic set of scenes** portraying everything from Prague Castle to Snow White and the Seven Dwarfs, as well as the Šatov coat of arms. Running off the main tunnel are five smaller rooms, each depicting a separate theme and carved and painted in painstaking detail.

It's almost as though Appeltauer was expecting to escape one day to his residence inside the cellar, celebrating his departure from life aboveground. Indeed, celebrating had already taken place inside the dark cellar, as the inscription VÍNO, ŽENY A ZPĚV, ZAHLADÍ VEŠKERÝ HNĚV ("Wine, women, and song will remove all anger") indicates. Legend has it that the cellar was once a popular place for the village men to idle away the hours and even entertain their lady friends from time to time. Wives searching for their husbands would enter, sending the girls scurrying into the subcellar. Local lore has it that Hitler visited the cellar when inspecting the military bunkers set up to defend his southern flank.

Appeltauer left the cellar for good in 1968 and died 4 years later, never realizing his next dream—to paint farther into the cellar. Some cans of paint and a few jars still sit idly by at the point where he stopped, untouched after nearly 40 years of waiting for his return.

The cellar tours are arranged by the **Znovín** winery ((C) **721-754-548;** www.znovin.cz; daily 10am–6pm), located at the edge of the village next to the train station. Book your tour over the telephone or on the website. Admission is 25Kč, which includes a glass of wine. To get to Šatov by car, take Highway 59 out of Znojmo to the south and turn right at the sign for Šatov. Buses and trains also run to the village from Znojmo on a regular basis.

At the edge of the embankment lies **Znojmo Castle**, which now houses the **Jiho-moravské Muzeum (South Moravian Museum)** exhibition (© 515-222-311). It focuses on the role of Znojmo through the ages, especially as a lookout against the Austro-Hungarian Empire. Admission is 45Kč adults, 25Kč students; if you take the tour, note that both sights are included in the tour price. Open May to September Tuesday to Sunday from 9am to 5pm, and in April Saturday and Sunday 9am to 5pm.

WHERE TO STAY

The quality of lodging in Znojmo has drastically improved in recent years. In addition to the properties listed below, there's now a raft of small family owned *pensions* behind the main square in and among the tiny lanes that overlook the river valley. The best bet if you turn up without a room is to roam around the center and see if something strikes your fancy. Except during wine festivals in the fall, you're unlikely to have a problem finding a room.

Althanský palác ★★ This romantic and tastefully reconstructed town palace is easily the nicest hotel in town. The location is dead center, and perfect for exploring the main squares or the tiny alleyways that overlook the river valley. Many of the rooms have retained their period details, like hardwood floors and beam ceilings. Ask to see a few before deciding. The beautiful "Blue Room," with pale blue walls and wood floors, goes for the price of an ordinary double. The in-house restaurant is one of the best around.

Horní nám. 3, 669 02 Znojmo. © **731-441-090.** www.althanskypalac.cz. 22 units. 1,950Kč double; 3,500Kč suite. AE, DC, MC, V. Amenities: Restaurant; bar; wine cellar; exercise room. *In room:* TV, Internet, minibar.

Hotel Dukla This is an old-style Communist high-rise 2km (1¼ mile) south of the center along the main highway to Vienna. The location makes it practical only for travelers with their own wheels and there are far more atmospheric places to choose from in the historic center of town. Still, the reconstructed rooms with new beds and updated bathrooms are decent value. One drawback: There's no Internet or Wi-Fi on the premises. Skip the hotel restaurant and instead walk across the parking lot to the "Styl" pizzeria if you're looking for something good, quick, and cheap.

Holandská 30, 671 81 Znojmo. © **515-227-239.** Fax 515-227-322. www.hotel-dukla.cz. 112 units. 1,000Kč unreconstructed double; 1,400Kč reconstructed double. AE, DC, MC, V. Free parking. **Amenities:** Restaurant. *In room:* TV.

Hotel Kateřina This former villa, now a hotel with a fitness center and a restaurant with a terrace that overlooks the river valley, is a welcome relief from the dreary hotels found throughout Znojmo. The rooms are small and a little sterile, but very bright; several have large bay windows. The "modern" furniture advertised by the hotel is not going to win any awards, but the beds are comfortable.

Na Valech 7, 669 02 Znojmo. © **515-220-307.** www.hotel-katerina.cz. 8 units. 1,100Kč double. AE, DC, MC, V. Free parking. **Amenities:** Restaurant; bar; summer terrace; exercise room; sauna. *In room:* TV, fridge.

WHERE TO DINE

Znojmo may have the pickles, but finding a decent rest of the meal is still tricky. The dining revolution that has swept much of the rest of the country, has yet to be felt here and most of the restaurants in town have the look and food of a Communist-era throwback. Fortunately, there's plenty of good wine on hand, and the beer—courtesy of local brewer Hostan—isn't bad either.

Na Věčností CZECH   This is a wine cellar, beer hall, and art gallery rolled into one. The food is simple but good and the laid-back vibe is the best in town. Lunchtime offers a rotating menu of traditional foods with modern updates and lots of vegetarian offerings. The place is nonsmoking.

Velká Mikulášská 11. ℂ **515-221-814.** Main courses 70Kč–180Kč. No credit cards. Mon–Sat 11am–9:30pm.

Fast Facts: Prague & the Czech Republic

AREA CODES There are no area or city codes in the Czech Republic. Each telephone number is a unique nine-digit number, usually written xxx-xxx-xxx. Numbers that begin with a "6" or "7" indicate a mobile phone.

BUSINESS HOURS Normal business and banking hours run from 9am to 5pm Monday to Friday. Stores in central Prague are typically open weekdays from 9am to 7pm and on Saturday from 9am until at least 1pm; larger stores and shopping centers are likely to be open on Sundays and holidays as well. Post offices are open from 8am until 7pm Monday to Friday. Some larger post offices have limited Saturday hours. Museums are almost always closed on Mondays. Tourist attractions may have shorter hours or shut down altogether during the winter (Nov–Apr).

DRINKING LAWS Alcohol (beer, wine, and spirits) is widely available at supermarkets, convenience stores, cafes, and bars. The legal age for buying and consuming alcohol is 18, though ID checks are not common. There are no set hours for when bars can operate. Traditional Czech pubs close around 11pm. More modern bars and clubs in Prague usually stay open until at least 1am or 2am. The blood-alcohol limit for driving a car is zero, and motorists face a stiff fine and loss of their driving license if caught.

DRIVING RULES See "Getting There & Getting Around," p. 33.

ELECTRICITY The Czech Republic operates on the standard European 220v using a two-pronged plug with round pins. Most U.S. appliances will need a transformer and a plug adaptor. Laptops will usually only require a plug adaptor.

EMBASSIES & CONSULATES All foreign embassies are located in the capital, Prague. The embassy of the **United States** is located at Tržiště 15, Prague 1, Malá Strana (© **257-022-000;** www.usembassy.cz). The embassy of **Canada** is at Muchova 6, Prague 6, Dejvice (© **272-101-800;** www.canada.cz). The embassy of the **United Kingdom** is at Thunovská 14, Prague 1, Malá Strana (© **257-402-111;** www.britain.cz). The local consular office of **Australia** is at Klimentská 10, Prague 1, Nové Město (© **296-578-350**).

EMERGENCIES Dial the following numbers in an emergency: **112** (general emergency, equivalent to U.S. 911); **155** (ambulance); **158** (police); **150** (fire); **1230, 1240** (emergency road service).

GASOLINE (PETROL) Gasoline, known as *benzín* in Czech is sold by the liter. Unleaded gas comes in two forms: regular (95 octane) and high-test (98 octane). Gasoline is expensive by U.S. standards. One liter costs around 30Kč, which works out to about $6.30 a gallon.

HOLIDAYS Public holidays include: New Year's Day (Jan 1); Easter Monday (March or April); Labor Day (May 1); Liberation Day (May 8); Sts. Cyril & Methodius Day (July 5); Death of Jan Hus Day (July 6); St. Wenceslas Day (Sept 28); the Founding of the Czechoslovak Republic (Oct 28); the Student Demonstrations of 1989 (Nov 17); Christmas (Dec 24, 25); and St. Stephen's Day (Dec 26).

HOSPITALS For emergency medical treatment, go to Nemocnice Na Homolce (Hospital Na Homolce) at Roentgenova 2, Prague 5, Smíchov (© **257-271-111;** www.homolka.cz). If you need nonurgent medical attention, practitioners in many fields can be found at the Canadian Medical Care center at Veleslavínská 1, Prague 6, Dejvice (© **235-360-133;** www.cmcpraha.cz). For dental service, call American Dental Associates at V Celnici 4, Prague 1, Nové Město (© **221-181-121;** www.americandental.cz), open 8am to 8pm Monday to Friday.

INSURANCE U.S., Canadian, and Australian citizens should obtain medical insurance with international coverage prior to arrival in the Czech Republic, as any doctor or hospital visits must be paid for out of pocket. Hospitals may demand cash pre-payment before rendering services, but be sure to save all of the paperwork for later reimbursements. The Czech Republic and the E.U. have a reciprocal health insurance agreement that covers U.K. citizens provided they have a European Health Insurance Card (EHIC).

North Americans with homeowner's or renter's insurance are probably covered for lost luggage. If not, inquire with Travel Assistance International (© **800/821-2828**) or Travelex Insurance Services (© **800/228-9792**). These insurers can also provide trip-cancellation, medical, and emergency evacuation coverage abroad.

For information on traveler's insurance, trip cancellation insurance, and medical insurance while traveling please visit www.frommers.com/planning.

INTERNET ACCESS Central Prague has several Internet cafes. Rates typically run from 1Kč to 2Kč per minute. Near Old Town Square, try Bohemia Bagel at Masná 2, Prague 1, Staré Město (© **224-812-560;** www.bohemiabagel.cz). They have a dozen PCs in a pleasant setting for 2Kč per minute; open daily from 8am to 11pm. Spika at Dlážděná 4, Prague 1, Nové Město (© **224-211-521;** http://net cafe.spika.cz) is open Monday to Friday 8am to midnight and Saturday and Sunday 10am to 11pm, and charges 20Kč for 15 minutes.

LANGUAGE Czech is a Slavic language, a distant cousin to Russian but more similar to Slovak and Polish. Nearly anyone who works in a hotel, restaurant or tourist center will be able to speak at least some English. Outside of the capital, English ability decreases, though nearly anyone under the age of 30 has had (in theory) several years of English instruction in the schools. German may also prove useful, particularly with older people.

Berlitz has a comprehensive phrasebook in Czech that is widely available locally in bookstores.

LAUNDROMATS Laundryland, Londýnská 71, Prague 2 (© **222-516-692**), offers dry cleaning as well as laundry service and costs about 60Kč a load to wash. Located 2 blocks from the náměstí Míru metro station and close to the I. P. Pavlova metro station, it's open daily from 8am to 10pm.

Prague Andy's Laundromat is nearby in Vinohrady at Korunní 14, Prague 2 (© **222-510-180**). Whirlpool washers and dryers cost 66 Kč a load to wash.

LEGAL AID Always keep your cool if you're stopped by the police. Acting angry or defensive is almost certain to backfire. Be sure to always carry your passport and driver's license and produce them when asked by a law-enforcement officer. Traffic violations are usually settled through a spot fine paid directly to the police officer. Ask for a receipt as a way of keeping the officer honest.

There are no specific agencies that offer legal services for visiting foreigners. The best advice for serious infractions is to contact your embassy as soon as you can.

MAIL Most post offices are open Monday through Friday from 8am to 7pm. The main post office (Hlavní pošta), at Jindřišská 14, Prague 1 (© **221-131-111**), is open 24 hours a day. You can receive mail, marked "Poste Restante" and addressed to you, in care of this post office. Postcards to the U.S. cost 19Kč; to any E.U. country, 18Kč. Rates for letters vary by weight and should be weighed at the post office to ensure proper postage. Mail service within Europe takes 3 to 5 days, and to the U.S. 7 to 10 days.

NEWSPAPERS & MAGAZINES Prague has two main English-language weekly newspapers: *The Prague Post* (www.praguepost.com) and the *Czech Business Weekly* (www.cbw.cz). The former has good restaurant, culture, and film reviews; the latter mostly concerns itself with business and politics. You'll find both at newsstands around town.

The *Prague Daily Monitor* (http://praguemonitor.com) is a daily online "newspaper," with both original content and reprints from other publications.

PASSPORTS A passport valid for at least 6 months is required to enter the Czech Republic. To replace a lost or stolen passport, contact your embassy immediately; see "Embassies & Consulates," above.

See www.frommers.com/planning for information on how to obtain a passport. For additional information, contact the following agencies:

For Residents of the United States To find your regional passport office, either check the U.S. State Department website or call the **National Passport Information Center** toll-free number (© **877/487-2778**) for automated information.

For Residents of Australia Contact the **Australian Passport Information**

Service at © **131-232,** or visit the government website at www.passports.gov.au.

For Residents of Canada Contact the central **Passport Office,** Department of Foreign Affairs and International Trade, Ottawa, ON K1A 0G3 (© **800/567-6868;** www.ppt.gc.ca).

For Residents of the United Kingdom Visit your nearest passport office, major post office, or travel agency or contact the **United Kingdom Passport Service** at © **0870/521-0410** or search its website at www.ukpa.gov.uk.

POLICE Dial the European Emergency Number © **112** from any phone in an emergency. For Czech police dial © **158.**

SMOKING Smoking is generally permitted in restaurants, bars, and cafes, though there has been discussion of imposing a blanket indoor smoking ban that may or may not be in force by the time of your visit. Restaurants are required to offer non-smoking seating, though this may not always be in the most desirable section of the restaurant. Note that it's illegal to smoke outdoors near bus and tram stops. This rule is rarely enforced, but the fine, 1,000Kč, is steep. Smoking is banned on all trains and public transportation.

TAXES All goods and services in the Czech Republic are levied a value-added tax (VAT, or *DPH* in Czech), ranging from 9% to 19% depending on the item. This tax is normally included in the price.

TELEPHONES Working public phones are rare thanks to the rapid growth of mobile phones. There are a few surviving coin-operated pay phones around town, but most public phones require a prepaid magnetic card. Find the cards at tobacco and magazine kiosks (cards are available for 200Kč–500Kč). Simply insert the card, listen for the dial tone, and dial. You can use pay phones with prepaid cards to dial abroad.

You can also dial abroad from the main post office (see "Mail," on previous page) or, more cheaply, over the Internet at many Internet cafes (see "Internet Access," p. 284). The country code for the Czech Republic is 420. To dial the Czech Republic from abroad, dial your country's international access code (011 in the United States) plus the unique 9-digit local number. Once you are here, to dial any number anywhere in the Czech Republic, simply dial the nine-digit number.

To make a direct international call from the Czech Republic, dial 00 plus the country code of the country you are calling and then the area code and number. The country code for the U.S. and Canada is 1; Great Britain, 44; and Australia, 61.

For directory inquiries regarding phone numbers within the Czech Republic, dial ℂ **1180.** For information about services and rates abroad, call ℂ **1181.**

TIME The Czech Republic is in the central European time zone, the same as Paris, Berlin, and Vienna, and 1 hour ahead of London (GMT), 6 hours ahead of New York (EST).

Daylight saving time is in effect from early spring until fall (the actual date varies from year to year). Daylight saving time moves the clock 1 hour ahead of standard time. The switch is made at 2am on a Sunday morning to cause the least disruption.

TIPPING In hotels, tip **bellhops** 20Kč per bag (more if you have a lot of luggage), and though it's not expected, it's a nice gesture to leave the **chamber staff** 20Kč per night (depending on the level of service). Tip the **doorman** or **concierge** only if he or she has provided a specific service (for example, calling a cab for you or obtaining difficult-to-get theater tickets).

In restaurants, bars, and nightclubs, tip **service staff or bartender** 10% of the check to reward good service. On smaller tabs it's easiest just to round up to the next highest multiple of 10. For example, if the bill comes to 72Kč, hand the waiter 80Kč and tell him to keep the change.

As for other service personnel, tip **cab drivers** 5% to 10% of the fare (provided he hasn't already overcharged you). Tip **hairdressers** and **barbers** 10% to 15%.

TOILETS Acceptably clean public pay toilets are scattered around tourist areas and can be found in every metro station. Expect to pay 5 Kč to 10Kč for the privilege. You'll find generally cleaner free toilets in restaurants, hotels, and fast-food outlets, but these are usually reserved for customers.

VISAS Currently, citizens of the U.S., Canada, the U.K., and Australia are not required to obtain a visa for short-term stays of 90 days or less within a six-month period, though a lingering dispute with Canada could change this for Canadian travelers.

Contact the Czech Ministry of Foreign Affairs website (www.mzv.cz) for up-to-date visa information or how to obtain a visa if required.

VISITOR INFORMATION The official tourist information service for the Czech Republic is the **Czech Tourist Authority,** known as CzechTourism (www.czechtourism.com). They have offices in several countries abroad and can help make basic travel arrangements and answer questions.

In the U.S., the CzechTourism office is at 1109 Madison Ave., New York, NY 10028 (ℂ **212/288-0830,** ext. 101).

In Canada: CzechTourism is at 2 Bloor St. W, Suite 1500, Toronto, M4W 3E2 (ℂ **416/363-9928**).

In the U.K., contact CzechTourism at 13 Harley St., London W1G 9QG (ℂ **0207-631-0427**).

The agency has no formal representation in Australia.

Once in Prague, the main tourist information center is the **Prague Information Service** (PIS; ✆ 221-714-444; www.prague-info.cz), with offices at the Old Town Hall on Old Town Square, several other points around the city, and at the main train station and airport. PIS hands out maps, organizes tours and can help book rooms.

Helpful websites include www.mapy.cz, an online map and journey planner that covers Prague and the entire Czech Republic. Simply type in an address and a map shows you exactly where it is. For the ins and outs of public transportation system, including maps and info on tickets and travel passes, go to www.dp-praha.cz/en.

The site www.idos.cz provides an online timetable for trains and buses, including international destinations. Just type in the city (using the Czech spellings, such as "Praha" for Prague, but note the diacritical marks are not required) and you'll get a complete listing of train and bus connections.

For the main website for the National Gallery in Prague, including practical information, admissions fees, and opening times for many of the city major museums, go to www.ngprague.cz.

WATER Tap water is fine to drink, but most restaurants won't serve it, preferring instead to charge for bottles of mineral water. Carbonated water is *"voda s bublínkami."* To order still water, say *"voda bez bublínek"* (literally: "water without bubbles").

1 AIRLINE, HOTEL & CAR-RENTAL WEBSITES

MAJOR AIRLINES

Aer Lingus
www.aerlingus.com

Aeroflot
www.aeroflot.ru

Air France
www.airfrance.com

Alitalia
www.alitalia.com

Austrian
www.aua.com

British Airways
www.british-airways.com

Czech Airlines
www.czechairlines.com

Delta Air Lines
www.delta.com

El Al Airlines
www.el.co.il

Finnair
www.finnair.com

Iberia Airlines
www.iberia.com

KLM
www.klm.com

Korean Air
www.koreanair.com

LOT
www.lot.com

Lufthansa
www.lufthansa.com

Malév
www.malev.hu

SAS
www.flysas.com

Swiss
www.swiss.com

TAP
www.flytap.com

Turkish Airlines
www.thy.com

BMI Baby
www.bmibaby.com

Brussels Airlines
www.brusselsairlines.com

easyJet
www.easyjet.com

GermanWings
www.germanwings.com

Jet2.com
www.jet2.com

Ryanair
www.ryanair.com

SmartWings
www.smartwings.com

Southwest Airlines
www.southwest.com

WizzAir
www.wizzair.com

MAJOR HOTEL CHAINS

Best Western International
www.bestwestern.com

Buddha Bar
www.buddhabar.com

Clarion Hotels
www.choicehotels.com

Courtyard by Marriott
www.marriott.com/courtyard

Crowne Plaza Hotels
www.ichotelsgroup.com/crowneplaza

Four Seasons
www.fourseasons.com

Hilton Hotels
www.hilton.com

Ibis Hotels
www.ibishotel.com

InterContinental Hotels & Resorts
www.ichotelsgroup.com

Kempinski Hotels
www.kempinski.com

Mandarin Oriental
www.mandarinoriental.com

Marriott
www.marriott.com

Mercure Hotels
www.mercure.com

Mövenpick Hotels
www.moevenpick-hotels.com

Novotel
www.novotel.com

Radisson Hotels & Resorts
www.radisson.com

Ramada Worldwide
www.ramada.com

Residence Inn by Marriott
www.marriott.com/residenceinn

Sheraton Hotels & Resorts
www.starwoodhotels.com/sheraton

Vienna International Hotels
www.vi-hotels.com

CAR-RENTAL AGENCIES

Avis
www.avis.com

Budget
www.budget.com

CS-Czechocar
www.czechocar.cz

Dvorak Rent-a-car
www.dvorak-rentacar.cz

Europcar
www.europcar.com

Hertz
www.hertz.com

Sixt
www.sixt.com

Thrifty
www.thrifty.com

Useful Terms & Phrases

Although Czech is a difficult language to master, you should at least make an attempt to learn a few phrases. Czechs will appreciate the effort and will be more willing to help you out.

1 BASIC PHRASES & VOCABULARY

CZECH ALPHABET

There are 32 vowels and consonants in the Czech alphabet, and most of the consonants are pronounced about as they are in English. Accent marks over vowels lengthen the sound of the vowel, as does the *kroužek*, the little circle that usually appears only over a "u."

A, a f*a*ther
B, b *b*oy
C, c get*s*
Č, č *ch*oice
D, d *d*ay
Ď, ď *Di*or
E, e n*e*ver
F, f *f*ood
G, g *g*oal
H, h un*h*and
Ch, ch Lo*ch* Lomond
I, i n*ee*d
J, j *y*es
K, k *k*ey
L, l *l*ord
M, m *m*ama

N, n *n*o
Ň, ň Ta*ny*a
O, o *aw*ful
P, p *p*en
R, r slightly trilled *r*
Ř, ř slightly trilled *r* + *zh* as in Per*si*an
S, s *s*eat
Š, š cru*sh*
T, t *t*oo
Ť, ť no*t y*et
U, u r*oo*m
V, v *v*ery
W, w *v*ague
Y, y funn*y*
Z, z *z*ebra
Ž, ž a*z*ure, plea*s*ure

CZECH VOCABULARY

Everyday Expressions

English	Czech	Pronunciation
Hello	**Dobrý den**	*doh*-bree den
Good morning	**Dobré jitro**	*doh*-breh *yee*-troh
Good evening	**Dobrý večer**	*doh*-bree *veh*-chair
How are you?	**Jak se máte?**	*yahk* seh *mah*-teh
Very well	**Velmi dobře**	*vel*-mee *doh*-brsheh
Thank you	**Děkuji vám**	*dyek*-ooee vahm
You're welcome	**Prosím**	*proh*-seem
Please	**Prosím**	*proh*-seem

English	Czech	Pronunciation
Yes	**Ano**	*ah*-no
No	**Ne**	neh
Excuse me	**Promiňte**	*proh*-min-teh
How much does it cost?	**Kolik to stojí?**	*koh*-leek taw *stoh*-ee
I don't understand.	**Nerozumím.**	*neh*-roh-zoo-meem
Just a moment.	**Moment, prosím.**	*moh*-ment, *proh*-seem
Goodbye	**Na shledanou**	*nah* skleh-dah-noh-oo

Traveling

English	Czech	Pronunciation
Where is the . . . ?	**Kde je . . . ?**	*gde* yeh . . .
bus station	**autobusové nádraží**	*au*-toh-boos-oh-veh *nah*-drah-zhee
train station	**nádraží**	*nah*-drah-zhee
airport	**letiště**	*leh*-tyish-tyeh
baggage check	**úschovna zavazadel**	*oo*-skohv-nah *zah*-vahz-ah-del
Where can I find a taxi?	**Kde najdu taxi?**	*gde nai*-doo *tahks*-eh
Where can I find a gas station?	**Kde najdu benzínovou pumpu?**	*gde nai*-doo *ben*-zeen-oh-voh *poomp*-oo
How much is the fare?	**Kolik je jízdné?**	*koh*-leek yeh yeesd-neh
I am going to . . .	**Pojedu do . . .**	*poh*-yeh-doo doh . . .
One-way ticket	**Jízdenka**	*yeez*-den-kah
Round-trip ticket	**Zpáteční jízdenka**	*zpah*-tech-nee *jeez*-den-kah
Car-rental office	**Půjčovna aut**	*poo*-eech-awv-nah ah-oot

Accommodations

English	Czech	Pronunciation
I'm looking for . . .	**Hledám . . .**	*hleh*-dahm . . .
a hotel	**hotel**	*hoh*-tel
a youth hostel	**studentskou ubytovnu**	*stoo*-dent-skoh *oo*-beet-ohv-noo
I am staying . . .	**Zůstanu . . .**	*zoo*-stah-noo . . .
a few days	**několik dnů**	*nyeh*-koh-leek dnoo
2 weeks	**dva týdny**	dvah tid-*neh*
a month	**jeden měsíc**	*yeh*-den *myeh*-seets
I have a reservation.	**Mám zamluvený nocleh.**	mahm *zah*-mloo-veh-ni *nohts*-leh
My name is . . .	**Jmenuji se . . .**	*meh*-noo-yee seh . . .
Do you have a room . . . ?	**Máte pokoj . . . ?**	*mah*-teh *poh*-koy . . .
for tonight	**na dnešek**	*nah* dneh-sheck

English	Czech	Pronunciation
for 3 nights	na tři dny	*nah* trshee dnee
for a week	na týden	*nah* tee-den
I would like . . .	Chci . . .	khtsee . . .
a single	jednolůžkový pokoj	*jed*-noh-loosh-koh-vee *poh*-koy
a double	dvojlůžkový pokoj	*dvoy*-loosh-koh-vee *poh*-koy
I want a room . . .	Chci pokoj . . .	khtsee *poh*-koy . . .
with a bathroom	s koupelnou	*skoh*-pehl-noh
without a bathroom	bez koupelny	*behz* koh-pehl-nee
with a shower	se sprchou	*seh* spur-choh
without a shower	bez sprchy	*bez* sprech-eh
with a view	s pohledem	*spoh*-hlehd-ehm
How much is the room?	Kolik stojí pokoj?	*koh*-leek *stoh*-yee *paw*-koy
with breakfast?	se snídaní?	*seh* snee-dan-nyee
May I see the room?	Mohu vidět ten pokoj?	*moh*-hoo *vee*-dyet ten *paw*-koy
The key	Klíč	kleech
The bill, please.	Dejte mi účet, prosím.	*day*-teh mee *oo*-cheht, *praw*-seem

Getting Around

English	Czech	Pronunciation
I'm looking for . . .	Hledám . . .	*hleh*-dahm . . .
a bank	banku	*bahnk*-oo
the church	kostel	*kohs*-tell
the city center	centrum	*tsent*-room
the museum	muzeum	*moo*-zeh-oom
a pharmacy	lékárnu	*lek*-ahr-noo
the park	park	pahrk
the theater	divadlo	*dee*-vahd-loh
the tourist office	cestovní kancelář	*tses*-tohv-nee *kahn*-tseh-larsh
the embassy	velvyslanectví	*vehl*-vee-slahn-ets-tvee
Where is the nearest telephone?	Kde je nejbližší telefon?	gde yeh *nay*-bleesh-ee *tel*-oh-fohn
I would like to buy . . .	Chci koupit . . .	khtsee *koh*-peet . . .
a stamp	známku	*znahm*-koo
a postcard	pohlednici	*poh*-hlehd-nit-seh
a map	mapu	*mahp*-oo

Emergencies

English	Czech	Pronunciation
I need a doctor	Potřebuji lékaře	*poh*-trzhe-boo-yee *leh*-kahrz-e
Hospital	nemocnice	nay-*mohts*-nee-tse

English	Czech	Pronunciation
Help!	Pomoc!	poh-*mohts*
Call the police	zavolejte policii	*zah*-vo-lay-te *pol*-ee-tsee-yee
I'm lost	atratil jsem se	ztrah-*teel* sem seh

Signs

No Trespassing   Cizím vstup zakázán
No Smoking   Kouření zakázáno
No Parking   Neparkovat
Arrivals   Příjezd/Přílet
Entrance   Vchod
Departures   Odjezd/Odlet
Exit   Východ
Toilets   Toalety
Information   Informace
Danger   Pozor, nebezpečí

Numbers

1	jeden (*yeh*-den)	16	šestnáct (*shest*-nahtst)
2	dva (dvah)	17	sedmnáct (*seh*-doom-nahtst)
3	tři (trzhee)	18	osmnáct (*aw*-soom-nahtst)
4	čtyři (*chtee*-rshee)	19	devatenáct (*deh*-vah-teh-nahtst)
5	pět (pyet)	20	dvacet (*dvah*-tset)
6	šest (shest)	30	třicet (*trshee*-tset)
7	sedm (*seh*-duhm)	40	čtyřicet (*chti*-rshee-tset)
8	osm (*aw*-suhm)	50	padesát (*pah*-deh-saht)
9	devět (*deh*-vyet)	60	šedesát (*she*-deh-saht)
10	deset (*deh*-set)	70	sedmdesát (*seh*-duhm-deh-saht)
11	jedenáct (*yeh*-deh-nahtst)	80	osmdesát (*aw*-suhm-deh-saht)
12	dvanáct (*dvah*-nahtst)	90	devadesát (*deh*-vah-deh-saht)
13	třináct (*trshee*-nahtst)	100	sto (staw)
14	čtrnáct (*chtur*-nahtst)	500	pět set (*pyet* set)
15	patnáct (*paht*-nahtst)	1,000	tisíc (tyee-seets)

Dining

English	Czech	Pronunciation
Restaurant	Restaurace	*rehs*-tow-rah-tseh
Breakfast	Snídaně	*snee*-dah-nyeh
Lunch	Oběd	*oh*-byed
Dinner	Večeře	*veh*-chair-sheh
A table for two, please. (Lit.: There are two of us.)	Jsme dva.	*ees*-meh dvah
Waiter	Číšník	*cheess*-neek
Waitress	Servírka	ser-*veer*-ka

English	Czech	Pronunciation	293
I would like . . .	Chci . . .	khtsee . . .	
a menu	jídelní lístek	*yee*-del-nee *lees*-teck	
a fork	vidličku	*veed*-leech-koo	
a knife	nůž	noosh	
a spoon	lžičku	lu-*shich*-koo	
a napkin	ubrousek	*oo*-broh-seck	
a glass (of water)	skleničku (vody)	*sklehn*-ich-koo (vod-*dee*)	
the check, please	účet, prosím	*oo*-cheht, *proh*-seem	
Is the tip included?	Je v tom zahrnuto sropitné?	yeh *ftohm*-zah *hur*-noo-toh s *proh*-peet-neh	

2 MENU TERMS

GENERAL

English	Czech	Pronunciation
Soup	Polévka	*poh*-lehv-kah
Eggs	Vejce	*vayts*-eh
Meat	Maso	*mahs*-oh
Fish	Ryba	*ree*-bah
Vegetables	Zelenina	*zehl*-eh-nee-nah
Fruit	Ovoce	*oh*-voh-tseh
Desserts	Moučníky	*mohch*-nee-kee
Beverages	Nápoje	*nah*-poy-yeh
Salt	Sůl	sool
Pepper	Pepř	*peh*-psh
Mayonnaise	Majonéza	*mai*-o-neza
Mustard	Hořčice	*hohrsh*-chee-tseh
Vinegar	Ocet	*oh*-tseht
Oil	Olej	*oh*-lay
Sugar	Cukr	*tsoo*-ker
Tea	Čaj	chye
Coffee	Káva	*kah*-vah
Bread	Chléb	khlehb
Butter	Máslo	*mahs*-loh
Wine	Víno	*vee*-noh
Fried	Smažený	*smah*-sheh-nee
Roasted	Pečený	*pech*-eh-nee
Boiled	Vařený	*vah*-rsheh-nee
Grilled	Grilovaný	*gree*-loh-vah-nee

Soup

Potato	**Bramborová**	Tomato	**Rajská**
Lentil	**Čočková**	Chicken	**Slepičí**
Goulash	**Gulášová**	Vegetable	**Zeleninová**

Meat

Steak	**Biftek**	Sausage	**Klobása**
Goulash	**Guláš**	Rabbit	**Králík**
Beef	**Hovězí**	Mutton	**Skopové**
Liver	**Játra**	Veal	**Telecí**
Lamb	**Jehněčí**	Veal Cutlet	**Telecí kotleta**
Duck	**Kachna**	Pork	**Vepřové**

Fish

Carp	**Kapr**	Pike	**Štika**
Caviar	**Kaviár**	Cod	**Treska**
Fish Filet	**Rybí filé**	Eel	**Úhoř**
Herring	**Sleď**	Oysters	**Ústřice**

Eggs

Scrambled Eggs	**Míchaná vejce**	Soft-boiled Eggs	**Vejce naměkko**
Fried Eggs	**Smažená vejce**	Bacon and Eggs	**Vejce se slaninou**
Boiled Eggs	**Vařená vejce**	Ham and Eggs	**Vejce se šunkou**

Salad

Bean Salad	**Fazolový salát**	Cucumber Salad	**Okurkový salát**
Mixed Green Salad	**Hlávkový salát**	Beet Salad	**Salát z červené řepy**

Vegetables

Potatoes	**Brambory**	Cauliflower	**Květák**
Celery	**Celer**	Carrots	**Mrkev**
Asparagus	**Chřest**	Peppers	**Paprika**
Onions	**Cibule**	Tomatoes	**Rajská jablíčka**
Mushrooms	**Houby**	Cabbage	**Zelí**

Dessert

Cake	**Koláč**	Apple Strudel	**Jablkový závin**
Cookies	**Cukroví**	Pancakes	**Palačinky**
Chocolate Ice Cream	**Čokoládová zmrzlina**		
Vanilla Ice Cream	**Vanilková zmrzlina**		

Fruit

Lemon	**Citrón**	Apple	**Jablko**
Pear	**Hruška**	Plum	**Švestka**
Strawberry	**Jahoda**		

Beverages

Tea **Čaj**

Coffee **Káva**

Milk **Mléko**

Wine **Víno**

Red **Červené**

White **Bílé**

Water **Voda**

Beer **Pivo**

INDEX

See also Accommodations and Restaurants, Cafes, and Pubs indexes, below